A SCIENTIFIC THEOLOGY

VOLUME I

NATURE

A SCIENTIFIC THEOLOGY

VOLUME I

NATURE

Alister E. McGrath

William B. Eerdmans Publishing Company
Grand Rapids, Michigan

Published in Great Britain by T&T Clark Ltd,
59 George Street, Edinburgh EH2 2LQ, Scotland
www.tandtclark.co.uk

This edition published 2001 in the USA
under license from T&T Clark Ltd by
Wm. B. Eerdmans Publishing Co.
255 Jefferson Ave. S.E., Grand Rapids, Michigan 49503
www.eerdmans.com

First published 2001

ISBN 0-8028-3925-8

Manufactured in Great Britain

FOR

THOMAS F. TORRANCE

A SCIENTIFIC THEOLOGIAN

Contents

PART TWO: NATURE

Preface

This trilogy had its origins in the long, hot and dry European summer of 1976. I was working at the University of Utrecht in the Netherlands, combining mastering the complex isolation of a protein thought to be implicated in phosphatidylcholine transport between biological membranes (which had been pioneered at Utrecht) with following through my continuing interest in the history and philosophy of the natural sciences, making use of Utrecht's excellent libraries.

I cannot recall quite how the idea came into my mind; it was as if a mental bolt of lightning flashed across my consciousness, eclipsing my thoughts on how best to apply Fourier Transforms to study the time-resolved anisotropy of a fluorescent probe that I had developed for studying lipid viscosity in biological membranes and their models. The idea that shot through my mind was simple: explore the relation between Christian theology and the natural sciences, using philosophy and history as dialogue partners. It would be grounded in and faithful to the Christian tradition, yet open to the insights of the sciences. This would be more than a mere exploration of a working relationship; it would be a proposal for a synergy, a working together, a mutal cross-fertilization of ideas and approaches – in short, a scientific theology.

Like all simple ideas, this turned out to be rather more difficult to put into practice than to conceive. The idea which came to me in a flash took twenty years to follow through. As the project which now follows is somewhat lengthy, it may be helpful to explain how it came to develop, and the form which it has taken.

By the age of eighteen, as someone about to leave high school and go up to university, I felt that I had sorted out the meaning of life, and so was free to move on to deal with other issues. One of the incorrigible certainties on which my life was based at this stage was that religion was outdated and irrelevant, if not actually harmful. My early views on this matter were shaped to no small extent by the writings of Karl Marx. I must confess, however, that I was probably influenced in my reading of Marx by his interpreters of the 1960s, who reworked Marx's vision of the working class as the vanguard of a socialist society. The working classes having signally failed to achieve what Marx had expected of them, Theodore Adorno and others suggested that students should be seen as inheriting their mantle. This appealed to teenagers such as myself in the late 1960s; it offered us a real role in the reshaping of history, as well as an excellent excuse for not being bothered by such wearisome matters as academic work. Who could fail to be seduced by being offered such an historic role? Whose ego could fail to be pampered by such a grandiose vision? It was also useful at a more mundane level. It allowed school students such as myself to suggest that we were far too busy creating a new world order to have time for such irrelevancies as homework.

The student riots in Paris and the United States suggested that real and permanent social change was not far away. In Northern Ireland, in which I had spent my entire youth, the events which gave birth to what were euphemistically termed 'the troubles' in 1968 were viewed by many more idealistic dreamers – myself included – as representing the dawn of a new era. It would be an era without religion. Marx had offered an explanation of the origins of religion which predicted its elimination through socio-economic change. Northern Ireland was notorious for its religious tensions; the elimination of religion would therefore lead to a new era of peace, co-operation and progress. It was impossible to overlook the compelling appeal of this world-view, and avoid being shaped by its vision. It was clear to me that Christianity was a relic of a past era, for which the future had no place. I was encouraged in this belief by a work which I had read in its second edition while a high school student – A. J. Ayer's powerful *Language, Truth and Logic*, which offered a vigorous rejection of metaphysics and elimination of any need to speak of God. Ayer's argument for atheism as the only intellectually credible and politically focused world-view for a thinking person seemed irrefutable.

Although I was interested in philosophy and politics while at school, my studies focused on the natural sciences. I had chosen to specialize in the sciences from the earliest moment possible within the British educational system, and at the age of eighteen was awarded a scholarship to study chemistry at Oxford University. The decision to study at Oxford is easily explained. It was widely regarded as offering the best university-level course in chemistry in Great Britain. In addition, it offered the possibility of a hugely stimulating intellectual environment in which to consolidate my atheistic views. A. J. Ayer, whom I so greatly revered, was professor of philosophy at this point; I would have the opportunity of attending his lectures. I had decided to study at Wadham College partly on account of the excellence of its chemists (J. R. Knowles and R. J. P. Williams were fellows of the college at this time), and partly on account of the college's association with left-wing politics at this time.

Looking back on those days, I find myself amazed at my arrogance and naïveté. How could I have hoped to have sorted out the great issues of life by the age of eighteen? On arriving at Oxford, I found my settled intellectual certainties were challenged. Doubts which I had suppressed concerning the intellectual credibility of atheism began to crystallize. Marxism seemed to offer answers which were simply too neat to relate to the complex and fuzzy realities of life. Although the intellectual discrediting of Marxism in British academia probably dates from around 1989, signs of decay and failure were everywhere evident at this earlier stage, for those who chose to notice them. It was intellectually fashionable to be a Marxist at this time in Oxford, which presumably explains why so many who claimed to have espoused it seemed to know little about it, or have any real commitment to its values. A disconcerting number of Wadham College's more prominent Marxists seemed to end up becoming merchant bankers, offering what seemed to me to be a rather lame justification for this remarkable about-turn – the aspiration of 'reforming the system from within'.

A. J. Ayer also turned out to be something of a disappointment. The radical philosophy which I had found so appealing as a teenager had, in effect, become the establishment position at Oxford. Although the Oxford guild of professional philosophers would not have seen it like this, the simple fact was that Oxford philosophy had become stuck in a rather boring rut. More interesting, creative and important things were happening elsewhere. As if that were not enough, I discovered that Ayer's reputation at Oxford in the early 1970s seemed to have rather more to do with his sexual proclivity than his philosophical creativity. The 'I've-slept-with-Freddy-Ayer' club was rumoured to be one of Oxford's less exclusive societies. New College students whom I knew took great pleasure in relating how Ayer had fallen into the habit of placing his shoes on the window sills of his rooms in New College when expanding the frontiers of human knowledge.[1]

By the end of my first term at Oxford, I was in a state of mental flux. I had suffered the immense inconvenience of discovering that Christianity could not be dismissed as easily as I had thought. In fact, it seemed to have rather a lot going for it. I underwent the kind of experience that Augustine describes so powerfully in his *Confessions*, which could be thought of as a 'twice-born' encounter with the Christian faith. While I continue to have difficulty in identifying the factors which brought about this decisive change in my outlook, I am quite clear that by the end of my first term at Oxford, I had firmly accepted the basic ideas of the Christian faith as both intellectually persuasive and personally fulfilling.

A huge amount of rethinking remained to be done, not least in relation to my interests in the natural sciences. Having previously thought, in rather uncritical terms which I now realize to have been shaped by Andrew Dickson White's hostile and inaccurate account of the relation of Christianity and the sciences,[2] that the natural sciences were the enemy of religion, I now began to realize that the situation was rather more complex (and interesting), demanding a more nuanced and informed response. My natural instinct was to abandon my studies of the natural sciences, and begin the detailed study of Christian theology. However, I was dissuaded from this, and in the end completed my first degree in chemistry and went on to gain a doctorate from Oxford in molecular biophysics. It was during a period spent working at the University of Utrecht on a European Molecular Biology Organization fellowship in 1976 that I began to think about the serious intellectual engagement between Christianity and the natural sciences, noted earlier, which would ensure that the theological, philosophical, historical and scientific aspects of the matter would be given full weight.

This demanded a serious engagement with Christian theology. On my return from Utrecht in August 1976, I began to plan how this might be realized. I had just been awarded a Senior Scholarship at Merton College, Oxford, for the period 1976–8. The scholarship in question allowed its holder either to undertake research work for an advanced degree of the University of Oxford, or to study for a second first degree,

---

[1] Some of these are documented in Ben Rogers, *A. J. Ayer: A Life*. London: Chatto & Windus, 1999. Some of the more interesting anecdotes circulating at the time appear to have been omitted, presumably for legal reasons.

[2] Andrew Dickson White, *The Warfare of Science*. London: Henry S. King & Co., 1867.

without limit of subject. I therefore asked the college authorities if it might be possible to fulfil both these possibilities, by continuing my research in molecular biophysics, while at the same time studying for the Final Honour School of Theology. In November 1976, the college agreed to this request.

At this stage, I was very much an amateur in matters of theology. I suspect that my interest in theology might well have proved to be short-lived, if not stillborn, had I begun my theological studies by reading some of the works which were typical of English-language theology of this time. However, redemption was at hand. Although I had left Wadham College in 1975 to take up a research scholarship at Linacre College, I remained in touch with its recently-appointed chaplain Tim Gorringe (now Professor of Theology at Exeter University). Gorringe was working on aspects of the theology of Karl Barth,[3] and suggested that I could do far worse than immerse myself in the *Church Dogmatics*. By the end of the first half-volume – which had just appeared in a new English translation, replacing the unsatisfactory translation originally published in 1936 – I knew that I was going to be excited by the study of theology. Barth's vision of theology might well have been controversial, and caused eyebrows to be raised within the English theological establishment of the time. But the vision was exciting, challenging and inspirational. Above all, I found myself impressed by the intellectual coherence of Barth's vision of 'theological science', and thrilled by the vision Barth offered of a sustained theological engagement with the past:[4]

> We cannot be in the church without taking responsibility for the theology of the past as much as for the theology of the present. Augustine, Thomas Aquinas, Luther, Schleiermacher and all the rest are not dead but living. They still speak and demand a hearing as living voices, as surely as we know that they and we belong together in the church.

With this in mind, I set out to ensure that I immersed myself in historical theology, as well as systematic theology, realizing that the latter could not be undertaken without the former, and that the former was incomplete without the latter. While I have misgivings about many aspects of Barth's theology – as I think these volumes will make clear – it is impossible to understate the positive impact which Barth had upon

---

[3] For a recent example of his writing in this area, see Timothy R. Gorringe, *Karl Barth: Against Hegemony*. Oxford: Oxford University Press, 1999.

[4] Karl Barth, *Die protestantische Theologie im 19. Jahrhundert: Ihre Vorgeschichte und ihre Geschichte*. 2nd edn. Zurich: Evangelischer Verlag, 1952, 3.

my estimate of, and enthusiasm for, theology as a serious intellectual discipline.

I went on to complete my doctorate in December 1977, and take first-class honours in theology in June 1978. My hope had been that I would be able to plunge into the debate about the relation of Christian theology and the natural sciences on the basis of a doctorate and publications in the latter,[5] and a first degree in the former. I had been elected to the Naden Studentship in Divinity at St John's College, Cambridge, and intended to use my time at Cambridge to study the Copernican debates of the second half of the sixteenth century. This, I hoped, would be good enough to allow me to get on with the project I had devised two years earlier. However, it soon became obvious that a mere first degree in theology was totally inadequate – although certainly better than nothing – as the basis for such an engagement. The problem was not simply mastering the ideas, but coming to terms with an extensive body of literature already written on the topics of direct relevance to my project, while at the same time keeping up with my reading in the history and philosophy of science. The task seemed totally unmanageable.

Happily, there proved to be a way of dealing with the immensity of the task by breaking it down into more manageable segments. Under the guidance of the late Gordon Rupp (then the *doyen* of English Luther studies, who had at that stage recently retired as Dixie Professor of Ecclesiastical History at Cambridge University), I began to develop an engagement with one major period in Christian theology (the Reformation), one major Christian theologian (Martin Luther), and the development throughout history of one specific Christian doctrine (the doctrine of justification).[6] Having dealt with these three related topics, it was relatively simple to use each as a platform for engaging with other periods, other theologians, and other doctrines. The approach

---

[5] For which see Benjamin de Kreef et al., 'Lipid Asymmetry, Clustering and Molecular Motion in Biological Membranes and Their Models', in S. Abrahamsson and I. Pascher (eds), *Nobel Foundation Symposium: Biological Membranes and Their Models.* New York: Plenum Press, 1977, 389–407; Alister E. McGrath, Christopher G. Morgan and George K. Radda, 'Photobleaching: A Novel Fluorescence Method for Diffusion Studies in Lipid Systems', *Biochimica at Biophysica Acta* 426 (1976), 173–85; Alister E. McGrath, Christopher G. Morgan and George K. Radda, 'Positron Lifetimes in Phospholipid Dispersions', *Biochimica at Biophysica Acta* 466 (1976), 367–72.

[6] See Alister E. McGrath, *Luther's Theology of the Cross: Martin Luther's Theological Breakthrough.* Oxford: Blackwell, 1985; idem, *The Intellectual Origins of the European Reformation.* Oxford: Blackwell, 1987; idem, *Iustitia Dei: A History of the Christian Doctrine of Justification.* 2nd edn. Cambridge: Cambridge University Press, 1998.

Rupp advocated also allowed me to grapple with the issue of the development of Christian doctrine in general.[7] By 1996 – some twenty years after the idea for the project was conceived – I finally felt ready to begin serious work in the field.

I began to set out some of my reflections on this relationship in an earlier work *The Foundations of Dialogue in Science and Religion* (1998), which may be regarded as an anticipation of the present, more substantial series of works.[8] This work represented an expanded version of a lecture I was invited to deliver at the University of Utrecht in January 1997 on 'The Relation of the Natural Sciences and Christian Theology', and can be seen as doing little more than clearing my own mind, preparatory to a more detailed engagement with the issues.

It was always clear to me that several volumes would be needed to do justice to the notion of a 'scientific theology', which sought to draw upon and interact with the methods of the natural sciences as an aid to theological reflection and analysis. Where medieval writers had extolled the virtues of philosophy as *ancilla theologiae*, I had come to the different – though clearly related – conclusion that it was a *natural* philosophy which would best serve this purpose.[9] To do justice to the theological, scientific, philosophical and historical issues involved, it was obvious from the outset that the traditional monograph was a quite inappropriate means of addressing this issue. Like many others, I had been frustrated by the brevity of many such existing discussions, and longed for the detailed and sustained engagement which a project of this magnitude demanded.

Such a work counters the trend towards the fragmentation of intellectual discourse and engagement by calling for the forging of links

---

[7] Alister E. McGrath, *The Genesis of Doctrine*. Oxford: Blackwell, 1990.

[8] Alister E. McGrath, *The Foundations of Dialogue in Science and Religion*. Oxford: Blackwell, 1998.

[9] On the important concept of 'natural philosophy', see Luciano Boi (ed.), *Science et philosophie de la nature: un nouveau dialogue*. Berne: Peter Lang, 2000. For older approaches, J. A. Bennett, 'Robert Hooke as Mechanic and Natural Philosopher', *Notes and Records of the Royal Society* 35 (1980), 33–48; L. W. B. Brockliss, 'Aristotle, Descartes and the New Science: Natural Philosophy at the University of Paris, 1600–1740', *Annals of Science* 38 (1981), 33–69; James W. Garrison, 'Newton and the Relation of Mathematics to Natural Philosophy', *Journal of the History of Ideas* 48 (1987), 609–27; P. M. Heimann, 'Nature is a Perpetual Worker: Newton's Aether and Eighteenth-Century Natural Philosophy', *Ambix* 20 (1973), 2–24; J. F. W. Herschel, *Preliminary Discourse on the Study of Natural Philosophy*. London: Longman, Rees, Orme, Brown & Green, 1830; James R. Jacob, 'The Ideological Origins of Robert Boyle's Natural Philosophy', *Journal of European Studies* 2 (1972), 1–21; J. R. Lucas, *Space, Time and Causality: An Essay in Natural Philosophy*. Oxford: Oxford University Press, 1984.

between four distinct, though related, disciplines. It can be thought of as a dialogue between theology and the natural sciences, with history and philosophy as respected and necessary partners to, and participants in, that discussion. A serious synthesis of this nature demands a considerable degree of space, especially if it is to avoid the superficiality and simplification which inevitably accompany briefer discussions of so complex an issue.

I must therefore apologize in advance for the length of the volumes which go to make up this analysis of 'scientific theology'. Their length results from the need to achieve a viable synthesis which recognizes and responds to the many issues which are involved. It is my hope that my readers will forgive the length of the work, and perhaps that they may capture something of my sense of intellectual excitement concerning the project.

The present work is fundamentally an attempt to explore the interface between Christian theology and the natural sciences, on the assumption that this engagement is necessary, proper, legitimate and productive. Its three volumes set out to explore the manner in which the working assumptions of the natural sciences can serve as a dialogue partner to the theological enterprise, in which there is a genuine interaction and interchange between the two disciplines, to the mutual benefit of both. It is fundamentally a sustained essay in theological method, in the sense of an attempt to explore the contours of a potentially interesting dialogue, not without its difficulties, which promises to be one of the more significant intellectual conversations of the twenty-first century. The interface between Christian theology and the natural sciences is not merely an intellectually habitable zone; this exploration is to be seen as an essential consequence of core Christian beliefs, which have defined Christianity throughout its long and complex history.

Interdisciplinary inquiry – whether this takes the form of the fusion of disciplines or the critical scrutiny of their boundaries – has become an increasingly important element of general intellectual activity. Yet it is reasonable to point out that some such inquiry is undertaken in something of a spirit of serendipity – a hope that the study of two apparently unrelated disciplines might yield new and exciting insights, inaccessible from the perspective of either on its own. Others, in contrast, are based on the perception that the two disciplines are fundamentally related to one another, so that the analysis of their mutual relationship may be expected from the outset to be realistic and profitable. It is the contention of this work that the relationship of Christian theology to the natural sciences is that of two fundamentally related disciplines, whose working methods reflect this common grounding in responding to a reality which lies beyond them, of which they are bound to give an ordered account.

This is not, as will become clear, a work of systematic theology. It is, however, a systematic work of theology – if this distinction may be allowed – which is primarily concerned with issues of method rather than substance. However, in that it is impossible to disentangle the manner in which knowledge arises from the specific knowledge thus attained, it will be clear that this difference has perhaps more to do with emphasis than substance. Theological assumptions cannot be isolated from theological method any more than the conclusions of the natural sciences may be disentangled from the methods used to infer them.

This work is written from an evangelical perspective, by which I mean an approach to theology which insists that 'theology must be nourished and governed at all points by Holy Scripture, and that it seeks to offer a faithful and coherent account of what it finds there'.[10] This task of rendering Scripture faithfully is, in my view, best carried out in dialogue with the 'great tradition' of Christian theology and in response to the challenges to the Christian faith which are raised by other disciplines – such as the natural sciences. Yet I have no doubt that many Christian theologians who would not wish to identify or style themselves as 'evangelical' will find much in these volumes that they will be able to welcome and appropriate. At its heart, after all, evangelicalism is fundamentally Christian orthodoxy, even though it may choose to place its emphases at points at which others might demur.[11]

The reader will notice that the work is generous in the amount of bibliographical information provided in footnotes. In view of the complexity and importance of many of the issues discussed in this work, I have felt it right to indicate the works which have led me to the conclusions set out in its pages. It is hoped that these references may

---

[10] Alister E. McGrath, 'Engaging the Great Tradition: Evangelical Theology and the Role of Tradition', in John G. Stackhouse (ed.), *Evangelical Futures: A Conversation on Theological Method.* Grand Rapids, MI: Baker, 2000, 139–58.

[11] On the complex issue of defining evangelicalism, see David Bebbington, *Evangelicalism in Modern Britain: A History from the 1730s to the 1980s.* London: Hyman, 1989; Stanley J. Grenz, *Revisioning Evangelical Theology: A Fresh Agenda for the 21st Century.* Downers Grove, IL: InterVarsity Press, 1992; Kenneth Hylson-Smith, *Evangelicals in the Church of England 1734–1984.* Edinburgh: T&T Clark, 1988; Alister E. McGrath, 'An Evangelical Evaluation of Postliberalism', in T. R. Philips and D. L. Okholm (eds), *The Nature of Confession: Evangelicals and Postliberals in Conversation.* Downers Grove, IL: InterVarsity Press, 1996, 23–44; John G. Stackhouse, *Canadian Evangelicalism in the Twentieth Century: An Introduction to Its Character.* Toronto: University of Toronto Press, 1993.

also be of some use to readers in developing their own thinking on these issues.

It will be obvious that I owe an enormous amount to those who have taught me, argued with me, and helped me see things more clearly. I can only begin to acknowledge these kindnesses. I owe thanks to Professors J. R. Knowles, G. K. Radda and R. J. P. Williams for instilling in me both a love and respect for the natural sciences, and a profound and healthy suspicion of ideas not grounded in an engagement with the real world. I owe an incalculable amount to those who helped me capture and sustain a sense of the excitement of theology, and wish to thank especially Professor Timothy Gorringe, Fergus Kerr OP, Professor Oliver M. T. O'Donovan, the late Professor E. G. Rupp, Professor Thomas F. Torrance, and Edward J. Yarnold SJ. Wycliffe Hall, Oxford, at which I have taught since 1983, has been an academically stimulating and spiritually supportive community, and has provided me with a secure base for research and writing. I am especially grateful to Mr Darren C. Marks (St Hugh's College, Oxford), who acted as my research assistant in the final stages of this work, and made invaluable suggestions for the improvement of the text. The John Templeton Foundation made funds available to support the research underlying these three volumes; without such generous assistance, this work could not have been written. What you, reader, make of them remains to be seen. It is my hope that you will find them interesting; I can at least be sure that it will take you less time to read this series than it has taken me to research and write it.

ALISTER E. McGRATH
Oxford, October 2000

PART ONE

Prolegomena

Chapter 1

The Legitimacy of a Scientific Theology

The present work is conceived as an extended essay which explores the contours of a possible approach to a scientific theology. It aims to examine, critically yet appreciatively, the way in which the working assumptions and methods of Christian theology and the natural sciences interact with and illuminate each other, and allow each other's distinctive characteristics to be appreciated, as an interesting means to the greater end of achieving at least a partial synthesis of their insights. There are often significant similarities in the issues faced by both Christian theology and the natural sciences as they go about their respective tasks. It is therefore of considerable interest to ascertain whether these disciplines might have anything to learn from each other. This series of volumes is not intended to offer some definitive statements concerning the relation of Christian theology and the natural sciences, but to offer some suggestions which will stimulate discussion, even if they do not command assent.

The structure of this trilogy should make it clear that this work is primarily concerned with theological method, rather than with specific theological topics. This structure takes the following form:

1. *Nature.* This opening volume clarifies the general position to be adopted, before moving on to a detailed engagement with the concept of 'nature', which is of such decisive importance in any discussion of the relation of the natural sciences and theology. 'Nature' is often treated as a fundamental resource for theology, on the basis of the assumption that it is an unmediated and uninterpreted concept. Yet there is a growing and settled view

that the concept of 'nature' actually represents a socially mediated construct. Nature is thus to be viewed as an interpreted notion, which is unusually vulnerable to the challenge of deconstruction. The implications of this for a 'theology of nature' are explored, with especial reference to the Christian understanding of nature as creation.

2. *Reality.* The second volume in the series deals with the issue of realism in science and theology, and sets out both a critique of anti- and non-realism, and a positive statement of a realist position. In the light of this, the nature of a scientific theology is explored, with particular emphasis being placed upon theology as an *a posteriori* discipline which offers an account of reality.

3. *Theory.* The third and final volume in the series deals with the manner in which reality is represented, paying especial attention to the parallels between theological doctrines and scientific theories. This volume considers the origin, development and reception of such doctrines and theories, and notes the important parallels between the scientific and theological communities in these important matters.

By its very nature, this series of works is lengthy and complex. So why undertake such a major publishing programme? The answer lies in the degree of interconnectedness of the matters to be considered, which is such that it would be quite inappropriate to consider them in isolation. What is under consideration is not a series of isolated ideas, but a complex web of interacting concepts and methods, which demand to be considered as a system. The issues to be considered are not purely scientific or theological, but involve careful analysis of certain historical developments and episodes, the role of communities in testing and receiving ideas, and philosophical debates.

The need for this extended study is evident from a number of general and more specific considerations. In general terms, the growing interest in the relation of the natural sciences has thrown up a number of fundamental issues which have yet to be addressed with the detail and precision which they demand. We shall note two, simply to illustrate the issues. Much is made of 'natural theology' and 'the investigation of nature' in such discussions.[1] Yet what is 'nature'? How does this

---

[1] See, for example, Ian G. Barbour, 'Experiencing and Interpreting Nature in Science and Religion', *Zygon* 29 (1994), 457–87; Albert Borgmann, 'The Nature of Reality and the Reality of Nature', in Michael E. Soulé and Gary Lease (eds), *Reinventing Nature: Responses to Postmodern Deconstruction.* Washington, DC: Island Press, 1995, 31–46; Frederick Gregory,

notion relate to the more specifically theological concept of 'creation'? What are the intellectual rivals to the Christian understanding of nature, and how did they arise? Is it not a matter for some concern that the concept of nature has failed to receive the full theological attention that it demands? It is therefore imperative that this project should begin with a major engagement with the question of what is to be understood by the highly elusive – yet immensely important – concept of 'nature'.

A second example is provided by the rise of what is often referred to as the 'postliberal' school of theology, which stresses the importance of communities and narratives in theological reflection.[2] There is an obvious parallel here with the natural sciences, especially in the manner in which scientific communities originate theories and hypotheses, subject them to critical examination, and finally receive them within the community as a whole. Yet such parallels have been sadly over-looked, despite the considerable light which they cast upon the theological enterprise. The whole question of the genesis, development and reception of doctrine is of incalculable importance to theology, especially to those theologians who see their responsibilities in the light of being answerable to a community of faith. Yet the parallel process within the global scientific community, both in the past and at present, has not been given due attention. The present project will thus deal with this matter in some detail.

Yet the contribution of this project does not lie in the identification of a series of areas which have been neglected; it lies in its insistence that these be correlated, and brought together in a coherent vision of a 'scientific theology'. Charles Gore once spoke of the 'coherence' of Christian doctrine, meaning that each individual aspect of the Christian world-view was not freestanding, insulated from its neighbours. Rather, it was part of an interconnected and interactive whole. The manner in which the doctrines of the Trinity and the person of

---

Nature Lost? Natural Science and the German Theological Traditions of the Nineteenth Century. Cambridge, MA: Harvard University Press, 1992; C. Jungnickel and R. McCormmach, *Intellectual Mastery of Nature: Theoretical Physics from Ohm to Einstein.* 2 vols. Chicago: University of Chicago Press, 1986; James L. Larson, *Interpreting Nature: The Science of Living from Linnaeus to Kant.* Baltimore: Johns Hopkins University Press, 1994.

   [2] George Lindbeck, *The Nature of Doctrine.* Philadelphia: Westminster, 1984. More generally, see Brad J. Kellenberg, 'Unstuck from Yale: Theological Method after Lindbeck', *Scottish Journal of Theology* 50 (1997), 191–218; Stephen L. Stell, 'Hermeneutics in Theology and the Theology of Hermeneutics: Beyond Lindbeck and Tracy', *Journal of the American Academy of Religion* 61 (1993), 679–703.

Christ relate to one another may be offered as one example of this phenomenon of interconnectedness. While it is unquestionably of interest to publish monographs dealing with individual aspects of the intellectual dialogue between Christian theology and the natural sciences, these must be seen as subsidiary to a process of integration and synthesis, leading to the formulation of a 'scientific theology' as a whole.

Were this project to have been published as a series of articles, a fatal fragmentation would have developed, at two levels. First, the articles would have been dispersed across a range of journals, dealing with such matters as the history and philosophy of science, the intellectual history of the sixteenth and eighteenth centuries, specialized aspects of patristic and medieval theology, classical philosophy, and the contemporary debate over the nature of 'postmodernity'. These discussions belong together, and require integration into a greater whole, in order to allow at least a partial glimpse of this greater perspective. Second, the ideas developed could not have been correlated with one another, and their importance for each other, and for the greater project as a whole, could not have been explored.

There have been several attempts to develop theological or ideological systems patterned on the natural sciences in the past. The most noted of these is Friedrich Engels' attempt to conceive Marxism as a science with a methodology similar to those of the natural sciences. This may have seemed attractive at the time; it was to prove a serious embarrassment to later Marxist writers. Georg Lukács, for example, rejected this approach, and urged a greater ontological modesty in Marxist claims.[3] Marxism was not to be seen as a universal theory of scientific method, applicable to nature in its totality, but a social theory, focused on a set of specific economic and social issues. The natural sciences were an inappropriate analogy for Marxist theory.

The present project argues, largely on the basis of a detailed analysis of a Christian doctrine of creation, that there are good reasons, grounded in the structure of the world as the creation of God, for developing an approach to theology which recognizes and welcomes convergences. There is, it will be argued, both an ontological foundation and imperative for dialogue between the disciplines, with important implications for the formulation and development of a scientific theology.

---

[3] Georg Lukács, *History and Class Consciousness*. Cambridge, MA: MIT Press, 1971, 24. For a discussion, see Steven Vogel, *Against Nature: The Concept of Nature in Critical Theory*. Albany, NY: State University of New York Press, 1996, 5–7, 15–20.

Science as the *ancilla theologiae*

Throughout its long history, Christian theology has found itself exploring its interface with other disciplines. The driving force behind this is not difficult to discern. The implicit claim on the part of the Christian faith to have a bearing on every aspect of human life, evident in both classics of Christian theology such as Augustine's *City of God*[4] and more recent works such as Abraham Kuyper's 1898 Stone Lectures at Princeton,[5] encouraged the direct engagement of Christian theology and other intellectual disciplines, on the understanding that the Christian doctrines of creation and redemption demanded precisely such an engagement as an integral element of discipleship. This process of interdisciplinary engagement has embraced philosophy, the arts, the social sciences, as well as the broad area of human intellectual endeavour usually described as 'the natural sciences'. Some, such as the thirteenth-century writer Roger Bacon, brought all together in a coherent vision of a comprehensive human engagement with reality, undergirded by a vigorous theological foundation.[6] For Bacon, *scientia* as a whole was the handmaiden of theology.

The natural sciences today offer to Christian theology today precisely the role that Platonism offered our patristic, and Aristotelianism our medieval forebears. A scientific theology will treat the working assumptions and methods of the natural sciences as offering a supportive and illuminative role for the Christian theological enterprise, both assisting theological reflection and identifying and allowing exploitation of apologetic possibilities and strategies.

The notion of the ancilla theologiae

Before beginning to examine the manner in which the natural sciences can now become the *ancilla theologiae nova*, we must consider the issues which arise in allowing any world-view to play such a role. To permit the natural sciences to act in this matter is to allot them a certain privilege, and it must be understood from the outset that its role is

---

[4] See Robert A. Marcus, *Saeculum: History and Society in St Augustine*. Cambridge: Cambridge University Press, 1970.

[5] Abraham Kuyper, *Lectures on Calvinism*. Grand Rapids, MI: Eerdmans, 1948. See further Peter Somers Heslam, *Creating a Christian Worldview: Abraham Kuyper's Lectures on Calvinism*. Grand Rapids, MI: Eerdmans, 1998.

[6] David C. Lindberg, 'Science as Handmaiden: Roger Bacon and the Patristic Tradition', *Isis* 78 (1987), 518–36.

limited, circumscribed and above all *supportive.* The natural sciences neither prove nor disprove Christianity; they are, however, a most profitable dialogue partner.

An early example of this process of intellectual engagement is provided through the expansion of Christianity into a Hellenistic milieu in the first centuries of its history, which led to the exploration of the contours of the relationship between Christianity and secular Greek philosophy.[7] Greek metaphysics had developed the idea of a god long before its encounter with Christianity, with the result that the proclamation of the God of Jesus Christ in this milieu involved somewhat tortuous negotiations with this metaphysical god, leading to a complex and nuanced history of identifications and differentiations.[8] Among these may be noted the distinct tendency to identify the figure of Christ with the mediating principle of Middle Platonism. It is perhaps unfair to suggest that this represents the dominance of rationalism or philosophy over the data of Christian revelation. There is a temptation for every generation of theologians to bring a cluster of inherited metaphysical commitments as self-evident, requiring no further justification, to the task of theology. The engagement of the Christian tradition with an already existing view of reality thus required that certain elements of the philosophical concept of God be critically refined, remastered and reappropriated.

The interaction between Christian theology and classical philosophy underwent further exploration during the Middle Ages, as Aristotelianism became increasingly the *ancilla theologiae* of preference. The works of Aristotle had been preserved in the Islamic world, and had become a resource of some considerable importance for the development of a number of Arabic sciences.[9] With the translation of these works into Latin, a major new intellectual resource was placed at the disposal of medieval theology. As a study of those western Christian theologians to have availed themselves of this new resource – such as Thomas Aquinas – makes clear, the interaction between Christianity

[7] Aloys Grillmeier, 'Hellenisierung-Judaisierung des Christentums als Deuteprinzipien der Geschichte des kirchlichen Dogmas', *Scholastik* 33 (1958), 321–55, 528–55. More generally, see the important overview of Henry Chadwick, *Early Christian Thought and the Classical Tradition.* Oxford: Clarendon Press, 1966.

[8] Wolfhart Pannenberg, 'The Appropriation of the Philosophical Concept of God as a Dogmatic Problem of Early Christian Theology', in *Basic Questions in Theology II.* London: SCM Press, 1971, 119–83.

[9] Shukri B. Abed, *Aristotelian Logic and the Arabic Language in Al-Farabi.* Albany, NY: State University of New York Press, 1991; Francis E. Peters, *Aristotle and the Arabs: The Aristotelian Tradition in Islam.* New York: New York University Press, 1968.

and Aristotelianism was by no means straightforward.[10] For example, Aquinas' use of Aristotelian physics – as in his argument *ex motu* – caused some difficulties for traditional themes of Christian belief.[11] It was clear that an uncritical appropriation of Aristotelian insights was not a realistic possibility for theology. This perception was strengthened by certain shifts in the reception of Aristotelianism in the later Renaissance, not without significance for Christian theology,[12] and by the growing hostility towards the use of Aristotle in the more Augustinian writers of the later Middle Ages.[13] In that Aristotle's corpus of writings embraced both physics and metaphysics, meteoreology and logic, it was inevitable that the interaction between Christian theology and Aristotelianism would go far beyond the confines of philosophy, and embrace the natural sciences.

In the late sixteenth and early seventeenth century, Protestant Orthodoxy – both Lutheran and Reformed – found Aristotelianism a congenial dialogue partner, especially in relation to issues of theological method.[14] The rival system of Pierre Ramus found favour with other Protestant theologians, especially within English Puritanism.[15] Nineteenth-century American evangelicalism, noted for its commitment to the supreme authority of Scripture, did not have any difficulty in using some of the leading ideas of the Scottish Enlightenment in defending and developing their proposals.[16] Rudolf Bultmann and Paul Tillich found the form of existentialism developed in the writings of

[10] William E. Carroll, 'San Tommaso, Aristotele e la creazione', *Annales Theologici* 8 (1994), 363–76; James A. Weisheipl, 'Aristotle's Concept of Nature: Avicenna and Aquinas', in Lawrence D. Roberts (ed.), *Approaches to Nature in the Middle Ages*. Binghamton, NY: Center for Medieval and Early Renaissance Studies, 1982, 137–60.

[11] Alister E. McGrath, 'The Influence of Aristotelian Physics upon St Thomas Aquinas' Discussion of the *Processus Iustificationis*', *Recherches de théologie ancienne et médiévale* 51 (1984), 223–9.

[12] Charles B. Schmitt, 'Towards a Reassessment of Renaissance Aristotelianism', *History of Science* 11 (1973), 159–93.

[13] Adolar Zumkeller, 'Die Augustinertheologen Simon Fidati von Cascia und Hugolin von Orvieto und Martin Luthers Kritik an Aristoteles', *Archiv für Reformationsgeschichte* 54 (1963), 13–37; Alister E. McGrath, *Luther's Theology of the Cross: Martin Luther's Theological Breakthrough*. Oxford: Blackwell, 1985, 136–41.

[14] Richard Schröder, *Johann Gerhards lutherische Christologie und die aristotelische Metaphysik*. Tübingen: Mohr, 1983.

[15] Brian G. Armstrong, *Calvinism and the Amyraut Heresy: Protestant Scholasticism and Humanism in Seventeenth-Century France*. Madison, WI: University of Wisconsin Press, 1969; Donald K. McKim, *Ramism in William Perkins' Theology*. New York: Peter Lang, 1987.

[16] Sidney E. Ahlstrom, 'The Scottish Philosophy and American Theology', *Church History* 24 (1955), 257–72; Mark Noll, *Princeton and the Republic, 1768–1822*. Princeton, NJ: Princeton University Press, 1989, 28–58.

Martin Heidegger to be theologically fruitful,[17] where Emil Brunner (much to the irritation of Karl Barth) exploited the dialogical personalism of Martin Buber.[18] This list could be extended without difficulty. The point at issue is that, throughout its long history, Christian theology has willingly drawn upon philosophical resources to assist it in its task of exploration, criticism and synthesis.

The issues which are raised by the theological adoption of such philosophies are quite well understood, and may be summarized briefly as follows.

- The *potential* of the approach is that it allows for rigorous exploration of ideas, allowing parallels with other spheres of human intellectual activity to be appreciated and appropriated. It also serves an important apologetic purpose, in that it allows the Christian proclamation to be related to a wider intellectual culture, by identifying linguistic and conceptual parallels through which the gospel may be preached more effectively. Providing that the *ancilla* is understood to function in a ministerial, rather than magisterial, capacity, the integrity of theology as a discipline can be maintained without undue difficulty.

- The *danger* of the approach is that ideas whose origins, nature and justification lie outside the Christian faith may come to have a significant or decisive influence over how the Christian faith is presented or conceived. The history of the Christian tradition offers us numerous examples of secular philosophy being allowed to play a magisterial, rather than ministerial, role, whatever the original intention in adopting it may have been. Adolf von Harnack argued that the influence of Greek metaphysics upon Christianity was such that an essentially Hebraic gospel was distorted through the gradual assimilation of the gospel to Hellenistic ways of thinking.[19] Martin Luther complained that much late medieval Christian theology rested on Aristotle, rather than the Bible.[20] For Karl Barth, leaning on any secular philosophy

[17] John Macquarrie, *An Existentialist Theology: A Comparison of Heidegger and Bultmann.* London: SCM Press, 1965.
[18] Bernhard Langemeyer, *Der dialogische Personalismus in der evangelischen und katholischen Theologie der Gegenwart.* Paderborn: Verlag Bonifacius-Druckerei, 1963; Roman Rössler, *Person und Glaube: Der Personalismus der Gottesbeziehung bei Emil Brunner.* Munich: Kaiser Verlag, 1965.
[19] E. J. Meijering, *Die Hellenisierung des Christentums im Urteil Adolf von Harnack.* Amsterdam: Kampen, 1985.
[20] McGrath, *Luther's Theology of the Cross: Martin Luther's Theological Breakthrough,* 136–41.

or methodology – to however moderate an extent – risked introducing anthropology into theology, and compromising theology's
distinctive character as a response to divine revelation.[21]

On the basis of this brief analysis, it will be clear that there exists a
well-established tradition within Christian theology of fostering interaction with intellectual resources which ultimately have their origins
and derive their legitimation from outside the Christian perspective.
The critical use of the methods and assumptions of the natural sciences
may thus be argued to conform to an acceptable pattern, providing
that they are understood to function in a ministerial capacity as a
theological resource. In what follows, we shall consider some aspects of
the debate over the use of such resources in greater detail.

The patristic debate over philosophy as the ancilla theologiae

An intensive debate took place during the patristic period over this
issue, and may be regarded as being of landmark importance. One of
the most important debates in the early church concerned the extent to
which Christians could appropriate the immense cultural legacy of the
classical world – poetry, philosophy, and literature. In what ways could
Platonism be used to communicate the Christian faith? The debate
went beyond the question of the *ideas* to be used in this matter to
include the *literary form* in which such ideas were deployed. In what
way could the *ars poetica* be adopted by Christian writers, anxious to
use such classical modes of writing to expound and communicate their
faith? Or was the very use of such a literary medium tantamount to
compromising the essentials of the Christian faith? It was a debate of
immense significance, as it raised the question of whether Christianity
would turn its back on the classical heritage, or appropriate it, even if
in a modified form.

One early answer to this important question was given by Justin
Martyr, a second-century writer with a particular concern to exploit
the parallels between Christianity and Platonism as a means of communicating the gospel. For Justin, the seeds of divine wisdom had
been sown throughout the world, which meant that Christians could
and should expect to find aspects of the gospel reflected outside the
church.[22]

---

[21] Arie L. Molendijk, 'Ein heidnische Wissenschaftsbegriff. Der Streit zwischen Heinrich
Scholtz und Karl Barth um die Wissenschaftlichkeit der Theologie', *Evangelische Theologie*
52 (1992), 527–45.

[22] Justin Martyr, *Apologia* I.xlvi.2–3; II.x.2–3; II.xiii.4–6.

We have been taught that Christ is the firstborn of God, and we have proclaimed that he is the Logos, in whom every race of people have shared. And those who live according to the Logos are Christians, even though they may have been counted as atheists – such as Socrates and Heraclitus, and others like them, among the Greeks . . . Whatever either lawyers or philosophers have said well, was articulated by finding and reflecting upon some aspect of the Logos. However, since they did not know the Logos – which is Christ – in its entirety, they often contradicted themselves . . . Whatever all people have said well belongs to us Christians. For we worship and love, next to God, the Logos, who comes from the unbegotten and ineffable God, since it was for our sake that he became a human being, in order that he might share in our sufferings and bring us healing. For all writers were able to see the truth darkly, on account of the implanted seed of the Logos which was grafted into them.

For Justin, Christians were therefore at liberty to draw upon classical culture, in the knowledge that whatever 'has been said well' ultimately draws upon divine wisdom and insight.

Important though Justin's argument may have been, it received a somewhat cool reception in many sections of the Christian church. The main difficulty was that it was seen to virtually equate Christianity with classical culture by failing to articulate adequate grounds for distinguishing them, apparently suggesting that Christian theology and Platonism were simply different ways of viewing the same divine realities. Justin's pupil Tatian (born *c.* 120) was sceptical concerning the merits of classic rhetoric and poetry, both of which he regarded as encouraging deception and a disregard for matters of truth. The most severe criticism of this kind of approach was to be found in the writings of Tertullian, a third-century Roman lawyer who converted to Christianity. What, he asked, has Athens to do with Jerusalem? What relevance has the Platonic academy for the church? The manner in which the question is posed makes Tertullian's answer clear: Christianity must maintain its distinctive identity by avoiding such secular influences.[23]

Philosophy provides the material of worldly wisdom, in boldly asserting itself to be the interpreter of the divine nature and dispensation. The heresies themselves receive their weapons from philosophy. It was from this source that Valentinus, who was a disciple of Plato, got his ideas about the 'aeons' and the 'trinity of humanity'. And it was from there that the god of Marcion (much to be preferred, on account of his

[23] Tertullian, *de praescriptione haereticorum*, 7.

tranquillity) came; Marcion came from the Stoics. To say that the soul is subject to death is to go the way of Epicurus. And the denial of the resurrection of the body is found throughout the writings of all the philosophers. To say that matter is equal with God is to follow the doctrine of Zeno; to speak of a god of fire is to draw on Heraclitus. It is the same subjects which preoccupy both the heretics and the philosophers. Where does evil come from, and why? Where does human nature come from, and how? . . . What has Athens to do with Jerusalem? What has the Academy to do with the church? Our system of beliefs comes from the Porch of Solomon, who himself taught that it was necessary to seek God in the simplicity of the heart. So much the worse for those who talk of a 'stoic', 'platonic' or 'dialectical' Christianity!

This wholesale rejection of every aspect of pagan culture had the advantage of being simple to understand. Christianity, according to Tertullian, was basically a counter-cultural movement, which refused to allow itself to be contaminated in any way by the mental or moral environment in which it took root.

Tertullian's basic question would find echoes throughout Christian history. For example, the English writer Alcuin rebuked the monks of Lindisfarne Abbey in 797 for reading too many Nordic sagas. 'What has Ingeld to do with Christ?', he asked, and by doing so, posed exactly the same question raised by Tertullian centuries earlier. Alcuin's remedy for the situation was direct and to the point: 'Let the words of God be read aloud at table in your refectory. It is the reader who should be heard there, not someone playing and fluting. It is the fathers of the church, and not the songs of the heathen, who should be heard.'

Yet there were difficulties with this consistently negative approach. It seemed to deny Christians access to or use of any of the intellectual and cultural heritage for a thoroughly laudable purpose – namely, the preaching of the gospel. Many early Christian writers studied classic rhetoric as a means of improving their preaching and writing, and thus facilitating the communication of the faith to those outside the church. Was Tertullian excluding this? Alongside this pragmatic approach could be found a more theological issue. Does not all true wisdom have its origins in God? And if so, should not Christians honour that truth where it is to be found? To his critics, Tertullian seemed to offer little in the way of response to these questions.

The matter became of greater significance with the conversion of the Roman emperor Constantine around the year 313. Christianity gradually came into favour, eventually to become the official religion of the Roman empire. The issue of the interaction of Christianity and classical culture now assumed a new significance. Rome was now the servant of the gospel; might not the same be true of its culture? If the Roman state could be viewed positively by Christians, why not also its cultural heritage? It seemed as if a door had opened upon some very interesting possibilities. Prior to 313, this possibility could only have been dreamt of. After 313, its exploration became a matter of urgency for leading Christian thinkers.

It is no surprise that the answer which would finally gain acceptance was set out by Augustine of Hippo, and can perhaps be best described as the 'critical appropriation of classical culture'. For Augustine, the situation of Christians in late classical culture was comparable to Israel fleeing from captivity in Egypt at the time of the Exodus. Although they left the idols of Egypt behind them, they carried the gold and silver of Egypt with them, in order to make better and proper use of such riches, which were thus liberated in order to serve a higher purpose than before. In much the same way, the philosophy and culture of the ancient world could be appropriated by Christians, where this seemed right, and thus allowed to serve the cause of the Christian faith. Augustine clinched his argument by pointing out how several recent distinguished Christians had made use of classical wisdom in advancing the gospel.[24]

> If those who are called philosophers, particularly the Platonists, have said anything which is true and consistent with our faith, we must not reject it, but claim it for our own use, in the knowledge that they possess it unlawfully. The Egyptians possessed idols and heavy burdens, which the children of Israel hated and from which they fled; however, they also possessed vessels of gold and silver and clothes which our forebears, in leaving Egypt, took for themselves in secret, intending to use them in a better manner (Exodus 3:21–22; 12:35–36) . . . In the same way, pagan learning is not entirely made up of false teachings and superstitions. It contains also some excellent teachings, well suited to be used by truth, and excellent moral values. Indeed, some truths are even found among them which relate to the worship of the one God. Now these are, so to speak, their gold and their silver, which they did not invent themselves, but which they dug out of the mines of the providence of God, which are scattered throughout the world, yet which are improperly and unlawfully prostituted to the worship of demons. The Christian, therefore, can separate these truths from their unfortunate associations, take them away, and put them to their proper use for the proclamation of the gospel . . . What else have many good and faithful people from

[24] Augustine of Hippo, *de doctrina Christiana*, II.xl.60–1.

amongst us done. Look at the wealth of gold and silver and clothes which Cyprian – that eloquent teacher and blessed martyr – brought with him when he left Egypt! And think of all that Lactantius brought with him, not to mention Marius Victorinus, Optatus and Hilary of Poitiers, and others who are still living! And look at how much the Greeks have borrowed! And before all of these, we find that Moses, that most faithful servant of God, had done the same thing: after all, it is written of him that 'he was learned in all the wisdom of the Egyptians' (Acts 7:22).

The fundamental theme is that of taking a way of thinking – or writing, or speaking – which had hitherto been put to pagan use, and liberating it so that it might be put to the service of the gospel. Augustine argues that what are essentially neutral yet valuable ways of thinking or self-expression have been quarried in 'the mines of the providence of God'; the difficulty is the use to which they were put within pagan culture, in that they had been 'improperly and unlawfully prostituted to the worship of demons'.

Augustine's approach thus laid the foundation for the assertion that whatever was good, true or beautiful could be used in the service of the gospel. It was this approach which would prove dominant in the western church, providing a theological foundation for the critical appropriation by Christian writers of philosophical ideas and literary genres whose origins lay outside the church. The scene was thus set for the creative interaction of Christian theology, liturgy and spirituality with the cultural tradition of the ancient world – unquestionably one of the most interesting and fertile examples of cultural cross-fertilization in human intellectual history.

The social sciences as ancilla theologiae?

Where the ancient world looked to the riches of the classical philosophical tradition in its quest for wisdom, the modern world has tended to find this in the social sciences. Certain theologians, generally disinclined to take seriously the claims to intellectual resilience on the part of the classical theological tradition, have sought to find a neutral and secure vantage point from which to undertake the theological enterprise. The desire is commendable; the chosen means of achieving this has proved flawed. Precisely on account of their radical and often aggressive commitment to a naturalist world-view, the social sciences offer a skewed perspective on religion which, in the first place, refuses to acknowledge an ancillary role to theology, and in the second place, denies the entire legitimacy of the theological project, as this is traditionally conceived.

Certain older sociologies of knowledge have laid particular interpretative weight upon the concepts of superstructure and substructure, reflecting the origins of many sociological concerns in the writings of Karl Marx. According to Marx, thought and knowledge are essentially a superstructure erected upon, or thrown up by, an underlying social reality.[25] They are protective ideational cocoons spun around themselves by vulnerable social groupings. Ideas are thus essentially an intellectual superstructure erected upon a determinative social or economic substructure. For the Durkheimian, religious ideas are erroneous cognitive responses to social structures. The historicist emphasis upon the fact that all knowledge is historically located – and hence historically determined (usually expressed using the terms *Standortsgebundenheit* and *Sitz im Leben*) – leads to an insistence upon the relativity of all perspectives upon human life. According to this viewpoint, no human thought is exempt from the pervasive (yet often unacknowledged) influence of ideology.[26]

It is, of course, equally important at this point to observe that sociology itself developed historically from the philosophical, moral and political concerns, presuppositions and methods of early nineteenth-century western Europe, and is subject to the same charge of *Standortsgebundenheit* levelled against other disciplines – including the suspicion that it may represent nothing more than a conceptual epiphenomenon of underlying economic, political and social realities. The tensions which this may create even within philosophies orientated towards social theory will be evident: it is thus particularly interesting to note the endemic dualism within much recent Marxist epistemology (for example, in the writings of Louis Althusser, Lucio Colletti and Jürgen Habermas) between thought as 'truth' on the one hand, and as historically situated on the other, apparently reflecting a reluctance to allow that Marxist frameworks of rationality themselves are simply the consequence of a given historical situation. The belief that such frameworks possess wider validity, despite the theoretical contradictions this might seem to imply, is deeply ingrained in many writings of the Frankfurt school.[27] In effect, Althusser and his colleagues appear to have little option but to smuggle the notion of some understanding of truth which is *not* dependent upon social location back into their reflections, in order to lend their

[25] Nicholas Lash, *A Matter of Hope: A Theologian's Reflections on the Thought of Karl Marx*. Notre Dame, IN: University of Notre Dame Press, 1982, 112–24.

[26] Peter L. Berger and Thomas Luckmann, *The Social Construction of Reality: A Treatise in the Sociology of Knowledge*. Harmondsworth: Penguin, 1971.

[27] Rolf Wiggershaus, *The Frankfurt School: Its History, Theories and Political Significance*. Cambridge: Polity Press, 1994.

theories the universal validity upon which their application ultimately depends.

So how can the social sciences function as the *ancilla theologiae*, as some clearly hope they may? Viewed from the perspective of the social sciences, Christian theology appears to be little more than an unwelcome and unimportant epiphenomenon, founded on social structures and dynamics. It is intellectually derivative, lacking any autonomy. One of the most influential myths of the modern period has been the belief that it is possible to locate and occupy a non-ideological vantage-point, from which reality may be surveyed and interpreted.[28] The social sciences have been among the chief and most strident claimants to such space, arguing that they offer a neutral and objective reading of reality, in which the ultimately spurious truth-claims of religious groupings may be deflated and deconstructed in terms of unacknowledged, yet ultimately determinative, social factors. The theological outcome of this engagement has thus been as predictable as it is unsatisfactory. A subtle reversal of roles took place, with the *ancilla* becoming the *domina*.

In his major study *Theology and Social Theory* (1993), John Milbank sets out a powerful critique of any attempt to ground theology in social theory.[29] Milbank offers both a critique of the foundations of social theory, and a positive statement of a programme for Christian theology based upon an incarnational ontology. For Milbank, there is no reality other than, or apart from, God; for that very reason, any attempt to construct a secular ontology must be doomed to failure, along with any theological system or approach foolish enough to become ideationally dependent upon such an ontology. Milbank argues that, whatever its proponents may think on the matter, sociology ultimately depends upon an unacknowledged theological foundation. 'Sociology is only able to explain, or even illuminate, religion to the extent that it conceals its own theological borrowings and its own quasi-religious status.'[30] Milbank finds this particularly well illustrated in Durkheim's interpretation of the nature of sacrifice, in which a concealed theological commitment is passed off as an objective social analysis:[31]

[28] Alister E. McGrath, *The Genesis of Doctrine*. Oxford: Blackwell, 1990, 81–102.

[29] John Milbank, *Theology and Social Theory. Beyond Secular Reason*. Oxford: Blackwell, 1993.

[30] Milbank, *Theology and Social Theory*, 52. See further Roland Spjuth, 'Redemption without Actuality: A Critical Interrelation between Eberhard Jüngel's and John Milbank's Ontological Endeavours', *Modern Theology* 14 (1998), 505–22.

[31] Milbank, *Theology and Social Theory*, 68.

Durkheim rejects as 'theological' or 'metaphysical' the usual religious or ethical accounts of sacrifice or crime, yet he can only do so by substituting a 'scientific' account which itself embodies a naturalized version of the myth of a universal expiatory law traceable back to *theological* positivism.

Milbank's critique has resonated with a new generation of theologians, impatient with the overstatements and aggressively reductionist agenda of social theory.[32] Of particular interest for the purposes of the present project, Milbank rightly discerns the need for a new statement of the relationship of nature and grace – a theme to which we shall return presently.[33]

The natural sciences as the ancilla theologiae

It is entirely understandable why the natural sciences should be considered a highly attractive dialogue partner for other intellectual disciplines. Wearied by the distortion of theory by prejudice in so many areas of intellectual activity, many have found the objectivity sought by the natural sciences to offer stability and sanity to their reflections. Israel Scheffler's reflections on the distinct character of the natural sciences help us understand why this might be the case:[34]

> A fundamental feature of science is its ideal of objectivity, an ideal that subjects all scientific statements to the test of independent and impartial criteria, recognizing no authority of persons in the realm of cognition. The claimant to scientific knowledge . . . is trying to meet independent standards, to satisfy factual requirements whose fulfilment cannot be guaranteed in advance.

Scheffler's comments raise some important questions – for example, just what is meant by 'objectivity'? Yet the vision offered is both attractive and compelling. It is hardly surprising that many have turned to the natural sciences – rather than to the *philosophie du jour* – for robust intellectual stimulation.

Christian theologians are no exception to this trend. The natural sciences seem to offer to contemporary Christian theology the same intellectual opportunities that earlier generations discerned within Aristotelianism or Cartesianism – the possibility of a dialogue partner with genuine insights to offer, which might be accommodated and

---

[32] See John Milbank, Catherine Pickstock and Graham Ward (eds), *Radical Orthodoxy: A New Theology*. London: Routledge, 1999.

[33] Milbank, *Theology and Social Theory*, 207–9.

[34] Israel Scheffler, *Science and Subjectivity*. Indianapolis: Bobbs Merrill, 1967, 1.

exploited within the theological enterprise. An established framework for this process of engagement already lay to hand, in the long tradition of the *ancilla theologiae*. It was merely necessary to alter the identity of the handmaid in question.

To appeal to the natural sciences as the handmaid of Christian theology is thus merely to modify the grand tradition of cultural engagement, in the sense that a different handmaid is being proposed. The general strategy is well understood; discussion is thus focused, not on the general strategy as such, but on the identity of the handmaid, and the specific opportunities and risks which this brings to the task at hand. One of those risks is that a failure to respect the distinct integrity of Christian theology could lead to it proceeding along routes which lead initially to Deism, and finally to atheism or some form of philosophical naturalism.[35] For certain of its anxious critics, any form of positive interaction between Christian theology and the natural sciences potentially represents a Faustian pact, in which Christian theology abandons the inner essence of its identity in order to gain some slight credibility among its scientifically literate despisers.

The pressure to articulate the Christian theological vision in terms congenial to the scientific spirit of the age can easily lead to the critical theological category of 'revelation' being restated as, and reduced to, the awareness of an order already present in creation – to mention only one aspect of this Faustian bargain which some theologians rightly discern and correctly fear. Revelation thus becomes the reduplication of nature, in a manner already associated with the most important early Deist writing, Matthew Tindal's 1730 work *Christianity as Old as Creation, or the Gospel a Republication of the Religion of Nature*. A scientific theology allots a ministerial, and religious naturalism a magisterial, role to the natural sciences.

The admission of the methods of the natural sciences into the operative logic of Christian theology is thus fraught with some danger, especially if there were to be a failure to take into account the provisionality of scientific judgements, and the likelihood of further 'paradigm shifts' – to use the ambivalent and contested phrase of Thomas Kuhn. We shall consider this further, in conjunction with the related danger of relying upon transient theological trends as a basis for a responsible scientific theology, at a later stage in this discussion.

---

[35] A development which Michael Buckley and others discern as underlying the evolution of modern atheism: see Michael Buckley, *At the Origins of Modern Atheism*. New Haven, CT: Yale University Press, 1987, 99–193.

These concerns are real, and must be given due weight in any formulation of a scientific theology. Yet these concerns represent only one
aspect of the issue, in that the points just made often assume that any
marriage between theology and the natural sciences is synthetic, rather
than natural, an artificial arrangement brought about by the intellectual
equivalent of Yenta the village matchmaker. Yet it is critical to realize
that any relationships between theology and the natural sciences in this
capacity are not arbitrary, as if they had been chosen merely on the
basis of a random search for a new dialogue partner for Christian
theology. There are excellent reasons for suggesting that such a dialogue
is not merely *legitimated* by Christian theology, but is actually *demanded*
on account of the Christian understanding of the nature of reality. In
what follows, we shall explore this point further.

The ontological imperative for theological engagement with the natural sciences

The present series of works argues for theological engagement with the
natural sciences, leading to the development of a scientific theology.
Some might argue that a dialogue between the natural sciences and
Christian theology is not demanded or imposed upon us by virtue of
the nature of reality itself; it rests upon a free decision that this dialogue
shall take place. The foundations of a positive interaction between these
disciplines thus rests upon an attitude, a 'blik', which we have freely
constructed, rather than representing a response to a situation which
exists whether we choose to acknowledge it, over which we have no
control. On the basis of this approach, to affirm such a dialogue is to
choose to adopt a certain attitude towards science and theology as an
expression of the sovereignty of individual choice. It is, according to
this view, an uncoerced decision of the human mind, resting upon
nothing more than the freedom of the individual to do what he or
she pleases, and the autonomy of the human imagination to construct
and invent whatever linkages or associations it finds to its liking,
profit or amusement. The grounds and foundations of such a dialogue
are thus to be seen as a projection of the free human mind, an affirmation
of the right of the individual to make choices without being fettered by
the limitations of evidence, warrant or external concerns.

Some, discontented with the apparent arbitrariness of this view,
might posit a more pragmatic approach. The dialogue is to be fostered
in that dialogue is in itself a good thing. Dialogue brings peace and
co-operation, ending the open warfare which has existed between the

natural sciences and Christian theology for many years. Such views – which, it has to be said, rest upon a rather uncritical acceptance of the outdated 'warfare' model of the interaction of the disciplines – at least have the advantage of offering some form of justification for the dialogue which goes beyond the free, and potentially arbitrary, decision and attitude of an individual. Others might wish to supplement this further, by arguing that the exploration of intellectual interstices is one of the most creative of intellectual adventures. Might not the fusion of the ancient traditions of Christian theology and the new insights of the natural sciences lead to a fusion of wisdoms?

The approach adopted in this study, which will be expounded and defended in detail in what follows, may be stated briefly as follows. *A positive working relationship between Christian theology and the natural sciences is demanded by the Christian understanding of the nature of reality itself* – an understanding which is grounded in the doctrine of creation. The Christian doctrine of creation demands a unitary approach to knowledge, while being responsive to diversity within that creation. If God made the world, which therefore has the status of being 'creation' as well as 'nature', it is to be expected that something of the character of God might be disclosed through that creation. This theme was developed during the Middle Ages, and can be shown to be an integral element of the theology of Thomas Aquinas, particularly in those of his writings which were directed towards a non-Christian audience.[36] In the sixteenth century, the emerging Reformed tradition developed a highly sophisticated theory of natural theology, which on the one hand stressed its subordinate role to divine revelation, while on the other noting its not insignificant apologetic implications and possibilities.

For Calvin, God reveals his glory, wisdom and power through the natural order, so that none might be without knowledge of his reality and significance for their lives.[37]

> There is within the human mind, and that by natural instinct, a sense of divinity. This we take to be beyond controversy. So that no-one might take refuge in the pretext of ignorance, God frequently renews and sometimes increases this awareness, so that all people, recognizing that

[36] An excellent example being the *Summa contra Gentiles*. See Norman Kretzmann, *The Metaphysics of Theism: Aquinas's Natural Theology in Summa contra Gentiles I*. Oxford: Clarendon Press, 1997. On the related issue of natural law, see Anthony J. Lisska, *Aquinas's Theory of Natural Law*. Oxford: Clarendon Press, 1996.

[37] *Institutes* I.iii.1, 2. The use made of Cicero in this connection is important: see Emil Grislis, 'Calvin's Use of Cicero in the *Institutes* I:1–5: A Case Study in Theological Method', *Archiv für Reformationsgeschichte* 62 (1971), 5–37.

there is a God and that he is their creator, are condemned by their own testimony because they have failed to worship him and to give their lives to his service . . . There are innumerable witnesses in heaven and on earth that declare the wonders of his wisdom. Not only those more arcane matters for the closer observation of which astronomy, medicine, and all of natural science (*tota physica scientia*) are intended, but also those which force themselves upon the sight of even the most unlearned and ignorant peoples, so that they cannot even open their eyes without being forced to see them.

Nevertheless, Calvin insists that this knowledge of God is neither complete nor saving; this full knowledge of God is only to be had through Scripture.[38] Calvin does not attempt to develop a natural theology in the sense of a source of knowledge of God which is autonomous, and can be arrived at independently of God's revelation in Scripture. Nevertheless, Calvin lays the foundation for the notion that something of God may be known from the natural order, and that the full revelation of God in Scripture confirms and completes this limited natural knowledge of God. Further development of the theme took place subsequently within the Reformation tradition, both at the Genevan Academy and in the Reformed schools of theology elsewhere, particularly in the Netherlands.[39]

This concept of natural theology received a particularly significant development within the confessional element of the Reformed tradition. The Gallic Confession of Faith (1559) argues that God reveals himself to humanity in two manners:[40]

First, in his works, both in their creation and their preservation and control. Second, and more clearly, in his Word, which was revealed through oracles in the beginning, and which was subsequently committed to writing in the books which we call the Holy Scriptures.

A related idea was set out in the Belgic Confession (1561), which expanded the brief statement on natural theology found in the Gallic

[38] *Institutes* I.vi.1. For a full discussion, see Edward A. Dowey, *The Knowledge of God in Calvin's Theology*. New York: Columbia University Press, 1952; T. H. L. Parker, *Calvin's Doctrine of the Knowledge of God*. 2nd edn. Edinburgh: Oliver & Boyd, 1969.

[39] See Michael Heyd, 'Un rôle nouveau pour la science: Jean Alphonse Turrettini et les débuts de la théologie naturelle à Genève', *Revue de théologie et philosophie* 112 (1982), 25–42; John Platt, *Reformed Thought and Scholasticism: The Arguments for the Existence of God in Dutch Theology*. Leiden: E. J. Brill, 1982; Martin Klauber, 'Jean-Alphonse Turrettini (1671–1737) on Natural Theology: The Triumph of Reason over Revelation at the Academy of Geneva', *Scottish Journal of Theology* 47 (1994), 301–25.

[40] *Confessio Gallicana*, 1559, article 2; in E. F. K. Müller (ed.), *Die Bekenntnisschriften der reformierten Kirche*. Leipzig: Böhme, 1903, 221–2.

Confession. Once more, knowledge of God is affirmed to come about by two means:[41]

> First, by the creation, preservation and government of the universe, which is before our eyes as a most beautiful book, in which all creatures, great and small, are like so many characters leading us to contemplate the invisible things of God, namely, his eternal power and Godhead, as the Apostle Paul declares (Romans 1:20). All of these things are sufficient to convince humanity, and leave them without excuse. Second, he makes himself known more clearly and fully to us by his holy and divine Word; that is to say, as far as is necessary for us to know in this life, to his glory and our salvation.

The two themes which emerge clearly from these confessional statements can be summarized as follows:

1. There are two modes of knowing God, one through the natural order, and the second through Scripture.

2. The second mode is clearer and fuller than the first.

It will be clear that this consideration is of no small importance in relation to the complex and contested historical question of whether Christianity is directly implicated in the origins of the natural sciences,[42] and the debate within Christian theology over the legitimate place and scope of natural theology (to be discussed later in this volume). There are excellent reasons for suggesting that a religious motivation may be discerned within the writings of many who actively promoted the natural sciences. However, it needs to be borne in mind that such religious motivations can be conceived in three different manners:

1. *A specifically theological perspective* – such as the ordering of the world in creation, or the contingency of the created order. T. F. Torrance is perhaps the most important of those who have argued that this perspective was of critical importance in the emergence

---

[41] *Confessio Belgica*, 1561, article 2; in Müller (ed.), *Bekenntnisschriften der reformierten Kirche*, 233.

[42] For the outlines of some aspects of this debate, see G. B. Deason, 'The Protestant Reformation and the Rise of Modern Science', *Scottish Journal of Theology* 38 (1985), 221–40; Edward Grant, *The Foundations of Science in the Middle Ages: Their Religious, Institutional and Intellectual Contexts*. Cambridge: Cambridge University Press, 1996; Peter Harrison, *The Bible, Protestantism, and the Rise of Natural Science*. Cambridge: Cambridge University Press, 1998; R. Hooykaas, *Religion and the Rise of Modern Science*. Edinburgh: Scottish Academic Press, 1972; Stanley L. Jaki, 'Science and Christian Theism: A Mutual Witness', *Scottish Journal of Theology* 32 (1979), 563–70; David C. Lindberg and Ronald L. Numbers, 'Beyond War and Peace: A Reappraisal of the Encounter between Christianity and Science', *Church History* 55 (1984), 338–54.

of the natural sciences.[43] While this assertion is historically vulnerable, it remains important and influential.

2. *A general cultural perspective*, in which some ideas of Christian theology have been absorbed, not necessarily with any awareness of their ultimate provenance, into western culture as a whole. The primary motivation for scientific study is primarily cultural, and secondarily theological.

3. *An indirect religious motivation* may be involved. For example, it is possible to argue that an aspect of the Puritan outlook on the world, ultimately theological in its origins, led to scientific research becoming socially acceptable. In its original form, the celebrated 'Merton Thesis' saw the origins of this new climate of acceptability as lying in the Reformed doctrine of election (rather than the doctrine of creation), which thus indirectly encouraged the emergence of the sciences.[44]

It would go beyond the available evidence to draw the conclusion that the Christian doctrine of creation was of critical importance towards the general emergence of the natural sciences. Perhaps theological reasons may be given as to why it *should* have been; yet history and theory do not often converge with quite the precision that theoreticians so earnestly covet. Yet it may still be noted that the Christian doctrine of creation was indeed a factor – among others – not least in that it can be shown to have had such a motivating and legitimating influence upon a number of individuals within the scientific community.

As we have seen, the Christian understanding of the ontology of creation demands a faithful investigation of nature. For this reason, the exploration of the interface between Christian theology and the natural sciences is to be regarded as ontologically motivated and legitimated. Yet the Christian doctrine of creation is not limited by the demand that we see nature as creation; it has a highly significant Christological component. The New Testament identifies an implicit continuity between creation and redemption, focused on the person and work of Christ.[45] The Christological dimensions of the doctrine of creation are

[43] See for example, Thomas F. Torrance, *Divine and Contingent Order*. Oxford: Oxford University Press, 1981, 2–5; idem, *The Ground and Grammar of Theology*. Belfast: Christian Journals Ltd, 1980, 52–60.

[44] For a basic account, see H. Floris Cohen, *The Scientific Revolution: A Historiographical Inquiry*. Chicago: University of Chicago Press, 1994, 314–21.

[45] Peter Stuhlmacher, 'Erwägungen zum ontologischen Charakter der *kaine ktisis* bei Paulus', *Evangelische Theologie* 27 (1967), 1–35.

such that the divine rationality – whether this is conceptualized as *logos* or as *ratio* – must be thought of as being *embedded in creation and embodied in Christ*. The same divine rationality or wisdom which the natural sciences discern within the created order is to be identified within the *logos* incarnate, Jesus Christ. Creation and Christ ultimately bear witness to the same God, and the same divine rationality.

As will become clear during this study, this kind of consideration leads to the possibility of seeing theology as a science in its own right, yet related to other sciences, each of which has its own distinctive subject-matters and means of investigation appropriate to that subject. Such a unitary conception of the human intellectual enterprise is not without its attractions and importance, just as it is not without accompanying difficulties. The exploration of this matter is therefore of considerable interest for the long-standing discussion of the theme of 'theology as a science', which we shall consider in more detail later. However, a preliminary clarification of one issue is required at this early stage.

The meanings of 'science'

The English word 'science' has shifted its meaning over the centuries. Once it meant an organized body of knowledge, or an intellectual discipline – a concept which continues to be expressed in the German term *Wissenschaft*. Dilthey's distinction between *Geisteswissenschaften* and *Naturwissenschaften* thus assumes that the investigation of the nature and achievements of the human spirit and the investigation of the natural world are both *Wissenschaften* and *wissenschaftlich* – sciences and scientific. Both the humanities and the natural sciences are to be regarded as 'sciences' – or 'disciplines', to use a less loaded term.

Yet in modern English, 'science' has now come to mean 'natural science'. The origins of this development can be traced to the middle of the nineteenth century. The *Oxford English Dictionary* records the first use of the term in this limited sense in 1867; prior to this, the term 'science' was generally taken to embrace every area of human knowledge. While the precise dating of this transition is contestable – it is not difficult to adduce citations in the decades prior to 1867 which suggest that 'science' has become regarded as synonymous for some writers with 'natural science' – the fact that it has taken place is beyond dispute. In ordinary English, terms such as 'scientist' are now taken to refer to the empirical sciences. This development has not taken place in other European languages – such as Dutch and German.

This raises considerable difficulties for English-language scholars engaging with continental works of theology. For example, consider Abraham Kuyper's celebrated Stone Lectures, delivered at Princeton Theological Seminary in October 1898.[46] The fourth of these lectures deals with the subject of 'Calvinism and Science'.[47] This is naturally taken by many readers to refer to the specific topic of the *natural* sciences; in fact, Kuyper uses the term 'science' to translate the Dutch term *Wetenschap*, which embraces both the natural sciences and the humanities. Perhaps more importantly, the celebrated debate between Karl Barth and Heinrich Scholtz over whether theology is *wissenschaftlich*[48] is often misunderstood to concern the specific relation of theology to the natural sciences. To avoid any misunderstanding of this nature, it is necessary to state explicitly that the present study is specifically and primarily concerned with the relation of Christian theology and the natural sciences – the cluster of disciplines that Wilhelm Dilthey designates, not simply as *Wissenschaften*, but specifically as *Naturwissenschaften*.

The fragmentation of intellectual discourse

The tumultous intellectual happenings of the sixteenth and seventeenth centuries made it clear that the interaction between Christian doctrine and the emerging theories of the natural sciences would be of some considerable importance. The rise of the Copernican world-view seemed, at least to some, to call into question traditional ways of reading certain biblical passages.[49] The further development of the heliocentric theory of the solar system under Galileo extended the debate to embrace the role of tradition in Christian theology, following the new emphasis upon doctrinal permanence espoused by the Council of Trent and leading Catholic writers such as Jacques Benigne Bossuet.[50] The emergence

[46] Abraham Kuyper, *Lectures on Calvinism*. Grand Rapids, MI: Eerdmans, 1948.
[47] See further Peter Somers Heslam, *Creating a Christian Worldview: Abraham Kuyper's Lectures on Calvinism*. Grand Rapids, MI: Eerdmans, 1998, 167–95.
[48] On which see the excellent study of Arie L. Molendijk, 'Ein heidnische Wissenschaftsbegriff. Der Streit zwischen Heinrich Scholtz und Karl Barth um die Wissenschaftlichkeit der Theologie', *Evangelische Theologie* 52 (1992), 527–45.
[49] T. S. Kuhn, *The Copernican Revolution*. New York: Random House, 1959; Jean Dietz Moss, *Novelties in the Heavens: Rhetoric and Science in the Copernican Controversy*. Chicago: University of Chicago Press, 1993; Robert S. Westman, 'The Melanchthon Circle, Rheticus and the Wittenberg Interpretation of the Copernican Theory', *Isis* 66 (1975), 165–93.
[50] Bruno Basile, 'Galileo e il teologo "Copernicano" Paolo Antonio Foscarini', *Rivista di letteratura italiana* 1 (1983), 63–96; Michael John Gorman, 'A Matter of Faith? Christoph Scheiner, Jesuit Censorship and the Trial of Galileo', *Perspectives on Science* 4

of the Newtonian world-view seemed, at least at first, to offer new hope to Christian theology, by demonstrating the coherence of the Christian doctrine of creation in the light of new insights into the universality of physical laws.[51] Yet as time progressed, the perceived apologetic value of Newtonianism began to diminish. The interest which the Newtonian world-view created in natural theology lessened.[52] Although William Paley's new approach to natural theology gave a new lease of life to the discipline, the growing public acceptance of the Darwinian concept of natural selection eroded its intellectual foundations.[53] The subsequent debate within the English and American academies over the implications of Darwinian theory for Christian theology[54] can be argued to demonstrate three important factors:

1. That this debate was of genuine intellectual significance;

2. That the relation between Christian theology and the natural sciences was ambivalent, in that the latter neither consistently affirmed nor consistently repudiated the former;

3. That relatively few were in a position to make an informed contribution to this debate, due to increasing professionalization and specialization within western academic life.

(1996), 283–320; Heinrich Karpp, 'Der Beitrag Keplers und Galileis zum neuzeitlichen Schriftsverständnis', *Zeitschrift für Theologie und Kirche* 67 (1970), 40–55; Olaf Pedersen, *Galileo and the Council of Trent*. Vatican City: Specolo Vaticana, 1983.

[51] I. B. Cohen, *The Newtonian Revolution*. Cambridge: Cambridge University Press, 1980; Henry Guerlac, 'Theological Voluntarism and Biological Analogies in Newton's Physical Thought', *Journal of the History of Ideas* 44 (1983), 219–30; Larry Stewart, 'Seeing through the Scholium: Religion and Reading Newton in the Eighteenth Century', *History of Science* 34 (1996), 123–65.

[52] John F. Carnell, 'Newton of the Grassblade? Darwin and the Problem of Organic Teleology', *Isis* 77 (1986), 405–21; James E. Force, 'The Breakdown of the Newtonian Synthesis of Science and Religion: Hume, Newton and the Royal Society', in R. H. Popkin and J. E. Force (eds), *Essays on the Context, Nature and Influence of Isaac Newton's Theology*. Dordrecht: Kluwer Academic Publishers, 1990, 143–63; John Gascoigne, 'From Bentley to the Victorians: The Rise and Fall of British Newtonian Natural Theology', *Science in Context* 2 (1988), 219–56.

[53] Neal C. Gillespie, 'Divine Design and the Industrial Revolution: William Paley's Abortive Reform of Natural Theology', *Isis* 81 (1990), 214–29; Daniel C. Dennett, *Darwin's Dangerous Idea: Evolution and the Meaning of Life*. New York: Simon & Schuster, 1995; Alvar Ellegard, *Darwin and the General Reader: The Reception of Darwin's Theory of Evolution in the British Periodical Press, 1859–1872*. Chicago: University of Chicago Press, 1990.

[54] On which see Thomas F. Glick, *The Comparative Reception of Darwinism*. Austin: University of Texas Press, 1972; David N. Livingstone, 'Darwinism and Calvinism: The Belfast-Princeton Connection', *Isis* 83 (1992), 408–28; James R. Moore, *The Post-Darwinian Controversies: A Study of the Protestant Struggle to come to terms with Darwin in Great Britain and America, 1870–1900*. Cambridge: Cambridge University Press, 1979.

It is this third point which concerns us especially at this juncture, as it can be seen to represent one of the most potent forces in modern intellectual life – the fragmentation of the human quest for knowledge.

The long history of human intellectual engagement is more often told in terms of fragmentation than synthesis. The case of Christian theology may serve as an example. The modern period has seen the emergence of both a distinction and separation within western Christian thinking between the two disciplines of 'theology' and 'spirituality'. It is a development which owes much to both social and academic pressures – such as the professionalization of the disciplines, the demand for detachment on the part of academically 'neutral' theologians, and the general trend towards diversification within the academy. Yet it has not always been so. For writers such as Evagrius, such a distinction was impossible: theology and prayer belonged together, and as a matter of both theory and fact could not be separated.[55] Other examples can easily be brought forward to illustrate this trend towards separation by evolution – that is, the general trend within the development of human thought for disciplines to diverge from one another over the course of their development.

Perhaps the greatest rift to open up in recent centuries has been between the natural sciences and the humanities. The origins of this bifurcation are not fully understood. A good case can be made for suggesting that it emerged in the late Renaissance Aristotelian commentaries, especially in the writings of Jacopo Zabarella (1533–89), on the basis of a distinction between the eternal world of nature and the world of human creativity. The former was the world of *scientiae*, the latter the world of *artes*.[56] *Scientia* thus deals with a world which is already in existence, and requires to be studied; *ars* has to do with the formation of things through human fashioning and imagination. Lying behind Zabarella's reflections on the distinction between science and art lies an important debate over the autonomy of the natural sciences

---

[55] On this point, see Philip Sheldrake, *Spirituality and Theology: Christian Living and the Doctrine of God*. London: Darton, Longman & Todd, 1998; Terry Tastard, 'Theology and Spirituality in the Nineteenth and Twentieth Centuries', in P. Byrne and L. Houlden (eds), *Companion Encyclopaedia of Theology*. London: Routledge, 1995, 594–619; Geoffrey Wainwright, *Doxology. The Praise of God in Worship, Doctrine and Life*. New York: Oxford University Press, 1980; Edward Yarnold, 'The Theology of Christian Spirituality', in C. Jones, G. Wainwright and E. Yarnold (eds), *The Study of Spirituality*. London: SPCK, 1986, 9–17.

[56] Heikki Mikkeli, 'The Foundation of an Autonomous Natural Philosophy: Zabarella on the Classification of Arts and Sciences', in Daniel A. Di Liscia, Eckhard Kessler and Charlotte Methuen (eds), *Method and Order in Renaissance Philosophy of Nature: The Aristotle Commentary Tradition*. Aldershot: Ashgate, 1997, 211–28.

at the University of Padua, in which the critical issue of contention was whether such sciences were dependent upon a prior acceptance of any given metaphysic.[57] A polemical intention – namely, to liberate the emergence of 'natural science' from what Zabarella termed 'divine science' (i.e. metaphysics) – can thus be discerned as underlying the increasing distance placed between the arts and sciences at the University of Padua, perhaps one of the most influential trend-setters of the late Renaissance.

In the nineteenth century, Wilhelm Dilthey (1833–1911) noted the development of what he clearly regarded as a seemingly unbridgeable divide between what he termed *Geisteswissenschaften* and *Naturwissenschaften*.[58] For Dilthey, the origins of this divergence lay in the subject-matters of the two disciplines. *Geisteswissenschaften* – the 'sciences of the human spirit' – were concerned with the human endeavour to understand the nature of humanity and society. By its very nature, this enterprise involved a high degree of affinity between the investigator and what was being studied, in that the human mind was being invited to explore the world and achievements of the human spirit. *Geisteswissenschaften* thus allowed the human mind to enter into a sympathetic understanding of what was being investigated. Thus the aim of *Geisteswissenschaften* is a process of 'indwelling', in which the experiences of another are sympathetically explored and amplified in the mind of the interpreter.[59]

On the other hand, *Naturwissenschaften* deal with precise descriptions, analyses and measurements, which are ultimately alien to us. The human understanding of nature is objective, external and detached, and is based upon the logical and rational investigation of physical objects with which we have no direct affinity or sympathy. This led Dilthey to draw the conclusion that the different roles played by the human mind in *Geisteswissenschaften* and *Naturwissenschaften* inevitably forced them apart.[60]

[57] Paolo Rossi, 'Aristotelici e "moderni": le ipotesi e la natura', in Luigi Oliveri (ed.), *Aristotelismo veneto e scienza moderna: atti del 25 anno accademico del Centro per la storia della tradizione aristotelica nel Veneto*. Padua: Antenore, 1983, 125–54.

[58] Wilhelm Dilthey, *Einleitung in die Geisteswissenschaften: Versuch einer Grundlegung für das Studien der Gesellschaft und der Geschichte*. Leipzig: Duncker & Humblot, 1883.

[59] See further Herbert A. Hodges, *The Philosophy of Wilhelm Dilthey*. London: Routledge & Kegan Paul, 1952; H. H. Groothoff, *Wilhelm Dilthey: Zur Erneuerung der Theorie der Bildung und des Bildungswesens*. Hannover: H. Schroedel, 1981.

[60] See P. A. Heelan, 'The Scope of Hermeneutics in Natural Science', *Studies in History and Philosophy of Science* 29 (1998), 273–98. For a more theological reflection, see Reinhold Niebuhr, 'The Tyranny of Science', *Theology Today* 10 (1954), 464–73.

Dilthey, then, distinguished the natural sciences and the humanities on account of their respective subject-matters, which demanded that these disciplines employed different methodologies. Others, however, have seen this as a potential oversimplification, ignoring the historical context within which this division arose. A more nuanced approach to the issue can be seen in the writings of Isaiah Berlin (1909–97), perhaps one of the most important polymaths of the twentieth century. In his 1974 lecture 'The Divorce between the Sciences and the Humanities', given at the University of Illinois, Berlin insisted that the separation between these disciplines arose, in part, on account of the agenda of the Enlightenment.[61] For Berlin, the agenda of the Enlightenment can be understood in a number of manners, not least through the lens of its critics, which often brought its distinctive and controversial aspects into sharp focus.[62] The Enlightenment regarded the advances of the natural sciences as paradigmatic for human knowledge as a whole, and sought to unify human knowledge on the basis of a unified methodology.

Critics of the Enlightenment – such as Giambattista Vico (1688–1744), Johann Georg Hamann (1730–88), and Johann Gottfried Herder (1744–1803) – sought to distance the humanities from the natural sciences in order to rebuff any such rationalist attempt to bring about the unification of human knowledge. Berlin suggests that Vico saw the discipline of history as offering the most effective means of resisting the Enlightenment demand for methodological uniformity across the disciplines. Where the Enlightenment enthroned reason, Vico sang the praises of imagination.[63] Vico's anti-rationalist polemic thus exposed a series of tensions between the disciplines, already present on account of their nature (thus endorsing Dilthey at this point), but polemically amplified and exploited on account of the context within which the debate took place:[64]

> The specific and unique versus the repetitive and the universal; the concrete versus the abstract; perpetual movement versus rest; the inner versus the outer; quality versus quantity; culture-bound versus timeless principles; mental strife and self-transformation as a permanent condition

---

[61] Isaiah Berlin, 'The Divorce between the Sciences and the Humanities', in *Against the Current: Essays in the History of Ideas*. London: Hogarth Press, 1979, 80–110.

[62] See especially Isaiah Berlin, *Three Critics of the Enlightenment: Vico, Hamann, Herder*. Princeton, NJ: Princeton University Press, 2000.

[63] Donald P. Verene, *Vico's Science of Imagination*. Ithaca, NY: Cornell University Press, 1981.

[64] Berlin, 'The Divorce between the Sciences and the Humanities', 109.

of man versus the possibility (and desirability) of peace, order, final harmony and the satisfaction of all rational human wishes – these are some of the aspects of the contrast.

Yet it is necessary to make some cautionary comments at this stage. Both the natural sciences and the arts have fallen into the habit of deploying a rhetoric of autonomy, insisting upon their intellectual independence. The situation is rather more complex, and points to a subtle and significant degree of interaction between the disciplines, even if this is ignored or suppressed for polemical reasons.

Many other examples could be brought forward to demonstrate that there is far more interaction between the natural sciences and other aspects of intellectual culture than has been appreciated. It may suit the purposes of some to suggest that philosophy is an autonomous discipline, which sets the rules of intellectual engagement for the natural sciences. Yet the truth is rather more complicated, and defies easy analysis. Cultural aspirations – such as a belief in unceasing social progress – and unacknowledged philosophical precommitments and agendas find their way into the reflections of natural scientists,[65] in much the same way as the findings of the natural sciences have had a considerable impact on philosophical reflection.[66] We shall illustrate these points by exploring both how Immanuel Kant's philosophy was shaped by the natural sciences, and how Kant's philosophy subsequently shaped the reflections of many natural scientists.

As Michael Friedman points out in his important study of Kant's relationship with the natural sciences, there has been a marked tendency to downplay or even to dismiss the importance of Kant's engagement with the natural science of his day. For Friedman, the reason for this reluctance to address this issue is not difficult to discern: the sciences which Kant knew were Euclidean geometry and Newtonian physics. Given that Kant's philosophical reflections were partly shaped by these outdated sciences, it is difficult to avoid the conclusion that the

---

[65] See the important study of Michael Ruse, *Monad to Man: The Concept of Progress in Evolutionary Biology*. Cambridge, MA: Harvard University Press, 1996, 19–41; 136–77. His earlier study should also be noted here: Michael Ruse, 'Darwin's Debt to Philosophy: An Examination of the Influence of the Philosophical Ideas of John F. Herschel and William Whewell on the Development of Charles Darwin's Theory of Evolution', *Studies in the History and Philosophy of Science* 66 (1975), 159–81.

[66] For example, note the important role of contemporary physics in relation to the origins of Cartesianism: Daniel Garber, *Descartes' Metaphysical Physics*. Chicago: University of Chicago Press, 1992. The value of studying the historical origins of certain philosophical trends is stressed by Gary Hatfield, 'The Importance of the History of Science for Philosophy in General', *Synthese* 11 (1995), 1–26.

validity of his philosophy in general must be questioned.[67] Kant treated
Euclidean geometrical axioms as non-empirical notions which therefore had the status of universal and necessary truths. The five axioms
of Euclidean geometry were held to give rise to a set of necessarily
true beliefs, which were not subject to the contingency of statements derived from experience. The Kantian categories are actually
those of Euclidean geometry and Newtonian mechanics, and do not
have the unique, universal and necessary character that Kant clearly
believed them to possess.[68] Perhaps the most familiar example of the
way in which Kant's philosophy was shaped by Newtonian physics
is provided by the important section in the *Critique of Pure
Reason* dealing with the category of space.[69] Kant accepts Newton's
problematic notion of 'absolute space' without reservation, and
argues that this concept is to be understood as 'pure *a priori* experience'.
It is significant that, in setting out his own approach to the category
of space, Kant merely restates Corollary V of Newton's *Principia
Mathematica*.[70]

Having noted that Kant's critical philosophy is unduly dependent
upon classical geometry and mechanics, we may now make the
additional point that this same critical philosophy exercised considerable influence over many German-speaking scientists of the late
nineteenth and early twentieth century.[71] Kant's view that the objects
of our knowledge are only appearances, and that things in themselves are unknowable, was of especial importance in this matter. For
Ernst Mach, the natural sciences concern that which is immediately
given by the senses. Science concerns nothing more and other than

---

[67] Michael Friedman, *Kant and the Exact Sciences.* Cambridge, MA: Harvard University
Press, 1992, xi–xii.

[68] At this point, the argument of Robert E. Butts should be noted, according to which
Kant liberalized the third and fourth antinomies of the first *Critique*. See Robert E. Butts,
*Kant and the Double Government Methodology: Supersensibility and Method in Kant's Philosophy
of Science.* Dordrecht: Reidel, 1986.

[69] For the background, see Murad D. Akhundov, *Conceptions of Space and Time.*
Cambridge, MA: Harvard University Press, 1986; Michael Friedman, *Foundations of Space–
Time Theories: Relativistic Physics and Philosophy of Science.* Princeton, NJ: Princeton
University Press, 1983.

[70] Immanuel Kant, *Kritik der reinen Vernunft.* Frankfurt am Main: Suhrkamp Verlag,
1968, 73. 'Also ist die ursprüngliche Vorstellung vom Raume Anschauung a priori, und
nicht Begriff.' Note that Newton states this principle in the form of a corollary, not an
axiom.

[71] Something of the nature of this influence can be understood from Alois Riehl, *Der
philosophische Kritizismus und seine Bedeutung für die positive Wissenschaft.* Leipzig:
Engelmann, 1887.

the investigation of the 'dependence of phenomena on one another'.[72] This led Mach to take a strongly negative view of the atomic hypothesis. In Mach's view, atoms were merely theoretical constructs which cannot be perceived. Nevertheless, Mach allows the use of 'auxiliary concepts' which serve as bridges linking one observation with another – provided it is assumed that they have no real existence, and must be thought of as 'products of thought' which 'exist only in our imagination and understanding'.[73] The impact of Kant's philosophy on Niels Bohr is also evident in the same respect, and may also have had a considerable impact on Bohr's emphasis on the need for *Anschaulichkeit* through the formulation of visual atomic models, rather than more abstract theories.[74] Perhaps the separation of the cultures of the humanities and the natural sciences is less impermeable than might at first be thought.

Whatever the origins of the perceived divide between the natural sciences and the humanities may be, and however valid this perception may be, there is no doubt that precisely this perception remains deeply embedded in western academic life and culture. As C. P. Snow pointed out in his 1959 Rede Lecture, the gulf between the arts and sciences had by then become so pronounced that it was necessary to speak of two distinct and non-interactive cultures in western society:[75]

The intellectual life of the whole of western society is increasingly being split into two polar groups . . . Literary intellectuals at one pole . . . at the other scientists, and as the most representative, the physical scientists. Between the two a gulf of mutual incomprehension.

Little seems to have changed since 1959. The debate continues, and raises the question as to whether there is any possibility of reversing –

[72] Ernst Mach, *History and Root of the Principle of the Conservation of Energy*. Chicago: Open Court Publishing Co., 1911, 63.

[73] Mach, *Principle of the Conservation of Energy*, 50–1. See further Erwin Hiebert, 'The Genesis of Mach's Early Views on Atomism', in R. Cohen and R. Seeger (eds), *Ernst Mach: Physicist and Philosopher*. Dordrecht: D. Reidel, 1970, 79–106.

[74] See David Favrholdt, 'Niels Bohr and Danish Philosophy', *Danish Yearbook of Philosophy* 13 (1986), 206–20; Jan Faye, *Niels Bohr: His Heritage and Legacy. An Anti-Realist View of Quantum Mechanics*. Dordrecht: Kluwer Academic Publishers, 1991; Dugald Murdoch, *Niels Bohr's Philosophy of Physics*. Cambridge: Cambridge University Press, 1987.

[75] C. P. Snow, *The Two Cultures and the Scientific Revolution*. Cambridge: Cambridge University Press, 1959, 3. For an evaluation of this lecture and its impact, see Armando Vitelli, *La cultura dimezzata*. Milan: Giordano, 1965. Snow's analysis is open to challenge at points, especially the way in which he contrasts Goethe and Newton: see Hannelore Schwedes, 'Goethe *contra* Newton', *Westermanns pädagogische Beiträge* 27 (1975), 63–73.

or at least eroding – the divorce between the natural sciences and humanities. Might there be a basis for proposing a unitary foundation for human knowledge, while avoiding the rationalist imperialism of the Enlightenment, so rightly derided and critiqued by its opponents? And might Christian theology offer such a basis? It will be clear that this is a question of the utmost importance for Christian theology, especially in its concern to relate a theological agenda to other areas of human knowledge.

In what follows, I shall set out the particular style of Christian theology which I believe to be especially appropriate to this major intellectual engagement.

Chapter 2

The Approach to Be Adopted

In the previous chapter, I set out an approach to theology which seeks to find illumination from the manner in which the natural sciences have grappled with the problems of epistemology – that is, with the question of how true knowledge is acquired, and what form that knowledge takes. Such a scientific theology involves a direct engagement between Christian theology and the natural sciences, not through some mediating discipline such as an allegedly 'universal' philosophy. No intellectual chaperone is required for the tryst between theology and the sciences.

It will be clear to the critical reader that such an approach legitimates a range of scientific theologies, reflecting in particular the long-standing debate within Christian theology over its sources, methods and tasks. It is therefore a matter of no small importance to clarify from the outset the particular style of scientific theology which this project adopts, and offer a justification for this approach.

The specific form of scientific theology which this project advocates is based on the affirmation of the intellectual resilience of traditional credal Christian orthodoxy, whose fundamental ideas are stated in the classic creeds of Christianity, and defended as living experienced realities by the great traditions of Christian theology – Catholicism, Orthodoxy and evangelicalism.[1] There are two particular considerations which lie behind this decision.

---

[1] For the possible relationships between these three streams, see especially J. I. Packer, 'On from Orr: The Cultural Crisis, Rational Realism, and Incarnational Ontology', *Crux* 32.3 (1996), 12–26.

1. Theologically, Christian orthodoxy must be considered to be the most authentic form of Christian theology, representing the consensus of the Christian communities of faith over an extended period of time. Christianity is a corporate faith, whose thought is governed both by Scripture and a long tradition of theological reflection, embodied and expressed in the creeds.

2. Historically, alternatives to Christian orthodoxy tend to be transient developments, often linked with specific historical situations whose passing leads to an erosion of plausibility of the variant of Christian theology being proposed.

The second of these points needs further exploration. When exploring the interaction of two domains of human thought which are in a state of flux, the nature of the interface is clearly highly dependent upon how those domains are perceived. It is all too easy to construct a scientific theology which turns out to rest upon provisional scientific conclusions which have been correlated with transient theological trends, leading to an outcome which is not of permanent value, but merely illuminates how both the natural sciences and Christian theology were understood in some quarters at some time. The critical question facing anyone proposing to develop a scientific theology is therefore the best means of evading such an inbuilt tendency to historical erosion.

In the two sections which follow, we shall consider the difficulties raised for the formulation of a scientific theology by the provisionality and transience of doctrines and trends within both disciplines.

The problem of transient theological trends

The intention of this project is to explore the interaction of the classic themes of Christian orthodoxy with the methods of the natural sciences as the basis for developing a scientific theology. A basic biblical and credal orthodoxy thus underlies this work. It is this concern to engage with the classic themes of Christian theology which explains the considerable attention paid throughout this project to writers such as Athanasius, Augustine and Thomas Aquinas and Karl Barth, as well as the concern to deal with some of the classic themes of philosophy, found in writers such as Plato and Aristotle. More recent trends are considered; however, the fatally flawed assumption that the most recent theological pronouncements are the best theological pronouncements has been studiously avoided. The reasons for taking this stance require explanation.

Many of those theologians who have contributed to the dialogue between the natural sciences and Christian theology have done so on the basis of the assumption that classic Christian theology is faced with serious limitations, which require to be transcended before any meaningful or significant dialogue may take place. Writers such as Ian Barbour and Arthur Peacocke – to mention two of the more distinguished twentieth-century contributors to this dialogue – have done so on the basis of significantly weakened variants of the classic statements of Christian orthodoxy.[2] The present study distances itself from such approaches, which can be argued to be vulnerable on two counts.

First, the decision to avoid classic Christian theological formulations often rests on discontents and perceptions of inadequacy which reflect a general cultural mood of restlessness with the past, rather than a sustained critique of traditional doctrines on theological grounds. For example, Barbour declines to talk about the 'two natures' or the 'substance' of Christ, preferring to talk about Christ's 'relationship with God'. Both Barbour and Peacocke owe a considerable theological debt to the British theologian Geoffrey W. H. Lampe, whose rather unorthodox approach to the identity of Christ was set out in his 1976 Bampton Lectures at Oxford University.[3] This was a period in which it was fashionable to express considerable doubts over the intellectual plausibility and spiritual benefits of the traditional doctrine of the incarnation – doubts which were perhaps most vigorously stated in the collection of essays *The Myth of God Incarnate* (1977), to which Lampe himself contributed.

Many theological writings of the 1960s and 1970s reflect the generally unquestioned assumption that the prevailing cultural trends of this remarkable period in western culture represented permanent features of the intellectual landscape, so that all future religious discourse would have to conform to their canons. In his magisterial study of English Christianity at this time, the noted religious historian Adrian Hastings points out that this period merely witnessed a temporary change of cultural mood, which some were unwise enough to treat as a permanent shift in the intellectual habits of humanity:[4]

[2] See the analysis in John Polkinghorne, *Scientists as Theologians: A Comparison of the Writings of Ian Barbour, Arthur Peacocke and John Polkinghorne*. London: SPCK, 1996.

[3] Geoffrey W. H. Lampe, *God as Spirit*. Oxford: Clarendon Press, 1977.

[4] Adrian Hastings, *A History of English Christianity 1920–1985*. London: Collins, 1986, 545.

In retrospect the dominant theological mood of that time in its hasty, slack rather collective sweep reminds one a little painfully of a flight of lemmings . . . A good deal of the more publicized theological writing in the sixties gives the impression of a sheer surge of feeling that in the modern world God, religion, the transcendent, any reliability in the gospels, anything which had formed part of the old 'supernaturalist' system, had suddenly become absurd. There were plenty of fresh insights but too little stringent analysis of the new positions. Everything was to be enthusiastically 'demythologized' in a euphoria of secularization which was often fairly soft on scholarly rigour.

With the benefit of hindsight, this precipitate and ill-considered abandoning of any element of the transcendent or supernatural can be seen to have been a capitulation to certain notions which, though dominant at the time, have proved to be transient. All periods of Christian thought are prone to be influenced by intellectual fashions, and it would be quite improper to criticize the dominant theological spirit of this period, with its restlessness over settled teachings and its impatience with traditional theological formulations, for this reason. Yet fashions change. What seemed to its proponents to be the settled consensus of a new era proved to be nothing of the sort. As a result, any attempt to forge a dialogue between Christian theology and the natural sciences on the basis of such transient trends leads to the results of such a dialogue being discredited on account of the outdated theological assumptions which shaped and guided it in the first place – including both the criticisms made of orthodox Christian theology, and the alternative theological stances adopted in its place. This brings us to the second misgiving we wish to express concerning the approach adopted by Barbour.

It is not merely that the forms of unease, disquiet and discontentment expressed with orthodox theology are generally shaped by cultural considerations; what is proposed in its place is often moulded and lent plausibility by the dominant ideology. The second concern which I wish to express concerning Barbour's approach is the disproportionate extent to which he relies upon process theology in the course of his analysis. Such has been Barbour's influence at this point that this unsatisfactory theology has almost come to be the 'establishment' position within institutions dedicated to fostering the dialogue between science and religion.

'Process theology' can be argued to have its origins in the thought of Alfred North Whitehead (1861–1947), and its subsequent development at Claremont Graduate School, Berkeley, and the University of Chicago

Divinity School.[5] Advocates of this style advocate a strongly revisionist approach to traditional Christian doctrines.[6] Process theology can be regarded as an important yet ultimately transitory phase in the development of Protestant English-language theology after the Second World War, which sought to recover the humanistic, immanentist trend of nineteenth-century theology in reaction against movements such as Barthianism or the neo-Thomist revival of the period.

The key aspect of process theology which Barbour appropriates is the rejection of the classic doctrine of God's omnipotence: God is one agent among many, not the sovereign Lord of all. As Barbour points out, process thought affirms 'a God of persuasion rather than compulsion', who 'influences the world without determining it'.[7] Barbour finds this approach (especially as it is set out in the writings of A. N. Whitehead) valuable in illuminating the manner in which science and religion interact. It allows God to be seen as present and active within nature, working within the limits and constraints of the natural order. It would be fair to categorize Barbour as a 'panentheist' at this point (meaning 'God is present in all things', and not to be confused with 'pantheism', the view that 'all things are divine'). Perhaps the most interesting way in which Barbour uses the distinctive ideas of process thought relates to the theory of evolution. Barbour argues that the evolutionary process is influenced by – but not directed by – God. This allows him to offer some form of explanation for the fact that the evolutionary process appears to have been long, complex and wasteful. 'There have been too many blind alleys and extinct species and too much waste, suffering and evil to attribute every event to God's specific will.'[8] God influences the process for good, but cannot dictate precisely what form it will take.

Attractive though Barbour finds this approach – and he has adopted it consistently throughout his career – others find it unconvincing, tired

[5] For a general overview, see Paul Fiddes, 'Process Theology', in A. E. McGrath (ed.), *The Blackwell Encyclopaedia of Modern Christian Thought*. Oxford: Blackwell, 1993, 472–6. For specific approaches, see John B. Cobb, *Process Theology: An Introductory Exposition*. Philadelphia: Westminster Press, 1976; Lewis S. Ford, *The Lure of God: A Biblical Background for Process Theism*. Philadelphia: Fortress Press, 1978; Bernard M. Loomer, 'Process Theology: Origins, Strengths, Weaknesses', *Process Studies* 16 (1987), 245–54.

[6] James J. Buckley, 'Revisionists and Liberals', in David F. Ford (ed.), *The Modern Theologians: An Introduction to Christian Theology in the Twentieth Century*, 2nd edn. Oxford: Blackwell, 1997, 327–42.

[7] Ian G. Barbour, *Religion in an Age of Science*. San Francisco: HarperSanFrancisco, 1990, 29, 224.

[8] Barbour, *Religion in an Age of Science*, 174.

and outdated.[9] It is, in my view, little more than a reworking of the central ideas of Ralph Cudworth's *True Intellectual System of the Universe* (1678) on the part of those who seem to have no idea that Cudworth had been there before them, or of the weaknesses which the historical critique of Cudworth's position exposed. The vague language about God's 'persuasive moral influence' over natural processes is stretched far beyond credibility when dealing with non-sentient entities. Its use of the language of 'persuasion' often appears to be little more than a lapse into unwarranted anthropomorphic modes of speech, which singularly lacks plausibility when applied at the molecular and sub-molecular levels.[10] Its plausibility can be argued to be linked to the values and norms of a specific historical situation. With the passing of that context, the attractiveness of process theology as a mediating principle in the dialogue between science and religion has waned correspondingly.

A more radical application of the Whiteheadian project to the dialogue between science and religion can be found in a recent work by David Ray Griffin.[11] Griffin's fundamental thesis is that both the scientific and religious (and, more specifically, the Christian) communities may harmonize their perspectives by adopting a Whiteheadian world-view. This approach – which Griffin refers to variously as 'theistic naturalism' or 'naturalistic theism' – argues that Whitehead's philosophy is capable of offering a credible aspect of every aspect of human experience through the belief that all actual entities directly perceive God through nonsensory prehension.[12] Developing this in a manner which some natural scientists will find alarming, Griffin contends that 'parapsychology is crucial for a form of liberal theology that effects a reconciliation of science with religion'.[13] Yet this is perfectly consistent with Griffin's general approach.

[9] See, for example, the comments of John Polkinghorne with specific reference to the dialogue between science and religion: John Polkinghorne, *Science and Christian Belief.* London: SPCK, 1994, 22.

[10] David Pailin is one of the few process theologians to admit that the use of mentalist language becomes meaningless at this level: David Pailin, 'Process Theology and Evolution', in Svend Andersen and Arthur Peacocke (eds), *Evolution and Creation: A European Perspective.* Aarhus: Aarhus University Press, 1987, 170–89, especially 182–8.

[11] David Ray Griffin, *Religion and Scientific Naturalism: Overcoming the Conflicts.* Albany, NY: State University of New York, 2000.

[12] Griffin, *Religion and Scientific Naturalism*, 96–101.

[13] Griffin, *Religion and Scientific Naturalism*, 183. Griffin here develops some ideas expounded earlier in his *Parapsychology, Philosophy and Spirituality: A Postmodern Exploration.* Albany, NY: State University of New York, 1997.

There are unquestionably valuable insights within this work, particularly in relation to Griffin's critique of the purely naturalistic approach to religion found in the writings of Willem Drees. Griffin correctly notes that Drees fails to offer adequate support for his central assumption that naturalism can account for all of human experience.[14] Nevertheless, Griffin's proposal ultimately amounts to a demand that an already outmoded philosophy be adopted by both scientists and theologians – one that neither community regards as a natural or obvious partner – before a meaningful dialogue can result.

The time has come to emancipate the dialogue from this Babylonian captivity. Process theology may be of interest to some; it is implausible to most, especially within the intellectually hard-nosed scientific community. Tomorrow's dialogue cannot be made conditional upon yesterday's intellectual fashions. Without wishing to give offence to anyone, I think it is time to offer a theological and scientific variant of Hans Christian Andersen's story of the 'Emperor's New Clothes', and suggest that process theology is an implausible construction which has probably alienated many scientists and orthodox Christian theologians from taking part in anything approaching a 'scientific theology' on account of the implausibility of the proposed intermediary. Both communities feel deeply uneasy – although for different reasons – about committing themselves to such an implausible notion as a necessary precondition of dialogue.

In any case, there is another question which demands attention at this point, which underlies the position developed in the present work of 'scientific theology'. Why should both natural scientists and Christian theologians be obligated to adopt *any* intermediate world-view – whether one as uncompelling as process theology, or the rather more resilient, plausible and interesting possibilities offered by Platonism – in entering into a productive dialogue? The position adopted in this project is to foster and sustain a *direct* rather than a *mediated* dialogue. When an intermediary is imposed upon the dialogue which the greater part of both sides regard with a mixture of puzzlement and ridicule, the quality of the ensuing dialogue is seriously prejudiced.

It is not my intention to pursue this specific theological trend in detail; my concern is to note a more general concern which underlies it – namely, the danger of basing the dialogue between the natural sciences and Christianity on a transient revision of a classic theological position.

[14] Griffin, *Religion and Scientific Naturalism*, 79.

The position adopted throughout this study is that the classic Christian formulations of faith are perfectly adequate to function as the basis of a scientific theology. The dynamic process of 'reception of doctrine' – to which we shall return in the third volume of this series – ensures that the maintenance of theological integrity is not equivalent to the wooden repetition of the doctrinal formulations of yesteryear.

This dynamic understanding of the nature of Christian truth has been appreciated since the earliest of times, and can be found in a nascent form in the writings of Irenaeus of Lyons, and in a more developed and nuanced form in Greek Orthodox theology. John Meyendorff (1926–92) sets out this critically important notion as follows:[15]

> Of necessity, any Orthodox theology and any Orthodox witness is *traditional,* in the sense that it is consistent not only with Scripture but also with the experience of the Fathers and the saints . . . However the term 'traditional theology' can also denote a dead theology, if it means identifying traditionalism with simple repetition . . . In fact, dead traditionalism cannot be truly traditional. It is an essential characteristic of patristic theology that it was able to face the challenges of its own time while remaining consistent with the original apostolic Orthodox faith. Thus simply to *repeat* what the Fathers said is to be unfaithful to their spirit and to the intention embodied in their theology . . . True tradition is always a *living* tradition. It changes while remaining always the same. It changes because it faces different situations, not because its essential content is modified.

A similar approach is set out in John Henry Newman's writings on the prophetic role of the church, and particularly his essay on the development of doctrine; these approaches have exercised a major influence on Catholic thinking subsequently, and are reflected in the statements of the Second Vatican Council.[16] Tradition is not – and, in order to be authentic, cannot be – a dead voice from the past; it is a living voice, which passes on the wisdom of the past to enrich the present.[17]

---

[15] John Meyendorff, *Living Tradition: Orthodox Witness in the Contemporary World.* Crestwood, NY: St Vladimir's Seminary Press, 1978, 7–8.

[16] Owen Chadwick, *From Bossuet to Newman: The Idea of Doctrinal Development.* Cambridge: Cambridge University Press, 1957; Hugo Meynell, 'Newman on Revelation and Doctrinal Development', *Journal of Theological Studies* 30 (1979), 138–52; Aidan Nichols, *From Newman to Congar: The Idea of Doctrinal Development from the Victorians to the Second Vatican Council.* Edinburgh: T&T Clark, 1990.

[17] A point made by Jaroslav Pelikan, *The Vindication of Tradition.* New Haven, CT: Yale University Press, 1984.

These insights might well be accepted without demur in Orthodox and Catholic circles. But what of evangelicalism, the third of the great orthodox streams of Christian theology to which this work is addressed, and from within which it is written? The concept of 'living tradition' might at first not seem to be entirely acceptable to evangelical writers, given the movement's celebrated emphasis upon a direct engagement with Scripture. However, it can be argued that the fundamental evangelical theme of obedient attentiveness to Scripture makes it all the more important to listen respectfully to the views of our forebears in the walk of faith, who paid such respectful attention to the biblical materials before us. A willingness to listen – not to agree uncritically, it must be stressed, but to *listen* – is of considerable importance in securing the stability of evangelical theological reflection. Such an approach can be found in the writings of many evangelical theologians who see themselves as standing within the 'great theological tradition', such as James Orr and J. I. Packer.[18]

The origins of such an approach may be found in the Reformation. Martin Luther once styled his reforming programme at Wittenberg as a return to 'the Bible and Augustine',[19] and regarded Augustine as something of a theological lodestar.[20] Luther's colleague Philip Melanchthon developed similar arguments, most notably that the Reformation could be seen as a return to the consensus of the early church, especially as found in the writings of Augustine and Ambrose.[21] A similarly high evaluation of the earlier Christian tradition can be found in the writings of Calvin.[22] Although especially concerned to

[18] The most significant studies of Orr have been Alan P. F. Sell, *Defending and Declaring the Faith: Some Scottish Examples, 1860–1920.* Exeter: Paternoster Press and Colorado Springs: Helmers & Howard, 1987, 137–71 and Glen G. Scorgie, *A Call for Continuity: The Theological Contribution of James Orr.* Macon: Mercer University Press, 1988. See also J. I. Packer, 'The Comfort of Conservatism', in M. Horton (ed.), *Power Religion.* Chicago: Moody, 1992, 283–99; idem, 'On from Orr: The Cultural Crisis, Rational Realism, and Incarnational Ontology', *Crux* 32/3 (September 1996), 12–26. On Packer, see Alister E. McGrath, 'The Importance of Tradition for Modern Evangelicalism', in D. Lewis and A. E. McGrath (eds), *Doing Theology for the People of God.* Downers Grove, IL: InterVarsity Press, 1996, 159–73.
[19] Alister E. McGrath, *Luther's Theology of the Cross: Martin Luther's Theological Breakthrough.* Oxford: Blackwell, 1985, 47–53.
[20] For detailed studies, see A. Hamel, *Der junge Luther und Augustin.* 2 vols. Gütersloh: Mohn, 1934–5; Bernhard Lohse, 'Die Bedeutung Augustins für den jungen Luther', *Kerygma und Dogma* 11 (1965), 116–35.
[21] Peter Fraenkel, *Testimonia Patrum: The Function of the Patristic Argument in the Theology of Philip Melanchthon.* Geneva: Droz, 1961.
[22] See the careful study of A. N. S. Lane, *John Calvin: Student of the Church Fathers.* Edinburgh: T&T Clark, 1999.

maintain fidelity to Augustine,[23] Calvin also had a positive evaluation of the thought of John Chrysostom.[24] This positive evaluation of the teachings and practices of the early church became of critical importance in the debate between Calvin and Sadoleto over the nature of the true church,[25] and is especially significant in relation to the Lausanne Disputation of October 1536.[26] At this important disputation, which took place shortly after Calvin's arrival at Geneva, a catholic critic of the evangelical reformers suggested that evangelicals despised the fathers (that is, the Christian writers of the first five centuries), regarding them as possessing no authority in matters of doctrine. Calvin declared that this was simply not true: not merely did the evangelicals respect the fathers more than their catholic opponents; they also knew them better. Reeling off a remarkable chain of references to their writings, including their location – apparently totally from memory – Calvin clinched the evangelical case in the eyes of those present. The vote was taken, and Lausanne opted for the Reformation.

The magisterial Reformation thus offers an approach to engaging with the 'great tradition' which has immense potential for their evangelical progeny today. Evangelical theology is not simply about giving total priority to the Bible; it is about valuing and engaging with those *in the past* who gave total priority to the Bible, and the ideas and values which they derived from that engagement. Quite simply, the mainline reformers believed that the Bible had been honoured, interpreted and applied faithfully in the past, and that evangelical theology was under an obligation to take their reflections into account as they forged their own.

The present study therefore takes its stand on the 'great tradition' of Christian theology, which seeks to be guided and governed at all points by Holy Scripture, and to offer a faithful and coherent account of what it finds there, using additional intellectual resources in a ministerial, rather than magisterial, manner. Theology is fundamentally a communal attentiveness to Scripture, and a desire to express and communicate what is to be found there to the church and the world, using forms of

---

[23] Luchesius Smits, *Saint Augustin dans l'oeuvre de Jean Calvin.* Assen: Van Gorcum, 1956.

[24] Alexandre Ganoczy, *Calvins handschriftliche Annotationen zu Chrysostomus: Ein Beitrag zur Hermeneutik Calvins.* Wiesbaden: Steiner, 1981.

[25] See J. C. Olin (ed.), *John Calvin and Jacopo Sadoleto: A Reformation Debate. Sadoleto's Letter to the Genevans and Calvin's Reply.* New York: Harper & Row, 1966.

[26] See E. Junod (ed.), *La Dispute de Lausanne 1536: La théologie réformée après Zwingli et avant Calvin.* Lausanne: Presses Centrals Lausannes, 1988.

language and conceptualities which are accessible to the envisaged audiences in an ancillary, not foundational, role. Christian theology is under an obligation to pay respectful and obedient attention to the biblical testimony, and allow itself to be shaped and reshaped by what it finds expressed there.

Yet the danger of basing a scientific theology upon what is little more than a transient theological trend has a direct counterpart within the natural sciences themselves. Both partners in the constructive dialogue which leads to a scientific theology are prone to historical erosion, resulting in a scientific theology which is trapped in a particular cultural or intellectual rut. The fallacy that underlies at least some of the less critical attempts to relate Christian theology to the natural sciences is the assumption that the way the sciences see things is the way they really are – and to overlook the continuing development of the sciences. Many attempts to relate theology and the natural sciences in the eighteenth and nineteenth centuries were based upon what were assumed to be the settled and permanently valid theories of classical physics, based upon the Newtonian paradigm. These attempts were seriously eroded, possibly fatally so, through the rise of the new physics of the twentieth century. Unlike Platonism and Aristotelianism, which can be taken as relatively settled outlooks, the natural sciences are continually evolving. So how can this important consideration be reflected within a scientific theology?

The provisionality of scientific conclusions

My concern throughout this work is to explore the *methodological* parallels between Christian theology and the natural sciences. How is knowledge gained, correlated and conceptualized? The focus of this work is thus the manner in which the various natural sciences seek to explore, understand and represent the world around us, rather than the specific understandings which result from that exploration. The reason for this particular focus needs to be considered in some detail.

A study of the history of science makes it clear that there is a significant degree of provisionality to the findings of the natural sciences. Each generation within the scientific community seems to have thought that the scientific enterprise was essentially complete; all that remained to be done was to achieve an increasing precision of measurement. In his 1871 inaugural lecture as the first Cavendish Professor of Physics at Cambridge University, James Clerk Maxwell spoke critically of a tendency he discerned among some of his fellow scientists:[27]

> This characteristic of modern experiments – that they consist principally of measurements – is so prominent, that the opinion seems to have got abroad that in a few years all the great physical constants will have been approximately estimated, and the only occupation which will then be left to men of science will be to carry on these measurements to another place of decimals.

Maxwell himself regarded this viewpoint, which he studiously avoids attributing to any of his colleagues, as unduly pessimistic. In his view, a combination of human creativity and the 'unsearchable riches of creation' meant that science was far from complete.

The view that all things worth knowing were already known may, however, be found in the writings of many noted nineteenth-century scientists. For example, Max Planck relates how he found himself uncertain what subject to study at the University of Munich in 1875. His inclination to study the natural sciences was rubbished by the then Professor of Physics at the university, who declared that nothing worthwhile remained to be discovered.[28] Robert A. Millikan – whose investigations of the electron broke new ground – recalls how physics was widely regarded as a 'dead subject' in American academic circles during the early 1890s.[29] Such views were widespread, and can be found in many scientific writings of the period. The leading American astronomer Simon Newcomb felt able to assert in 1888 that more or less everything of importance had been seen and measured; what remained was to consolidate this body of knowledge:[30]

> So far as astronomy is concerned, we must confess that we do appear to be fast approaching the limits of our knowledge. True, there is still a great deal to learn. Every new comet that appears must be found by some one, and I do not grudge the finder the honors awarded him. At the same time, so far as we can see, one comet is so much like another that we cannot regard one as adding in any important degree to our knowledge. The result is that that work which really occupies the attention of the

---

[27] W. D. Niven (ed.), *The Scientific Papers of James Clerk Maxwell*. 2 vols. Cambridge: Cambridge University Press, 1980, vol. 2, 244.

[28] Max Planck, *A Scientific Autobiography*. New York: Philosophical Library, 1949, 8.

[29] Robert A. Millikan, *The Autobiography of Robert A. Millikan*. New York: Houghton, Mifflin, 1950, 23–4. On Millikan, see Robert Hugh Pargon, *The Rise of Robert Millikan: Portrait of a Life in American Science*. Ithaca, NY: Cornell University Press, 1982.

[30] Simon Newcomb, 'The Place of Astronomy among the Sciences', *The Sidereal Messenger* 7 (1888), 69–70.

astronomer is less the discovery of new things than the elaboration of those already known, and the entire systemization of our knowledge.

With the passage of time, there has been increasing recognition of the *provisionality* of scientific understanding.[31] As Karl Popper has pointed out, part of the paradox of the scientific method is that while science is the most critically tested and evaluated form of knowledge available, it is nevertheless tentative and provisional.[32] Science is to be seen as an 'unended quest', whose findings may be up to date but are never final. As techniques are refined and conceptual frameworks modified, the understandings of one generation of natural scientists give way to those of another. Although there is a clear degree of continuity between the understandings of successive generations, this can be argued to be based more on the methods which they applied than the outcome of their application.

The history of the scientific enterprise makes it abundantly clear that theories which were widely accepted in one generation – on the basis of the best evidence available – were superseded in following eras. For example, Newtonian mechanics and his theory of universal gravitation were widely regarded as correct in the eighteenth and nineteenth centuries, not on account of any sociological factors predisposing the scientific community to accept them, but simply because they offered the best explanation of the available observations. Yet the Newtonian world-view has now been superseded by the Einsteinian, on account of the explanatory and predictive successes of the general theory of relativity. Perhaps the most famous example of this overconfidence in existing scientific paradigms is Lord Kelvin's assertion, made in the closing years of the nineteenth century, that all that remained for physics to achieve was to fill in the next decimal place.[33] The abandonment of the concept of 'ether' and advent of quantum mechanics would demonstrate the provisionality of much of what appeared to be settled at the end of that century.[34]

---

[31] For some useful reflections on this theme, see John Maddox, *What Remains to be Discovered: Mapping the Secrets of the Universe, the Origins of Life, and the Future of the Human Race*. New York: Free Press, 1998.

[32] Karl R. Popper, *Conjectures and Refutations: The Growth of Scientific Knowledge*. London: Routledge & Kegan Paul, 1963.

[33] See William Dampier, *A History of Science*. Cambridge: Cambridge University Press, 1938, 382; Lawrence Badash, 'The Completeness of Nineteenth-Century Science', *Isis* 63 (1973), 48–58.

[34] A. A. Michelson and E. W. Morley, 'On the Relative Motion of the Earth and Luminiferous Ether', *American Journal of Science* 34 (1887), 333–45; S. Goldberg and R. Stuewer, *The Michelson Era in American Science, 1870–1930*. New York: American Institute

Similarly, Newton's corpuscular theory of light was widely accepted in the eighteenth century, before being displaced by Fresnel's elastic solid ether theory, which envisaged a wave model of light. Fresnel's theory was strikingly successful in terms of its predictions and explanations, and also possessed the admirable qualities of simplicity and coherence. Yet the light-theories of both Newton and Fresnel were both ultimately superseded by the quantum approach to light, developed by Einstein as a means of explaining the photoelectric effect.[35] There have thus been radical discontinuities in understanding in the history of the natural sciences, even though the fundamental methods of investigation of the world, and their accompanying assumptions, have remained unchanged, save for technological advances.

It will thus be clear that to base the interaction of theology and the natural sciences on the basis of the outcome of the application of their methods runs the risk of characterizing and defining the nature of that interaction on provisionalities. The inevitable result of this would be an understanding of the interaction which is temporary and potentially superficial. By their very nature, the natural sciences are breaking new ground, gradually rendering obsolete those understandings of the world which once seemed secure. Yet the methods and assumptions by which those provisional understandings are gained remain virtually the same – namely, that there is an independent reality to the world, the ordering and structure of which can be investigated empirically and expressed mathematically by the human mind.

A theology which is grounded in the alleged 'certain findings' of the natural sciences will therefore find itself outdated with every advance in scientific understanding. The many eighteenth-century British theologians who sought to forge an alliance between Newtonian physics and Christian theology are nowadays regarded with a degree of pity mingled with historical curiosity, not to mention a slight dash of *Schadenfreude*. While there is no doubt that the early eighteenth-century

of Physics, 1988; Stanley Goldberg, 'Poincaré's Silence and Einstein's Relativity', *British Journal for the History of Science* 5 (1970), 73–84; T. Hirosige, 'Theory of Relativity and the Ether', *Japanese Studies in the History of Science* 7 (1968), 37–53; T. Hirosige, 'The Ether Problem, the Mechanistic World View, and the Origins of the Theory of Relativity', *Historical Studies in the Physical Sciences* 7 (1976), 3–82; Andrew Warwick, 'The Sturdy Protestants of Science: Larmor, Trouton and the Earth's Motion through the Ether', in Jed Z. Buchwald (ed.), *Scientific Practice: Theories and Stories of Doing Physics*. Chicago: University of Chicago Press, 1995, 300–43.

[35] On which see Albert Einstein, 'Über einen die Erzeugung und Verwandlung des Lichtes betreffenden heuristischen Gesichtspunkt', *Annalen der Physik* 17 (1905), 132–48.

proponents of a Newtonian-style natural theology, or some variant of a 'physico-theology', developed ideas which are of purely historical interest, it is important to realize that these were seen as being at the cutting edge of advanced theological speculation by their proponents and at least some of their contemporary public. What now seems quaint and hopelessly outmoded was then seen as thoroughly up to date.

Without in any way endorsing the intensely problematical assumptions of Thomas Kuhn's model of scientific revolutions, there can be no doubt that Kuhn has demonstrated that today's scientific certainties are routinely overthrown by a later generation.[36] 'Today, most scientists believe that . . .' – prefaced to a statement that is taken to be correct – has a disconcerting tendency, with the passage of time, to become 'Yesterday, most scientists believed that . . .', prefaced to a statement which is now taken to be wrong – even though it was once believed to be right within the scientific community. A theology which is derived from, or justified with reference to, such 'certainties' is thus destined for oblivion with the passage of time.

The study of the history of Christian theology indicates the need to avoid becoming committed to the accepted scientific wisdom of the day. As we have already noted, English theologians of the eighteenth century developed quite sophisticated understandings of the interaction of science and theology, based on the assumption that the Newtonian world-view had been demonstrated to be correct beyond reasonable doubt.[37] Similarly, both William Paley's *Natural Theology* and the *Bridgewater Treatises* were thoroughly contemporary in terms of their scientific assumptions; the erosion of those scientific assumptions inevitably entailed a corresponding reduction in the plausibility of the appended – and dependent – theology.[38] Going back further, the development of medieval theology often shows an unsettling dependence upon certain widely-held (yet largely non-empirical)

[36] See Thomas Kuhn, *The Structure of Scientific Revolutions*. Chicago: University of Chicago Press, 1962. For indications of some concerns over Kuhn's proposals, see Paul Hoyningen-Huene, 'Kuhn's Conception of Incommensurability', *Studies in History and Philosophy of Science* 21 (1980), 481–92; Maben Walter Poirier, 'A Comment on Polanyi and Kuhn', *The Thomist* 53 (1989), 259–79; Cordell Strug, 'Kuhn's Paradigm Thesis: A Two-Edged Sword for the Philosophy of Religion', *Religious Studies* 20 (1984), 269–79.

[37] John Gascoigne, 'From Bentley to the Victorians: The Rise and Fall of British Newtonian Natural Theology', *Science in Context* 2 (1988), 219–56; Larry Stewart, 'Seeing through the Scholium: Religion and Reading Newton in the Eighteenth Century', *History of Science* 34 (1996), 123–65.

[38] John Hedley Brooke, 'Science and the Fortunes of Natural Theology: Some Historical Perspectives', *Zygon* 24 (1989), 3–22; Neal C. Gillespie, 'Divine Design and the Industrial Revolution: William Paley's Abortive Reform of Natural Theology', *Isis* 81 (1990), 214–29.

'scientific' assumptions, deriving from the Aristotelian physics of the period. The biblical exegesis and theological analysis of that period tend to reflect the unconscious incorporation of Aristotelian ideas on the basis of the implicit assumption that these were 'correct'.[39] As a result, there was intense resistance to new approaches to biblical interpretation which called these settled Aristotelian presuppositions into question. Through a subtle and largely unconscious process of reasoning, a text which was originally interpreted *in the light of Aristotelian presuppositions* subsequently became regarded as *proof of those Aristotelian presuppositions.*[40]

The procedure adopted in this work is not to base an account of a scientific theology upon the allegedly secure findings of the natural sciences, but upon the methods and working assumptions which underlie those sciences – supremely a belief in the regularity of the natural world, and the ability of the human mind to uncover and represent this regularity in a mathematical manner. We may now move on to explore why this interaction concerns Christian theology – rather than the more vague category of 'religion' – and the natural sciences.

Engaging with Christian theology, not 'religions'

This work aims to explore the creative and constructive interface between the natural sciences and Christian theology, rather than the more elusive category of 'religion'. In part, this reflects a specific concern to respect the integrity of the Christian faith, and ensure that its distinctive character is maintained and explored. More significantly, however, this stance reflects an informed awareness of the failure of past attempts to offer a reliable and warranted definition of 'religion', rendering intensely problematic any attempt to bring precision to the theme 'science and religion'.

[39] L. W. B. Brockliss, 'Aristotle, Descartes and the New Science: Natural Philosophy at the University of Paris, 1600–1740', *Annals of Science* 38 (1981), 33–69; William E. Carroll, 'San Tommaso, Aristotele e la creazione', *Annales Theologici* 8 (1994), 363–76; Edward Grant, *The Foundations of Science in the Middle Ages: Their Religious, Institutional and Intellectual Contexts.* Cambridge: Cambridge University Press, 1996; Alister E. McGrath, 'The Influence of Aristotelian Physics upon St Thomas Aquinas's Discussion of the Processus Iustificationis', *Recherches de théologie ancienne et médiévale* 51 (1984), 223–9; James A. Weisheipl, 'Aristotle's Concept of Nature: Avicenna and Aquinas', in Lawrence D. Roberts (ed.), *Approaches to Nature in the Middle Ages.* Binghamton, NY: Center for Medieval and Early Renaissance Studies, 1982, 137–60.

[40] Alister E. McGrath, *The Foundations of Dialogue in Science and Religion.* Oxford: Blackwell, 1998, 118–20.

There has been a depressing tendency on the part of certain writers in this field to accept the most recent definition of 'religion' offered by a scholar claiming to base her findings upon 'scientific' and 'objective' research. Despite the fact that these are clearly provisional and contested, such writers develop often ambitious models of the interaction of science and religion on the basis of these definitions. Today's assuredly 'scientific' findings have a curious habit of becoming tomorrow's discarded hypotheses. Despite the fact that there has hardly been a shortage of definitions of religion offered over the last century or so, each of which has duly announced itself as being 'scientific' or 'objective', none has been sufficiently resilient or representative to command continuing support, save in the niches and ghettos of certain social sciences.[41]

Furthermore, the polemical intentions of those offering accounts of the nature and origins of religion cannot be overlooked. Definitions of religion are rarely neutral, but are often generated to favour beliefs and institutions with which one is in sympathy and penalize those to which one is hostile.[42] They too often depend upon the 'particular purposes and prejudices of individual scholars'.[43] Certain of these have been strongly reductionist, generally reflecting the personal or institutional agendas of those who developed them. Karl Marx's critique of religion rests upon a series of assumptions concerning its social role and genesis which have proved vulnerable to even modest scholarly inquiry.[44] Sigmund Freud's account of the origins of religion has proved to be more resilient,[45] even though it has generally been abandoned as an

---

[41] See, for example, Peter Harrison, *'Religion' and the Religions in the English Enlightenment.* Cambridge: Cambridge University Press, 1990; Tomoko Masuzawa, *In Search of Dreamtime: The Quest for the Origin of Religion.* Chicago: University of Chicago Press, 1993; Daniel L. Pals, *Seven Theories of Religion.* New York: Oxford University Press, 1996; Samuel J. Preus, *Explaining Religion: Criticism and Theory from Bodin to Freud.* New Haven, CT: Yale University Press, 1987.

[42] Philip E. Devine, 'On the Definition of "Religion"', *Faith and Philosophy* 3 (1986), 270–84.

[43] Peter B. Clarke and Peter Byrne, *Religion Defined and Explained.* London: St Martin's Press, 1993, 3–27.

[44] On Marx, see Hans Bosse, *Marx, Weber, Troeltsch. Religionssoziologie und marxistische Ideologiekritik.* Munich: Kaiser Verlag, 1971; Reinhard Buchbinder, *Bibelzitate, Bibelanspielungen, Bibelparodien, theologische Vergleiche und Analogien bei Marx und Engels.* Berlin: Schmidt, 1976; Sergei Nikolaevich Bulgakov, Donald W. Treadgold and Virgil R. Lang, *Karl Marx as a Religious Type: His Relation to the Religion of Anthropotheism of L. Feuerbach.* Belmont: Nordland Publishing Co., 1979; Werner Post, *Kritik der Religion bei Karl Marx.* Munich: Kösel, 1969; Charles Wackenheim, *La faillité de la religion d'après Karl Marx.* Paris: Presses universitaires de France, 1963.

[45] Peter Gay, *A Godless Jew: Freud, Atheism, and the Making of Psychoanalysis.* New Haven, CT: Yale University Press; Hans Küng, *Freud and the Problem of God.* New Haven, CT: Yale University Press, 1979; William Lloyd Newell, *The Secular Magi: Marx, Freud, and*

objective – as opposed to polemical – explanation of the issues.[46] Durkheim's definition of religion as 'beliefs with no super-empirical or supernatural reference' has fallen out of favour, having been subjected to severe criticism by writers such as Mircea Eliade on account of their failure to relate adequately to the real world of religious life and thought.[47] The contribution of writers specializing in fieldwork anthropology (such as E. E. Evans-Pritchard and Clifford E. Geertz) must be noted at this point; they have offered more complex and reflective models of religion, even if these remain provisional and partial.[48] The term 'religion' has now generally been accepted to refer to 'beliefs and practices with a supernatural referent';[49] this modest and provisional definition, however, is hardly adequate as the basis of a sustained and systematic engagement with the issue of science and religion.

Discussions of the complex interaction of science and religion are often rendered problematic through the false assumption that the word 'religion' designates a universal phenomenon or category. While there is no doubt that the word is used in this vague sense in everyday English, attempts to offer a more precise definition have crumbled in the face of innumerable difficulties. David Tracy notes the vulnerability of this approach, pointing out that, as a matter of simple observation, there 'is no single essence, no one content of enlightenment or revelation, no one way of emancipation or liberation' to be discerned within the religions of the world.[50] Again, John B. Cobb, Jr, a pioneer of Christian–Buddhist dialogue, comments:[51]

> I see no a priori reason to assume that religion has an essence or that the great religious traditions are well understood as religions, that is, as traditions for which being religious is the central goal. I certainly see no

Nietzsche on Religion. New York: Pilgrim Press, 1986; Joachim Scharfenberg, *Sigmund Freud and his Critique of Religion.* Philadelphia: Fortress Press, 1988.

[46] See, for example, Fraser Watts and Mark Williams, *The Psychology of Religious Knowing.* Cambridge: Cambridge University Press, 1988.

[47] Robert Towler, *The Need for Certainty: A Sociological Study of Conventional Religion.* London: Routledge & Kegan Paul, 1984; Christian Wachtmann, *Der Religionsbegriff bei Mircea Eliade.* Frankfurt am Main/Berlin: Peter Lang, 1996.

[48] Eric J. Sharpe, *Comparative Religion: A History.* New York: Charles Scribner's Sons, 1975.

[49] Michael L. Peterson, *Reason and Religious Belief: An Introduction to the Philosophy of Religion.* Oxford: Oxford University Press, 1991, 4–5.

[50] David Tracy, *Plurality and Ambiguity.* San Francisco: Harper & Row, 1987, 90.

[51] John B. Cobb, 'Beyond "Pluralism"', in Gavin D'Costa (ed.), *Christian Uniqueness Reconsidered: The Myth of a Pluralistic Theology of Religions.* Maryknoll, NY: Orbis Books, 1990, 81–95; 84.

empirical evidence in favour of this view. I see only scholarly habit and the power of language to mislead.

John Milbank argues persuasively that, while the 'assumption about a religious genus' is central to some late-twentieth-century attempts to defend a theology of religious pluralism, the notion is so seriously flawed as to be virtually indefensible.[52]

> It would be a mistake to imagine that it arose simultaneously among all the participants as the recognition of an evident truth. On the contrary, it is clear that the other religions were taken by Christian thinkers to be species of the genus 'religion', because these thinkers systematically subsumed alien cultural phenomena under categories which comprise western notions of what constitutes religious thought and practice. These false categorizations have often been accepted by western-educated representatives of the other religions themselves, who are unable to resist the politically imbued rhetorical force of western discourse.

Ninian Smart has also made the point that much of the loose talk about 'classical' religion actually means '*western* classical' religion, and is therefore a reflection of the specifics of western culture.[53] It cannot be regarded as a universal category. In much the same way, Paul Knitter notes how, in his own thinking, he regards himself as having been guilty of 'implicitly, unconsciously, but still imperialistically imposing our notions of Deity or the Ultimate on other believers who, like many Buddhists, may not even wish to speak about God or who experience the Ultimate as *Sunyata*, which has nothing or little to do with what Christians experience and call God'.[54]

John Hick, easily the most prolific defender of the thesis of the homogeneity of religious beliefs, has devoted considerable attention to identifying similarities between the various religious traditions of the

[52] John Milbank, 'The End of Dialogue', in Gavin D'Costa (ed.), *Christian Uniqueness Reconsidered: The Myth of a Pluralistic Theology of Religions*. Maryknoll, NY: Orbis Books, 1990, 174–91; 176.

[53] Ninian Smart, 'Truth and Religions', in John Hick (ed.), *Truth and Dialogue: The Relationship between the World Religions*. London: Sheldon Press, 1974, 45–58; 57. See further Mark S. Heim, *Salvations: Truth and Difference in Religion*. Maryknoll, NY: Orbis Books, 1995; Alvin Plantinga, 'Pluralism: A Defense of Religious Exclusivism', in Thomas Senor (ed.), *The Rationality of Belief and the Plurality of Belief*. Ithaca, NY: Cornell University Press, 1995, 191–215.

[54] Paul F. Knitter, 'Toward a Liberation Theology of Religions,' in John Hick and Paul F. Knitter (eds), *The Myth of Christian Uniqueness*. Maryknoll, NY: Orbis Books, 1987, 178–200; 184. For an assessment of Knitter, see Reinhold Bernhardt, 'Ein neuer Lessing? Paul Knitters Theologie der Religionen', *Evangelische Theologie* 49 (1989), 516–28.

world. Hick argues that there is a common core structure to all religions, which 'are fundamentally alike in exhibiting a soteriological structure. That is to say, they are all concerned with salvation/liberation/enlightenment/fulfilment.'[55] All the 'great traditions' are declared to be 'more or less equally effective' soteriologically; their truth is held to lie 'in soteriological effectiveness'.[56]

This position has been subject to considerable criticism, and is simply incapable of sustaining the epistemic weight that some choose to place upon it. For example, how does Hick *know* that all religions are 'more or less equally effective' soteriologically? What evidence has led him to this conclusion, apart from a politically correct – yet theologically spurious – wish not to give offence to any faith community? As Keith Ward demonstrates, Hick's highly ambivalent notion of 'soteriological efficacy' can only be interpreted in terms of fostering 'moral heroism or the achievement of spectacular virtue'.[57] Yet Marxism-Leninism and Nazism – among many other more exotic ideologies – inspired many to precisely such heroic conduct. Ward rightly concludes that 'moral efficacy may be one test of an acceptable belief; but it is not even a necessary condition of a belief's being true, much less a sufficient one'.

Hick makes much of the highly abstract notion of 'the Real' in his approach to religions, arguing that the same 'Real' may be discerned as lying behind the various responses to that 'Real' within the world's highly diverse and divergent religious communities. 'The great world traditions constitute different conceptions and perceptions of, and responses to, the Real from within the different ways of being human.'[58] Yet Hick is coy precisely where his theory demands he must be precise: just *what* do we know about the 'Real'?

In his critique of Hick's approach, Keith Ward points out that Hick's failure to offer anything specific concerning the critically important notion of the 'Real' renders his position untenable.[59] As Ward points out, Hick seems to make the ultimate elusiveness and ineffability of the ultimately vacuous notion of the 'Real' the ground of his assertion that all statements concerning it are equally valid.[60]

[55] John Hick, *The Second Christianity*. London: SCM Press, 1983, 86.
[56] John Hick, *An Interpretation of Religion*. London: Macmillan, 1989, 369, 373.
[57] Keith Ward, *Religion and Revelation: A Theology of Revelation in the World's Religions.* Oxford: Clarendon Press, 1994, 316.
[58] Hick, *An Interpretation of Religion*, 376.
[59] Ward, *Religion and Revelation*, 310–24.
[60] Ward, *Religion and Revelation*, 313.

If X is indescribable by me, and Y is indescribable by me, it does not follow that X is identical with Y. On the contrary, there is no way in which X can be identical with Y, since there are no criteria of identity to apply. It is rather like saying, 'I do not know what X is; and I do not know what Y is; therefore X must be the same as Y.' If I do not know what either is, I naturally do not know whether they are the same or different. To assert identity is thus to commit the quantifier-shift fallacy, of moving from 'Many religions believe in an ineffable Real' to 'There is an ineffable Real in which many religions believe.'

A similar difficulty arises in the approach favoured by Wilfrid Cantwell Smith, in which the somewhat opaque category of 'the Transcendent' plays a role analogous to 'the Real'. Lesslie Newbigin notes the intense difficulties that the unknowability of this 'Transcendent' raises for this position.[61]

> It is clear that in Smith's view 'The Transcendent' is a purely formal category. He, she, or it may be conceived in any way that the worshipper may choose. There can therefore be no such thing as false or misdirected worship, since the reality to which it is directed is unknowable. Smith quotes as 'one of the theologically most discerning remarks that I know' the words of the *Yogavasistha*: 'Thou art formless. Thy only form is our knowledge of Thee'. Any claim for uniqueness made for one concept of the Transcendent, for instance the Christian claim that the Transcendent is present in fullness in Jesus (Colossians 1:19), is to be regarded as wholly unacceptable. There are no criteria by which different concepts of the Transcendent may be tested. We are shut up to a total subjectivity: the Transcendent is unknowable.

As Newbigin points out, until and unless the 'full reality which relativizes all the claims of the religions' is made publicly available and subjected to intense empirical analysis, the claim that all the religions somehow represent embodiments of its various aspects is little more than an unverified claim without any legitimate basis. Indeed, it represents both an unverifiable and unfalsifiable claim, an intrusion into the world of speculation rather than solid empirical research.

Other criticisms have been directed against Hick's unwillingness to recognize genuine and significant divergences between religions. As Kathryn Tanner shrewdly observes, Hick's approach fails to treat

---

[61] Lesslie Newbigin, *The Gospel in a Pluralist Society*. Grand Rapids, MI: Eerdmans, 1989, 159–61, 168–70.

religious traditions with integrity, seizing on their similarities and failing to honour or give full weight to their clear divergences.[62]

> Pluralist generalizations about what all religions have in common conflict with genuine dialogue, in that they prejudge its results. Commonalities, which should be established in and through a process of dialogue, are constructed ahead of time by pluralists to serve as presuppositions of dialogue. Pluralists therefore close themselves to what people of other religions might have to say about their account of these commonalities. Moreover . . . a pluralist focus on commonalities slights differences among the religions of the world. The pluralists' insistence on commonalities as a condition of dialogue shows an unwillingness to recognize the depth and degree of diversity among religions, or the positive importance of them.

Hick's reluctance to accept religious belief systems as they are is particularly well illustrated by his vigorous rejection of some of the core teachings of historical Christianity. The doctrines of the incarnation and the Trinity – regarded as the defining beliefs of the Christian faith by orthodox Christian theologians, whether Catholic, Orthodox or evangelical – are judged to be at best peripheral to the Christian faith, and may be dispensed with. Having eliminated the central dogmas – in the technical sense of that word – of the Christian faith, Hick is able to demonstrate without undue difficulty that Christianity appears to show remarkable similarities to other religious belief systems. Yet it requires a considerable act of theological empathy, not to mention a suspension of the critical faculties, to concede that it is *Christianity* which is being compared in this manner to its religious rivals. Having eliminated what is distinctive about Christianity, it is not entirely surprising that Hick finds it to be religiously undistinctive. Hick's presuppositions determine his conclusions with admirable logical consistency.

Hick's strongly conceptual approach to the issue of the relation of the religions rests primarily upon a comparison of their ideas. Yet the question of how those ideas are derived and justified cannot be ignored. Hick's approach is strongly a-historical, minimizing the role of the Christian narrative in generating and shaping Christian doctrine. The decision to minimize the theological function of the biblical narrative was typical of the Enlightenment agenda,[63] which Hick replicates – in

---

[62] Kathyrn Tanner, 'Respect for Other Religions: A Christian Antidote to Colonialist Discourse', *Modern Theology* 9 (1993), 1–18; quotation at 2.

[63] See the classic study of Hans Frei, *The Eclipse of Biblical Narrative*. New Haven, CT: Yale University Press, 1974, and the literature which it engendered, including Gary Comstock, 'Two Types of Narrative Theology', *Journal of the American Academy of Religion* 55 (1987), 687–717; Mark Ellingsen, *The Integrity of Biblical Narrative*. Minneapolis: Fortress Press, 1990.

effect, treating 'religion' as a universal category, which can be abstracted from its historical context. This grand retreat from history, typical of the Enlightenment, has been countered by the realization of the integral place of the Christian narrative – which, awkwardly for Hick, focuses upon Jesus Christ – in the genesis of Christian doctrine.[64] It may also be pointed out that Christianity is characterized by a distinctive tradition of prayer and worship, in which Christian ideas are related to and embodied in certain definite doxological traditions.[65] The distinction between Christianity and, for example, Islam or Buddhism is thus located at the level of praxis, as well as theory.

I have no intention of basing a serious discussion of the interaction of the natural sciences and religion upon such a biased and flawed account of the nature of religion in general, or the specific place of Christianity in particular. The present project avoids the question of the relationship of Christianity to other religions. This is not to suggest that this question is of no significance. The point being made is that it is a complex and highly contested question, which cannot be discussed adequately within the compass of the project as it is currently envisaged. An analysis of the Christian theological tradition is, however, entirely manageable.

Unfettered by the perverse and distorting controlling assumption that all religious traditions must be saying substantially the same thing, this study will thus focus on the Chalcedonian definition of the Christian faith, the integrity of which will be treated with the greatest respect. Rather than laying down what Christianity *ought* to be in order to advance a partisan agenda, I shall instead focus on what Christianity has understood itself to be, and allow its representatives to speak for themselves rather than dismissing their views when they happen to be inconvenient for my purposes. I have no doubt that equally useful studies from a Jewish and Islamic perspective could and will be written, avoiding the intellectual inadequacies of the position associated with Hick.

---

[64] See the points made in Alister E. McGrath, *The Genesis of Doctrine*. Oxford: Blackwell, 1990.

[65] On this important point, see Andrew Louth, *Discerning the Mystery: An Essay on the Nature of Theology*, Oxford: Oxford University Press, 1983; Robin Maas and Gabriel O'Donnell, 'An Introduction to Spiritual Theology: The Theory that undergirds our Practice', in R. Maas and G. O'Donnell (eds), *Spiritual Traditions for the Contemporary Church*. Nashville, TN: Abingdon, 1990, 11–21; Philip Sheldrake, *Spirituality and Theology: Christian Living and the Doctrine of God*. London: Darton, Longman & Todd, 1998. Such approaches are resisted by Hick in his *A Christian Theology of Religions: The Rainbow of Faiths*. Louisville, KY: Westminster/John Knox Press, 1995.

There is no doubt that the three religions which, as a simple matter of historical observation, have been of particular significance in relation to the development of the natural sciences are Christianity, Islam and Judaism. It is perhaps no accident that these religions share what can at least be argued to be some common insights, most notably in relation to monotheism and a doctrine of creation. It is for this reason that the thirteenth century is perhaps one of the most creative periods in the history of Christian theology, in that – for historical reasons – conditions arose which encouraged and fostered the interaction of Christian, Islamic and Jewish thought, particularly at the University of Paris.[66] The introduction of Arabic philosophy into Europe proved to be one of the most important catalysts to the development of medieval theology and philosophy.[67] It must nevertheless be stressed that these three traditions – which may, for our limited purposes at this point, be linked with the persons of Thomas Aquinas, Avicenna (Ibn Sina) and Maimonides – show both convergence and divergence.[68] It may also be pointed out that some of those convergences may reflect shared philosophical assumptions, typical of the intellectual culture of the day; a common respect for Aristotelian metaphysics, for example, was not without its implications for the theological conclusions reached on their basis.[69]

While not in any way wishing to underplay either these important convergences between Christianity, Islam and Judaism, it is important to note that their divergences are, in the first place, significant and

[66] See the important studies of Georges Anawati, *Islam et christianisme: la rencontre de deux cultures en occidente au Moyen-Âge*. Cairo: Institute dominicain d'études orientales, 1991; Roger Arnaldez, *A la croisée des trois monothéismes: une communauté de pensée au Moyen-Âge*. Paris: Albin Michel, 1993; Avital Wohlman, *Thomas d'Aquin et Maïmonide: un dialogue exemplaire*. Paris: Editions du Cerf, 1988.
[67] See the materials assembled in Charles Butterworth and Blake André Kessel (eds), *The Introduction of Arabic Philosophy into Europe*. Leiden: E. J. Brill, 1994.
[68] David B. Burrell, *Freedom and Creation in Three Traditions*. Notre Dame, IN: University of Notre Dame, 1993; Herbert Davidson, *Proofs for Eternity, Creation and the Existence of God in Medieval Islamic and Jewish Philosophy*. Oxford: Oxford University Press, 1987.
[69] See in particular David B. Burrell, *Knowing the Unknowable: Ibn Sina, Maimonides, Aquinas*. Notre Dame, IN: University of Notre Dame Press, 1986; Marvin Fox, *Interpreting Maimonides: Studies in Methodology, Metaphysics and Moral Philosophy*. Chicago: University of Chicago Press, 1990. The condemnation of Aristotle by Bishop Etienne Tempier in 1277 was thus of particular importance in relation to the development of scholastic theology: see Luca Bianchi, *Il vescovo e i filosofi: la condanna parigini del 1277 e l'evoluzione dell'Aristotelismo scolastico*. Bergamo: Pierluigi Lubrina, 1990; John Murdoch, 'The Condemnation of 1277, God's Absolute Power and Physical Thought in the Late Middle Ages', *Viator* 10 (1979), 211–44.

decisive, and, in the second, are of considerable importance both to the general issue of the interaction of science and religion, and also to the specific agenda of this project. Two divergences of importance may be singled out for comment. These are illustrative, not exhaustive, and indicate the importance of respecting the integrity of the beliefs of a religious community, rather than polemically minimizing them for the purposes of advancing some theological agenda.

1. Islam tends to reject any notion of a 'natural knowledge of God', largely on the grounds that this diminishes or challenges the place of the Qu'ran. Although there was a period during the Middle Ages in which Islamic philosophers were receptive to the ideas of Greek philosophy, including the concept of 'natural theology',[70] these notions were generally viewed with intense suspicion by the more militant defenders of Islamic orthodoxy, such as al-Ghazālī (1058–1111). It is important to appreciate that many of the more prominent Islamic scientists and natural philosophers of the medieval period were supported by royal patronage, and thus shielded from the attacks and denunciations of local religious leaders, who regarded their views as threats to Islam.[71] As al-Ghazālī points out in the brief conclusion to his major work *On the Incoherence of the Philosophers*, the conclusion must be drawn that 'anyone who believes in them ought to be branded with infidelity, and punished with death'.

2. The decisive place and role of Jesus Christ in orthodox Christian thought must be fully acknowledged, along with the implications of this emphasis for Christianity's relation with Judaism and Islam. This is particularly clear in relation to the doctrine of the incarnation.[72] Thus orthodox Christianity envisages a strong

---

[70] A. I. Sabra, 'The Appropriation and Subsequent Naturalization of Greek Science in Medieval Islam: A Preliminary Statement', *History of Science* 25 (1987), 223–43; idem, 'Science and Philosophy in Medieval Islamic Theology', *Zeitschrift für Geschichte der Arabisch-Islamischen Wissenschaften* 9 (1994), 1–42.

[71] See Francis E. Peters, *Aristotle and the Arabs: The Aristotelian Tradition in Islam*. New York: New York University Press, 1968; Edward Grant, *The Foundations of Science in the Middle Ages: Their Religious, Institutional and Intellectual Contexts*. Cambridge: Cambridge University Press, 1996, 176–82.

[72] Jacob Neusner, *Telling Tales: The Urgency and Basis for Judeo–Christian Dialogue*. Louisville, KY: Westminster/John Knox Press, 1993, argues that the doctrine of the incarnation, along with the distinctively Jewish notion of the divine vocation of Israel, has often been ignored in Jewish–Christian dialogue, on account of the difficulties which it raises for the notion of a homogeneous 'Judeo-Christian tradition'. I would also point out that the critically important doctrine of *creatio ex nihilo* only gained widespread acceptance

theological link between the doctrine of creation and Christology. This is evident in the statement of the Nicene Creed, which declares that it is Christ 'through whom all things are made'. The Christological orientation of the doctrine of creation is a common theme of Christian writers down the ages, and may be regarded as common to Catholic, Orthodox and evangelical approaches to Christian theology.[73] Judaism, in contrast, sees creation in terms of the impression of the *Torah* – the law of Moses – upon the created order.[74] We shall explore this point further at a later point in this chapter.

The particular perspective of the present study thus reflects a concern to ensure that it is grounded on the distinctive ideas of Christianity, some of which can be argued to have been of importance to the historical development of the natural sciences, rather than attempting to identify a set of universal religious beliefs, common to all faiths – an undertaking, it must be added, which has failed to achieve its stated objectives with any degree of conviction. This position cannot be finally refuted as wrong; yet it is so flawed and contested that it cannot conceivably act as the basis of a critical and systematic engagement of the relation of Christianity – or, for that matter, any religion – and the natural sciences.

The sciences as a stimulus to theological reflection

While stressing the importance of the faithful interpretation of Scripture as of central importance to the development of Christian theology, the importance of the stimulus received from outside the Christian community in relation to the development of doctrine has always been conceded. In John Henry Newman's *Essay on the Development of Christian Doctrine* (1845), we find this notion expressed in terms of the stimulus that is provided to theological reflection by the challenges

---

as a cardinal dogma within Judaism in the late fifteenth century, more than a millennium after the Christian church had given such a status to the doctrine. See Menachem M. Kellner, *Dogma in Medieval Judaism from Maimonides to Abravanel.* Oxford: Oxford University Press for the Littmann Library of Jewish Civilization, 1986, 213–17.

[73] Kenneth Cauthen, 'Christology as the Clarification of Creation', *Journal of Bible and Religion* 33 (1965), 34–41.

[74] Hava Tirosh-Samuelson, 'Theology of Nature in Sixteenth-Century Italian Jewish Philosophy', *Science in Context* 10 (1997), 529–70, especially 544–52. For some of the more mystical and kabbalistic ways in which this was interpreted, see Moshe Idel, *Golem: Jewish Magical and Mystical Traditions on the Artificial Anthropoid.* Albany, NY: State University of New York, 1990, 9–26;

posed to existing ways of thinking within the church by intellectual currents dominant within its cultural milieu.[75] Newman does not hold that such external stimuli lead to Christian theology mimicking the ideas and values of the secular world. Rather, he argues that they act as a catalyst for the church to explore the revelation entrusted to it, and reconsider whether it has indeed fully understood it or properly expressed it.

In one sense, the natural sciences can be seen as offering a stimulus to Christian theology, to consider whether it has, in fact, achieved a correct interpretation of its foundational resources on points of importance. Augustine of Hippo (354–430) is of especial importance in this matter, in that Augustine noted the importance of respecting the conclusions of the sciences in relation to biblical exegesis. In his commentary on Genesis, Augustine pointed out that certain passages were genuinely open to diverse interpretations, without calling into question any fundamental doctrines of the church. It was therefore important to allow further scientific research to assist in the determination of which was the most appropriate mode of interpretation for a given passage:[76]

> In matters that are so obscure and far beyond our vision, we find in Holy Scripture passages which can be interpreted in very different ways without prejudice to the faith we have received. In such cases, we should not rush in headlong and so firmly take our stand on one side that, if further progress in the search for truth justly undermines our position, we too fall with it. We should not battle for our own interpretation but for the teaching of the Holy Scripture. We should not wish to conform the meaning of Holy Scripture to our interpretation, but our interpretation to the meaning of Holy Scripture.

Augustine therefore urged that biblical interpretation should take due account of what could reasonably be regarded as established facts.

This approach to biblical interpretation can be argued to prevent Christian theology from becoming trapped in a pre-scientific worldview, or improperly committing itself to a specific scientific outlook which would become outmoded through progress. Edward Grant has shown the importance of this point in relation to the development of medieval cosmology over the period 1200–1687, noting in particular

[75] Owen Chadwick, *From Bossuet to Newman: The Idea of Doctrinal Development.* Cambridge: Cambridge University Press, 1957, 157–63.

[76] Tarsicius van Bavel, 'The Creator and the Integrity of Creation in the Fathers of the Church', *Augustinian Studies* 21 (1990), 1–33; quotation at 1–2.

the manner in which Augustine's approach was endorsed and developed by Thomas Aquinas.[77] The general approach set out by Augustine was adopted by several influential Roman Catholic theologians of the sixteenth century, including a highly significant commentary on Genesis which is known to have influenced Galileo's developing views on biblical interpretation.[78] Nevertheless, it was an approach which was not without its difficulties, not least of which was the question of whether an allegedly 'scientific' belief was a permanently valid insight into the nature of the world, or simply a culturally conditioned response to events, a traditional belief resting on the authority of an acknowledged master, or a fallacy which would be discarded by subsequent generations.

It can be shown without difficulty that all three such categories of 'scientific' beliefs had a considerable influence on the Christian interpretation of the Bible, especially during the Middle Ages. The rediscovery of Aristotle seemed to make available a body of highly respectable 'scientific' findings, whose validity seemed assured – a belief in which theologians were encouraged to believe by other academics of the time.[79] In consequence, medieval biblical exposition and systematic theology can be shown to have followed Augustine's advice in deferring to science, and thus perpetuated what can now be recognized to be the unscientific influence of Aristotle.[80]

It is sometimes argued that the controversy over the view of Copernicus and Galileo arose partly because biblical exposition took no account of the natural sciences. While this viewpoint is not totally without merit, a much more plausible and satisfactory reading of the historical data is that the controversy arose precisely because too much weight was given to what early generations of theologians and philosophers had been led to understand were the established certainties of the sciences. In particular, it is important to note the immense

[77] Edward Grant, *Planets, Stars and Orbs: The Medieval Cosmos, 1200–1687*. Cambridge: Cambridge University Press, 1996, 90–1.

[78] Richard J. Blackwell, *Galileo, Bellarmine and the Bible*. Notre Dame, IN: University of Notre Dame Press, 1991, 20–2.

[79] Etienne Gilson, *History of Christian Philosophy in the Middle Ages*. London: Sheed & Ward, 1978, 181–410.

[80] Edith Dudley Sylla, 'The a posteriori Foundations of Natural Science. Some Medieval Commentaries on Aristotle's *Physics*', *Synthese* 40 (1979), 147–87; L. W. B. Brockliss, 'Aristotle, Descartes and the New Science: Natural Philosophy at the University of Paris, 1600–1740', *Annals of Science* 38 (1981), 33–69; Alister E. McGrath, 'The Influence of Aristotelian Physics upon St Thomas Aquinas's Discussion of the Processus Iustificationis', *Recherches de théologie ancienne et médiévale* 51 (1984), 223–9; William E. Carroll, 'San Tommaso, Aristotele e la creazione', *Annales Theologici* 8 (1994), 363–76.

influence of the Aristotelian commentators on the intellectual life of the period.[81] When those 'scientific' foundations were challenged, biblical interpretation became intensely difficult at points. How could Augustine's maxim be applied confidently and meaningfully, when there was controversy over what the sciences were saying? Christian biblical exposition had allowed itself to assume that the sciences had established certain matters as fact, which could then be used as the basis of the interpretation of related biblical passages.

Augustine's legacy to biblical interpretation thus proved to be ambivalent. Designed to ensure that biblical interpretation was alert to what the sciences had established, it proved capable of enslaving Christian theology to what previous generations of scientists had believed. We have already stressed the dangers posed to responsible theological reflection by transient developments in the history of science; it is therefore of no small importance to ensure that Christian theology incorporates the necessary safeguards to protect itself against being misled by such trends.

The situation became more complex in the aftermath of the Council of Trent (1545–63). Responding to the challenges posed by the rise of Protestantism in the first half of the sixteenth century, the Roman Catholic Church stressed the importance of maintaining continuity with the medieval church. Intending to undermine the credibility of Protestant interpretations of certain critical biblical passages (such as those relating to the disputed doctrine of justification by faith), the Council insisted that the consensus of previous generations of theologians should remain normative.[82] This weapon was intended to discredit Protestant teachings, which were in effect treated as theological innovations. However, there was an unintended side-effect of this approach. Augustine's maxim – designed to maintain openness to the sciences – now trapped theologians in the world of medieval science, rather than liberating them from the tyranny of prevailing (and often transient) scientific assumptions. If, for example, the consensus of theologians had been that the sun rotated around the earth, Trent's stipulations could only mean that that consensus must be maintained. An indirect and unintended casualty of Trent's polemic against

---

[81] Charles B. Schmitt, *The Aristotelian Tradition and Renaissance Universities*. London: Variorum, 1984; Nicholas Jardine, 'Keeping Order in the School of Padua: Jacopo Zabarella and Francesco Piccolomini on the Offices of Philosophy', in Daniel A. Di Liscia, Eckhard Kessler and Charlotte Methuen (eds), *Method and Order in Renaissance Philosophy of Nature: The Aristotle Commentary Tradition*. Aldershot: Ashgate, 1997, 183–209.

[82] Blackwell, *Galileo, Bellarmine and the Bible*, 5–22.

Protestantism was thus the ability of theology to grasp and respond to the theological significance of *new* developments in the sciences. The results were as tragic as they were unintended. Galileo was right, and those who insisted that the Bible was to be interpreted as teaching that the sun revolved around the earth were wrong.

The natural sciences thus offer an important resource to Christian theology, in that they invite the church continually to reconsider its present interpretations of Scripture, in order to ensure that the settled scientific assumptions of earlier generations – now known or suspected to be incorrect – have not inadvertently been incorporated into the teachings of the church. The importance of this role of the natural sciences is recognized by many theologians, including the influential evangelical writer Benjamin B. Warfield.[83] Yet there is another manner in which the natural sciences offer illumination to theological development, which will be considered in more detail in the third volume of this work. This concerns the important parallels between the development of doctrine and the development of scientific theories.

It is a matter of observable fact that both scientific theories and Christian doctrines have undergone development.[84] This development is complex and nuanced, involving important judgements concerning the criteria to be used for evaluation, and especially the role of communities in the genesis, development and reception of theories. The present study therefore devotes considerable space to considering the factors which affect these processes within both the scientific and theological communities, and how they might cast light on issues faced within each other. This major topic has received substantially less attention than it merits, and led to the decision to devote an entire volume to the exploration of this important matter.

The essentialist fallacy

The interaction of religious and scientific communities and their leading representatives has been far from simple. Polemical distortions of the

---

[83] David N. Livingstone, 'B. B. Warfield, the Theory of Evolution and Early Fundamentalism', *Evangelical Quarterly* 58 (1986), 69–83.

[84] P. M. Harman, *Energy, Force, and Matter: The Conceptual Development of Nineteenth-Century Physics.* Cambridge: Cambridge University Press, 1982; Christopher Knight, 'An Authentic Theological Revolution? Scientific Perspectives on the Development of Doctrine', *Journal of Religion* 74 (1994), 524–41; David Park, *The How and the Why: An Essay on the Origins and Development of Physical Theory.* Princeton, NJ: Princeton University Press, 1988; Pierre Rousselot, 'Petit théorie du dévelopement du dogme', *Recherches de science religieuse* 53 (1965), 355–90; H. E. W. Turner, *The Patristic Doctrine of Redemption: A Study of the Development of Doctrine during the First Five Centuries.* London: Mowbray, 1952.

histories abound, both from those who wish to perpetuate the myth that the two disciplines have been in a state of perpetual warfare,[85] and those who prefer the equally mythical view that the two disciplines have generally existed in a harmonious and mutually productive relationship.[86] The truth is more messy, complex and interesting than either of these polemical simplifications allows. There is no doubt that, at times, Christianity – whether we take this to refer either to Christian theological positions or to ecclesiastical institutions – has sought to inhibit scientific advance; equally, at others it has sought to advance it. It is impossible to impose a single grand narrative upon the complex history of the interaction of science and religion without serious distortion or omission.

Yet some have taken the view that the relation between science and Christian theology is permanently defined, at least in its fundamental respects, by the essential nature of the two disciplines. It is argued that, once the essential nature of the two disciplines is grasped, their mutual relationship can be inferred as a matter of course. Underlying these 'essentialist' accounts of the interaction of science and religion is the unchallenged assumption that each of these terms designates something fixed, permanent and essential, so that their mutual relationship is determined by something essential to each of the disciplines, unaffected by the vagaries of time, place or culture.[87]

This tendency to attribute fixed and unchanging defining qualities to both science and religion – and hence to determine the nature of their relationship on the basis of these allegedly 'essential' attributes – is seriously deficient, and has been successfully challenged by a series of rigorous historical studies. These have demonstrated the diversity, occasional inconsistency, and sheer complexity of understandings of the mutual relationship of science and religion since about 1500. No single account or 'metanarrative' may be offered of this relationship,

---

[85] For the origins of this stereotype, see John William Draper, *History of the Conflict between Religion and Science*. New York: Daniel Appleton, 1874. For more thoughtful and critical reflections on the model, see C. A. Russell, 'The Conflict Metaphor and its Social Origins', *Science and Christian Faith* 1 (1989), 3–26; Frank Miller Turner, 'The Victorian Conflict between Science and Religion: A Professional Dimension', *Isis* 69 (1978), 356–76; Fraser Watts, 'Are Science and Religion in Conflict?', *Zygon* 32 (1997), 125–38.

[86] A view which tends to underlie Reijer Hooykaas' important studies of the origins of modern science: R. Hooykaas, *Religion and the Rise of Modern Science*. Edinburgh: Scottish Academic Press, 1972; idem, *Fact, Faith and Fiction in the Development of Science*. Dordrecht: Kluwer Academic Publishers, 1999.

[87] For a sustained critique of this position, richly illustrated with historical case studies, see John Brooke and Geoffrey Cantor, *Reconstructing Nature: The Engagement of Science and Religion*. Edinburgh: T&T Clark, 1998.

precisely because the variety of relationships that have existed reflect prevailing social, political, economic and cultural factors.

This unhistorical approach to the issue has led to the totally unacceptable retrojection of the polemical concerns of the late nineteenth century onto earlier periods of history, leading to a number of serious historical distortions. Thus the 'Galileo Affair' is widely read by anti-religious activists as a classic example of 'science versus religion'.[88] This viewpoint arises through five serious errors:

1. Through treating 'science' and 'religion' as essentially fixed and unchanging entities, whose relationship is permanently defined by their subject-matter. The discrediting, if not the elimination, of this 'essentialist fallacy' must be regarded as one of the most significant achievements of recent studies in the history and philosophy of science.

2. Through assuming that this relationship may be universally defined in terms of the 'warfare' imagery of the nineteenth century, using this as a controlling metanarrative, a prism through which all related intellectual engagements throughout history are to be viewed, permanently adversarial.

3. Through failing to draw a distinction between the institution of the Christian church and the ideas of Christian theology, especially during the late Middle Ages, and failing to appreciate that the political decisions of the former often rest on considerations which have little to do with the latter. To critique the leading ideas of Christian theology on the basis of the actions of certain late medieval ecclesiastical figures is to assume a simple, direct, and linear connection between these entities which rarely existed in practice.

4. Through overlooking the complex social dynamics of the period, both within the ecclesiastical establishment itself, and within the Italian courts which often acted as patrons of scientific research.[89]

5. Through failing to appreciate the critically important role played by influential individuals in shaping attitudes in debates over the relation of science and theology. This can be illustrated from

---

[88] Brooke and Cantor, *Reconstructing Nature*, 106–38.

[89] For example, consider the role of political and ecclesiastical patronage in the Galileo affair: Mario Biagioli, *Galileo, Courtier: The Practice of Science in the Culture of Absolutism*. Chicago: University of Chicago Press, 1993.

the Galileo debate, in which it is clear that Galileo's personal relationship to figures of influence within papal circles was of no small importance in shaping official attitudes towards him. More recently, the same factor can be seen in the shaping of late nineteenth-century Presbyterian attitudes to Darwinism.[90] The generally positive attitudes adopted at Princeton, and the rather more stridently negative attitudes found in Belfast, can be put down to the influence of certain personalities who exercised considerable sway in the cloisters of power.

Since the church represented the social, political and intellectual establishment in Europe in the sixteenth century, as it did in England during the early nineteenth century, it should not be any cause for surprise that the social location of the church was a significant factor in generating at least the perception of conflict between the church and the sciences. Science is, almost by definition, a subversive activity, in that its advance is virtually uncontrollable by vested interests and power groups – a point famously stated in a lecture delivered in February 1923 to the 'Society of Heretics' at Cambridge by the biologist J. B. S. Haldane.[91] Yet the target of this rebellion is historically determined, not permanently fixed. What is being challenged is determined by the contingencies of historical and social factors, rather than some allegedly 'essential' factors. As Freeman Dyson points out in his important essay 'The Scientist as Rebel', the interaction of science with culture – including religion – is conditioned by local factors.[92] A common element of most visions of science is that of 'rebellion against the restrictions imposed by the local prevailing culture'.

This can easily be illustrated from the history of the interaction of science and culture. For the Arab mathematician and astronomer Omar Khayyám, science was a rebellion against the intellectual constraints of

[90] David N. Livingstone, 'Darwinism and Calvinism: The Belfast-Princeton Connection', *Isis* 83 (1992), 408–28. For further aspects of this matter, see his additional studies 'B. B. Warfield, the Theory of Evolution and Early Fundamentalism', *Evangelical Quarterly* 58 (1986), 69–83; *Darwin's Forgotten Defenders: The Encounter between Evangelical Theology and Evolutionary Thought.* Grand Rapids, MI: Eerdmans, 1987; 'The Idea of Design: The Vicissitudes of a Key Concept in the Princeton Response to Darwin', *Scottish Journal of Theology* 37 (1984), 329–57

[91] On this group, see P. Sargant Florence, 'The Cambridge Heretics 1909–1932', in A. J. Ayer (ed.), *The Humanist Outlook.* London: Pemberton Publishing Co., 1968, 223–39. The group tended to focus primarily on issues of religion, philosophy and art, but occasionally ventured into the territories of the natural sciences.

[92] Freeman Dyson, 'The Scientist as Rebel', in John Cornwell (ed.), *Nature's Imagination: The Frontiers of Scientific Vision.* Oxford: Oxford University Press, 1995, 1–11.

Islam; for nineteenth-century Japanese scientists, science was a rebellion against the lingering feudalism of their culture; for the great Indian physicists of the twentieth century, their discipline was a powerful intellectual force directed against the fatalistic ethic of Hinduism (not to mention British imperialism, which was then dominant in the region). And in western Europe, scientific advance inevitably involved confrontation with the culture of the day – including its political, social and religious elements. In that the west has been dominated by Christianity, it is thus unsurprising that the tension between science and western culture has often been viewed as a confrontation between science and Christianity.

The manner in which the interaction of science and religion is socially conditioned can be illustrated from any number of historical situations. For example, the polarity between the two disciplines which developed in England during the early nineteenth century can be seen in sociological – rather than 'essentialist' – terms as reflecting a struggle between two élites in early nineteenth-century English society.[93] From a sociological perspective, scientific knowledge can be seen as a cultural resource which was constructed and deployed by particular social groups towards the achievement of their own specific goals and interests.[94] This approach casts much light on the growing competition between two specific groups within English society in the nineteenth century: the clergy and the scientific professionals. The clergy were widely regarded as an élite at the beginning of the century, with the 'scientific parson' a well-established social stereotype.[95] The rise of the professional scientist posed a challenge to this hegemony, just as the continued existence of the gentleman clerical scientist posed a perhaps less serious threat to the professional guild of scientists. Conflict was inevitable, given the social factors involved – factors, of course,

[93] See the important studies of Frank Miller Turner, 'Rainfall, Plagues and the Prince of Wales: A Chapter in the Conflict of Science and Religion', *Journal of British Studies* 13 (1974), 46–65; idem, 'The Victorian Conflict between Science and Religion: A Professional Dimension', *Isis* 69 (1978), 356–76. More generally, see Claude Welch, 'Dispelling Some Myths about the Split between Theology and Science in the Nineteenth Century', in W. Mark Richardson and Wesley J. Wildman (eds), *Religion and Science: History, Method, Dialogue.* New York: Routledge, 1996, 29–40.

[94] See, for example, Martin J. S. Rudwick, *The Great Devonian Controversy: The Shaping of Scientific Knowledge among Gentlemanly Specialists.* Chicago: University of Chicago Press, 1985; idem, 'Senses of the Natural World and Senses of God: Another Look at the Historical Relation of Science and Religion', in Arthur R. Peacocke (ed.), *The Sciences and Theology in the Twentieth Century.* London: Oriel Press, 1981, 241–61.

[95] S. F. Cannon, *Science in Culture: The Early Victorian Period.* New York: Science History Publications, 1978.

which were determined by the contingencies of English social history, rather than the necessities of the allegedly 'fixed' natures of science and religion.

Furthermore, it is clear that many facets of the historical interaction of Christianity and the natural sciences have reflected the institutional agenda of the church, rather than been the direct consequence of Christian beliefs. For example, the historically contingent association between the Roman Catholic Church and Aristotelian philosophy was of no small importance in relation to the Galilean controversy. The challenge posed to the Aristotelian – *not* Christian – belief in the incorruptibility and immutability of the heavens by the astronomical observations of Galileo and others was substantial.[96] Yet the linkage between Aristotelianism and the ecclesiastical establishment at this time was contingent, and was being challenged by influential figures within the church and university.[97] It is quite inaccurate to suggest that Christianity itself was somehow being called into question by Galileo's discoveries. A challenge was certainly posed to one of the many temporary alliances forged between Christian theology and secular philosophies over the period of many centuries; the challenge, however, related to the propriety and utility of such an alliance, rather than the intellectual integrity of the faith itself.

The interaction of Christianity and the natural sciences is thus not totally conditioned or determined by their essential natures – if these could be satisfactorily determined, and shown to be independent of time and culture, which is very much open to question[98] – but is modulated by the social situation in which they find themselves. This inevitably leads to the conclusion that a given view of the relation of science and religion is partly a social construction – that is, that it has been shaped by the context in which the interaction takes place. The relation of the disciplines is thus open to at least some degree of reconstruction by their interpreters. Despite the assertions of some,

---

[96] See the important material assembled and analysed in Jean Dietz Moss, *Novelties in the Heavens: Rhetoric and Science in the Copernican Controversy.* Chicago: University of Chicago Press, 1993.

[97] See the essays collected in Charles B. Schmitt, *The Aristotelian Tradition and Renaissance Universities.* London: Variorum, 1984.

[98] This is well illustrated by the inconclusive debate over whether there exists an 'essence' of Christianity and, if so, what this might be. For a useful overview, see Guglielmo Forni, *The Essence of Christianity: The Hermeneutical Question in the Protestant and Modernist Debate (1897–1904).* Atlanta, GA: Scholars Press, 1995; Stephen Sykes, *The Identity of Christianity: Theologians and the Essence of Christianity from Schleiermacher to Barth.* Philadelphia: Fortress Press, 1984.

for their own purposes – in that the historical evidence most certainly does not warrant any such positions – 'science' and 'religion' have neither been locked permanently in battle, nor in a tender embrace.

The limitations of controlling paradigms

A number of paradigms or 'models' have been proposed to account for the relation of the natural sciences and religion in general, including Christian theology in particular.[99] The present work avoids precommitment to any of these models, in that there are certain serious difficulties associated with this unduly stipulative approach to the interaction. The present work takes the view that a dialogue between the natural sciences and Christian theology is both appropriate and potentially fruitful. However, this does not necessarily entail the acceptance of any of the specific models which are currently proposed in the literature. Three particular concerns should be noted here.

First, as has just been noted, some of the existing models – especially the 'warfare' paradigm – are little more than projections from specific historical situations which are improperly treated as timeless and permanent, corresponding to the alleged 'essences' of science and religion. It is ludicrous to allow the twenty-first-century discussion of such issues to be fettered by the accumulated baggage of the past – for example, by imposing nineteenth-century stereotypes upon what might otherwise be a creative discussion. The past has the ability to imprison, as much as to illuminate. In commending the importance of learning from history, I have no intention of repeating its darker moments.

Second, there is a risk of historical distortion. Precommitment to any one such model of the interaction of science and religion generally ends up by leading to certain historical episodes being prioritized or interpreted in such a way that they are accommodated to fit the requirements of the model.[100] Those committed to demonstrating the fundamental harmony of science and religion tend to end up emphasizing the religious faith of those at the forefront of scientific advance; those preferring to see the two disciplines as being permanently opposed to each other tend to dwell more on the conflicts and tensions of the past

---

[99] Among which may be noted Ian G. Barbour, *Religion in an Age of Science*. San Francisco: HarperSanFrancisco, 1990, 3–30; Jacques Fantino, 'La rencontre entre science et théologie', *Revue des sciences religieuses* 71 (1997), 60–78; Ted Peters, 'Theology and the Natural Sciences', in David F. Ford (ed.), *The Modern Theologians: An Introduction to Christian Theology in the Twentieth Century*, 2nd edn. Oxford: Blackwell, 1997, 649–68.

[100] This point is stressed by John Hedley Brooke, *Science and Religion: Some Historical Perspectives*. Cambridge: Cambridge University Press, 1991, 16–51.

and present, arguing that religious beliefs and institutions are opposed to scientific advance. Both faith and conflict are unquestionably present in the history of this interaction; the model adopted by the historian, however, leads to a certain accentuation of parts of the story, so that the full story is not told.

Third, there is a risk of intellectual restriction, in that a given model might be taken as being *prescriptive* rather than *descriptive*, and hence used to 'police' – to borrow a heavily nuanced term from Michel Foucault – a particular understanding of the science–theology interaction, without due regard for the complexity of the situation. The theologian must be free to develop an approach to the natural sciences which is believed to be coherent and responsible, without regard to any alleged inconsistency with a prevailing paradigm of discourse or stereotypical viewpoints. Models can be illuminating and helpful; sadly, they can also become a barrier to understanding and obstacles in the way of creative and constructive theological reflection and development.[101]

A realist perspective

A scientific theology adopts a realist perspective, affirming that its task is to offer an *a posteriori* account of what it encounters or is made known to it. One of the most important working assumptions of the natural sciences is that there exists a reality, independent of the human mind, of which some account may be given. This commitment within the natural sciences to some form of realism is of immense importance to this investigation, and will be considered in detail in the second volume of this work. However, in view of its importance, it is appropriate to reflect briefly on this matter at this early point.

Most active natural scientists espouse what is recognizably a form of realism, even if they fail to – or prefer not to – articulate this in a

---

[101] The weakness of this obsession with categorizing ideas and approaches can be seen from the difficulties experienced in forcing T. F. Torrance, perhaps the most important theological advocate of dialogue between Christian theology and the natural sciences, into these procrustean paradigms. Ian G. Barbour offers four different paradigms for understanding the relationship: Barbour, *Religion in an Age of Science*, 3–30. Torrance fits awkwardly into the somewhat arbitrary categorization set out in this work, and ends up being assigned to two of the four supposedly distinct categories. In any case, Roland Spjuth rejects one of these categorizations outrght, arguing that it rests upon a misconstrual of Torrance's relation to Barth: Roland Spjuth, *Creation, Contingency and Divine Presence in the Theologies of Thomas F. Torrance and Eberhard Jüngel*. Lund: Lund University Press, 1995, 84 n. 80.

self-consciously philosophical manner. This process of critical reflection often leads to a series of distinctions, divisions and debates which can often create the impression that 'realism' is at best an incoherent, or even an indefensible, position. As Jarrett Leplin once commented wryly, 'scientific realism is a majority position whose advocates are so seriously divided as to appear a minority'.[102] Yet the varieties of realism espoused within the more philosophically reflective sections of the scientific community must not be allowed to obscure the fact that the community of experimentally-active scientists is wedded to a realist understanding of the world.

The remarkable explanatory and predictive successes of the natural sciences are widely held to point to the independent reality of what they describe. Even the most dedicated anti-realist philosopher, crossing the Atlantic Ocean to deliver an eagerly-awaited intellectual demolition of realism, will be forced to concede that the airplane boarded to reach that destination flies – and it flies, at least in part, on account of the relation between pressure and kinetic energy first set out by Daniel Bernouilli in 1738. The television and radio networks which he or she relies upon to carry reports of the lecture work, at least in part, on account of the predictions made by Maxwell's theory of electromagnetic radiation. Curiously, the technological means required to propagate an anti-intellectual standpoint rest upon an implicit acceptance of its antithesis. That the anti-realist can live with this tension is an excellent witness to the ability of the human mind to overlook matters which it finds challenging – a phenomenon, interestingly, often associated with religious fundamentalism.

A long list of technological developments, widely regarded as essential to modern western existence, can be argued to rest upon the ability of the natural sciences to develop theories which may initially explain the world, but subsequently allow us to transform it. And what more effective explanation may be offered for this success than the simple assertion that what scientific theories describe is really present? As John Polkinghorne comments:[103]

> The naturally convincing explanation of the success of science is that it is gaining a tightening grasp of an actual reality. The true goal of scientific endeavour is understanding the structure of the physical world, an

---

[102] Jarrett Leplin (ed.), *Scientific Realism*. Berkeley, CA: University of California Press, 1984, 1.

[103] John Polkinghorne, *One World: The Interaction of Science and Theology*. Princeton: Princeton University Press, 1986, 22.

understanding which is never complete but ever capable of further improvement. The terms of that understanding are dictated by the way things are.

The simplest explanation of what makes theories work is that they relate to the way things really are. If the theoretical claims of the natural sciences were not correct, their massive empirical success would appear to be totally accidental, or at best a stunning concatenation of co-incidences.[104]

The dialogue between natural scientists – who are generally realists in outlook – and theologians has thus led to a renewal of the debate over realism in theology, with T. F. Torrance representing an especially vigorous proponent of the realist position. Yet an important point must be made in this matter. What compels most working scientists to adopt a realist outlook is the outcome of their experimental procedures – such as the replicability of experimental results, and the ability of mathematics to provide a means by which these may be represented and accounted for. Realism is not a position adopted through group pressure or personal whim; it results from the relentless accumulation of experimental data, and the successful design and development of experiments to explore matters further.

To put the matter bluntly, natural scientists are realists because of the force of evidence, not on account of pressure within the scientific community or the force of inherited assumptions. My own experience in the biochemical laboratories of Oxford University would make it very difficult for me to take an anti-realist position seriously, due to the dissonance between its assumptions and the outcome of the experimental work of my colleagues in my own research group, and others within the university.

Yet many of those engaging in the dialogue between science and theology from a theological perspective lack any first-hand experience of laboratory culture, or the design and implementation of experiments. The natural sciences are about *praxis* not just *theoria*; indeed, it can easily be argued that *theoria* is dependent upon *praxis*, in that the natural sciences tend to adopt a robustly *a posteriori* approach to the question of knowledge. As Rom Harré points out, it is necessary to draw a somewhat pointed distinction between experimentally active scientists and those who 'confine themselves to the study of printed scientific

---

[104] Michael Devitt, *Realism and Truth*. Oxford: Blackwell, 1984, 108: 'If scientific realism, and the theories it draws on, were not correct, there would be no explanation of why the observed world is as if they were correct; that fact would be brute, if not miraculous.'

texts'.[105] Perhaps unwisely, some of these latter individuals have suggested that Kant's critique of realism excuses their disengagement with the world of the experiment. This is not an especially convincing argument. While the Kantian challenge to certain forms of realism has received much attention in the writings of philosophers, the serious challenge posed to Kant's epistemology by the natural sciences has received considerably less attention, and will be considered in some detail in the second volume of this work.

While I would not dream of breathing a word against those philosophers and theologians who have yet to be inducted into the experimental culture of the scientific community, I cannot help but feel that their discussions of realism and its alternatives will be less than fully informed. While it is doubtless interesting to learn that the assumptions of some working scientists are in some way 'philosophically flawed' or 'theologically incoherent', the force of such criticisms will be immeasurably reduced if the hypothetically immaculate philosopher in question has no idea why the force of experimental evidence has compelled the scientist to adopt such a 'flawed' position in the first place. One might also point out that the historical advance of the natural sciences has been accompanied by both philosophical and theological retreat, as allegedly 'incoherent' or 'flawed' assumptions are shown to be perfectly acceptable, in the light of the advance of human knowledge.

Perhaps the most fundamental and significant perspective adopted by this study is its undisguised and unapologetic commitment to a realist position. Theology is to be viewed as a discipline which offers an account of reality. It must be conceded immediately that 'realism' is a multivalent term, and the form of realism to be adopted will be clarified in the second volume of this work. However, the acceptance of a realist perspective is not to be seen as an arbitrary expression of human autonomy; rather, it is – for reasons which will be explained in the second volume of this series – to be seen as the outcome of a series of considerations which lead to the conclusion that some such doctrine is required, in order to account for the tasks and responsibilities of both Christian theology and the natural sciences.

Especially during the 1970s and 1980s, some religious (and anti-religious) writers argued that 'God' and 'religion' were essentially human constructs, and proceeded to draw the conclusion that human dignity and freedom could best be advanced by the systematic deconstruction

---

[105] Rom Harré, *Varieties of Realism*. Oxford: Blackwell, 1986, 323–4.

of both of these notions.[106] Reality is something which we construct, not something to which we respond. It therefore follows that we are at liberty to reconstruct realities as we please, in that they represent autonomous human creations. As Don Cupitt, perhaps the most noted popular critic of any form of religious realism, asserts: 'We constructed all the world-views, we made all the theories . . . They depend on us, not we on them.'[107] The suggestion that religious worlds are purely human constructions (and may thus be reconstructed in manners congenial to the *Zeitgeist* or the concerns of the postmodern self) clearly has an attraction for many; nevertheless, it remains a contested issue. Cupitt gives little indication of, or interest in, the very serious challenges posed for his self-constructed world by the natural sciences. The present series of volumes takes seriously what Cupitt disregards, believing that it offers important insights to the contemporary restatement of Christian theology.

Three general claims may be seen as underlying the form of realism adopted in this study.

1. *Ontologically*, it is held that there exists a reality or realities, the existence of which is independent of and external to the inquiring human mind. This reality awaits our discovery or response, and is not called into being, constructed, projected or invented by the human mind.

2. *Epistemologically*, it is held that this reality or realities can be known, however approximately, and that statements which are made concerning it cannot be regarded totally or simply as subjective assertions concerning personal attitudes or feelings. It is possible to gain at least some degree of epistemic access to a reality which exists 'objectively', while at the same time conceding that the manner in which this is apprehended or conceptualized may, to some extent, be conditioned by cultural, social and personal factors.

3. *Semantically*, it is held that this reality may be depicted, described or in some manner represented, however inadequately or

---

[106] The most widely cited non-realist publication to date from this period continues to be R. B. Braithwaite, 'An Empiricist's View of the Nature of Religious Belief', in Basil Mitchell (ed.), *The Philosophy of Religion*. Oxford: Oxford University Press, 1970, 72–91.

[107] Don Cupitt, *Only Human*. London: SCM Press, 1985, 9. For a vigorous critique of Cupitt at this point, see Rowan Williams, "Religious Realism": On Not Quite Agreeing with Don Cupitt', *Modern Theology* 1 (1984), 3–24; Anthony C. Thiselton, *Interpreting God and the Postmodern Self: On Meaning, Manipulation and Power*. Edinburgh: T&T Clark, 1995.

provisionally, so that it is possible to make statements concerning this reality which may be described at least as approximations to the truth. While fully conceding the limitations placed upon human language, it is held that this is neither inadequate nor inappropriate as a means of making meaningful statements concerning reality.

It is quite unrealistic to engage in any serious philosophical discussion concerning the merits of any form of realism without engaging with the explanatory and predictive successes of the natural sciences, and their apparent implications for an understanding of the nature of the world, and the ability of the human mind to grasp and represent it, however provisionally. Cupitt's failure to deal adequately with this question is puzzling, to say the least – perhaps best to be explained in terms of an implicit awareness of the severe difficulties raised for his position by the natural sciences.

One of the most important defences of theological realism in the twentieth century is due to Thomas F. Torrance (born 1913).[108] Torrance is widely credited with having formulated the most highly developed version of realism available to modern theology. In that the present work represents an attempt to develop and extend Torrance's vision of theological science, it is appropriate to explore some aspects of Torrance's understanding of the realism of a scientific theology at this early point. For Torrance, true knowledge must be understood to represent a genuine disclosure to the mind of that which is objectively real. Both Christian theology and the natural sciences understand genuine knowledge to have 'ontological foundations in objective reality'. Any responsible intellectual discipline – including both the natural sciences and Christian theology – is thus under an intrinsic obligation to give an account of that reality:[109]

> The concept of truth enshrines at once the real being of things and the revelation of things as they are in reality. The truth of being comes to bear in its own light and in its own authority, constraining us by the power of what it is to assent to it and acknowledge it for what it is in itself. St Anselm, who developed that further in a more realist way, held truth to be the reality of things as they actually are independent of us before God, and therefore as they ought to be known and signified by us.

---

[108] See Alister E. McGrath, *Thomas F. Torrance: An Intellectual Biography*. Edinburgh: T&T Clark, 1999.
[109] Thomas F. Torrance, *Reality and Scientific Theology*. Edinburgh: Scottish Academic Press, 1985, 141.

Torrance's affirmations on the theme of 'responding to reality' convey an almost moral imperative: it is necessary and proper to be attentive and responsive to things as they actually are, and to ensure that an accurate and objective account of things is rendered, in a manner appropriate to the reality being investigated.

Torrance argues that theology and the sciences share a common commitment to a realist epistemology, to which they respond in manners which are appropriate to the nature of that reality. The precise nature of this approach varies from one discipline to another, and is determined by the engagement itself.[110]

> [Theology and the sciences recognize] the impossibility of separating out the way in which knowledge arises from the actual knowledge that it attains. Thus in theology the canons of inquiry that are discerned in the process of knowing are not separable from the body of actual knowledge out of which they arise. In the nature of the case a true and adequate account of theological epistemology cannot be gained apart from substantial exposition of the content of the knowledge of God, and of the knowledge of man and the world as creatures of God . . . This means that all through theological inquiry we must operate with an *open* epistemology in which we allow the way of our knowing to be clarified and modified *pari passu* with advance in deeper and fuller knowledge of the object, and that we will be unable to set forth an account of that way of knowing in advance but only by looking back from what has been established as knowledge.

The position set out in this series of works may be regarded as an exposition of a scientific theology representing a sympathetic yet critical response to the imposing and stimulating contribution made to the dialogue between theology and the natural sciences by Torrance, widely regarded as the greatest British theologian of the twentieth century.

So where do we begin? There is little doubt that one of the most significant theological failures of the twentieth century has been the virtual absence of any extended engagement with the concept of nature. It is impossible to even begin to deal with the relation of Christian theology and the natural sciences, or deal with the theme of 'natural theology', without addressing the issue of what is meant by nature, and

---

[110] Thomas F. Torrance, *Theological Science*. Oxford: Oxford University Press, 1969, 10. For some early responses to this position, see Thomas A. Langford, 'T. F. Torrance's *Theological Science*: A Reaction', *Scottish Journal of Theology* 25 (1972), 155–70; Frank D. Schubert, 'Thomas F. Torrance: The Case for a Theological Science', *Encounter* 45 (1984), 123–37.

how this relates to the Christian notion of creation. The first volume in this project therefore represents a direct and sustained engagement with the concept of nature – to which we now turn.

PART TWO

Nature

Chapter 3

The Construction of Nature

I t is impossible to address the relation of Christian theology and the natural sciences without a thorough examination of the complex notion of nature itself.[1] While the issue of the formulation of a scientific theology is of no small importance, it will be clear that exploration of the concept of nature is of immense interest in other respects. The concepts of natural theology and natural law rest upon a proper understanding of what is implied by the deliberate use of the word 'natural'. Equally, an evaluation of the role of the concept of the 'supernatural' in the writings of significant twentieth-century writers, such as Karl Rahner and Henri de Lubac, requires a careful weighing of the implications of the related notion of the 'natural'. Perhaps more importantly, the idea of 'doing what comes naturally' has highly important cultural overtones,[2] which often rest upon an intuited notion of 'nature'.

Even a superficial analysis of the substantial body of literature to make reference to the concept of 'nature' can be shown to understand it in at least three different senses:[3]

---

[1] For the best general survey of the idea, see C. S. Lewis, *Studies in Words.* 2nd edn. Cambridge: Cambridge University Press, 1967, 24–74. There is no direct Hebrew word corresponding to the modern term 'nature', rendering it problematic to offer an account of the Old Testament understanding of this concept: see Joel P. Weinberg, 'Die Natur im Weltbild des Chronisten', *Vetus Testamentum* 31 (1981), 324–45. The preferred Old Testament paradigm is that of 'creation'.

[2] See Stanley Fish, *Doing What comes Naturally: Change, Rhetoric, and the Practice of Theory in Literary and Legal Studies.* Oxford: Clarendon Press, 1989.

[3] I here follow (though with some slight reservations) the useful analysis of Kate Soper, *What is Nature? Culture, Politics and the Non-Human.* Oxford: Blackwell, 1995, 155–6.

1. Used as a realist concept, 'nature' refers to the structures, processes and causal powers that are constantly operative within the physical world, and are studied by the natural sciences.

2. Used as a metaphysical concept, 'nature' denotes a category which allows humanity to posit its distinctive nature and identity in relation to the non-human.

3. Used as a 'surface' concept, the term refers to ordinarily observable features of the world. This is perhaps the most widely used sense of the term in modern ecological discourse, in which a contrast is often drawn between nature and an urban or industrial environment, often to highlight how nature has been violated, and thus to emphasize the need for conservation and preservation of the natural habitats that remain.

In view of the highly significant implications of the concept of nature for our project, the present chapter of the work offers a major engagement with this idea. The term 'nature' is generally used in theological literature without the critical analysis that the term clearly demands, or any awareness of the extent to which the concept has been shaped by social concerns and ideological agendas. Given the potency of the idea of nature, it is not surprising that there have been many calls for a 'theology of nature' within the Christian tradition. Curiously, these seem to have failed to deliver anything even remotely approaching what seems to be promised.[4] This should not be taken as an implied criticism of those exploring this field, but rather points to the considerable difficulties attending this enterprise in the first place. In what follows, we shall begin to consider what these problems might be.

The many faces of nature

In modern western thought, the term 'nature' has acquired tones of innocence and nostalgia, perhaps evoking the memory of a distant rural past, whose idealized simplicities contrast sharply with the harsh realities of life in the urban west. The simplicity and beauty of nature is contrasted with the artificiality and ugliness of human conventions and

---

[4] One cannot help but express disappointment at the failure of a recent collection of essays to live up to the promise of its title: Niels H. Gregersen, Michael W. S. Parsons and Christoph Wassermann (eds), *The Concept of Nature in Science and Theology*. Geneva: Labor et Fides, 1997. This overlooks the very serious issues raised, for example, by Neil Evernden, *The Social Creation of Nature*. Baltimore, MD: Johns Hopkins University Press, 1992.

creations. Indeed, it can be argued that the concept of nature adopted by a culture has a shadowy, darker side – the concepts of will and intelligence, to which nature is understood to be antithetical.

This contrast between nature and construction is not a new phenomenon; it can be seen clearly in the way in which English writers depicted an ideal country in the early modern period.[5] Jean-Jacques Rousseau's demand to return to nature can be argued to represent a deep underlying alienation from the political and religious life of Geneva in the eighteenth century, culminating in the longing to return to a rationalist paradise.[6] The discovery of Tahiti had a profound influence on this debate, with the islands of the South Pacific being depicted (for example, in the writings of Denis Diderot) as a naturalist paradise, perhaps reflecting a golden age in the history of humanity which could be recovered through social and ethical engineering.[7] More recently, a similar theme emerges in the federal Wilderness Act (1964), which sets out an important contrast between a region 'affected primarily by the forces of nature' and 'areas where man and his own works dominate the landscape':[8]

A wilderness, in contrast with those areas in which man and his own works dominate the landscape, is hereby recognized as an area where the earth and its community of life are untrammeled by man, where man himself is a visitor who does not remain. An area of wilderness is further defined to mean in this Act an area of undeveloped federal land retaining its primeval character and influence, without permanent improvements or human habitation, which is protected and managed so as to preserve its natural conditions, and which generally appears to have been affected primarily by the forces of nature, with the imprint of man's work substantially unnoticeable.

Nature is here defined in terms of an absence of human influence – a theme which is considered by both Plato and Aristotle in terms of τέχνη.

---

[5] Niels Bugge Hansen, *That Pleasant Place: The Representation of Ideal Landscape in English Literature from the 14th to the 17th Century.* Copenhagen: Akademisk Forlag, 1973.

[6] Jürgen von Stackelberg, *Jean-Jacques Rousseau. Der Weg zurück zur Natur.* Munich: Fink, 1999. See also the classic study of Daniel Mornet, *Le sentiment de la nature en France de J.-J. Rousseau à Bernardin de Saint-Pierre: essai sur les rapports de la littérature et des moeurs.* Paris: Hachette, 1907.

[7] Bernard Smith, *European Vision and the South Pacific, 1768–1850.* London: Oxford University Press, 1960.

[8] John C. Hendee, George H. Stankey and Robert C. Lucas, *Wilderness Management.* Miscellaneous Publication (United States Dept. of Agriculture) No. 1365. Washington, DC: Forest Service, US Department of Agriculture, 1978, 82.

The romanticization of nature began in earnest in the late eighteenth century, initially in the writings of German Romantics such as Goethe and Novalis.[9] Yet the trend is probably seen at its most pronounced in English Romanticism,[10] as in the famous lines from William Wordsworth's 'The Tables Turned' (1798):

> One impulse from a vernal wood
> May teach you more of man,
> Of moral evil and of good,
> Than all the sages can.

A similar theme can be found in a series of recent writings which foster sentimentalism about nature, which suggest that Arcadian nature – as opposed to the pillaged and mutilated version we now know – is the only responsible moral education for modern youth. Where science and capitalism mislead and destroy, nature leads its followers onwards to personal fulfilment and environmental integrity.[11]

This strongly idealized conception of nature played a major role in the shaping of American attitudes to the wilderness from which an emerging nation was being hewed. As Perry Millar points out in his classic study of the shaping of American concepts of and attitudes towards nature,[12] the concept of American as 'nature's nation' began to emerge in the nineteenth century, along with a belief that the natural order could educate and safeguard the moral standards of the new nation. As Walt Whitman saw things in January 1840:[13]

> America can progress indefinitely into an expanding future without acquiring sinful delusions of grandeur simply because it is nestled in Nature, is instructed and guided by mountains, is chastened by cataracts . . . So then – because America, beyond all nations, is in perpetual touch with Nature, it need not fear the debauchery of the artificial, the urban, the civilized.

---

[9] Alfred Schmidt, *Goethes herrlich leuchtende Natur: philosophische Studie zur deutschen Spätaufklärung*. Munich: Hanser, 1984; Dennis F. Mahoney, *Die Poetisierung der Natur bei Novalis: Beweggründe, Gestaltung, Folgen*. Bonn: Bouvier, 1980.

[10] See the interesting analysis and literature review provided by Mario John Lupak, *Byron as a Poet of Nature: The Search for Paradise*. Toronto, ON: Edwin Mellen Press, 1999.

[11] Gerald Weissmann, 'Ecosentimentalism: The Summer Dream beneath the Tamarind Tree', in Paul R. Gross, Norman Levitt and Martin W. Lewis (eds), *The Flight from Science and Reason*. New York: New York Academy of Sciences, 1996, 483–9.

[12] Perry Millar, 'The Romantic Dilemma in American Nationalism and the Concept of Nature', *Harvard Theological Review* 48 (1955), 239–54.

[13] Walt Whitman; as summarized in Millar, 'Romantic Dilemma', 247.

Such attitudes can easily be discerned to lie not far beneath the surface of American naturalism, both philosophical and literary.[14]

In older writings, however, nature is portrayed in more hostile terms, as an aggregate of untamed and hostile forces threatening to destroy and overwhelm humanity, shattering its precarious hold on existence. This can be seen in much Anglo-Saxon poetry.[15] Nature is here not depicted as a delightful garden in which stressed courtiers may find repose, as in the English pastoral tradition. The garden is an image of nature tamed and subdued; in older writings such as *Beowulf,* thought to date from the ninth century, we find nature portrayed as a menacing force, which heroes are obliged to battle and conquer.[16] Where Wordsworth saw nature as a moral educator, Tennyson suggested it lacked any ethic, save that of survival. The familiar lines from Canto 5 of *In Memoriam* make this point powerfully:

> Man . . .
> Who trusted God was love indeed
> And love Creation's final law –
> Though Nature, red in tooth and claw
> With ravine, shrieked against his creed.

The so-called 'naturalist' tradition in modern American fiction also reflects this ambivalence within nature itself, tending to depict a destructive, mechanistic Darwinian world within which it was assumed that most modern Americans struggled to prosper and survive.[17] The works of the leading naturalist Theodore Dreiser were often critiqued

---

[14] Donald Pizer, *The Theory and Practice of American Literary Naturalism: Selected Essays and Reviews*. Carbondale, IL: Southern Illinois University Press, 1993; Christophe Den Tandt, *The Urban Sublime in American Literary Naturalism*. Urbana, IL: University of Illinois Press, 1998.

[15] The classic study remains Emile Pons, *Le thème et le sentiment de la nature dans la poésie anglo-saxonne*. Strasbourg: Publications de la Faculté des lettres de l'Université de Strasbourg, 1925.

[16] Bernard F. Huppé, 'Nature in *Beowulf* and *Roland*', in Lawrence D. Roberts (ed.), *Approaches to Nature in the Middle Ages*. Binghamton, NY: Center for Medieval and Early Renaissance Studies, 1982, 3–41.

[17] V. L. Partington, *The Beginnings of Critical Realism in America*. New York: Harcourt Brace, 1930, 327. The terms 'realism' and 'naturalism' are used with quite different meanings in sociology, literary criticism and philosophy, and confusion can easily result: see Roy Bhaskar, *The Possibility of Naturalism: A Philosophical Critique of the Contemporary Human Sciences*. 3rd edn. London/New York: Routledge, 1998, 2–4; René Wellek, 'The Concept of Realism in Literary Scholarship', in *Concepts of Realism*. New Haven, CT: Yale University Press, 1963, 222–55; George Levine, 'Realism Reconsidered', in John Halperin (ed.), *The Theory of the Novel: New Essays*. New York: Oxford University Press, 1974, 233–56.

at the time as offering an animal theory of human motivation and conduct, implying that humanity was trapped within an uncontrollable nature as a victim, rather than a master.[18]

Against this, we must note the point made by C. S. Lewis, especially in relation to his analysis of the cultural associations of the concept of 'nature' – namely, that 'nature' is the term we use to describe what we have mastered, whether intellectually or physically.[19]

> We reduce things to mere Nature *in order that* we may conquer them. We are always conquering Nature, *because* 'Nature' is the name for what we have, to some extent, conquered. The price of conquest is to treat a thing as mere Nature. Every conquest over Nature increases her domain. The stars do not become Nature till we can weigh and measure them: the soul does not become Nature till we can psychoanalyse her. The wresting of powers *from* Nature is also the surrendering of things *to* Nature.

Lewis' point is contestable; nevertheless, it illuminates the immense difficulties in treating the notion of 'nature' as a self-evident category. For some, nature is what humanity has failed to control; for others, it is the name applied to what humanity has conquered.

The concept of 'nature' is thus profoundly ambivalent, reflecting the aspirations, longings and fears of those who appeal to it. These values, hopes and longings have been projected onto the essentially neutral canvas of 'nature'. In the absence of a strong ontology, which affirms that certain things are intrinsically true of nature, the concept has become what its champions choose it shall be. It is thus potentially meaningless to speak of nature – along with cognate notions such as 'natural' and 'naturalism' – unless there are reasons for supposing that it is more than a free construction of human minds which are at liberty to create what they please. That is to say, the articulation of an ontology of nature is the essential prerequisite for any appeal to 'nature' as a legitimate category of discourse, along with any normative claims which might be linked with natural order. Yet there is a point to be noted in this respect. If such an ontology may indeed be discerned, might the term 'nature' not be displaced or moderated by another, more appropriately related to the ontology in question?

---

[18] See the famous essay of Stuart P. Sherman, 'The Barbaric Naturalism of Mr Dreiser', in *On Contemporary Literature*. New York: Holt, 1917, 93–4.

[19] C. S. Lewis, *The Abolition of Man*. London: Collins, 1978, 43. More generally, see Michael D. Aeschliman, *The Restitution of Man: C. S. Lewis and the Case against Scientism*. Grand Rapids, MI: Eerdmans, 1998.

The present analysis will develop the argument that the concept of 'nature' is a socially mediated notion, not an objective entity in its own right. Unless the potentially meaningless or conceptually fluid notion of 'nature' is given an ontological foundation through the more rigorous Christian doctrine of creation, the continued appeal to 'nature' is without intellectual justification or merit. The Christian doctrine of creation is perhaps the only viable means by which the notion of 'nature' may be salvaged, and placed on a sustainable intellectual foundation. Without an ontological foundation, 'nature' is simply one person's construction and projection, and what is 'natural' a restatement of that person's own moral vision, which has been read into – and not out of – an ethically and philosophically amorphous world.

The importance of this point can be seen by a careful examination of the linkages between Aristotle's *Ethics* and *Metaphysics*, in which Aristotle's metaphysics of human nature determine his understanding of what is 'natural', and hence ethical.[20] Aristotle's understanding of nature leads him to make a number of important statements of an ethical or political nature, based on what may be said to be 'natural'. 'Nature' easily slips from a description of what is observed to a prescription of what ought to be the case. Thus we are informed that human beings are defined, by nature, as being 'political' animals[21] – although the Greek phrase ἄνθρωπος φύσει πολιτικὸν ζῷον should really be understood to imply that human beings, by nature, are urban animals, preferring to dwell in cities. Rather more controversially, in the same section of the *Politics* Aristotle tells us that slavery is an entirely natural institution. Yet such normative statements rest ultimately upon a specific and socially conditioned understanding of the categories of nature and the natural. The plausibility of Aristotle's effortless transition from a description of what is observed to be the case to prescriptions of what ought to be the case often rests upon social conventions and attitudes – such as attitudes to slavery and women – which more recent generations find intensely problematic.

Yet this is not to be taken as a critique of Aristotle, as if this classic philosopher conspicuously failed where others have triumphed. The all-important category of 'nature' is not merely vague and ill-defined; it lies beyond definition in terms of its intrinsic identity, and is thus left

---

[20] Ed Halper, 'The Substance of Aristotle's Ethics', in May Sim (ed.), *The Crossroads of Norm and Nature: Essays on Aristotle's Ethics and Metaphysics*. Lanham, MD: Rowman & Littlefield, 1995, 3–28.

[21] Aristotle, *Politics* I, 1253a 2–3.

open to be defined by those who have vested interests in doing so. This 'definition' rests primarily upon the free choice of the individual, rather than some intrinsic property of nature itself. This will doubtless strike some readers as a rather radical and overstated position. While I am naturally sorry for any distress that this view may occasion, I cannot see how the conclusion is to be avoided. Having worked carefully through the immense amount of material, primary and secondary, relating to this theme, it has become clear to me that the concept of 'nature' is a serious candidate for the most socially conditioned of all human concepts. A study of the development of the concept of nature indicates that there is no self-evidently correct definition of this term which can serve as the basis of any system of thought. The concept of nature is constructed by various groupings, largely to serve their own ends and lend intellectual legitimation to their enterprises.

In what follows, we shall explore this matter in more detail, before moving on, in the following chapter (Ch. 4), to offering a theological defence of nature-as-creation, which avoids the ultimate naturalist fallacy – namely, the belief that there is some objective concept of 'nature' in the first place, which may be discovered by unbiased observation and reflection.

The history of the concept of nature

It is often assumed that the idea of 'nature' is so self-evident that it requires no further discussion. Nature designates the external world of material things (an idea perhaps corresponding more to the Greek term κόσμος than to φύσις), and may therefore be contrasted with such notions as the 'supernatural' or 'metaphysical'. Thus the Hippocratic theorists argued that the causes of human diseases were natural – as opposed to being the result of divine or demonic influence – and were hence open to natural explanation and a natural cure. Alternatively, the realm of the 'natural' may be defined as 'that which has not been artificially created by human beings'. The contrast now proposed is between the world as we encounter it, and the world as transformed by the creative activity of humanity. Nature thus stands opposed to culture.

It will be obvious that the term 'nature' has moral overtones. To suggest that something is 'natural' is to imply that it acts in such a way that is in accordance with its nature. In their careful study of the critically important role played by the concept of φύσις in classical Greek moral reflection, Lovejoy and Boas note how, in effect, the entire discussion became ensnared in something of a linguistic trap, with important conceptual implications:[22]

> It was, in a sense, a historical accident that, when Greek thinkers had occasion to formulate the demand for objectively true principles, in contrast with mere conventions or subjective prejudices in the realm of moral judgements, the term which they found made ready for them by the cosmologists and the theorists about sense-perception was 'nature'. It is a historical accident in the sense that it is quite conceivable that the expression chiefly used for 'the objective' might have been some other word – some much more inert and colorless and less ambiguous word – than 'nature'. If it had happened so, the history of European thought in many fields would doubtless have had a very different course.

The distinction between what is natural and what is deviant could thus rest upon a prior understanding of precisely how this nature might be defined, on the assumption that there is an objective 'nature' which determines this matter, independent of existing social conventions or personal whims. As Geoffrey Lloyd points out in his overview of Greek attitudes to nature, there has always been a chorus of voices who[23]

> . . . invoked the natural to contrast it with the deviant, to justify their own particular attitudes, beliefs and behaviour, including, not least, their prejudices on gender differences and on sexual practices, where what passes for natural to insiders appears to outsiders as all too obviously culturally determined. What a writer such as Artemidorus tells us about what some Greeks thought *natural* sexual intercourse is enough to jolt one out of any unreflecting assumption that the Greeks were very much like us.

To speak of 'natural philosophy', 'natural theology', 'natural law' or 'natural science' is to invite discussion of what the immensely important term 'natural' might denote. It is also to raise precisely the question noted by Lloyd in the above analysis – namely, whether the concept of 'nature' can be defined essentially, or whether it is fundamentally a social construction. Some Greek writers contrasted φύσις with νόμος, seeing the former as something given, in itself stable and immutable, which humans were free to investigate; and the latter as either arbitrary

---

[22] Arthur O. Lovejoy and George Boas, *Primitivism and Related Ideas in Antiquity*. New York: Octagon Books, 1973, 110.

[23] Geoffrey E. R. Lloyd, 'Greek Antiquity: The Invention of Nature', in John Torrance (ed.), *The Concept of Nature*. Oxford: Oxford University Press, 1992, 1–24; 2.

or self-serving conventions established by humanity (Antiphon), or as laws which reflect some deeper reality, to which humans are obligated to respond (Plato).[24]

In that part of the task of this project is to clarify the contribution of Christian theology in defining the concept of nature, it is essential to gain an understanding of the evolution of the notion of nature from the classic period to the present day. We therefore begin our study by exploring the understanding of φύσις encountered in the Greek antiquity.

Classic Greek concepts of nature

Though all areas of scholarly investigation are intrinsically interesting, some have the added virtue of being useful even to the point of relevance. The philosophical and theological importance of the investigation of the classic Greek understanding of nature is brought out clearly by a series of articles published by the Oxford philosopher Michael B. Foster (1903–59), in which he argued that the Christian doctrine of creation, especially when contrasted with Greek philosophies of nature, played an essential role in the evolution of the natural sciences.[25] We shall be assessing Foster's analysis presently, with a view to correcting, developing and extending it to offer a Christian understanding of the concept of nature, and its implications for the nature of the theological enterprise itself, for the historical development of the natural sciences, and for the mutual interaction of theology and those sciences.

It is perhaps too obvious a truth that there is no single 'Greek concept of nature', but a number of such concepts, competing for acceptance within a constantly changing web of ideas. Part of the task of this present chapter is to explore these concepts of nature, and examine their implications for the task we have set ourselves. The term φύσις was used in a variety of ways in the pre-Socratic tradition. The term is found in Homer, where its sense is unclear: the word is used with reference to a plant, and could be argued to refer either to the concept of 'growth' or to the 'distinctive character' of the plant in question.[26] Some pre-Socratics wished to limit the use of φύσις to one of the four

[24] Lloyd, 'Greek Antiquity: The Invention of Nature', 12–14.
[25] Michael B. Foster, 'The Christian Doctrine of Creation and the Rise of Modern Science', *Mind* 43 (1934), 446–68; idem, 'Christian Theology and Modern Science of Nature (I)', *Mind* 44 (1935), 439–66; idem, 'Christian Theology and Modern Science of Nature (II)', *Mind* 45 (1936), 1–27.
[26] Homer, *Odyssey* X, 302; see Lloyd, 'Greek Antiquity: The Invention of Nature,' 3.

elements – fire, earth, water and air; others, including Empedocles, argued that the term could be applied to a composite entity, made up of any combination of these elements.[27] Although a limited degree of clarification of the concept can be discerned within the writings of Plato, it is in the Aristotelian corpus that we find the first major systematic engagement with the notion.

Plato

Plato's use of the term φύσις is far from easy to understand, and may possibly be inconsistent. For Plato, all that exists may be said to come about through one of three agencies: art (τέχνη), nature (φύσις) or chance (τύχη).[28] This can be seen to mark a significant move away from the earlier Greek philosophical tradition, which tended to see events within the world as being attributed solely to φύσις, understood as a blind and non-directive force, which operated by chance. For Plato, a failure to disentangle these three agencies would inevitably lead to the deplorable view that the beauty of nature and the regularity of the heavenly bodies were to be ascribed to nature and chance, failing to do justice to the creative and ordering activity of some divinity. Plato argued that his predecessors, by attributing the world and its events to chance, failed to give due place to the activity of God, as the true nature.[29]

Plato thus gave art (τέχνη) pre-eminence over nature (φύσις) and chance (τύχη), and argued that the material universe was to be seen as a product of the creative action of God. It was something that had been purposefully and intelligently created. To deny such a notion was to lead young people away from a proper belief in God.[30]

While there is a very serious danger of simplifying Plato's ideas at this point, and giving priority to the tenth book of the *Laws* over other sections of his dialogues, it seems that Plato generally thought of nature as something which was to be opposed to intelligence and art. Divine intelligence is anterior to the existence of the world, and is reflected in the precise mode of its fashioning and operating. The human intellect

---

[27] Hermann Diels, *Die Fragmente der Vorsokratiker.* 5th edn. Berlin: Weidman, 1934, 31 B, fragment 8. See further John Burnet, *Early Greek Philosophy.* 4th edn. London: A&C Black, 1945, 205–6, n. 4.

[28] Plato, *Laws* 10.888E. For the full context of this, see *Laws* 884A–913D.

[29] Plato, *Laws* 898D–E.

[30] *Laws* 884A–913D. I assume that this same concern can be discerned in the passage in Aristophanes' *Clouds*, which speaks of Zeus being dethroned, and δίνη reigning in his stead (*Clouds* 828). See Burnet, *Early Greek Philosophy*, 338–47.

is capable of discerning such ordering. For Plato, the primary concept which requires to be invoked in the explanation of the natural world is thus not φύσις, but the divine ψύχη, which produces the world and directs its development by τέχνη.[31]

Plato's emphasis upon human reason and the divine soul led him to take a generally negative attitude towards what we would nowadays call the natural order.

Aristotle

It is with Aristotle that we find the first sustained engagement with the concept of nature. Aristotle's influence over the development of the natural sciences, and Christian understandings of the possibility of interaction with these sciences, is such that it is imperative to engage with his ideas in considerable detail.[32] In that Aristotle appears to reject virtually every aspect of Plato's account of nature,[33] it is perhaps not necessary to dwell on the manner in which he interacts with Plato, although it may be helpful to note that Aristotle tends to offer φύσις as an explanation of what Plato explains on the basis of ψύχη.[34] Yet there is a more profound general point underlying Aristotle's analysis. In the face of Plato's charge that natural philosophy – at least as practised by the φυσιολόγοι – was little more than myth-making or story-telling – deserving only to be regarded as 'opinion', and failing the rigorous demands of ἐπιστήμη – Aristotle sought to restore the investigation of nature as a truly rational and honourable intellectual undertaking. It was perfectly legitimate, he argued, to seek a rational explanation of the ways things are in this world we inhabit, without having recourse to the Platonic device of appealing to the divine soul as the ultimate ground of intelligibility. There was something about the world which rendered it capable of being understood.

---

[31] See further *Republic* 7.522A and *Timaeus* 27D, especially in the light of the comments of J. A. Weisheipl, 'The Concept of Scientific Knowledge in Greek Philosophy', in *Mélanges à la mémoire de Charles de Konick.* Quebec: Les Presses de l'Université Laval, 1968, 487–507.

[32] For the best studies, see Augustin Mansion, *Introduction à la physique aristotélicienne.* 2nd edn. Paris: Vrin, 1946; Friedrich Solmsen, *Aristotle's System of the Physical World: A Comparison with his Predecessors.* Ithaca, NY: Cornell University Press, 1960; Helen S. Lang, *The Order of Nature in Aristotle's Physics: Place and the Elements.* Cambridge: Cambridge University Press, 1998.

[33] Lang, *The Order of Nature in Aristotle's Physics,* 45.

[34] André Pellicer, *Natura: étude sémantique et historique du mot latin.* Paris: Presses Universitaires de France, 1966, 17–39; Friedrich Solmsen, *Aristotle's System of the Physical World,* 93.

On the basis of his understanding of nature, Aristotle sets forth a general account of the method to be followed in a natural philosophy which has been as influential as it is obscure:[35]

> In the science of nature, our first task will be to try to determine what relates to its principles. The natural way of doing this is to begin from those things that are more knowable and clear to us, and to proceed towards those things that are clearer and more knowable to us by nature. For the same things are not knowable relatively to us and knowable without qualification. So we must follow this method, and move on from what is more obscure by nature, but clearer to us, towards what is more clear and more knowable by nature.

The twenty-two lines of this opening chapter in Aristotle's *Physics* have been the subject of intense discussion, especially during the later Renaissance. What, it was asked, did Aristotle mean by this distinction between what is 'clear to us' and what is 'clear by nature'?[36]

In that Aristotle saw himself as countering Plato's critique of natural philosophy, it was perhaps inevitable that Aristotle's exposition of the concept of nature should be based upon the same triad that we encountered in Plato: art (τέχνη), chance (τύχη), and nature (φύσις). These three may be explained as follows:

1. Art (τέχνη). Aristotle uses this term to refer to any action or product which results from a human mind acting upon reality. While the term can be used to refer to static objects which arise from human craft – such as statues or pictures – it is to be understood in the more general sense as designating any human intervention in the world. Thus one could legitimately say that a stone being thrown in the air moves upwards as a result of human τέχνη, even though the act of throwing a stone upwards would not count as 'art' in the modern sense of the term. For Aristotle, the term means simply that an event may be accounted for by human activity or agency. Matter has no innate or intrinsic propensity towards artistic form; an agent must therefore impose such form upon it.

---

[35] Aristotle, *Physics* I, 1, 184a15–20. For detailed comments on this difficult passage, see Johann Fritsche, *Methode und Beweisziel im ersten Buch der 'Physikvorlesung' des Aristoteles*. Frankfurt am Main: Hain, 1986.

[36] See Neil Gilbert, *Renaissance Concepts of Method*. New York: Columbia University Press, 1960.

2. Chance (τύχη). Aristotle recognizes that certain events in the world are unpredictable, unexpected and unintended. While this notion does not play a major positive role in his thinking he clearly regards it as important to recognize that not every action in the world can be adequately explained. Yet Aristotle is clear that there are relatively few events which can be assigned to chance;[37] the vast majority are to be assigned to natural causes – to which we now turn.

3. Nature (φύσις). By this, Aristotle means 'that which is given'. In one sense, Aristotle tends to use this category to refer to those aspects of the world which cannot be accounted for by human actions or chance. Once these two categories have been eliminated, what remains is to be explained on the basis of the innate nature of things, which is in itself a primary source of action. 'Nature is a source or cause of being moved or being at rest . . . in virtue of itself, and not accidentally.'[38]

Aristotle's most fundamental claim is that φύσις gives the world both its ordering and its intelligibility: 'nature is everywhere a cause of order.'[39] Aristotle does not offer any kind of proof or demonstration of this assertion. There are two important arguments in book nine of the *Metaphysics* which provide at least some support;[40] yet Aristotle apparently assumes that the force of his statement will be accepted as self-evidently true by his readers. There is always a reason for something happening naturally; as Aristotle stresses, nature – like God – does nothing without a purpose (ἀτελές) or uselessly (μάτην).[41]

To establish the nature of an entity is thus to make a series of potentially significant statements concerning both what that entity is, and what it ought to do – where 'ought' bears the meaning of 'do what is appropriate to its specific nature'. Once human nature has been defined, a series of ethical and political statements may thus be made. As we noted earlier: Aristotle asserts that human beings are by nature

---

[37] Aristotle, *Physics* I, 8, 198b35.

[38] Aristotle, *Physics* II, 1, 192b22–3. There is a serious translation difficulty here, in that the all-important Greek verb κινεῖσθαι can be interpreted to be present either in the middle or the passive forms in this passage, and others of critical importance. In that these forms are homographic, it is impossible to distinguish between them. For a good discussion of the problems this raises, see Lang, *The Order of Nature in Aristotle's Physics*, 40–6.

[39] Aristotle, *Physics* VIII, 1, 252a12, 17. See further Mansion, *Introduction à la physique aristotélicienne*, 92.

[40] Summarized in Lang, *The Order of Nature in Aristotle's Physics*, 291–2.

[41] Aristotle, *Politics* I, 1256b 20–1.

urban animals (ἄνθϱοπος φύσει πολιτικὸν ζῷον).[42] Aristotle defends this important statement by tracing the development of the city-state from the family and village, in order to show that this development was 'by nature'. Living in a city-state is essential to the pursuit of the good life, partly on account of the environment which it provides for the actualization of human capacities.

John Philoponus: a Christian response to Aristotle

One of the most important responses to Aristotle's concept of nature dates from the sixth century, and is found in the writings of John Philoponus of Alexandria (*c.* 490 – *c.* 570). Philoponus is remembered primarily for his contribution to the Monophysite debate, and for theological works such as *de opificio mundi*. In recent years, there has been renewed interest in Philoponus on account of his critique of Aristotle,[43] and his general approach to the relation of Christian theology and the natural sciences.[44] In his *de aeternitate mundi contra Aristotelem*, Philoponus offers a severe criticism of Aristotle's doctrine of the eternity of the world, and also of Aristotle's notion of 'ether'. Philoponus clearly saw his task as being the refinement of Aristotle's teaching in the light of Christian theology; at points, this demanded the rejection of Aristotelian ideas, and at others their modification. Our concern at this point, however, relates to Philoponus' criticisms of Aristotle's definition of φύσις.[45]

Philoponus is concerned to emphasize that the visible order of the world, and the matter from which that world is constituted, are not eternal, but were brought into being through the creative activity of God. For Philoponus, nature is to be understood as a 'life or power'. He criticizes Aristotle's definition of φύσις on the grounds that it is functional, not ontological. It merely tells us what nature does, not what nature actually is. The passage in which this point is made needs to be carefully considered. After setting out Aristotle's definition of nature as 'a source or cause of being moved or being at rest', he comments:[46]

---

[42] Aristotle, *Politics* I, 1253a 2–3.
[43] See the important material gathered together in Richard Sorabji (ed.), *Philoponus and the Rejection of Aristotelian Science*. London: Duckworth, 1987.
[44] On which see especially Thomas F. Torrance, 'John Philoponos of Alexandria, Sixth Century Christian Physicist', *Texts and Studies* vol. 2, London: Thyateira House, 1983, 261–5.
[45] We here follow E. M. Macierowski and R. F. Hassing, 'John Philoponus on Aristotle's Definition of Nature: A Translation from the Greek with Introduction and Notes', *Ancient Philosophy* 8 (1988), 73–100.
[46] Macierowski and Hassing, 'John Philoponus on Aristotle's Definition of Nature', 81–2.

This, therefore, is the definition of nature. Now it is worth stopping to consider that this definition does not express what nature is, but rather the activity of nature. For by learning that it is a principle of motion and rest, we did not learn what nature is, but rather what it does. Therefore, so that we may also present the definition of the substance itself (τῆς οὐσίας αὐτῆς), it is necessary to speak in this way: nature is a life or power (ἐστίν ἡ φύσις ζωὴ ἤτοι δύναμις) having descended through bodies, shaping them and governing them, being a principle of motion and rest in that in which it is primarily, *per se* and not *per accidens*.

Philoponus' position is distinguished from that of Stoicism by his insistence that nature is something which 'descends through' things, rather than something which is 'diffused within' them. It is also distinguished from Aristotle's position through its ontological identity as distinct from those bodies in which it operates. Philoponus clearly regards nature as having existence prior to and independently of that in which it works – hence the language of 'descending through' things.

The essence of Philoponus' modification of Aristotle's definition of 'nature' is this. While agreeing with Aristotle that there is some quality of things which governs the way in which they behave, Philoponus indicates that this quality cannot be simply regarded as intrinsic to the matter in question. The question of where this quality comes from cannot be overlooked. Nature is described in terms of a force – a life or power (ζωὴ ἤτοι δύναμις). This leads Philoponus to speak of nature in terms of an *eidopoetic* – that is, a 'trans-formal' or 'form-making' – activity, paralleling the action of an artisan in fashioning a work of art from raw material. Nature is thus like an artisan forming and shaping his materials.[47]

The result of this modification of Aristotle's definition of 'nature' is highly important. For Aristotle, 'nature' is something intrinsic to entities, which governs their motion and rest, and gives order to things. Philoponus does not have especial difficulties with Aristotle's account of what nature *does*; his concern is that Aristotle fails to address and offer an adequate account of what nature *is*. In place of Aristotle's rather functional account of φύσις, Philoponus offers an ontological foundation for the notion, which he clearly believes to be acceptable to Christian theology, precisely because it is grounded in a Christian doctrine of creation. 'The monistic and formative power pervading bodies will be the instrument of God, the divine artisan.'[48]

---

[47] Macierowski and Hassing, 'John Philoponus on Aristotle's Definition of Nature', 86–7.
[48] Macierowski and Hassing, 'John Philoponus on Aristotle's Definition of Nature', 87.

Having diverged from Aristotle on the ontology of nature, and laid the foundations for a Christian approach to the issue, Philoponus proceeds to develop his understanding of how the distinctive nature of a body can be studied. A distinction is drawn between the properties of a body which are 'in accordance with the *logos* of its own nature' and those which arise from outside its nature. Thus in the case of the concept of 'imperishability', Philoponus argues that two senses of the term may be distinguished:[49]

1. That which has imperishability in accordance with the *logos* of its own nature;

2. That which is receptive of destructive or dissolution, but which has gained imperishability in addition as a further addition.

This can be seen clearly in the following extract from *de aeternitate*:[50]

Just as in these cases, each of the things mentioned has two senses, (1) joined essentially to the subject from its nature, and (2) having come to it as a further acquisition, in this way it is necessary for 'imperishable' to have a double sense, either (1) belonging to something in accordance with its essence, or (2) having come to something as a further acquisition and not from the *logos* of its proper nature.

We can see here a clear anticipation of the scholastic discussion of the relation of nature and grace, beginning to explore the notion of certain qualities which are added to nature by God's grace, rather than on account of the intrinsic quality of the created material itself. However interesting that point might be, our concern here relates to Philoponus' understanding of the importance of the category of nature in relation to scientific investigation. Especially in his *de aeternitate*, Philoponus uses a variety of phrases to indicate his basic conviction that each subject must be studied according to its own nature – and that this nature is itself ontologically grounded, having its origins in God. As his discussion of 'imperishability' makes clear, Philoponus is prepared to draw a distinction between intrinsic and acquired qualities. However, the essential point is that 'nature' is something that is established or bestowed by God through creation. It is therefore possible to explore

---

[49] See the careful analysis of Lindsay Judson, 'God or Nature? Philoponus on Generability and Perishability', in Richard Sorabji (ed.), *Philoponus and the Rejection of Aristotelian Science*. London: Duckworth, 1987, 179–96.

[50] Translation from Judson, 'God or Nature?', 186.

the God-given ordering of the world through studying each subject 'in accordance with the *logos* of its own nature'. It will be clear that Philoponus' use of the theologically loaded term *logos* is of considerable moment. The *logos* which determines the 'nature' of an entity is clearly understood to be grounded in the divine *logos*, which was incarnate in Christ. This insight, which can be discerned in earlier Alexandrian writers from Clement of Alexandria through Athanasius, indicates the correlatedness of the concept of 'nature', a Christian doctrine of creation, and a robust doctrine of the incarnation – a point which has not been lost on more recent theologians, concerned to explore such issues.[51]

Limits upon space do not permit us to explore the remarkably complex development of both the Platonic and Aristotelian concepts of nature in the Middle Ages, nor the fascinating dynamics of the interaction of both with Christian theology.[52] It is perhaps enough to note that the respect in which both writers were held was sufficient to ensure that their ways of thinking persisted throughout the Middle Ages and Renaissance, until the force of observational evidence began to indicate that revision was necessary. The traditional view – according to which the Aristotelian tradition was overthrown by these observations – has now been displaced, through a closer reading of the textual evidence of the period, especially the Aristotelian commentaries, which has led to the growing acceptance of the view that Renaissance Aristotelianism was actually a positive force in the development of the modern scientific world-view.[53]

In view of the continuity of the Aristotelian tradition throughout the Middle Ages, we propose to move directly to the seventeenth century, which witnessed a new understanding of nature through the rise of the scientific revolution.

---

[51] See, for example, Thomas F. Torrance, *The Ground and Grammar of Theology*. Charlottesville, VA: University of Virginia Press, 1980, especially 95–100.

[52] See, for example, Alexander Murray, 'Nature and Man in the Middle Ages', in John Torrance (ed.), *The Concept of Nature*. Oxford: Oxford University Press, 1992, 25–62; James A. Weisheipl, 'Aristotle's Concept of Nature: Avicenna and Aquinas', in Lawrence D. Roberts (ed.), *Approaches to Nature in the Middle Ages*. Binghamton, NY: Center for Medieval and Early Renaissance Studies, 1982, 137–60.

[53] Charles B. Schmitt, 'Towards a Reassessment of Renaissance Aristotelianism', *History of Science* 11 (1973), 159–93; Heikki Mikkeli, 'The Foundation of an Autonomous Natural Philosophy: Zabarella on the Classification of Arts and Sciences', in Daniel A. Di Liscia, Eckhard Kessler and Charlotte Methuen (eds), *Method and Order in Renaissance Philosophy of Nature: The Aristotle Commentary Tradition*. Aldershot: Ashgate, 1997, 211–28.

The autonomy of nature: the seventeenth century

In his important study of the scientific revolution of the seventeenth century, Richard S. Westfall demonstrated that the concept of nature which now came to predominate had four distinct features:[54]

1. *Quantification.* One of the most important achievements of the period was the demonstration that the patterns of natural behaviour – such as the motions of the planets, or the falling of objects – could be described mathematically. Alexandre Koyré's phrase 'the geometrization of nature' serves as an admirable summary of this achievement, even if the geometry in question was resolutely Euclidean, and hence soon to be displaced. Both Kepler and Galileo argued for the ability of geometry to render the character of the universe, that latter in particular affirming that the 'book of the universe' was 'written in the language of mathematics, and its characters are triangles, circles and other geometric figures'.

2. *Mechanization.* Descartes and other writers of the period abandoned any notion of nature as an organic entity, and compared it to a mechanism – such as that of a clock (an image popularized by Robert Boyle). Nature was a world of passive matter, made up of individual particles or atoms, whose behaviour was governed by mechanical laws.[55] Even human beings could be thought of as machines. Giovanni Alfonso Borelli offered an account of the human skeletal and muscular system which treated it as a system of levers and applied forces. Archibald Pitcairne argued that the human circulatory system was simply a type of hydraulic machine. Christiaan Huygens argued that the universe was constructed of one common matter, which expressed itself in different sizes, shapes and motions.

3. *Nature as 'other'.* Part of Descartes' intellectual programme was the development of a conception of nature as 'the other', through a fundamental challenge to any suggestion of a genuine affinity between the natural order and its human observer. As the century developed, the 'otherness' of nature was reinforced primarily

---

[54] Richard S. Westfall, 'The Scientific Revolution of the Seventeenth Century: A New World View', in John Torrance (ed.), *The Concept of Nature*. Oxford: Oxford University Press, 1992, 63–93.

[55] James R. Jacob, 'Boyle's Atomism and the Restoration Assault on Pagan Naturalism', *Social Studies of Science* 8 (1978), 211–33.

through a growing awareness of the size of the universe. In 1698, Francis Roberts suggested that the light from the nearest star would take at least as long to reach the earth as a ship would take to reach the West Indies – namely, six weeks. As the speed of light was then reckoned to be about 48,000 leagues per second, it is clear that the age possessed at least some apprehension of the vastness of the universe.

4. *Secularization.* At this point, Westfall finds himself in some superficial difficulty, due to the remarkably large number of works dating from the later seventeenth century stressing the consonance of the new natural philosophy and the Christian faith. Westfall's point, however, is that there was a growing trend to accept the authority of experimental observations, and reflection upon them, in dealing with questions of science, rather than in turning to religious sources of authority.

Given the misleading associations of the term 'secularization', Westfall's final point is probably better expressed in terms of a growing emphasis on the autonomy of nature. Nature was to be examined and explained on its own terms. Those explanations might well resonate with the traditional teachings of Christian theology – and the seventeenth-century English scientific establishment was certainly persuaded that this was the case. But nature was now considered to be an autonomous entity, to be studied on its own terms, and observations to be explained by analogy with similar phenomena within nature.

The locus of authority within the natural sciences was thus located within the *saeculum* – the world of nature – rather than the world of revelation or faith. Considerable emphasis was thus placed upon the role of secondary causes within the natural order, with a growing marginalization of any discussion of God as the first cause.[56] Without necessarily drawing any specific conclusions concerning the origins of the world, the later seventeenth century was increasingly convinced of its explanatory autonomy. The world could explain its properties with reference to itself, rather than require the invocation of God. The Newtonian world-view thus encouraged the view that, although God may well have created the world, there was no further need for divine involvement in its government or explanation. The discovery of

---

[56] For the background, see Robert. H. Kargon, *Atomism in England from Hariot to Newton.* London: Oxford University Press, 1966, 96–7; 104–5.

the laws of conservation in physics – and similar ideas in biology[57] – seemed to imply that God had endowed the creation with all the mechanisms which it required in order to continue. While the concept of God was held to be significant in relation to accounting for the creation of the world, it seemed to have no necessary place in the conservation or subsequent explanation of the natural order. It was thus but a small step – if, indeed, a further step was required – to the famous statement of LaPlace, made in relation to the idea of God as a sustainer of planetary motion: *nous n'avons pas besoin de cette hypothèse-là.*[58]

In concluding his survey of the developments of the seventeenth century, Westfall comments:[59]

> A world conceived as the arena in which Christians pursue the ultimate goal of eternal salvation had been quantified, mechanized, perceived to be other, secularized, that is, altered beyond recognition, all in the short space of a hundred years.

The principal casualty of this development was an older view of nature as a living organism, often articulated in terms of the personification of *natura* as a female figure, possessed of at least some degree of divinity.

Not all were happy with the developments of the seventeenth century, especially its reductionist agenda as portraying nature in mechanistic terms. An alternative lay to hand; the depiction of nature as a living organism was a traditional metaphor, which the 'mechanical philosophy' had discarded. However, this was generally seen as unrealistic. The intellectual climate had shifted irreversibly. This did not, however, prevent a reconceptualization of nature in vitalist terms – that is, asserting the fundamental organic unity of nature.

This development took place in two quite distinct manners. The Cambridge Platonists – such as Henry More and Ralph Cudworth – accepted the dualistic structure of mind and matter postulated by Descartes;[60] the fissure between these two realms was understood to be

---

[57] Samuel A. Barnett, *Biology and Freedom: An Essay on the Implications of Human Ethology.* Cambridge: Cambridge University Press, 1988.

[58] Roger Hahn, 'LaPlace and the Vanishing Role of God in the Physical Universe', in Harry Woolf (ed.), *The Analytic Spirit.* Ithaca, NY: Cornell University Press, 1981, 85–95.

[59] Westfall, 'The Scientific Revolution of the Seventeenth Century', 86–7.

[60] On this movement, see Ernst Cassirer, *Die Platonische Renaissance in England und die Schule von Cambridge.* Leipzig, Berlin: B. G. Teubner, 1932; G. A. J. Rogers, Jean-Michel Vienne and Yves Charles Zarka, *The Cambridge Platonists in Philosophical Context: Politics, Metaphysics, and Religion.* Dordrecht; Boston: Kluwer Academic Publishers, 1997.

bridged by the 'spirit of nature' and the concept of 'plastic nature'. [61]
More's 'spirit of nature' was a spiritual principle that pervaded the
universe, directing the movement and direction of matter, and shaping
it through its plasticizing powers. In his *True Intellectual System of the
Universe* (1678), Cudworth sets his idea of 'cosmoplastic stoicism', which
likened nature to 'a great plant or vegetable'. [62] Nature was thus a living
entity – but an entity which could be controlled and mastered.

Vitalism was framed in terms of a critique of Cartesian dualism,
which postulated a dead nature being investigated by living agents.
The specific form of monistic vitalism found in the *Principles* (1692) of
Anne Conway (1631–79) is specifically presented as a refutation of the
Cartesian elimination of life from nature:[63]

> [The Cartesian philosophy] says that every body is a dead mass, not only
> void of all kind of life and sense, but utterly incapable thereof to all
> eternity. This grand error is also to be imputed to all those who affirm
> body and spirit to be contrary things, and inconvertible one into another,
> so as to deny a body all life and sense.

Vitalism regarded nature as possessing gradations of soul or spirit, so
that the entire natural order was to be regarded as a living entity. Nature
could not be accounted for simply as the sum of its material parts; it
was endowed – whether from without or within – with some additional
'vital force', which could not be observed or verified.[64]

In view of the importance of the ideas of nature as 'female' and a
'mechanism', we shall turn to explore some of the images of nature
found in western culture, and note their relevance to our theme.

Images of nature

The way in which a culture chooses to visualize abstract entities often
allows us insights into the culture as much as the abstraction itself. A
cluster of images of nature can be discerned within western culture,

---

[61] Robert Greene, 'Henry More and Robert Boyle on the Spirit of Nature', *Journal of the
History of Ideas* 23 (1962), 451–74.

[62] Ralph Cudworth, *The True Intellectual System of the Universe*. 2 vols. New York: Gould
& Newman, 1938, vol. 1, 225. See further Lydia Gysi, *Platonism and Cartesianism in the
Philosophy of Ralph Cudworth*. Berne: Peter Lang, 1962.

[63] Anne Conway, *The Principles of the Most Ancient and Modern Philosophy concerning
God, Christ and the Creatures*. The Hague: Martinus Nijhoff, 1982, 147.

[64] For the issues this raised, see J. A. van Ruler, *The Crisis of Causality: Voetius and
Descartes on God, Nature, and Change*. Leiden: E. J. Brill, 1995.

each reflecting a complex amalgam of religious beliefs, popular sentiment, and the vestiges of a classical culture. For example, the late Renaissance found the image of the *theatrum mundi* or *theatrum naturae* a compelling metaphor for the natural order.[65] Perhaps its most celebrated instance is found in Shakespeare's *As You Like It*, in which the image dominates the soliloquy of Jaques at the end of Act 2:

> All the world's a stage,
> And all the men and women merely players:
> They have their exits and their entrances;
> And one man in his time plays many parts,
> His acts being seven ages.

The image, however, was widely used in religious contexts, to convey the idea that the world is a theatre in which God displays power and wisdom for the edification of its human audience. John Calvin argued that God 'created the world for this end, so that it might be a theatre of his glory'.[66] For Jean Bodin, 'the Theatre of Nature is nothing other than a sort of table of the things created by the immortal God, placed before the eyes of everyone, so that we may contemplate and love the majesty, power, goodness, wisdom of the author himself'.[67]

A second metaphor which found wide application in the sixteenth and seventeenth centuries was that of the book. The origins of this metaphor lie in the desire to set nature alongside Scripture as two distinct, yet related, sources of knowledge of God. The metaphor is deployed in the writings of Pierre Viret (1511–71), who gained a reputation as a popularizer of the theology of Calvin. For Viret, reading the book of nature posed some difficulties; nevertheless, it was there, and was meant to be read:[68]

> In Scripture, the Spirit of God often portrays this whole visible world as a great book of nature and of true natural theology, as preachers and universal witnesses to God their creator, and his works and glory. There are, however, few whose eyes are able to read this book, and few whose ears are adapted to hearing the voices and sermons of these natural

---

[65] Lynda G. Christian, *Theatrum Mundi: The History of an Idea.* New York: Garland Publishing, 1987.

[66] John Calvin, *Institutes* I.v.1–2; I.vi.2–4. On the imagery, see Susan Elizabeth Schreiner, *The Theater of His Glory: Nature and the Natural Order in the Thought of John Calvin.* Durham, NC: Labyrinth Press, 1991.

[67] Jean Bodin, *Universae naturae theatrum.* Frankfurt: Wechel, 1597, sig. 3v. For a full discussion of this image, see Ann Blair, *The Theater of Nature: Jean Bodin and Renaissance Science.* Princeton, NJ: Princeton University Press, 1997, 153–79.

[68] Pierre Viret, *Instruction chrestienne.* 2 vols. Geneva: Jean Rivery, 1564, fol. 106 r.

preachers – even among those who have pursued research into nature, and have advanced the farthest in the knowledge of the things of nature, the liberal arts, and human philosophy.

This basic framework is of considerable importance in relation to the development of the 'two books' tradition within Christian theology, especially in England, which regarded nature and Scripture as two complementary sources of our knowledge of God. Thus Francis Bacon commended the study of 'the book of God's word' and the 'book of God's works' in his *Advancement of Learning* (1605). This latter work had considerable impact on English thinking on the relation of science and religion.

In his 1674 tract *The Excellency of Theology compared with Natural Theology*, Robert Boyle noted that 'as the two great books, of nature and of scripture, have the same author, so the study of the latter does not at all hinder an inquisitive man's delight in the study of the former'.[69] At times Boyle referred to the world as 'God's epistle written to mankind'. This metaphor of the 'two books' with the one divine author was of considerable importance in holding together Christian theology and piety and the emerging interest and knowledge of the natural world in the seventeenth and early eighteenth centuries.[70] There can be no doubt that it offered a major theological motivation and incentive to the committed investigation of the natural theology by Christians, persuaded that the study of the works of God led to a glimpse of the mind of God. The image is also of importance in relation to the postmodern deconstruction of nature: if nature is a book, must not this text, in common with all others, be open to multiple readings on the part of its autonomous readers? We shall return to this point presently.

A third metaphor to find wide application was that of the mirror.[71] The phrase 'the mirror of nature' was widely used to refer to attempts to understand nature (natural philosophy), to depict nature (especially in landscape painting) or to refer to the impact which nature had upon people's perceptions of themselves.[72]

---

[69] Robert Boyle, *Works* ed. R. Birch. 6 vols. London: Rivingtons, 1882, vol. 4, 1–66.

[70] See, for example, Frank E. Manuel, *The Religion of Isaac Newton*. Oxford: Clarendon Press, 1974, 31; Arthur R. Peacocke, *Creation and the World of Science*. Oxford: Oxford University Press, 1979, 1–7.

[71] Herbert Grabes, *The Mutable Glass: Mirror-Imagery in Titles and Texts of the Middle Ages and English Renaissance*. Cambridge: Cambridge University Press, 1982.

[72] John I. H. Baur, *A Mirror of Creation: 150 Years of American Nature Painting*. New York: Friends of American Art in Religion, 1980; John Walsh and Cynthia P. Schneider, *A Mirror of Nature: Dutch Paintings from the Collection of Mr and Mrs Edward William Carter.*

In what follows, we shall consider two further metaphors in more detail, with the aim of showing how changing social conditions and technological innovation offered new metaphors for the visualization of the natural world.

The female

In the Middle Ages, nature was regularly portrayed as female – a process no doubt assisted by the grammatical femininity of the noun *natura*.[73] The twelfth-century poet Bernard Silvestris portrays *natura* as a female potentiality which requires ordering and direction by a male *nous*. Primal matter is formless, until it is ordered in a definite form. Geoffrey Chaucer, followed by many Renaissance writers – including Shakespeare – thought of nature in characteristically female terms.[74] The earth was to be conceived as a nurturing mother, who sustained and supported humanity throughout their time of sojourn in the world. The world itself could be thought of as a womb, within which metallic ores came into existence, awaiting the discovery of human miners. The familiar image of 'mother nature' has its origins in this context, although the English writers of the Renaissance preferred the phrase 'Dame Nature'.[75] Many later Renaissance writers developed the image of the earth, if not as a mother, then as a nurse, picking up some themes found in Hermes Trimegistus. The following citation from the noted Cambridge Platonist Henry More (1614–87) shows this image being deployed in a number of manners; More here picks up on some themes developed in Girolamo Cardan's *de varietate rerum* (1557), which developed the thesis of the interrelatedness of all forms of things, organic and inorganic, in and on the earth.[76]

> Though we should admit, with Cardan and other naturalists, that the earth at first brought forth all manner of animals as well as plants, and

New York: Los Angeles County Museum of Art, 1992; Virgil K. Whitaker, *The Mirror up to Nature: The Technique of Shakespeare's Tragedies*. San Marino, CA: Huntington Library, 1965; Rose A. Zimbardo, *A Mirror to Nature: Transformations in Drama and Aesthetics, 1660–1732*. Lexington: University Press of Kentucky, 1986.

[73] Winthrop Wetherbee, 'Some Implications of Nature's Femininity in Medieval Poetry', in Lawrence D. Roberts (ed.), *Approaches to Nature in the Middle Ages*. Binghamton, NY: Center for Medieval and Early Renaissance Studies, 1982, 47–62.

[74] Carolyn Merchant, *The Death of Nature: Women, Ecology, and the Scientific Revolution*. New York: Harper & Row, 1980, 1–41.

[75] See the famous French work by Sylvain Maréchal, *Dame Nature à la Barre de l'Assemblée Nationale*. Paris: Chez les Marchands de Nouveautés, 1791.

[76] Henry More, *A Collection of Several Philosophical Writings of Dr Henry More*. 2nd edn. London: James Flesher, 1697, 65.

that they might be fastened by the navel to their common mother the earth, as they are now to the female in the womb; yet we see she is grown sterile and barren, and her births of animals are now very inconsiderable. Wherefore what can it be but a providence, that while she did bear, she sent out male and female, that when her own prolific virtue was wasted, yet she might be a dry nurse, or an officious grandmother, to thousands of generations?

The Enlightenment writer Denis Diderot found the image of nature as a female attractive in another way. In his essay *De l'interpretation de la nature* (1753–4), he suggested that the scientific enterprise could be compared to undressing a woman, in which items of clothing are removed, one at a time, 'giving a hope to those who follow her assiduously that they will one day know her entire person'.

Not surprisingly – especially in the light of Diderot's comment – the use of feminine imagery in relation to nature has been heavily criticized by many modern feminist writers as improperly perpetuating the social structures of earlier generations. Sandra Harding, for example, argues that sexist sexual metaphors played a decisive role in the rise of modern science, and draws the conclusion that the writings of such early modern scientists as Francis Bacon are laden with 'rape and torture metaphors'. Nature, she argues, is too often portrayed as a passive, compliant and exploitable woman, and the scientist as an exploitative male.[77] 'Francis Bacon appealed to rape metaphors to persuade his audience that experimental method is a good thing.'[78] The demand for revision of the traditional natural imagery must serve to remind us that nature is neither male nor female – nor, indeed, anything in particular. It is simply something that has been described, defined and debated using terms and images which various ages and writers have found congenial for their audiences, agendas and purposes.

The extent to which the use of the female as an image of nature is shaped by social conventions of earlier eras has been brought out clearly by Sherry Ortner.[79] Ortner stresses that the process of socialization

[77] See in particular Sandra Harding, *The Science Question in Feminism*. Ithaca, NY: Cornell University Press, 1986; idem, *Whose Science? Whose Knowledge? Thinking from Womens' Lives*. Cornell: Cornell University Press, 1991.

[78] Harding, *Whose Science? Whose Knowledge?*, 43. For a response to this inaccurate statement, see Alan Soble, 'In Defense of Bacon', in Noretta Koertge (ed.), *A House Built on Sand: Exposing Postmodernist Myths about Science*. New York: Oxford University Press, 1998, 195–215.

[79] Sherry B. Ortner, 'Is Female to Male as Nature is to Culture?', in Michelle Zimbalist Rosaldo and Louise Lamphere (eds), *Woman, Culture and Society*. Stanford, CA: Stanford University Press, 1974, 67–87.

shapes gender roles, and hence is of critical importance in determining what is 'male' and 'female'. Biological factors – such as reproduction and lactation – are unquestionably of importance in shaping part of the female role; nevertheless, other aspects are determined by social forces. Any comparison of nature to a female – or culture to a male – thus reflects an amalgam of biological and social factors, which is inherently unstable over time and across cultural boundaries. In short: the image is mediated through social constructs.

The mechanism

The image of nature as a female was closely linked with the notion of it being a living organism, which could be harmed in certain ways – for example, by mining. The reaction against the idea of nature as an organism is generally thought to have begun in earnest in France during the early seventeenth century, as a new fascination with machinery began to have important consequences for the visualization of the world. René Descartes (1596–1650), Pierre Gassendi (1592–1655) and Marin Mersenne (1588–1648) advocated the metaphor of the machine as a means of conceptualizing the abstract notion of nature.[80] Nature was increasingly viewed in impersonal and mechanical terms. Instead of being unpredictable, nature was now viewed as an inert, reliable and ordered mechanism, which could be controlled and regulated. Pascal's invention of the adding machine (1642) led many writers to suggest that the human brain was simply a more complex version of such a device.

This understanding of nature was given a substantial impetus through the development of Newtonian mechanics, and especially through its remarkable explanatory successes.[81] Newton's arguments in favour of universal gravitation encouraged the view that the universe was a single uniform mechanism, governed at all times and in all places by the same fundamental laws of motion.[82] This approach to nature was

[80] See Robert Lenoble, *Mersenne ou la naissance du mécanisme*. Paris: Librarie J. Vrin, 1943; Margaret Osler, 'Descartes and Charleton on Nature and God', *Journal of the History of Ideas* 40 (1979), 445–56; E. J. Dijksterhuis, *The Mechanization of the World Picture: Pythagoras to Newton*. Princeton, NJ: Princeton University Press, 1986.

[81] Marie Boas, 'The Establishment of the Mechanical Philosophy', *Osiris* 10 (1962), 442–520. See also Keith Thomas, *Man and the Natural World: Changing Attitudes in England, 1500–1800*. Harmondsworth: Allen Lane, 1983.

[82] I. B. Cohen, *The Newtonian Revolution*. Cambridge: Cambridge University Press, 1980; James W. Garrison, 'Newton and the Relation of Mathematics to Natural Philosophy', *Journal of the History of Ideas* 48 (1987), 609–27; A. Rupert Hall, *Isaac Newton: Adventurer in Thought*. Cambridge: Cambridge University Press, 1996.

profoundly hostile to the empathetic and more holistic conception of nature found in the Middle Ages, and reflected in the literature of the Renaissance. As E. A. Burtt points out, the new understanding of nature as a mechanism swept away earlier attempts to conceive nature as endowed with human qualities – such as 'wisdom' or 'harmony':[83]

> The gloriously romantic universe of Dante and Milton, that set no bounds to the imagination of man as it played over space and time, had now been swept away. Space was identified with geometry, time with the continuity of number. The world that people had thought themselves living in – a world rich with colour and sound, redolent with fragrance, filled with gladness, love and beauty, speaking everywhere of purposive harmony and creative ideals – was crowded now into minute corners in the brains of scattered organic beings. The really important world outside was a world hard, cold, colourless, silent, and dead; a world of quantity, a world of mathematically computable motions in mechanical regularity. The world of qualities as immediately perceived by man became just a curious and quite minor effect of that infinite machine beyond.

A further point may be noted here. Newton's account of celestial mechanics seemed to many to suggest that the world was best understood as a self-sustaining mechanism which had no need for divine governance or sustenance for its day-to-day operation. The mechanism might have been constructed and set in motion by God; God's presence was, however, no longer required. This point was recognized at an early stage by one of Newton's interpreters, Samuel Clark. In his correspondence with Leibniz, Clark expressed concern over the potential implications of the growing emphasis on the regularity of nature:[84]

> The notion of the world's being a great machine, going on without the interposition of God, as a clock continues to go on without the assistance of a clockmaker; is the notion of materialism and fate, and tends (under the pretence of making God a supramundane intelligence) to exclude providence, and God's government in reality of the world.

The image of God as a 'clockmaker'[85] (and the associated natural theology which appealed to the regularity of the world) was thus seen

---

[83] Edwin A. Burtt, *The Metaphysical Foundations of Modern Physical Science*. Garden City, NY: Doubleday Anchor, 1954, 238–9. See also the important reflections of C. S. Lewis, *The Discarded Image*. Cambridge: Cambridge University Press, 1967, 93–4.

[84] H. G. Alexander, *The Leibniz–Clark Correspondence*. Manchester: Manchester University Press, 1956, 14.

[85] On which see Otto Mayr, *Authority, Liberty and Automatic Machinery in Early Modern Europe*. Baltimore: Johns Hopkins University Press, 1986.

as potentially leading to a purely naturalist understanding of the universe, in which God had no continuing role to play. Clarke's concerns may, with the benefit of hindsight, be seen to be well founded. Although Newton's natural philosophy was initially viewed as entirely to the benefit of Christian theology, the passage of time led to a growing alienation between theology and natural philosophy as God was gradually eliminated from the machine of nature.[86] The increasing interest in machinery which resulted from the Industrial Revolution led to the final triumph of the metaphor of nature as a machine, forcing writers such as William Paley to develop mechanical apologetics in order to reassert the credibility of the Christian faith in this context.[87]

The point we wish to highlight is the following: the metaphor of nature as a machine arose in the 1630s, and gradually emerged as triumphant over the next two hundred years. Its origins and plausibility lie in the world created by humanity – in the realm of human construction. Carolyn Merchant has identified both the implications and consequences of this important development:[88]

> The rise of mechanism laid the foundation for a new synthesis of the cosmos, society and the human being, construed as ordered systems of mechanical parts subject to governance by law and to predictability through deductive reasoning. A new concept of the self as a rational master of the passions housed in a machinelike body began to replace the concept of the self as an integral part of a close-knit harmony of organic parts related to the cosmos and society. Mechanism rendered nature effectively dead, inert and manipulable from without. As a system of thought, it rapidly gained in plausibility during the second half of the seventeenth century.

The purpose of this brief exploration of the iconography of nature has been to show how the metaphors used are socially constructed and mediated. The image of the female reflects an idealization of female and male roles, shaped by the popular culture of the Middle Ages. The later image of the machine reflects a series of social concerns of the period, including the desire to *control* nature, along with a growing

---

[86] James E. Force, 'The Breakdown of the Newtonian Synthesis of Science and Religion: Hume, Newton and the Royal Society', in R. H. Popkin and J. E. Force (eds), *Essays on the Context, Nature and Influence of Isaac Newton's Theology*. Dordrecht: Kluwer Academic Publishers, 1990, 143–63; John Gascoigne, 'From Bentley to the Victorians: The Rise and Fall of British Newtonian Natural Theology', *Science in Context* 2 (1988), 219–56.

[87] Neal C. Gillespie, 'Divine Design and the Industrial Revolution: William Paley's Abortive Reform of Natural Theology', *Isis* 81 (1990), 214–29.

[88] Carolyn Merchant, *The Death of Nature*, 214.

interest in the new mechanisms devised by human ingenuity for navigation, timekeeping and astronomical observations. A complex set of social mediations lies between the observer and 'nature'. Nature is not, and cannot be, a 'thing-in-itself'; it always appears reflected through the prism of a particular social order, and subject to a set of social mediations.

Such perceptions are not entirely novel. In the seventeenth century, Robert Boyle protested against the reification of nature.[89] 'Nature' is a fictitious entity, which exists to no greater extent than the 'astral beings' of some of the more exotic schools of philosophy of his day. 'Nature', for Boyle, is merely a conventional way of referring to an external reality consisting of an aggregate of individual entities. Trees, elephants and other such bodies can be considered to make up 'nature'; yet there is no substance or self-sufficient entity of 'nature', existing in and of itself. 'Nature is the aggregate of bodies, that make up the world.'[90] Boyle sets this against vitalist or organic conceptions of nature, which take nature to be a self-sufficient reality – for example, the idea that 'nature is a most wise being', possessed of reason, intelligence and purpose.

The variety of models of nature deployed during the last 500 years points to both the inherent plasticity of the concept, and the potency of the agendas of those who appeal to them. To define nature is to impose a meaning upon it, reflecting the vested interests of those in positions of cultural and intellectual power and influence. The definition in question is not a consequence of the intrinsic qualities of what is loosely referred to as 'nature', but is imposed upon an essentially formless aggregate of constituent parts by those with intellectually potent conceptions of what nature *ought* to be. The definition of nature is thus about the exercise of power.

It is therefore the cause for little surprise that many in the second half of the twentieth century came to the conclusion that 'nature' was socially constructed by power groups. Given the agenda of postmodernity, it was inevitable that this would lead to demands for the subsequent deconstruction of nature.

The deconstruction of nature

The deconstruction of nature is to be set against the broader issue of the postmodern critique of allegedly 'objective' concepts and values,

---

[89] J. E. McGuire, 'Boyle's Conception of Nature', *Journal of the History of Ideas* 33 (1972), 523–42, especially 528–30.
[90] Boyle, *Works*, vol. 4, 370–2.

with the intention of exposing and neutralizing the societal norms and agendas which they express.[91] This can be seen in Roland Barthes' reflections on the famous exhibition of photographs created by Edward Steichen for the Museum of Modern Art in the 1950s. In reflecting on the concept of the 'human condition' – which the exhibition was intended to illustrate – Barthes commented that the fundamental notion of 'nature' was to be seen as a human construction, rather than something that was somehow 'given'. Classic humanism grounded itself on the notion of an ontologically given human nature; postmodernity, however, recognized that this was merely a cultural or linguistic construction:[92]

> Any classic humanism postulates that in scratching the history of men a little, the relativity of their institutions or the superficial diversity of their skins . . . one very quickly reaches the solid rock of a universal human nature. Progressive humanism, on the contrary, must always remember to reverse the terms of this very old imposture, constantly to scour nature, its 'laws' and its 'limits', in order to discover History there, and at last to establish Nature itself as historical.

Barthes' importance for our theme can be summarized in that luminous statement of intention – 'to establish Nature as historical'. All 'natural' norms and ideals are to be seen as free human creations. Where 'classic humanism' argued that, beneath the immense variety and diversity of human beliefs and values, a common given human nature could be discerned, 'progressive humanism' proclaims this to be a myth. The reality is that nature is not possessed of the epistemological finality and inevitability implied by the category of the *given*; it is created in the process of historical construction, and may be reconstructed as and when required.

In a similar manner, Michel Foucault has argued that the distinction between 'natural' and 'unnatural' is a fundamentally linguistic construction.[93] In that the term 'nature' has been interpreted in a variety of

[91] For a general overview of the movement and issues, see Terry Eagleton, *The Illusions of Postmodernism.* Oxford: Blackwell, 1996; Horace L. Fairlamb, *Critical Conditions: Postmodernity and the Question of Foundations.* Cambridge: Cambridge University Press, 1994; Mark Gottdiener, *Postmodern Semiotics.* Oxford: Blackwell, 1995; David Harvey, *The Condition of Postmodernity: An Enquiry into the Origins of Cultural Change.* Oxford: Blackwell, 1989; David Lyon, *Postmodernity.* Buckingham: Open University Press, 1994.

[92] Roland Barthes, *Mythologies.* London: Paladin, 1973, 108.

[93] For Foucault, the issue of what constitutes 'natural' sexual practices was a matter of no small personal importance: see David H. J. Larmour, Paul Allen Miller and Charles Platter, *Rethinking Sexuality: Foucault and Classical Antiquity.* Princeton, NJ: Princeton University Press, 1998.

different manners during different historical periods and in different cultural contexts, it follows that the term is a cultural construct. Far from being independent of socially mediated discourse, the concept of nature is its product. For Foucault, this necessarily means that the concept of 'nature' is not natural, but the product of human culture. The instability of the concept of 'nature' reflects the fact that it does not possess any fixed reference, but is defined by communities of discourse.

This point is reinforced by Jacques Derrida's argument that all philosophical categories are binary dependencies.[94] The importance of this will be obvious in the light of our observation that 'nature' is often defined in terms of the antithesis of 'technology', with the 'natural' being defined in a binary or antithetical manner as the 'other' of 'the human', 'the artificial', or 'the cultural'. The category of the natural is thus argued to rest upon a series of prior social constructions – again, allowing Foucault to draw the conclusion that this category is culturally constructed and socially mediated. The paradox of which Foucault demands acceptance is that the one thing that is not natural is nature itself.

In part, the success of the social deconstruction of nature rests upon developments within the philosophy of science. The assumption that 'nature' designates an observable reality can be seen as paralleling Moritz Schlick's category of 'observation statements' – that is, neutral reports which are the basis of theoretical reflection. However, this notion has been subjected to a withering critique. N. R. Hanson argued that, far from being a neutral process, observation was assumption-laden.[95] Perception is a patterning, dependent upon a prior conceptual system. Observation is not simply about *seeing*; it is about *seeing as*. There is no neutral view of the world, in that observation of that world is conditioned, perhaps to an indeterminate extent, by the belief systems and patterns of thought of the observer. We all 'have spectacles behind our eyes'. Hanson thus argues that the notion of 'brute empiricism' is unsustainable.

Hanson thus suggests that Ptolemy and Copernicus would therefore observe a sunrise in a different manner. Each would see the same phenomenon; they would, however, see it *as* something quite distinct, reflecting their different understandings of the relative positions and

---

[94] Julia De Nooy, *Derrida, Kristeva, and the Dividing Line: An Articulation of Two Theories of Difference.* New York: Garland, 1998.
[95] See especially N. R. Hanson, *Patterns of Discovery: An Inquiry into the Conceptual Foundations of Science.* Cambridge: Cambridge University Press, 1961.

motions of the earth and sun within the solar system. Similarly, one might argue that William Paley and Charles Darwin see the same set of natural phenomena, while seeing it *as* something quite different – Paley as the result of special creation, Darwin as the result of natural selection. Others had seen the finches of the Galapagos before Darwin; they did not, however, see them in quite the same way.[96]

'Nature' is thus not a neutral entity, having the status of an 'observation statement'; it involves seeing the world in a particular way – and the way in which it is seen shapes the resulting concept of 'nature'. Far from being a 'given', the idea of 'nature' is shaped by the prior assumptions of the observer. One does not 'observe' nature; one constructs it. And once the importance of socially mediated ideas, theories and values is conceded, it is impossible to avoid the conclusion that the concept of nature is, at least in part, a social construction. If the concept of nature is socially mediated – to whatever extent – it cannot serve as an allegedly neutral, objective or uninterpreted foundation of a theory or theology. *Nature is already an interpreted category.*

The fact that nature is, at least in part, socially constructed is reflected in many ways. Many have praised the natural landscapes of France, Greece and New England, seeing in them some kind of pristine purity, contrasting with the ghastliness of human constructions – a reworking, incidentally, of the classic Aristotelian contrast between φύσις and τέχνη. Others have sought inspiration in the great natural wonders of North America, which display nature at its finest – such as Yellowstone National Park, the Mississippi River, or the Niagara Falls. Such landscapes and natural wonders are portrayed as independent of humanity, possessing an integrity and simplicity which contrasts with the crude artefacts of humanity.[97]

Yet the reality of the situation is completely different. These 'natural' landscapes and features are socially mediated. The English natural landscapes which evoked so powerful a reaction in Romantic poets such as Coleridge had been tamed by centuries of human presence and agricultural work, and included buildings – primarily churches.[98] The

---

[96] Frank J. Sulloway, 'Darwin and his Finches: The Evolution of a Legend', *Journal of the History of Biology* 15 (1982), 1–53.

[97] For some interesting reflections, see Marjorie Hope Nicolson, *Mountain Gloom and Mountain Glory: The Development of the Aesthetics of the Infinite*. Seattle: University of Washington Press, 1997.

[98] Raimonda Modiano, *Coleridge and the Concept of Nature*. Tallahassee, FL: Florida State University Press, 1985, 8–27.

so-called 'natural' landscapes of New England and Europe are the result of human habitation and transformation, with the imprint of human civilization evident at point after point.[99] The features of the landscape of the Great American west owes far more to human activity than is acknowledged by those who long for nature at its purest;[100] nature has been tamed, transformed, and is now being marketed to city-dwellers. Yellowstone National Park is not allowed to manage itself; it is managed by well-intentioned human beings, whose views as to whether naturally-occurring forest fires should be extinguished or allowed to burn themselves out are determined by current fashions of thought as to what counts as 'natural'.[101] The flow of both the Niagara and Mississippi is not determined by natural forces, but by government agencies, including the US Army Corps of Engineers.[102] Nature, it seems, is perhaps better suited as the basis of empathetic feeling than critical discursive reasoning.[103]

Yet there is a further point that needs to be made in stressing the social mediation of the concept of 'nature'. It is certainly true that there are vast domains of the world which are still thought of as 'nature' – one thinks, for example, of the great oceans of the world. In one sense, it is possible to argue that these have yet to be affected by human τέχνη. Yet this is not entirely true. The oceans that were seen by writers of the sixteenth- and seventeenth-century as vast and untamed are now mere inconveniences to global travel, which can be flown over in a matter of hours. Reading Andrew Marvell's classic poem *Bermudas* (1652) brings home how things have changed.[104] The Bermudas – a small group of uninhabited islands in the Atlantic, discovered in 1515 –

[99] William Cronon, *Changes in the Land: Indians, Colonists, and the Ecology of New England*. New York: Hill & Wang, 1983; René J. Dubos, *The Wooing of Earth*. New York: Charles Scribner's Sons, 1980; J. Donald Hughes, *Ecology in Ancient Civilizations*. Albuquerque: University of New Mexico Press, 1975; idem, *North American Indian Ecology*. 2nd edn. [El Paso]: Texas Western Press, 1996.

[100] Mark Fiege, *Irrigated Eden: The Making of an Agricultural Landscape in the American West*. Seattle: University of Washington Press, 1999; William G. Robbins, *Landscapes of Promise: The Oregon Story, 1800–1940*. Seattle: University of Washington Press, 1997.

[101] Alston Chase, *Playing God in Yellowstone: The Destruction of America's First National Park*. San Diego, CA: Harcourt Brace Jovanovich, 1987.

[102] John A. McPhee, *The Control of Nature*. New York: Noonday Press, 1990; George A. Seibel and Olive M. Seibel, *Ontario's Niagara Parks 100 Years: A History*. Niagara Falls, ON: Niagara Parks Commission, 1985, 166–73.

[103] A point made in the interesting essay of Michael Reid, 'The Call of Nature', *Radical Philosophy* 64 (1993), 13–18.

[104] For the text and comment, see Alister E. McGrath (ed.), *Christian Literature: An Anthology*. Oxford: Blackwell, 2000, 454–6.

come to play an almost mythical role in this poem. They are seen as a symbol of an unspoilt paradise, in which weary exiles from England can find peace and freedom. The Atlantic Ocean is portrayed as a hostile force, at one and the same time threatening the very existence of the refugees, yet offering them their only hope of escape from religious persecution in England. Today, the Bermudas are a holiday resort for elderly and rich Americans, and the Atlantic Ocean has lost the mystique and fear which earlier generations knew so well through the advent of airliners.

Nature is what we perceive it to be, and that perception is defined by social structures (including technological advances). Thus today's city-dwellers express delight when admiring the vast forests of the Pacific north-west, forgetting that earlier generations saw these forests as posing serious risks to life, concealing predatory animals and other such threats. We can enjoy nature only when it no longer poses a threat to us.

A survey of conceptions of nature thus reveals the remarkable plasticity and instability of the notion. Even the brief survey of western attitudes to the matter offered within these pages reveals this diversity; it could easily be developed further by considering the various concepts of nature which are found in eastern religions and philosophies.[105] 'Nature', in common with other hitherto supposed universals – such as rationality and justice[106] – has been viewed by postmodernity as a socially conditioned construct.

This has caused considerable concern to many within the environmental movement, which here finds itself in open conflict with postmodernity over the status of nature. Postmodern cultural theory and criticism have been intensely suspicious of any attempt to reify what is in reality merely a convention, and have insisted that nature is to be seen as linguistically constructed. The ecological movement, on the other hand, has tended to see nature as a conceptually self-sufficient domain of intrinsic value, truth and authenticity, and has been somewhat dismissive of questions of representation and conceptuality. In the absence of any consensus concerning the ontology of nature, such notions as 'the environment' become socially constructed entities. Nature is under siege – both physically (through bulldozers) and intellectually (through deconstruction), in that the very existence of the

---

[105] While simplifications are notoriously unreliable, it would be important to note the unitary conceptions of nature which are often held to underlie Japanese approaches to the issue. See, for example, H. Watanabe, 'The Conception of Nature in Japanese Culture', *Science* 183 (1967), 1203–7.

[106] Alasdair MacIntyre, *Whose Justice? Which Rationality?*. London: Duckworth, 1988.

category has been challenged.[107] The defences offered by well-meaning environmentalists are generally pragmatic ('this will lead to further exploitation of the environment'), and have failed to appreciate that the real issue lies much deeper – the need for an ontology of nature.

The need for an ontology of nature

This point is illustrated in an important 1982 discussion of the necessity to respect the environment from an ecofeminist known as Starhawk. In the course of her analysis of the options available, she suggests that human beings would have greater respect for the world if they were to treat it as a Goddess. She then comments as follows:[108]

> When I say 'Goddess' I am not talking about a being somewhere outside of this world, nor I am proposing a new belief system. I am talking about choosing an attitude: choosing to take this living world, and creatures in it, as the ultimate meaning and purpose of life, to see the world, the earth and our lives as sacred.

The passage vividly illustrates the need for an ontology. According to this author, there is nothing about the world that demands we view it or treat it as sacred. It is a matter of our free decision to view it in this manner. We choose to project onto the earth the view that it is divine, and respond appropriately. But this is a divinity of our own choosing and making, and which evaporates when we choose to view things otherwise. An ontology is clearly demanded, setting out what the world *is*, so that our response is determined by the external constraints of reality, not simply an internal decision to view matters in certain, potentially arbitrary, manners.

At this point, we cannot ignore the insights of critical theory – the tradition of German western Marxism which includes such leading luminaries as Georg Lukács, Theodor Adorno and Jürgen Habermas.[109] While such writers differ on precisely how 'nature' is to be understood, the recognition of the social construction of nature undergirds much of

---

[107] See Gary Lease, 'Nature under Fire', in Michael E. Soulé and Gary Lease (eds), *Reinventing Nature: Responses to Postmodern Deconstruction*. Washington, DC: Island Press, 1995, 3–16; and Michael E. Soulé, 'The Social Siege of Nature', in Soulé and Lease (eds), *Reinventing Nature*, 137–70.

[108] Starhawk, *Dreaming the Dark: Magic, Sex, and Politics*. Boston: Beacon Press, 1982, 11. See also her earlier work *The Spiral Dance: A Rebirth of the Ancient Religion of the Great Goddess*. San Francisco: Harper & Row, 1979.

[109] See the careful study of Steven Vogel, *Against Nature: The Concept of Nature in Critical Theory*. Albany, NY: State University of New York Press, 1996.

their writing. In the end, we are obliged to recognize the merit of the point made by Georg Lukács: namely, that modern western thought has been marked by 'reification', understood as a pattern of thought that demands and expects to separate subjects from object, and that sees any recognition of the importance of *praxis* as destroying an object's true being – instead of creating it.[110] If Lukács is correct, modern western culture is doomed, by its refusal to recognize the role of social mediation and construction, to pursue 'nature' as an unconstructed immediacy with the same passion and ultimate outcome as an earlier generation pursued the Holy Grail. 'Nature', which we hoped with Aristotle and Rousseau would play a foundational role in philosophy, politics and theology, turns out to be something elusive, about which we can say rather little, yet feel the need to say rather a lot.

The deconstruction of nature has been resisted by many, and it is fair to point out some observations that have been made in response to the postmodern onslaught on the concept. In the first place, it can be argued that, simply because 'nature' is always presented to us as mediated through the 'social', it does not necessarily follow that 'nature' is totally subordinated to the category of the 'social'. That, as the Italian philosopher Sebastiano Timpanaro pointed out some years ago, would be simply 'idealist sophistry'.[111] Secondly, it can be argued that the dialectic between 'nature' and 'culture' cannot be resolved by reducing nature to a mere cultural epiphenomenon. As Kate Soper has pointed out, the position that nature is a totally socially constructed notion has to assume the existence of the very entities which it denies in order to have any plausibility.[112] These points are fair, and must be given due weight. Nevertheless, they are not sufficient to deflect the main thrust of the postmodern case, which rests in part upon the undeniable fact that 'nature' has been understood in different ways by different groups at different points in history.

Multiple readings of the 'book of nature'

One of the images of nature to have enjoyed wide currency since the early modern period is that of the 'book of nature'. Galileo affirmed that 'philosophy is written in this grand book, the universe, which stands

---

[110] Andrew Arato, 'Lukács's Theory of Reification', *Telos* 11 (1972), 25–66; J. M. Bernstein, 'Lukács' Wake: Praxis, Presence and Metaphysics', in Tom Rockmore (ed.), *Lukács Today: Essays in Marxist Philosophy*. Philadelphia: Temple University Press, 1992, 167–95.

[111] Sebastiano Timpanaro, *On Materialism*. London: New Left Books, 1975, 45.

[112] Soper, *What is Nature?*, 132–3.

continually open to our gaze'.[113] Similar thoughts can be found expressed in Sir Thomas Browne's 1643 classic *Religio Medici*:[114]

> There are two books from whence I collect my divinity. Besides that written one of God, another of his servant, nature, that universal and publick manuscript, that lies expansed unto the eyes of all. Those that never saw him in the one have discovered him in the other.

Writers such as Browne argued that their divinity was based on the reading of two texts – Scripture and nature. The image of nature as a book, however, has proved vulnerable to some of the core assumptions of the postmodern deconstruction of both texts and their authors.

Postmodern writers have challenged the assumption that there exists some reality outside the text, and argued for the legitimacy of multiple readings of all texts. The identity and intentions of the author of a text are declared to be an irrelevance to the interpretation of the text; in any case, no fixed meaning can be found within it. Such ideas can be seen as arising as a result of Jacques Derrida's reading of the works of Martin Heidegger in the late 1960s,[115] which led him to conclude that texts convey meaning which the author did not intend and could not have intended, and that the author cannot adequately put into words what he or she meant in the first place. Perhaps the most celebrated manner of expressing the priority of the reader over the text can be found in Roland Barthes' proclamation of the 'death of the author'.[116] Yet Derrida's slogan *il n'y a pas de hors-texte* can be seen as making substantially the same point – namely, that there is no extra-textual reality which can be invoked to determine whether a text has been read 'correctly'.

All textual interpretations are thus to be regarded as possessed of equal validity.[117] There is no reality outside the text which dictates how

---

[113] *The Assayer: Discoveries and Opinions of Galileo*, translated and edited by Stilman Drake. Garden City, New York: Doubleday, 1957, 237–8.

[114] Sir Thomas Browne, *Religio Medici*, II.xiv–xviii.

[115] On this, see Paul de Man, *Allegories of Reading*. New Haven, CT: Yale University Press, 1979; J. Hillis Miller, *The Ethics of Reading*. New York: Columbia University Press, 1987, and especially Christopher Norris, *Deconstruction and the Interests of Theory*. London: Pinter Publishers, 1988.

[116] For the origins and fortunes of this idea, see Sean Burke, *The Death and Return of the Author: Criticism and Subjectivity in Barthes, Foucault and Derrida*. Edinburgh: Edinburgh University Press, 1998.

[117] For a close reading of the presuppositions and implications of this approach, see Christopher Norris, 'Kant Disfigured: Ethics, Deconstruction and the Text Sublime', in *The Truth about Postmodernism*. Oxford: Blackwell, 1993, 182–256.

that text is to be interpreted. The issue concerns how the reader chooses to read the text. The attempt to discern or impose a specific meaning upon a text is suggested to have certain parallels with Fascism. This approach rode the crest of a cultural wave in post-Vietnam America, as is clear from the writings of Paul de Man, Geoffrey Hartman, Harold Bloom and J. Hillis Miller.[118] For Barthes, 'the death of the author' encapsulated the freedom of the reader to interpret a text without reference to authorial intention. The text, he argued, belonged to its readers, not its author.

The impact of this approach on the reading and interpretation of the Bible has been substantial.[119] It can be illustrated from the recent literary analysis of virtually any biblical text. To give some weight to this point, we shall consider some recent writings on the book of Job.[120] The standard critical approach, which reached its zenith in the 1960s, was dominated by historico-critical issues, aiming at detemining the meaning of the text by a rigorous investigation of its redactions.[121] This approach has now been virtually abandoned, in part on account of the literary issues we have just considered.[122] Thus Norman Habel uses an essentially narrative approach, based on the insights of new literary theory, and ignores the traditional debates over issues of authorship, dating and redaction.[123] In marked contrast, David Clines makes extensive use of reader response criticism, to offer an interpretation of Job which is open to a substantial variety of readings – including, he playfully suggests, feminist, vegetarian, materialist and Christian readings.[124] All of these, he argues, may legitimately be discerned within the text by those with prior ideological commitments. This approach is taken a stage further in a study from Edward Good, which argues for indeterminacy of meaning. The interpretation

---

[118] For an excellent analysis of this trend, see David Lehman, *Signs of the Times*. London: André Deutsch, 1991.

[119] For the issues, see David Seeley, *Deconstructing the New Testament*. Leiden: E. J. Brill, 1994; Stephen D. Moore, *Poststructuralism and the New Testament: Derrida and Foucault at the Foot of the Cross*. Minneapolis, MN: Fortress Press, 1994.

[120] I here base myself on the excellent study of Carol A. Newsom, 'Job and Ecclesiastes', in James Luther Mays, David L. Petersen and Kent Harold Richards (eds), *Old Testament Interpretation: Past, Present and Future*. Nashville, TN: Abingdon Press, 1995, 177–94.

[121] An excellent example of this older approach is to be found in Georg Fohrer, *Das Buch Hiob*. Kommentar zum Alten Testament, vol. 16. Gütersloh: Gerd Mohn, 1963.

[122] See the useful survey in L. Alonso Schökel and José Luis Sicre, *Job: comentario teológico y literario*. Madrid: Cristiandad, 1983, 36–43.

[123] Norman C. Habel, *The Book of Job*. Philadelphia: Westminster Press, 1985.

[124] David J. A. Clines, *Job 1–20*. Word Bible Commentary. Dallas, TX: Word Books, 1989, 48–56.

of the text is to be thought of as 'free play' with an 'open text', characterized by 'a certain purposelessness'.[125] This idea can also be found in Alan Cooper's study of how Job is to be interpreted, in which he suggests that this biblical book is a puzzle with many possible solutions. No single such solution is demanded by the text itself, so that the emphasis falls upon the creativity of the interpreter in *constructing* solutions which she finds congenial to her outlook. 'Those readers who are willing to pursue its diverse leads will never arrive at *the* meaning of the book of Job, but they will surely learn something about the meaning of their own lives.'[126]

The point being made here is that postmodernity has strongly encouraged the view that the text's meaning is incoherent, indeterminate, or is to be decided by the reader. There is no 'meaning in the text'; the meaning is discerned, supplied or imposed by the active reader.[127] Yet it has not been appreciated that the same issues apply to the 'book of nature'. The intimation of the textuality of nature is laden with interpretative significance – not least in that Derridean deconstruction, applied to the 'book of nature', leads to the assertion that there is no reality external to this text, which is open to a wide variety of cultural readings. There is no means of assessing such readings, as this would involve the imposition of a metanarrative, limiting the freedom of the reader of the text. The indeterminacy associated with the act of reading applies to nature as much as to the Bible, or any other text. The identity and intentions of the author are not of significance, and a variety of constructions – including the Christian reading of the 'book of nature' as God's creation – may be placed upon the reading of this textual analogue. The concept of nature, it would therefore be argued within postmodernity, is imposed upon a reading of the natural world, not discerned within it. There is no external reality that we may legitimately denote as 'nature'; at best, this is to be seen as one way of reading the world among many others.

The considerations outlined above do not pose any insurmountable challenge to Christian theology. While any claims it might make to

[125] Edward M. Good, *In Turns of Tempest: A Reading of Job, with a Translation*. Stanford, CA: Stanford University Press, 1990, 180.

[126] Alan Cooper, 'Reading and Misreading the Prologue to Job', *Journal for the Study of the Old Testament* 46 (1990), 67–79; quotation at 75.

[127] For a well-informed critical evaluation of this trend in biblical interpretation, see Kevin J. Vanhoozer, *Is there a Meaning in this Text?: The Bible, the Reader, and the Morality of Literary Knowledge*. Grand Rapids, MI: Zondervan, 1998.

privileged status would be contested, the specific doctrines which it affirms are more resilient to the postmodern critique than has been appreciated. Yet the postmodern approach to texts and their analogues radically undermines those who assert that the category of 'nature' is an intellectually stable external reality, which can act as the basis of theoretical reflection and speculation. Derrida and Barthes both insist that this manner of reading the world is to be seen as a free construction of the human mind, reflecting the right of the reader to frame the text as he or she pleases. Nature is a construction of the reader, reflecting the reader's theoretical precommitments; it is not an autonomous reality, which can be the objective basis of theoretical reflection. Suggestions such as these radically undermine the plausibility of world-views which hold that 'nature' is an objective reality, capable of functioning as the basis of a world-view. If anything, 'nature' is itself the outcome of a world-view. Without an ontology of nature, the concept has little value in critical intellectual discourse.

The attempt to deconstruct the natural sciences

The postmodern programme can easily be extended from 'nature' itself to the natural sciences. In the postmodern world-view, the natural sciences – in common with other disciplines – merely relate stories or describe constructs which do little more than articulate the existing prejudices of the narrator. Postmodern theory provides a critique of representation and the modern belief that theory mirrors reality. In the place of this approach, postmodern writers offer what might be termed 'perspectivist' and 'relativist' positions, to the effect that theories at best provide partial perspectives on their objects, and that all cognitive representations of the world are historically and linguistically mediated. Some postmodern theorists accordingly reject the totalizing macro-perspectives on society and history favoured by modern theory in favour of microtheory and micropolitics. Postmodern theory rejects modern assumptions of social coherence and notions of causality in favour of multiplicity, plurality, fragmentation, and indeterminacy. It stresses the radical 'situatedness' of all human thought. In all of these respects, it may be regarded as a conscious and deliberate reaction against the totalization of the Enlightenment project.

The leading general feature of postmodern theory is generally agreed to be the deliberate and systematic abandonment of centralizing narratives – what Jean-François Lyotard styles *les grands récits*. The general differences between modernity and postmodernity have been summarized in terms of a series of stylistic contrasts, including the following:[128]

Modernism	Postmodernism
Purpose	Play
Design	Chance
Hierarchy	Anarchy
Centring	Dispersal
Selection	Combination

Note how the terms gathered together under the 'modernism' category have strong overtones of the ability of the thinking subject to analyse, order, control and master. Those gathered together under the 'postmodernism' category possess equally strong yet antithetical overtones, affirming both the *inability* of the thinking subject to master or control, and the *impropriety* of doing so in the first place. The outcome of this is the assertion that things need to be left as they are, in all their glorious and playful diversity. Postmodern theory thus abandons the rational and unified subject postulated by much modern theory in favour of a socially and linguistically decentred and fragmented subject.

It will therefore be clear why the natural sciences are such a significant issue for postmodern writers. The assertion that the natural sciences are able to offer an empirical approach to reality which is independent of culture, gender, class and language poses a formidable challenge to the postmodern rejection of universal truth. It is therefore easy to understand why so much effort has been directed by the academic left towards the demonstration that the natural sciences represent culturally-conditioned opinions, in common with other disciplines.

It is therefore important to note that the postmodern critique of the natural sciences has achieved a very limited degree of success.[129] It has not been especially difficult for natural scientists to argue that the explanatory and predictive successes of the natural sciences rest upon a real connection to the way things actually are – a point which we shall

[128] Ihab Hassan, *The Dismemberment of Orpheus: Toward a Postmodern Literature*. New York: Oxford University Press, 1982, 267–8. See also his 'Culture of Postmodernism', *Theory, Culture and Society* 2 (1985), 119–32, especially 123–4.

[129] See, for example, Paul R. Gross, and Norman Levitt, *Higher Superstition: The Academic Left and its Quarrels with Science*. Baltimore, MD: Johns Hopkins University Press, 1998; Paul R. Gross, Norman Levitt and Martin W. Lewis (eds), *The Flight from Science and Reason*. New York: New York Academy of Sciences, 1996; Noretta Koertge (ed.), *A House built on Sand: Exposing Postmodernist Myths about Science*. New York: Oxford University Press, 1998.

be considering in much greater detail in the second volume of this project. Reality acts as a constraint upon the reflections and theories of the natural sciences, which restrains them from presenting as 'true' theories which can be shown to be arbitrary, random, or an expression of the unbounded imagination.

The natural sciences are thus a serious headache for those who have difficulties with the idea of a universal, objective reality which may be, at least in part, apprehended and described. Aware of this difficulty, Lyotard argues that the natural sciences depend upon 'paralogy' – that is, faulty or even contradictory reasoning, which abandons any claim to be in possession of or governed by centralizing narratives.[130]

> Postmodern science – by concerning itself with such things as un-decidables, the limits of precise control, conflicts characterized by incomplete information, *fracta*, catastrophes and pragmatic paradoxes – is theorizing its own evolution as discontinuous, catastrophic, non-rectifiable, and paradoxical. It is changing the meaning of the word *knowledge*, while expressing how such a change can take place. It is producing not the known, but the unknown.

It has proved somewhat difficult for natural scientists to take seriously this bizarre account of the methods, goals and achievements of the natural sciences. As Steven Connor points out, there is a serious disjunction between Lyotard's approach and the realities of the empirical sciences.[131]

> Lyotard paints a picture of the dissolution of the sciences into a frenzy of relativism in which the only aim is to bound gleefully out of the con-finement of musty old paradigms and to trample operational procedures underfoot in the quest for exotic forms of illogic. But this is simply not the case. If some forms of the pure sciences, mathematics and theoretical physics again being the obvious examples, are concerned with the exploration of different structures of thought for understanding reality, then this still remains bound, by and large, to models of rationality, consensus and correspondence to demonstrable truths.

While the postmodern attempt to deconstruct the natural sciences has met with little success, save among those with little knowledge of those sciences or first-hand experience of laboratory culture, the same

---

[130] Jean-François Lyotard, *The Postmodern Condition: A Report on Knowledge*. Manchester: Manchester University Press, 1992, 60.
[131] Steven Connor, *Postmodernist Culture: An Introduction to Theories of the Contemporary*. Oxford: Blackwell, 1989, 35.

is not true of the postmodern criticisms directed against the concept of nature. The postmodern agenda, when brought to bear on central concepts such as 'nature' and 'wilderness', has exposed a series of extremely disturbing issues over who has the right to define such concepts, and precisely what vested interests underlie these notions in both their traditional and more recent expressions.[132] The 'reinvention' of nature involves a deliberate decision of power and privilege, in determining whose views are to be preferred, and for what reasons – reasons which are often directly linked with the core values of cultures, peoples, communities or academies. There is no such thing as 'nature' – only various conceptions of what nature is, or ought to be, reflecting the agendas of various pressure groups.

The mediation of social constructs between the observer and the natural order thus causes serious difficulty for the idea that we can somehow directly encounter nature directly, as an uninterpreted entity. To accord epistemological privilege to the concept of 'nature' is to grant a derivative priority to the social values, attitudes and ideologies which shape our understanding of the notion. The importance of this point can be seen by considering the philosophy generally known as 'naturalism', in which a significant appeal is made both to nature and to the natural sciences as the basis of human knowledge.

The phenomenon of naturalism

Earlier, we considered the distinction between *Naturwissenschaften* and *Geisteswissenschaften*, especially in the thought of Wilhelm Dilthey. A thoroughgoing naturalism would dispute any such distinction, holding that everything that exists or happens is[133]

> . . . susceptible to explanation through methods which, although paradigmatically exemplified in the natural sciences, are continuous from domain to domain of objects and events. Hence naturalism is polemically defined as repudiating the view that there exists or could exist any entities or events which lie, in principle, beyond the scope of scientific explanation.

---

[132] See the following: David E. Goodman and Michael R. Redclift, *Refashioning Nature: Food, Ecology and Culture*. New York: Routledge, 1991; Donna J. Haraway, *Simians, Cyborgs and Women: The Reinvention of Nature*. New York: Routledge, 1991; William McKibben, *The End of Nature*. New York: Random House, 1989; Max Oelschlager, *The Idea of Wilderness*. New Haven, CT: Yale University Press, 1991.

[133] I here draw on the definition offered by Arthur C. Danto, 'Naturalism', in P. Edwards (ed.), *Encyclopaedia of Philosophy*. 8 vols. New York: Macmillan, 1967, vol. 5, 448–50.

This emphasis on the continuity across and within domains of knowledge undermines any notion of a given domain of knowledge – such as philosophy, sociology, theology or the natural sciences – possessing privileged status. There is only one way to knowledge and truth.[134]

The explicit rejection of any form of dualism is thus of central importance to naturalism. Aristotle's important distinction between φύσις and τέχνη is to be rejected as resting upon a false construal of nature, as is the classic distinction drawn in Thomistic philosophical theology between *natura* and *gratia*. Nature is to be defined as what *is*, without any distinction. There is no realm of the supernatural, no division of the 'natural' order into non-interacting magisterial domains, no division between science and arts, so special pleading for any area of human reflection as being exempted from the control of nature. Ethics, for example, is to be defined in such terms as to deliberately exclude any reference to the transcendent, supernatural, or divine, holding simply and consistently that 'there are no values in the world that are not reducible to or explainable away in terms of the naturalistic conceptual scheme of things'.[135] Nothing, it is argued, lies beyond the scope of scientific explanation.[136] Sterling Lamprecht defines naturalism as 'a philosophical position, empirical method, that regards everything that exists or occurs to be conditioned in its existence or occurrence by causal factors within one all-encompassing system of nature'.[137]

The intellectual pedigree of naturalism is complex, and brings together a number of elements. In the first place, naturalism has a natural resonance with both empiricism and scepticism in modern philosophy, especially in regard to the systematic exclusion of metaphysics from philosophical and ethical reflection.[138] In the second place, naturalism builds upon the materialist tradition in metaphysics, without necessarily embracing reductive materialism.

Whereas earlier forms of naturalism did not necessarily make an explicit and extended appeal to the explanatory power and successes of

[134] For an excellent survey of older naturalist discussions of this point, see John H. Randall, 'The Nature of Naturalism', in Yervant H. Krikorian (ed.), *Naturalism and the Human Spirit*. New York: Columbia University Press, 1945, 354–82.

[135] Elie M. Adams, *Ethical Naturalism and the Modern World-View*. Chapel Hill, BC: University of North Carolina Press, 1960, 6.

[136] Danto, 'Naturalism', 448.

[137] Power Lamprecht Sterling, *The Metaphysics of Naturalism*. New York: Appleton-Century-Crofts, 1967, 160.

[138] Paul Kurtz, *Philosophical Essays in Pragmatic Naturalism*. Buffalo, NY: Prometheus Books, 1990, 12–13.

the natural sciences,[139] a growing awareness of these issues contributed in no small way to the growing conviction that a philosophical and ethical system rooted simply in nature was viable. As the noted naturalist philosopher Paul Kurtz puts this point: 'What is common to naturalistic philosophy is its commitment to science. Indeed, naturalism might be defined in its more general sense as *the philosophical generalization of the methods and conclusions of the sciences.*'[140] It is important to note that the natural sciences are subtly dethroned from any position of privilege in the discussion of what 'nature' might be. Although the natural sciences are held to exemplify the naturalist approach particularly well, these cannot be held to *define* such an approach. Other naturalist writers have been more cautious in their statements about the relation of the movement to the natural sciences, preferring to speak of 'the scientific method, *broadly understood*' – meaning (as in the writings of John Dewey) an appeal to 'the method of intelligence' which embraces philosophy and the social sciences, as well as the natural sciences.

It will be clear that the notion of 'nature' plays a critically important – even to the point of definitive – role within naturalist reasoning. It is, however, a concept which eludes definition with anything like the precision or consensus which would be required for a workable philosophical system. In order to make the category of 'nature' viable for philosophical or ethical reflection, it needs to be seen in a certain way. In the case of naturalism, the general definition offered can be summarized as follows: nature is what the empirical methods of the natural sciences disclose it to be, and nothing more.

The naturalist exclusion of transcendence

Nature is not necessarily defined ontologically by this tradition, but tends to be conceived in terms of what may be known, or grasped through experience. As Danto stresses, naturalism 'is ontologically neutral in that it does not prescribe what specific kinds of entities there must be in the universe'. Nature is defined in terms of what is experienced at the level of nonreflective encounter. A 'principle of exclusion' is deployed, limiting reality to what can be experienced and directly interpreted. Naturalism purposefully limits itself to an investigation of relationships within the natural order, excluding the possibility that anything within that system can be taken as pointing to something beyond it. What is experienced can be explained in terms of other

---

[139] Jonathan Kemp, *Ethical Naturalism: Hobbes and Hume.* London: Macmillan, 1970.
[140] Kurtz, *Philosophical Essays in Pragmatic Naturalism*, 12.

aspects of experience. This can be understood as *methodological naturalism*, in that it prescribes the means by which knowledge is to be derived, rather than the precise form which that knowledge might take.

Nevertheless, it is clear that many naturalist philosophers would make ontological claims on the basis of the application of a naturalist method. Danto was perfectly prepared to concede that naturalism, conceived as a 'methodological rather than an ontological dualism', left many options open, including the possibility that naturalists might be 'idealists, materialists, atheists, or non-atheists'.[141] (Note the curious construction 'non-atheist'; one assumes that a person who does not deny the existence of God might be allowed to be a theist.) Others, however – perhaps the majority – have insisted that ontological precommitments are implicit within such an approach, and must be made explicit at every point. Reality is to be defined as that which may be known through the methods of natural sciences (although there is often a certain opaqueness to how this criterion is to be understood and applied).

Most of those committed to naturalism insist that it necessarily excludes any notion of the supernatural or the transcendent. Niklas Luhmann, of no small importance to this discussion, suggests that a naturalized epistemology is, by its very nature, 'detranscendentalized'.[142] John H. Randall, perhaps one of the more distinguished philosophers in this tradition, asserts that 'naturalism finds itself in thoroughgoing opposition to all forms of thought which assert the existence of a supernatural or transcendent Realm of Being, and which make knowledge of that realm of fundamental importance to human living'.[143] Randall and his colleagues, it should be noted, are not suggesting that such realms may indeed exist, but are of no interest to philosophy; they are emphatic that they do *not* exist.

The result of this is entirely predictable. In that God cannot be observed by the methods of the natural sciences, God does not exist. Those who make statements which refer to God are therefore mistaken in doing so, and a purely natural explanation of those statements is to be sought. Drawing on the long line of anti-theistic reductionist strategies devised by writers such as Ludwig Feuerbach, Karl Marx and Sigmund Freud, language about God is easily shown to be a social construction, reflecting the needs of those individuals and communities

---

[141] Danto, 'Naturalism', 448.
[142] Niklas Luhmann, *Die Wissenshaft der Gesellschaft*. Frankfurt am Main: Suhrkamp, 1990, 15–16.
[143] Randall, 'The Nature of Naturalism', 358.

which make them.[144] Statements about God having been declared invalid in advance, it only remains to offer a reductionist explanation based on the canons of the social sciences. While naturalism generally has little difficulty with religious language and behaviour, this is tolerated only on the assumption that it refers to and arises from social factors and other considerations which can be studied by the natural (and, in this case, the social) sciences.

Willem B. Drees offers a defence of naturalism which he believes allows important statements to be made concerning the proper relationship between science and religion. Drees distinguishes three possible levels of naturalism – methodological, epistemological and ontological – before indicating his commitment to the last:[145]

> The natural world is the whole of reality that we know of and interact with; no supernatural or spiritual realm distinct from the natural world shows up *within* our natural world, not even in the mental life of humans. This claim I will call *ontological naturalism.*

Drees then offers a naturalist account of both the natural sciences and religion, which offers a functional view of religion more or less informed by sociobiology. While Drees states that this functionalist account of religions does 'not necessarily' deny that their 'central terms refer to realities', he makes it clear that references to supernatural realities are to be treated with great suspicion, and to be explained away on essentially sociobiological grounds:[146]

> On the naturalist view there is no locus for particular divine activities in a similar ostensible way. Thus it is extremely unlikely that our ideas about gods would correspond to their reality . . . Hence an evolutionary view challenges religions not only by offering an account of their origin, but also by undermining the credibility of their references which would transcend the environments in which the religions arose.

Drees here follows the general naturalist trend towards the elimination of God, and the explanation of religion on social grounds.[147]

---

[144] See, for example, William Lloyd Newell, *The Secular Magi: Marx, Freud, and Nietzsche on Religion.* New York: Pilgrim Press, 1986; Samuel J. Preus, *Explaining Religion: Criticism and Theory from Bodin to Freud.* New Haven, CT: Yale University Press, 1987.

[145] Willem B. Drees, *Religion, Science and Naturalism.* Cambridge: Cambridge University Press, 1995, 12.

[146] Drees, *Religion, Science and Naturalism*, 250–1.

[147] See the excellent study of William M. Shea, *The Naturalists and the Supernatural: Studies in Horizon and an American Philosophy of Religion.* Macon, GA: Mercer University Press, 1984.

Drees' account of the relation of science and religion proceeds on the assumption that, since there can be no gods, any human discussion of or reference to gods must rest upon the false construal of social factors. A similar approach is taken by Paul Kurtz in his writings on 'pragmatic naturalism':[148]

> The naturalist does *not* deny the existence of reverence, awe, piety or of mystical ecstasy, nor does he deny that the experience can be prized or cherished by individuals who undergo them. The key epistemological issue, however, concerns what these experiences point to and what they assert, if anything, about the universe. It is one thing to *have* an experience, it is another to endow the universe with qualities in its name. And here we must proceed with caution, lest we read into nature any and all human experiences . . . Naturalists tend to be humanists, for they believe that religious experiences are natural and that they can be explained with reference to natural processes and events.

The approach offers a recognizable variant on the Feuerbachian and Marxian critiques of religion, which hold that any human reference to God must have its origins in individual personal consciousness or the individual's socio-economic environment. But *why*? How do we *know* that the real is only the natural? Or that the observable is the whole of reality? Drees offers us little by way of justification of his approach, and is best read as an exploration of the implications of a thoroughgoing naturalism for science and religion, rather than a serious defence of its presuppositions.

A preliminary critique of naturalism

Naturalism holds that 'the natural world is the whole of reality that we know of and interact with' (Drees). This position is defended particularly clearly by Frederick Woodbridge, in his 1940 naturalist manifesto *An Essay on Nature*.[149] Woodbridge insists that knowledge arises from what is accessible to the senses; in doing so, he seems to come dangerously close to the Humean view that the foundations of philosophy are sensist postulates, a view which most naturalists are anxious to avoid, given the known weaknesses of the position. In the second volume of this work, we shall set out a detailed critique of

---

[148] Kurtz, *Philosophical Essays in Pragmatic Naturalism*, 37.
[149] Frederick J. E. Woodbridge, *An Essay on Nature*. New York: Columbia University Press, 1940, 60–73. For further comment, see William Frank Jones, *Nature and Natural Science: The Philosophy of Frederick J. E. Woodbridge*. Buffalo, NY: Prometheus Books, 1983; Shea, *Naturalists and the Supernatural*, 143–70.

naturalism, including an attempted clarification of the often blurred distinction between ontological naturalism and methodological naturalism. However, it is clearly appropriate to offer some preliminary points of criticism at this stage.

The first major point which must be made is that there is a self-serving circularity to the naturalist approach. To assert that 'the natural world is the whole of reality that we know of and interact with' (Drees) is usually taken to mean that the findings of the natural sciences – which, of course, provide a direct engagement with the natural world – are epistemologically privileged, to the point of eclipsing other disciplines. Setting aside, for one moment, the not inconsiderable difficulty of defining what constitutes a 'natural' science and what does not, it is critically important to note that, in addition to making an affirmation concerning how reality may be known, Drees' statement smuggles in an implicit view of reality. That which is real is that which may be known through the natural sciences. This implicit ontological reductionism has important implications, as we shall demonstrate later in this work.

At this stage, we may simply point out that the kind of approaches commended by Drees and Woodbridge merely highlight the critical question which naturalism cannot ignore: how do we know that the world which may be known by the senses is the whole of reality? This goes beyond what may reasonably be claimed to be a scientific outlook, which is concerned primarily with the question of the investigation of reality. Naturalism smuggles an essentially materialist philosophy into its allegedly 'scientific' account of reality. It places an embargo on the transcendent, without offering any scientific justification for doing so. The movement aimed to settle by stipulation in advance of the evidence precisely those issues which required to be settled on the basis of empirical evidence.[150]

So what is the evidence for naturalism? In a foreword to a somewhat disappointing study of the interaction of evolutionary theory and theology, Gerhard Vollmer suggests that one of its chief deficiencies is the simple fact that it fails to offer any persuasive reasons for wishing to adopt a theological approach in the first place.[151] No justification is offered for the introduction of theological categories, which are clearly

---

[150] For additional comments, see Alvin Plantinga, *Warrant and Proper Function*. New York: Oxford University Press, 1993, 194–237; Kevin Schilbrack, 'Problems for a Complete Naturalism', *American Journal of Theology and Philosophy* 15 (1994), 269–91.

[151] Gerhard Vollmer, in Ulrich Lüke, *Evolutionäre Erkenntnistheorie und Theologie*. Stuttgart: Wissenschaftliche Verlag, 1990, 6.

out of place in a purely naturalist account of things. So, playfully to invert this question, what justification may be offered for naturalism, drawn from outside naturalism itself? The system may possess an internal coherence – along with many other such theories, including Christianity and Marxism – but that is not enough to justify the theory.

Naturalists have been disappointingly coy on this crucial matter. In his discussion of this matter, Drees considers the question: 'Can one offer – independently from a naturalist view – a justification for holding a naturalist view?'[152] The question is critical, and underlies the remainder of his rather ambitious book. Drees then devotes an entire three sentences to dealing with this issue, before drawing the astonishing conclusion that 'a completely independent justification of naturalism is impossible, since naturalism attempts to deal with everything'. Well, so does Marxism. And does that solve the problem of its justification? And Drees knows full well that the naturalist's definition of 'everything' is really rather limited, since it is confined to what may be known through the senses.

Happily, others – including Richard Rorty and Hilary Putnam – have been more than willing to discuss this critically important question, and raise some telling concerns. However, at this stage, we may note a significant assault on the position which Drees seems happy to accept, even if he fails to offer us any plausible, let alone compelling reasons for doing so. The issue at stake is whether any justification for naturalism can be offered from a naturalist perspective. George Myro has argued that naturalism must be recognized as self-defeating, in that a naturalist cannot coherently assert the naturalist thesis.[153] From a naturalist point of view, there are no adequate grounds for asserting that naturalism is true. There are legitimate claims concerning the nature of justification which lie beyond the purview of the natural sciences, and any derivative philosophical system or method. A similar point is made by Steven Wagner, who points out that naturalism remains locked into this self-defeating matrix, even if subtle redefinitions of the naturalist enterprise are proposed.[154]

---

[152] Drees, *Religion, Science and Naturalism*, 23. For a critique, see David Ray Griffin, 'A Richer or Poorer Naturalism? A Critique of Willem Drees' *Religion, Science and Naturalism*', *Zygon* 32 (1997), 595–616.

[153] George Myro, 'Aspects of Acceptability', in Steven J. Wagner and Richard Warner (eds), *Naturalism: A Critical Appraisal*. Notre Dame, IN: University of Notre Dame Press, 1993, 197–210.

[154] Steven J. Wagner, 'Why Realism Can't Be Naturalized', in Steven J. Wagner and Richard Warner (eds), *Naturalism: A Critical Appraisal*. Notre Dame, IN: University of Notre Dame Press, 1993, 211–53.

In the end, naturalism is a *blik* – an outlook, or way of conceiving, the world, which is, at least in part, socially mediated. If 'nature' is a socially mediated notion, that notion will be, to a greater or lesser extent, constructed in terms of the social world of the interpreter of nature. The observer's beliefs, prejudices, values and precommitments will be brought to bear, perhaps unconsciously, on the interpretation of the world. What might therefore be asserted to be an objective entity, and potentially the foundation of philosophical or ethical norms, is itself constructed partly in the light of precisely such norms – whether these are acknowledged or not. 'Naturalism' can thus easily become – if it is not already so – potentially little more than an *a posteriori* validation of the existing notions and values of the allegedly neutral observer. We shall return to such points in much greater detail as part of our discussion in the next volume in this series, dealing with the nature of reality and the means by which this may be known.

From nature to creation

In pointing out that 'nature' is a socially mediated concept, we are noting that nature is necessarily viewed through a prism of beliefs and values, reflecting the historical and social location of the observer, which inevitably skews the resulting notion. If one believes – as many did in the Middle Ages, and some continued to believe in the early seventeenth century – that the world is a harmonious living organism, in which all parts work together for the common good, one tends to adopt a perspective on the natural order which is rather different from that encouraged by a reading of Malthus and Darwin, in which the natural world tends to be seen as a bloody and wasteful struggle for survival, with victory going to the best adapted. As Holmes Rolston points out, from this viewpoint there would seem to be a complete absence of any deep morality within nature itself:[155]

> Wildness is a gigantic food pyramid, and this sets value in a grim, death-bound jungle. Earth is a slaughterhouse, with life a miasma rising over the stench. Nothing is done for the benefit of another . . . Blind and ever urgent exploitation is nature's driving force.

This contrasts sharply with what Robert Boyle termed the 'vulgar notion of nature', which stressed that 'nature is a most wise being, that does

---

[155] Holmes Rolston, *Environmental Ethics: Duties to and in the Natural World*. Philadelphia: Temple University Press, 1988, 218. See also the important discussion of Darwinian ethics in Michael Ruse, *Taking Darwin Seriously: A Naturalistic Approach to Philosophy*. New York: Prometheus Books, 1998, 82–93.

nothing in vain', and refused to countenance anything within nature which was not ultimately directed towards the 'public good'.[156] What is observed within nature thus cannot be dissociated from how nature itself is understood.

The position adopted in this study is not that the concept 'nature' is totally socially or culturally constructed, but that the notion is partly shaped by socially mediated factors. This process of mediation means that our perception of what 'nature' means – or what it means to be 'natural' – is covertly shaped by a series of influences, which deny us direct access to an allegedly neutral or self-sufficient notion of 'nature' itself. How can nature shape our values and ideas, when that same nature has already been shaped by them? How can we construct a philosophy based on nature, when nature has already been constructed by our philosophical ideas?

For reasons such as these, the concept of nature has lost its intuitive intellectual plausibility, and, for many, has become little more than a synonym for 'the totality of all things'. It is therefore a category which offers little promise as a basis – or even a dialogue partner – for a scientific theology. Nature itself offers no ontology as a means of categorical justification. It is an interpreted and socially mediated category. For the theologian, this raises the critical question: given that 'nature' is an interpreted and mediated notion, what interpretation is to be preferred? The Christian theologian will wish to explore another category as a means of reclaiming the concept of 'nature' as an intellectually viable category, while at the same time interpreting it in a Christian manner. The category? Creation.

[156] Boyle, *Works*, vol. 4, 370.

Chapter 4

The Christian Doctrine of Creation

There is no doubt that there is a need for a specifically Christian approach to what has come to be known as 'nature'.[1] Wolfhart Pannenberg has both argued for the need for this question to be addressed, and also offers a provisional response – a response, however, which is more than a little puzzling in tone. For Pannenberg, theology ought to avail itself of the category of 'nature', rather than 'creation':[2]

> The fundamental task of theology in this case is better characterised as a 'theology of nature'. With this, the concept of 'creation' is by no means surrendered. It designates a possible result of a theology of nature, of a theological interpretation of natural reality . . . From many aspects, the word 'creation', or in any case its usual understanding, is not very appropriate for a theology of nature.

This is a bold statement, and one that is not satisfactorily justified in Pannenberg's subsequent discussion. The following points may be made in response to Pannenberg's line of argument:

1. Pannenberg is right to point out that 'nature' is the category employed in public discourse concerning the world, and that

[1] See George Hendry, *The Theology of Nature*. Philadelphia: Westminster Press, 1980; Jan-Olav Henriksen, 'How is Theology about Nature "Natural"?', *Studia Theologica* 43 (1989), 179–209; Claude Y. Stewart, *Nature in Grace: A Study in the Theology of Nature*. Macon, GA: Mercer University Press, 1983. One of the best studies to deal with this issue is the neglected work of Christian Link, *Die Welt als Gleichnis: Studien zum Problem der natürlichen Theologie*. Munich: Kaiser Verlag, 1976.
[2] Wolfhart Pannenberg, *Toward a Theology of Nature: Essays on Science and Faith*. Philadelphia: Westminster/John Knox Press, 1993, 72.

theology, if it is to avoid being relegated to an intellectual ghetto, ought to use this public language. Yet for Christian theology to absorb this term, with its implicit associations, is inevitably to weaken any distinctive Christian evaluation of the concept. The first stage in the elimination of Christianity's public role in the world is to force it to use the language of that world, in that the elimination of a vocabulary is the first stage in the elimination of the conceptualities it embodies. The surrender of its language is the precondition for the elimination of a world-view. Christianity is perfectly capable of adapting its language for the public arena, while retaining its own language *intra muros ecclesiae*. Pannenberg has made a good case for ensuring that Christianity is able to speak to and be understood by the public arena; he has not, however, shown that this apologetic task can only be undertaken by the replacement of Christian terms by their secular equivalents, and the inevitable imposition of the associations of the latter upon the former.[3]

2. It is entirely possible that misunderstandings of the term 'creation' may lead to miscommunication and other such difficulties in relation to the Christian community's conversations with the world. This is not, however, a valid reason for abandoning this, or any other theological term. The important point is to ensure that it is correctly understood. The apologetic task of the Christian community demands that it explain its terms, and offer provisional translations into the languages of modern culture.

3. Most importantly Pannenberg's analysis does not take account of the profound ambivalence of the notion of 'nature', which was explored in the previous chapter (Ch. 3). The term 'nature' is itself open to the same type of misunderstandings which Pannenberg represents as being associated with the term 'creation'. In addition, Pannenberg seems to overlook the fact that the concept of 'nature' is socially mediated, apparently holding that there is some uncontested observable reality in the public arena called 'nature'. Yet in the previous chapter (Ch. 3), we noted the difficulty in seeing 'nature' without an interposed

---

[3] I think Pannenberg might agree with this observation. Thus Pannenberg's recent three-volumed work of systematic theology – for which a Christian readership is clearly presupposed – gives priority to the theological category of creation, and makes little use of the notion of 'nature': e.g., see Wolfhart Pannenberg, *Systematic Theology*. 3 vols. Grand Rapids, MI: Eerdmans. Edinburgh: T&T Clark, 1994, 1998, vol. 2, 1–174.

socially-mediated framework, which results in the world being viewed in a certain way. Nature cannot be thought of as a neutral or uninterpreted entity, in that it is *seen as* something (Hanson).

In contrast to Pannenberg, we wish to affirm that a Christian 'theology of nature' is contained and subsumed in the insight that the natural order, including humanity, is God's creation.[4] Christians see *nature* as *creation*. There is thus already a perfectly good 'theology of nature' available to Christians. It is called a doctrine of creation. The use of some such phrase as a 'theology of nature' may have some value in explaining what Christians mean by a doctrine of creation to those *extra muros ecclesiae*, in much the same way that one might speak of a 'theology of destiny' to convey the essence of a Christian doctrine of providence to an audience more familiar with secular ways of speaking. The apologetic aspect of the matter having been noted, however, it may be pointed out that this usage is not particularly helpful theologically, in that the Christian tradition has tended to use a different idiom on account of the secular overtones or associations of other modes of discourse.

The Christian approach to nature is to see it as God's creation. In a paragraph added in 1543 to his preface to Olivetan's translation of the New Testament (1534), Calvin argues that Scripture provides us with spectacles through which we may view the world as God's creation and self-expression. Calvin is clearly working with the idea of 'creation' as a *theory-laden* reading or viewing of nature. He argues that Christian doctrine provides us with spectacles through which we may view and interpret the natural world as God's creation, in much the same way as N. R. Hanson regards scientific theories as spectacles through which the process of observation takes place.[5]

Everyone views the natural order in some interpreted manner; the question which we are under obligation to address is which of the many perspectives on the natural world are we to adopt? For the purposes of this project, nature is to be seen through the prism of revelation as

---

[4] The sustained use of the category of 'creation', rather than the mimicking of secular discourse concerning 'nature', is one of the most welcome features of the excellent 'Evangelical Declaration on the Care of Creation' (1994). For the text and comment, see R. J. Berry (ed.), *The Care of Creation*. Leicester: InterVarsity Press, 2000.

[5] Dudley Shapere, 'The Concept of Observation in Science and Philosophy', *Philosophy of Science* 49 (1982), 485–525; N. R. Hanson, *Patterns of Discovery: An Inquiry into the Conceptual Foundations of Science*. Cambridge: Cambridge University Press, 1961.

God's creation. David Novak makes a similar point in his fine study of natural law in Judaism:[6]

> Nature is not an object right before us about which we can argue using the truth criteria of correspondence. It is something that can only be grasped abstractly from without our historical present, a present whose content is continually provided by revelation.

This does not posit a tension between 'nature' and 'creation'. To speak of 'nature', as we have stressed, is to speak of an *interpreted* entity, which is mediated through a series of social constructs. Only if 'nature' itself is interpreted in some specific manner, and if that interpretation is then improperly designated 'nature', can there be a tension of such a type. 'Creation' is a specific way of viewing 'nature', which stands opposed to certain other ways of reading nature. In what follows, we shall outline this specific way of reading the book of nature, and explore its importance for a scientific theology.

Towards a Christian view of nature: M. B. Foster

In beginning to set out a Christian understanding of nature, we may take some cues from a series of writings of the English philosopher Michael Beresford Foster (1903–59). Foster spent virtually his entire academic career at Oxford, and developed an interest in the importance of a Christian doctrine of creation in relation to the development of the natural sciences. Although not a scientist himself, Foster clearly recognized the growing importance of these disciplines at Oxford and elsewhere, and was concerned to explore the implications of the concept of 'nature' which lay behind them.

Foster's interest in the concept of creation was stimulated by his reading of R. G. Collingwood's classic work *The Idea of Nature*, which suggested that the ancient Greek conception of nature was that of an organism, the growth and development of which was determined by the 'nature' of that object. In two important essays, dating from the last twelve months of his life, Foster attempted to set out the main themes to distinguish the Christian and Greek views of nature, and identify their importance for the natural scientist.[7]

---

[6] David Novak, *Natural Law in Judaism*. Cambridge: Cambridge University Press, 1998, 144–5.

[7] Michael Foster, 'Man's Idea of Nature', *The Christian Scholar* 41 (1958), 361–6; idem, 'Greek and Christian Ideas of Nature', *The Free University Quarterly* 6 (1959), 122–7.

Foster located the most fundamental distinction between the Greek and Christian conceptions of nature as lying in the concept of creation. To assert that the world is created is to make a series of significant statements concerning nature:[8]

> Nature, on the Greek view, includes everything. It includes men and gods (men and gods are fellow-citizens of the universe, says Cicero, reproducing a Stoic view; men and gods spring from a common origin, said Hesiod) . . . Science of nature is a contemplative study; it proceeds from sensuous contemplation of the appearances of divinity to intellectual contemplation of the divine in itself . . .

> On the Christian conception, on the other hand, nature is made by God, but *is not* God. There is an abrupt break between nature and God. Divine worship is to be paid to God alone, who is *wholly other than nature*. Nature is not divine.

Foster was no Barthian, but it is impossible to miss the affinities with Karl Barth's insistence that God is 'wholly other', to be radically distinguished from nature and from culture. One can surely hear echoes of what Kierkegaard called the 'infinite qualitative distinction' between time and eternity in Foster's statements at this point.

Given this view of nature, Foster argues that 'we can never say *a priori* how God must act, and therefore can never say *a priori* how his creations must behave'.[9] The natural sciences and the Bible both see themselves as proceeding *a posteriori*, whereas Greek science tended to adopt an *a priori* approach to knowledge, based on the assumption that there was some fundamental kinship between humanity and divinity. Interestingly, Foster chooses to stress a number of biblical texts which stress the hiddenness of God: 'Thou art a God that hidest thyself' (Isaiah 45:15); 'His ways are past finding out' (Romans 11:33); and 'His thoughts are not our thoughts' (Isaiah 55:7). All these verses – apparently cited from memory, and hence slightly inaccurately – stress the *otherness* of the divine and the inability of the natural order to disclose the divine to humanity.[10]

In an earlier series of articles written over the period 1934–6, Foster set out some themes of a Christian understanding of nature which he believed to be of some importance, both to the historical question of

---

[8] Foster, 'Greek and Christian Ideas of Nature', 123–4. Emphasis in original.

[9] Foster, 'Greek and Christian Ideas of Nature', 125.

[10] Foster appears to have spent the academic year 1927–8 studying at Dresden, and it is possible that he may have encountered Barthian ideas at that point.

the evolution of the natural sciences in the west, and to the more general question of the relation of Christian theology and the natural sciences.[11] The essays are remarkable in many respects, chiefly in that they do not appear to have been occasioned by any specific controversy at the time. The articles appeared in the journal *Mind*, which had not given any consideration to this issue prior to the appearance of Foster's articles. In the articles, Foster set out his understanding of how a Christian doctrine of creation impacted upon the sciences. While Foster's approach has been critiqued in several important respects, it remains an important discussion of the theme.[12]

Foster argued that a Christian doctrine of creation made possible a specific outlook to nature which encouraged the rise of the natural sciences. The doctrine of creation *ex nihilo* allowed the scientist to approach nature with the expectation that the divine rationality would be reflected in its structures and workings:[13]

> Hence are derived two assumptions which will easily be recognized to be fundamental assumptions of modern scientific method: the first the assumption that the scientist has to look nowhere beyond the world of material nature itself in order to find the proper objects of his science; the second (which is really a corollary of the first) that the intelligible laws which he discovers there admit of no exception. Both are consequences of the doctrine that the material world is the work, not of a Demiurge, but of an omnipotent creator. It is because a Demiurge has to work in an alien material that he never wholly realizes in it the idea which his reason conceives, so that the observer of the product, the object of whose search is to discover the idea of the producer, can never discover in the material product the object of his search . . . But a divine Creator who is not limited by a recalcitrant material can embody his ideas in nature with the same perfection in which they are present to his intellect.

Important though Foster's arguments may be, he seems to have failed to develop them as effectively as he might. For example, one might ask the following question: is not such an approach characteristic of any religious world-view which affirmed the created character of the natural order? Might not a Jewish writer adopt a similar perspective to Foster's

---

[11] Michael B. Foster, 'The Christian doctrine of Creation and the Rise of Modern Science', *Mind* 43 (1934), 446–68; idem, 'Christian Theology and Modern Science of Nature (I)', *Mind* 44 (1935), 439–66; idem, 'Christian Theology and Modern Science of Nature (II)', *Mind* 45 (1936), 1–27.

[12] See Rolf Gruner, 'Science, Nature and Christianity', *Journal of Theological Studies* 26 (1975), 55–81.

[13] Foster, 'Christian Theology and Modern Science of Nature (II)', 14–15.

Christian model? This point, it will be clear, is of importance to the present study, which is concerned to respect the integrity and distinctiveness of religious traditions.

In fact, this question may be answered – and answered in the negative. In a highly important recent study of the theology of nature in Jewish philosophy of the late Renaissance, Hava Tirosh-Samuelson stresses that Judaism did not interpret its doctrines of creation as necessitating any such conclusions.[14] While Jewish writers of the fifteenth century were clear that God, in creating the natural order, had 'impressed' laws into the creation – laws which had their origin and character in the uncreated realm of the Godhead itself:[15]

> Unlike Protestant theologians, who highlighted the absolute power of God in their insistence on the total dependence of humans on God's salvation, and mechanist philosophers, who held, against Aristotle, that nature is not a being capable of any power and purpose apart from the hands of God, Jewish thinkers continued to attribute intrinsic powers and purpose to the world, as Aristotle had done, anthropomorphize nature (e.g. when they called nature 'wise'), and allow for material processes to take place on their own without a direct intervention from God.

As Tirosh-Samuelson, points out, this means that Jewish theologians of the sixteenth century were still committed to an 'organismic and intellectualistic conception of the universe, based on the correspondence of Torah, nature, and Israel' which prevented them from interpreting the doctrine of creation in the manner which Foster discerns as being essential to the scientific study of nature.

Foster's arguments are clearly of great interest, and indicate the potential importance of seeing nature as God's creation. The remainder of the present section is therefore devoted to a discussion of the grounds and character of a Christian doctrine of creation, before moving on to explore the implications of this doctrine for a scientific theology (Ch. 5).

The biblical concept of creation

The theme of 'God as creator' is of major importance within the Old Testament.[16] While attention has often focused on the opening two

[14] Hava Tirosh-Samuelson, 'Theology of Nature in Sixteenth-Century Italian Jewish Philosophy', *Science in Context* 10 (1997), 529–70.

[15] Tirosh-Samuelson, 'Theology of Nature in Sixteenth-Century Italian Jewish Philosophy', 549.

[16] See, for example, R. J. Clifford, 'The Hebrew Scriptures and the Theology of Creation', *Theological Studies* 46 (1985), 507–23; I. J. Stadelmann Luis, *The Hebrew Conception of the World: A Philological and Literary Study*. Rome: Pontifical Biblical Institute, 1970.

chapters of the book of Genesis as somehow providing a definitive statement of the Old Testament understanding of creation, it is important to appreciate that the creation motif is deeply embedded in the wisdom and prophetic literature, and is not confined to any one genre of biblical writing, or to any specific location in the canon.

The Old Testament deploys a rich range of Hebrew verbs to convey the notion of creation, each associated with a lexical and semantic field which makes precise translation a hazardous business. One cannot conceivably base one's understanding of the Old Testament concept of creation simply on the basis of an analysis of one such verb – *bārā'* being an especial favourite for some. The following, along with what are generally accepted as the best English translations, may be noted:[17]

'āsá	make
bārā'	create
yāsar	form
yāsad	establish
qānâ	create
kûn	found
pā'al	make

It will be clear that a number of ideas are brought together through this assemblage of terms, including both the notion of 'bringing into being', 'the imposition of form', and 'the assembly of a structure'. Each of these has quite different resonances and nuances, and must serve to remind us that it is simply not acceptable to treat the Old Testament idea of creation simply as concerning origination – the themes of 'ordering' and 'assembly' are embraced within this all-important notion.

Yet before setting out the concepts of creation found in the Old Testament, it is important to establish a fundamental point of interpretation. For Christians, the Old Testament is to be read in the light of the New Testament, and especially in the light of Christ. Scripture centres on and enfolds Christ, who can be known definitively only through its medium. Karl Barth is but one of the great theologians of the Christian tradition to affirm this point:[18]

> When Holy Scripture speaks of God, it does not permit us to let our attention or thoughts wander at random ... When Holy Scripture

---

[17] For a detailed study, see Andreas Angerstorfer, *Der Schöpfergott des Alten Testaments: Herkunft und Bedeutungsentwicklung des hebraischen Terminus bara, 'schaffen'.* Frankfurt am Main: Peter Lang, 1979.

[18] Karl Barth, *Church Dogmatics* II/2, 52–4.

speaks of God, it concentrates our attention and thoughts upon one single point and what is to be known at that point . . . If we ask further concerning the one point upon which, according to Scripture, our attention and thoughts should and must be concentrated, then from first to last the Bible directs us to the name of Jesus Christ.

Scripture, when rightly interpreted, leads to Christ; Christ can be known properly only through Scripture. As Luther put it, Christ is 'the mathematical point of Holy Scripture',[19] just as Scripture 'is the swaddling clothes and manger in which Christ is laid'.[20] John Calvin made a similar point: 'This is what we should seek . . . throughout the whole of Scripture: to know Jesus Christ truly, and the infinite riches which are included in him and are offered to us by God the Father.'[21]

Considerations such as this raise a question of considerable importance. Emil Brunner raises this in a very focused form – namely, whether Genesis 1–2 is the foundational statement of a Christian doctrine of creation:[22]

> The uniqueness of this Christian doctrine of Creation and the Creator is continually being obscured by the fact that theologians are so reluctant to begin their work with the New Testament; when they want to deal with the Creation, they tend to begin with the Old Testament, although they never do this when they are speaking of the Redeemer. The emphasis on the story of Creation at the beginning of the Bible has constantly led theologians to forsake the rule which they would otherwise follow, namely, that the basis of *all* Christian articles of faith is the Incarnate Word, Jesus Christ. So when we begin to study the subject of Creation in the Bible we ought to start with the first chapter of the Gospel of John, and some other passages of the *New* Testament, and not with the first chapter of Genesis.

[19] *D. M. Martin Luthers Werke. Kritische Gesamtausgabe: Tischreden*, vol. 2. Weimar: Böhlau, 1883– , 439.

[20] *D. M. Martin Luthers Werke. Kritische Gesamtausgabe: Deutsche Bibel*, vol. 8. Weimar: Böhlau, 1883– , 12.

[21] *Ioannis Calvini opera quae supersunt omnia*, 59 vols. Brunschweig and Berlin: Schwetschke, 1863–1900, vol. 9, 815. There are some thoughtful explorations of related themes to be found in John D. Morrison, 'John Calvin's Christological Assertion of Word Authority in the Context of Sixteenth Century Ecclesiological Polemics', *Scottish Journal of Theology* 45 (1993), 465–86. For the Christocentric orientation of the Reformation doctrine of Scripture in general, see J. K. S. Reid, *The Authority of Scripture*. New York: Harper & Row, 1957, 29–72; Brian A. Gerrish, 'The Word of God and the Words of Scripture: Luther and Calvin on Biblical Authority', in *The Old Protestantism and the New*. Chicago: University of Chicago Press, 1982, 51–68.

[22] Emil Brunner, *The Christian Doctrine of Creation and Redemption*. London: Lutterworth Press, 1952, 6.

Brunner's argument is important, and must not be dismissed as a typical concern of the theological school which he represents. As we shall see, there are good reasons for suggesting that the Old Testament, read on its own terms rather than in the light of the New Testament, tends to affirm a doctrine of creation through the conquest of pre-existing chaotic forces or the ordering of pre-existent matter. The New Testament allows such accounts to be read in a different light.

We thus begin our discussion with a consideration of the various understandings of creation found in the Old Testament, before moving on to consider the New Testament witness to the issue.

The Genesis accounts

The two creation accounts of the book of Genesis are perhaps the most famous of the texts traditionally brought into play in discussions of the doctrine of creation. Doubtless the canonical ordering of the Old Testament encouraged this development, in that it placed Genesis as the first biblical work to be encountered by the reader of the Bible. This has led to what must be regarded as a less than adequately justified practice in explorations of the doctrine of creation – the assumption that these specific texts somehow articulate all that needs to be said on the matter, or that they are in some sense 'privileged' on account of their specific location within the canon of Scripture.

The first creation account takes the form of a prologue, followed by two major sections. After an opening statement depicting the chaotic nature before the act of creation (Genesis 1:1–2),[23] a first section sets out a series of four creative word-deeds or speech-acts, set over a period of three days (vv. 3–13). This is followed by a second section, again consisting of four word-deeds, set over three days. The chaotic waste or void (*tōhû wābōhû*) constitutes the background to the divine creative activity. It is characterized as a potentially uncontrollable chaos, mingling primal uncreated darkness and a watery depth. The use of the images of 'darkness' and 'water' are widely thought to be indicative of the forces of chaos, which other biblical passages depict God as conquering.

The literary style of the passage is of considerable importance, and merits careful study in its own right.[24] Our concern, however, is to

[23] On which, see David T. Tsumura, *The Earth and the Waters in Genesis 1 and 2: A Linguistic Investigation.* Sheffield: Sheffield Academic Press, 1989.

[24] Bernhard W. Anderson, 'A Stylistic Study of the Priestly Creation Story', in George W. Coats and Burke O. Long (eds), *Canon and Authority: Essays in Old Testament Religion and Theology.* Philadelphia: Fortress Press, 1977, 148–62; Walther Eichrodt, 'In the Beginning:

identify some theological motifs of importance for our theme. The first such theme is as elementary as it is critical – *the created order is not divine*. The creation is carefully distinguished from God; at no point is there any suggestion that the creation is an extension of God, or that it represents the refashioning of part of the divine substance. The creation is ontologically distinct from God. It is especially important to note that the sun and moon – the greater and lesser lights in the firmament – are firmly identified as having been created by God (Genesis 1:16). Where some worshipped the sun and moon as divine, Israel would see them as created by – and hence subordinate to – God as their creator.

The prophetic tradition

The theme of creation is of considerable importance to the prophetic tradition. The fact that the covenant God of Israel is the creator of the entire world is used at a number of points to undergird the universal authority of God over the nations and empires around Israel,[25] especially at points at which Israel's continuing existence seems under threat or in doubt. The theme appears, for example, at Isaiah 40, which affirms that Israel – though in exile in Babylon – has not been forgotten by the Lord.[26] In that the Lord is creator, he is sovereign over the nations and their destinies, and can be relied upon to redeem Jerusalem from her bondage (Isaiah 40:25–31):

> 'To whom will you compare me? Or who is my equal?' says the Holy One. 'Lift your eyes and look to the heavens: Who created all these? He who brings out the starry host one by one, and calls them each by name. Because of his great power and mighty strength, not one of them is missing. Why do you say, O Jacob, and complain, O Israel, "My way is hidden from the LORD; my cause is disregarded by my God"? Do you not know? Have you not heard? The LORD is the everlasting God, the Creator of the

---

A Contribution to the Interpretation of the First Word of the Bible', in Bernhard W. Anderson and Walter Harrelson (eds), *Israel's Prophetic Heritage*. London: SCM Press, 1962, 1–10.

[25] See the important discussion of the role of the doctrine in Amos by Gerhard Pfeiffer, 'Jahwe als Schöpfer der Welt und Herr ihrer Mächte in der Verkündigung des Propheten Amos', *Vetus Testamentum* 41 (1991), 475–81.

[26] I use this construction in preference to 'YHWH' to render the covenant name of God. The tetragrammaton is a proper noun which occurs 6,823 times in the Old Testament, and is never used generically to refer to a deity, but is used specifically and personally to refer to the covenant God of Israel. See G. H. Parke-Taylor, *The Divine Name in the Bible*. Waterloo, ON: Wilfrid Laurier University Press, 1975.

ends of the earth. He will not grow tired or weary, and his
understanding no one can fathom. He gives strength to the weary
and increases the power of the weak. Even youths grow tired and
weary, and young men stumble and fall; but those who hope in
the LORD will renew their strength. They will soar on wings like
eagles; they will run and not grow weary, they will walk and not
be faint.'

One theme which emerges as being of especial importance in the
prophetic tradition is the theme of 'creation as ordering', especially the
notion of an order resulting from the divine victory over chaotic forces
of disorder.[27] The world is to be regarded as ordered on account of the
divine act of creation; indeed, the emphasis within many biblical
passages dealing with the theme of creation can be argued to be more
concerned with 'the imposition of order' than 'bringing into being'.[28]
While this theme can be discerned at points outside the prophetic
tradition, it appears to play an especially important role within it.

Two major paradigms for the divine mastering of chaos can be
discerned.[29] First, chaos is depicted as an essentially inert yet formless
mass, which requires to be shaped. Order is thus imposed through the
creation of a specific structure. It is possible to argue that this theme
can be discerned throughout the first Genesis creation account, where
the images of 'darkness' and 'water' can be taken as relating to chaos,
which is subsequently ordered through the divine creative action.
However, its most familiar form is encountered in the image of God as
the potter, moulding formless clay into an ordered structure (Isaiah
29:16; Jeremiah 18:1–6). This image stresses both the ordering of the
clay, and the authority of the creator over the ensuing creation –
'creation' here being understood as matter which has now assumed a
definite form as a result of purposeful action.

The second paradigm depicts chaos as personal forces. Chaos is here
personified as a dragon or monster variously named 'Behemoth',

---

[27] John Day, *God's Conflict with the Dragon: Echoes of a Canaanite Myth in the Old
Testament.* Cambridge: Cambridge University Press, 1985; Susan Niditch, *Chaos to Cosmos:
Studies in Biblical Patterns of Creation.* Chico, CA: Scholars Press, 1985.

[28] D. A. Knight, 'Cosmogony and Order in the Hebrew Tradition', in R. W. Lovin and
F. E. Reynolds (eds), *Cosmology and Ethical Order: New Studies in Comparative Ethics.*
Chicago: University of Chicago Press, 1985, 133–57; P. D. Millar, 'Cosmology and World
Order in the Old Testament: The Divine Council as Cosmic-Political Symbol', *Horizons in
Biblical Theology* 9 (1987), 53–78.

[29] I here follow Jon D. Levenson, *Creation and the Persistence of Evil: The Jewish Drama
of Divine Omnipotence.* Princeton, NJ: Princeton University Press, 1994.

'Leviathan', 'Nahar', 'Rahab', 'Tannim' or 'Yam' who must be subdued. These themes are found within the wisdom literature (see Job 3:8; 7:12; 9:13; 40:15–32; Psalm 74:13–15; 139:10–11), but are found used to particular effect within the prophetic corpus (see, for example, Isaiah 27:1; 51:9–10; Ezekiel 29:3–5; 32:2–8; Habakkuk 3:8–15; Zechariah 10:11).[30] It is clear that there are parallels between the Old Testament account of God engaging with the forces of chaos and Ugaritic and Canaanite mythology. Nevertheless, there are highly significant differences, not least in the Old Testament's insistence that the forces of chaos are not to be seen as divine. Creation is not to be understood in terms of different gods warring against each other for mastery of a (future) universe, but in terms of God's mastery of chaos and ordering of the world. These chaotic forces are understood to be independent of God, and to exist prior to God's act of creation. The act of creation is then understood as the subjugation of chaos and the imposition of order, rather than a bringing of all things – including these chaotic entities – into being.

The creation-theme – generally expressed as the ordering of chaos – plays an especially important role in Isaiah 40–55 (Deutero-Isaiah).[31] An appeal is often made to the Lord as creator to exercise that same divine power in the protection of Israel (Isaiah 51:9–10):[32]

> Awake, awake! Clothe yourself with strength, O arm of the LORD; awake, as in days gone by, as in generations of old. Was it not you who cut Rahab to pieces, who pierced that monster through? Was it not you who dried up the sea, the waters of the great deep, who made a road in the depths of the sea so that the redeemed might cross over?

While the general thrust of all the Old Testament passages to deal with the divine defeat of chaos in creation assumes that chaotic forces exist prior to the act of creation, it is important to note that one text appears to state that chaos is itself created by God (Isaiah 45:7):

---

[30] See the references within Rainer Albertz, *Weltschöpfung und Menschenschöpfung: Untersucht bei Deuterojesaja, Hiob und in den Psalmen.* Stuttgart: Calwer, 1974.

[31] P. B. Harner, 'Creation Faith in Deutero-Isaiah', *Vetus Testamentum* 17 (1967), 298–306; T. M. Ludwig, 'The Traditions of Establishing of the Earth in Deutero-Isaiah', *Journal of Biblical Literature* 92 (1973), 345–57; B. C. Ollenburger, 'Isaiah's Creation Theology', *Ex Auditu* 3 (1987), 54–71; Rolf Rendtorff, 'Die theologische Stellung des Schöpfungsglaubens bei Deuterjesaja', *Zeitschrift für Theologie und Kirche* 51 (1954), 2–13.

[32] Rolf Rendtorff, '"Where Were You when I laid the Foundations of the Earth?" Creation and Salvation History', in *Canon and Theology: Overtures to an Old Testament Theology.* Minneapolis, MN: Fortress Press, 1993, 92–113.

I form the light and create darkness (*hōsek*), I bring prosperity and create disaster; I, the LORD, do all these things.

Some scholars suggest that this verse is to be read as a deliberate quali-fier, modifying other texts which could be read in such a way as to suggest that chaos existed prior to creation.[33] For example, Genesis 1 presupposes that the darkness – an image of chaos – existed prior to creation; Isaiah 45:7 suggests that this darkness is itself brought into being by God. One of the difficulties faced by this viewpoint is that the text is embedded in a context which is saturated with the notion that the Lord creates by defeating or ordering an already existent chaotic entity (e.g. see Isaiah 42:15–16; 43:16–21; 51:9–10). Assuming the literary unity of this section of Isaiah, the only conclusion that may reasonably be drawn is that the prophet is critiquing himself, as much as anyone else.

The most satisfactory solution to this difficulty is to challenge the assumption that 'darkness' is here to be understood as a metaphor of chaos, and to see it specifically as referring to an aspect of the created order. The verse identifies two pairs of antithetically formulated aspects of creation: light and darkness; prosperity and disaster. The entire spectrum of created entities and possibilities are thus affirmed to lie within God's scope and authority as creator. A similar structure can be discerned elsewhere in the Old Testament – for example, Psalm 74:16–17:

> The day is yours, and yours also the night;
> you established the sun and moon;
> it was you who set all the boundaries of the earth;
> you made both summer and winter.

Here, we find three sets of contrasted pairs: day and night; things in the heavens and things on earth; summer and winter. The simple point being made is that the extremities of the creation, and all that these embrace, are the work and are under the authority of God.

The major theme to emerge from the prophetic creation tradition is that of *ordering*. Creation represents the imposition of order upon formless matter, or the defeat of forces of disorder. It is certainly true that this *Chaoskampf* reflects beliefs which were once current in Ugarit and Mesopotamia; nevertheless, the prophetic tradition places a

---

[33] For the debate, see Michael Deroche, 'Isaiah 45:7 and the Creation of Chaos', *Vetus Testamentum* 42 (1992), 11–21.

distinctive stamp upon these ideas.[34] No longer is creation the result of a war between gods; it represents the free decision of a covenant God to create an ordered world – and that theologically grounded order is to be expressed politically, socially and legally.[35]

The wisdom literature

If any genre of Old Testament writing places a premium upon the theology of creation, it is the wisdom literature.[36] God did not merely create the world; it was created 'in wisdom' (Proverbs 3:19) – and traces of that wisdom can be discerned by the humble. Wisdom is portrayed as searching for regularity within the world, and appears to make no real distinction between the human, the socio-historical and the natural realms. The fundamental belief which undergirds the wisdom literature is that certain patterns may be discerned by the wise within the vast ambit of life, and that such discernment is profitable for human education and reflection.[37]

While the book of Ecclesiastes includes much reflection on the nature of creation,[38] the more important discussions of the theme are to be found in Job and the Psalms.[39] A number of passages may be singled out for special comment. The Psalter is especially rich in material relating to the doctrine of creation. Psalm 19:1 asserts that 'the heavens declare the glory of God', clearly implying that Israel should be able to discern the divine glory through the study of the created order. Many Psalms make reference to the act of creation itself, often portraying this

[34] See the important study of H. H. Schmid, 'Jahweglaube und altorientalisches Weltordnungsgedanken', in *Altorientalische Welt in der alttestamentlichen Theologie*. Zurich: Theologischer Verlag, 1974, 31–63.

[35] See Fritz Stolz, *Strukturen und Figuren im Kult von Jerusalem: Studien zur altorientalischen, vor- und frühisraelitischen Religion*. Berlin: de Gruyter, 1970, 12–101 for a full analysis.

[36] This is true of the genre beyond the Old Testament: see H. Brunner, 'Die Weisheitsliteratur', in Bertold Spuler (ed.), *Handbuch der Orientalistik*. Leiden: E. J. Brill, 1952, 90–110, especially 93, which stresses that 'primal order' is of central important to the ancient wisdom corpus. More generally, see Hans Heinrich Schmid, *Gerechtigkeit als Weltordnung: Hintergrund und Geschichte des alttestamentlichen Gerechtigkeitsbegriffs*. Tübingen: Mohr, 1968, 24–46.

[37] See here John Day, *Wisdom in Ancient Israel: Essays in Honour of J. A. Emerton*. Cambridge: Cambridge University Press, 1995; Gerhard von Rad, *Wisdom in Israel*. Nashville, TN: Abingdon Press, 1972; Franz-Josef Steiert, *Die Weisheit Israels – ein Fremdkörper im Alten Testament? Eine Untersuchung zum Buch der Sprüche auf dem Hintergrund der ägyptischen Weisheitslehren*. Freiburg im Breisgau: Herder, 1990.

[38] Mathias Schubert, *Schöpfungstheologie bei Kohelet*. Frankfurt am Main: Peter Lang, 1989.

[39] See Albertz, *Weltschöpfung und Menschenschöpfung*.

as the triumphant outcome of a conflict with the forces of chaos. Psalm 89:9–14 declares that the same Lord who destroyed the forces of chaos in the act of creation is still able to deal with those same forces. The divine conquering of the primal chaotic flood is not to be seen simply as a past event. Psalm 104:1–30 sets out a comprehensive survey of the created order, and the way in which the entire universe is dependent upon the wisdom and watchfulness of God. The doxological importance of the Psalter should be noted in this context: the Psalms often articulate the praise of Israel to the Lord, as the one who created the world, redeemed Israel from Egypt, and continues to care for Israel providentially.[40] The frequent affirmation that 'the Lord is king' can be seen as a statement of the Lord's continuing authority over the forces of the world (Psalm 93:1–5).[41] Kingship itself was seen as a powerful stabilizing force, promoting social and political order in a potentially chaotic world. The divine ordering of the creation sets boundaries for all the forces contained within its bounds. Creation thus can be understood to involve a conflict between the creator and something which is older than the creation – where 'creation' is understood as 'the establishment of order'. Human kings are often understood as divine surrogates in texts from the ancient near east, including a substantial number of biblical texts, in that at the political and social level the defeat of disorder and chaos is seen as an extension of the divine creation. This also allows us to understand why creation is not understood by biblical writers as a complete act in the past, but as a continuing process, embracing what some would now term a doctrine of providence. Ordering is both a past event and a present necessity.

The divine speeches in the book of Job (Job 38–41) are often regarded as being a particularly important statement of a wisdom theology.[42] God is both creator (Job 38:22 – 39:12) and sustainer of the world (Job 39:13–30). The diversity of the created order is rehearsed, and the authority of God over its various elements reasserted – for example,

---

[40] Norbert Lohfink, 'God the Creator and the Stability of Heaven and Earth: The Old Testament on the Connection between Creation and Salvation', in *Theology of the Pentateuch*. Edinburgh: T&T Clark, 1994, 116–35.

[41] See here the important study of Jörg Jeremias, *Das Königtum Gottes in den Psalmen: Israels Begegnung mit dem kanaanäischen Mythos in den Jahwe-König-Psalmen*. Göttingen: Vandenhoeck & Ruprecht, 1987, which stresses the importance of the kingship-motif in both constructive and polemical contexts.

[42] Gerhard von Rad, 'Job 38 and Ancient Egyptian Wisdom', in *The Problem of the Hexateuch and Other Essays*. Edinburgh: Oliver & Boyd, 1966, 281–91; Scott L. Harris, 'Wisdom or Creation? A New Interpretation of Job 38:27', *Vetus Testamentum* 33 (1983), 419–27.

limits have been set to the sea (Job 38:8–11). The world has been ordered, and chaos has been at least brought under control, if not totally excluded. The world is therefore ordered, and this ordering may be discerned by enlightened human beings, leading to the praise and adoration of its creator. Job may not be able to understand every aspect of the created order – but he is clearly expected to accept that, despite the apparent disordering at points, God is indeed present and active in the midst of things.

The doctrine of creation thus undergirds much of the wisdom literature. Whereas the historical works place an emphasis upon the covenant established between the Lord and Israel – in effect making this the arbiter of belief and conduct – the wisdom literature makes little reference to this theme, preferring instead to affirm that the Lord created the world in wisdom, and that the wholesome ordering of the world could be identified, summarized and attributed. Human wisdom is able to discern the wisdom of the creator in the creation.

How important is the theme of creation in the Old Testament?

In a major essay, originally published in 1936, Gerhard von Rad argued that the most characteristic insight of the Old Testament was that the Lord was sovereign over history, especially the history of Israel.[43] In the Old Testament, faith in the Lord is not *Schöpfungsglaube* but *Heilsglaube* – faith in a God who acts within, and is sovereign over, cosmic human history. While von Rad is careful to stress that the faith of Israel included reference to creation, the primary emphasis lay on the Lord bringing Israel out of Egypt and into Canaan. The doctrine of creation takes its place as a secondary, ancillary doctrine, providing a certain context for the affirmation of the divine lordship over history. Although the Hexateuch opens with statements concerning the creative activity and authority of the Lord, von Rad argues that the essential theological message of these historical books is summarized in a confessional recital found in Deuteronomy 26:5–9:

> My father was a wandering Aramean, and he went down into Egypt with a few people and lived there and became a great nation, powerful and numerous. But the Egyptians mistreated us and made us suffer, putting us to hard labour. Then we cried out to the

---

[43] Gerhard von Rad, 'Das theologische Problem des alttestamentlichen Schöpfungs-glaubens', in *Gesammelte Studien zum Alten Testament*. Munich: Kaiser Verlag, 1958, vol. 1, 136–47.

LORD, the God of our fathers, and the LORD heard our voice and saw our misery, toil and oppression. So the LORD brought us out of Egypt with a mighty hand and an outstretched arm, with great terror and with miraculous signs and wonders. He brought us to this place and gave us this land, a land flowing with milk and honey.

The affirmation of the creative action and authority of the Lord is seen as setting the context for this redemptive activity. Yet creation here functions as a subsidiary and secondary teaching, lending context to the more fundamental belief that the Lord brought Israel out of Egypt. Creation is seen as an aspect of the *Vorbau* to this event, just as the patriarchal narratives act as an *Ausbau* and the Sinai narratives as an *Einbau*. The Lord's rule over the creation is always affirmed, yet as an aspect of the divine rule over history in particular. As Ludwig Köhler has argued, 'creation in the Old Testament is not a statement about the natural sciences, but about human history'. The creation story is therefore not an answer to the question: 'How did the world come into existence?' Rather, it deals with the question: 'From what does the history of the people of God derive its meaning?' – to which the answer is 'from the creation'.[44] This understanding of the theological role of the doctrine of creation within the Old Testament has been very influential. In general terms, Old Testament scholarship has tended to regard the doctrine of creation as being theologically secondary and chronologically late.

It is possible to argue that polemical considerations may underlie both the lack of emphasis on the doctrine of creation within the Old Testament, and also the particular animus with which von Rad pointed this out. In the latter case, it may be noted that specific theological anxieties concerning an excessive emphasis upon the doctrine of creation had been expressed by Karl Barth in 1934, following the political triumph of National Socialism in Germany.[45] Von Rad's essay was originally delivered as a lecture at a conference in Göttingen in 1935, when concern about the theological role of the doctrine of creation was widespread. An appeal to the doctrine of creation was seen as laden with risk, not

---

[44] Ludwig Köhler, *Theologie des Alten Testaments.* 3rd edn. Tübingen: Mohr, 1953, 71: 'Die Schöpfung ist . . . nicht eine naturwissenschaftliche, sondern eine menschheits-geschichtliche Aussage.'

[45] See Karl Barth and Emil Brunner, *Natural Theology.* London: SCM Press, 1947; Joan O'Donovan, 'Man in the Image of God: The Disagreement between Barth and Brunner Reconsidered', *Scottish Journal of Theology* 39 (1986), 433–59.

least the possibility that the 'orders of creation' – including the German state – might be taken as legitimating certain unacceptable theological conclusions.

However, it is the Old Testament context itself which is of greater significance. It is clear that one of the most fundamental motivations governing the beliefs and conduct of ancient Israel around the time of the conquest was the desire to separate and distinguish itself from the religious beliefs and practices of the Canaanites. While much remains to be learned concerning Canaanite religion, it is clear that its emphasis upon *El* as the creator God, responsible for the fertility of the earth, would have caused Israel some difficulties in relation to attaching any decisive importance to the doctrine of creation.[46] Thus when Hosea or the Deuteronomic historian engage in controversy with Canaanite religion over, for example, the fertility of the land, the debate is conducted not in terms of an appeal to the Lord as creator (and hence as the one who safeguards the fertility of the land), but through an appeal to the Lord as redeemer, who led Israel into this land – and is therefore also the one who will ensure the land's fruitfulness (Deuteronomy 8:7–9; Hosea 2:8–9). Israel's distinctiveness was better affirmed through rehearsing the acts in history by which Israel was guided and formed, rather than by appealing to concepts – such as the divine creatorship – which were shared with neighbouring nations, and could hence become the basis of syncretism. Just as Israel's language about her deity was designed to prevent confusion with rival claimants to this title from the nations around her, so her emphasis upon *Heilsglaube* rather than *Schöpfungsglaube* was equally intended to preserve and maintain the religious distinctiveness of Israel.[47]

It should also be pointed out that the title 'the Lord, creator of heaven and earth' is an extremely old title for the God of Israel, possibly conflating two older titles – 'Lord of heaven' and 'creator of earth'.[48] The early history of the title may be considered to reflect Israel's insistence that it was her God – not those of Canaan and other nations

---

[46] G. W. Ahlstrom, *Aspects of Syncretism in Israelite Religion.* Lund: C. W. K. Gleerup, 1963; Robert du Mesnil du Buisson, *Nouvelles études sur les dieux et les mythes de Canaan.* Leiden: E. J. Brill, 1973.

[47] It is therefore of particular interest to note that one of the relatively few Old Testament texts which gives emphasis to creation is Jonah 1:9, in which Jonah cries 'I am a Hebrew and I worship the Lord, the God of heaven, who made the sea and the land'. This statement is made in the presence of Gentiles, who presumably would know nothing of Israel's distinctive history, but were open to a more general description of her God.

[48] Norman C. Habel, ' "Yahweh, Maker of Heaven and Earth": A Study in Tradition Criticism', *Journal of Biblical Literature* 91 (1972), 321–37.

– who created heaven and earth. If this is the case, the term is partly polemical in nature. It is thought that the prototype of the formula may lie in Genesis 14:19. Later developments of the theme are to be found in liturgical contexts, such as those offered by Psalm 115:15; 121:2; 124:8; 134:3; and 146:5–6. In these later contexts, the emphasis appears to be more upon the rehearsal and celebration of the great acts of the Lord in history, rather than upon the notion of creation. However, in Deutero-Isaiah, we find the title being used in a polemical manner, to affirm the sovereignty and ultimate final triumph of the Lord over the gods of Babylon.

In a series of studies comparing the world-views of the ancient near east with that of Israel,[49] Hans Heinrich Schmid stresses the importance of an orderly world, and its correlation to a doctrine of creation. The political, social, legal and spiritual realms were all governed by the need for order, and the avoidance of chaos. The Old Testament bears witness to the distinctive nature and beliefs of Israel, especially in relation to the covenant between Israel and the Lord – yet those distinctive beliefs are set alongside a shared belief in a doctrine of creation, which Israel understood in a specific manner, consistent with its concept of the sovereignty of the Lord.

There can be little doubt that such a doctrine of creation was de-emphasized at points to avoid any threat of religious syncretism, especially in the Canaanite context. Yet at other points in Israel's history – particularly during the exilic period, when issues of global development became of critical importance – the doctrine of creation assumed a much higher profile. The doctrine was always there; the issue was what profile it would be given, in the light of the context to be addressed.

So what general conclusions may be drawn from this survey of the Old Testament on creation?

1. The Old Testament employs a rich diversity of terminology to discussion of the notion of creation, embracing the concepts of both origination and ordering. Creation is thus to be understood not merely in terms of the raw material out of which the world is composed, but as the order and coherence in which it is composed.

---

[49] See Schmid, *Gerechtigkeit als Weltordnung: Hintergrund und Geschichte des alttestamentlichen Gerechtigkeitsbegriffs*; idem, 'Jahweglaube und altorientalisches Weltordnungsgedanken'.

2. The Old Testament studiously avoids any suggestion that the world is made out of God, or that the created order can be considered divine. The created world may indeed point to its creator; it belongs, however, to a different level of existence.

3. The doctrine of creation is often used in a polemical, rather than constructive manner, in that it is used to erode and discredit claims to authority on the part of rival divinities, whether during the Canaanite period or the period of exile in Babylon.

4. The theme of ordering is of major importance to Old Testament conceptions of creation. The world is affirmed to be an ordered totality. By virtue of the fact that there is a creator, there is also a creation that is ordered to its creator, a world which exists as his creation and in no other way, so that by its very existence it points to God. Yet the Old Testament links God's work of creation with the work of redemption, set within a covenantal framework, and tends to place the emphasis upon God's saving, rather than creative, activities. In part, this reflects polemical considerations; yet it also points to the fundamental emphasis upon salvation which is so distinctive a feature of the Old Testament itself.

The New Testament

In Christian perspective, the Old Testament is to be interpreted in the light of the New, along the general lines of Augustine's maxim that 'the New Testament is hidden in the Old; the Old is made accessible by the New' (*in Vetere Novum latet et in Novo Vetus patet*). The New Testament is seen as offering a framework by which the Old Testament may be interpreted – for example, in terms of the fulfilment of prophecy in Christ. In the case of the doctrine of creation, the New Testament may be seen as offering two distinctive perspectives, which can be argued to lead to a significant disjuncture between Jewish and Christian doctrines of creation. In the first place, the New Testament recognizes a Christological dimension to the doctrine of creation; in the second, it points to a pattern of divine activity which is expressed in the doctrine of creation *ex nihilo*. We shall be considering both these perspectives later in this chapter.

The Christian understanding of the interpretation of the Old Testament is of particular importance in relation to the doctrine of creation, not least in that it demonstrates a significant divergence between Christian and Jewish understandings of the nature of creation. The distinguished British theologian Rowan Williams sets out the consensus within theological scholarship on the matter of creation as follows: 'The belief that God created the world out of nothing was unquestionably a *distinctive* Jewish and Christian view in the late antique world.'[50] This may be a widespread opinion, but it is nonetheless incorrect. Williams is correct in what he affirms concerning Christian views on creation, but not in his views on the Jewish approach to the matter. Awkward though it may be for some, the Jewish tradition on this matter was divided. *Creatio ex nihilo* was one such position; it was most emphatically not the only such option, nor even the dominant. The final commitment of the Jewish tradition to such a doctrine dates from as late as the fifteenth century. It is of no small importance, both historically and theologically, to avoid imposing the increasingly settled consensus of Christian theology upon the rather more fluid Jewish exegesis of this period.

As the history of Jewish exegesis of what Christians know as the Old Testament makes clear, the most compelling reading of the Old Testament affirmations concerning creation is not a doctrine of creation *ex nihilo*. At best, this is one option among many, with the dominant theme being that of creation as the divine subjugation of primeval chaotic forces, thereby imposing the order which is now to be discerned within the framework of the creation. The possible re-emergence of the forces is thus seen as a serious threat at several points. The order of the cosmos is a fragile matter, sustained only by the compassion and power of God.

Yet when the Old Testament is read in the light of the New, a different grid comes to be imposed upon its affirmations. The strongly Christological interpretative framework of the Christian tradition, grounded in the New Testament,[51] results in a *logocentric* conception of creation, which has considerable implications for a Christian understanding of both the basis of creation and the nature and characteristics of the ensuing created order. These issues will be addressed in some detail in the present chapter. At this stage, we wish to draw out some of the characteristics of the creation theme as expressed in the New Testament writings. The Christian reading of the Old Testament thus represents a not insignificant divergence from the Jewish consensus of the intellectual world of late classical antiquity.

---

[50] Rowan Williams, *On Christian Theology*. Oxford: Blackwell, 2000, 67.

[51] Luther's Christological exegesis of the Old Testament is a case in point; see Gerhard Ebeling, 'Die Anfänge der Luthers Hermeneutik', in *Lutherstudien I*. Tübingen: Mohr, 1971, 1–66.

At first sight, the New Testament does not appear to attach quite the same importance to the doctrine of creation as the Old. In their canonical forms, the Old Testament opens with an affirmation of the divine creation of the world; the New opens with the genealogy of Jesus Christ. Yet the matter is not quite as clear as might initially appear: if read in a certain manner, this genealogy can be argued to represent a careful and considered exposition of Christ as the fulfilment of God's creation.[52] The theme of creation, however, is more explicitly addressed in the prologue to John's gospel (John 1:1–18), which offers a striking verbal parallel to the opening verses of Genesis 1,[53] which it can be regarded as interpreting in a specifically Christological manner. The *Logos*, which existed before the work of creation, became flesh and sojourned within human history. The *Logos* by whom God created all things is affirmed to be uncreated, existing prior to the work of creation itself. Related thoughts can be found elsewhere in the New Testament, most notably at Philippians 2:6, Colossians 1:15 and Hebrews 1:3. Creation and redemption are affirmed to be the work of the same divine *Logos*, embodied in Christ.[54]

The Christian doctrine of the incarnation is, in part, a sustained reflection on the affirmation that 'the *Logos* became flesh (ὁ λόγος σὰρξ ἐγένετο)' (John 1:14). While it would be quite incorrect to suggest that this single verse has had a disproportionate influence over the Christian articulation of this theme, there can be no doubt that Christian theologians found in this specific verse a succinct and focused account of the New Testament witness to the identity and significance of Christ. The *Logos* through whom God created the world became incarnate in the historical figure of Jesus of Nazareth.

The theme of creation can be discerned as important at several other junctures, perhaps most importantly in the writings of Paul,[55] for whom the concept of a 'new creation' (2 Corinthians 5:17; Galatians 6:15) plays an especially important role. In affirming that, through faith, there is a 'new creation', Paul is clearly developing a correlation of creation and

[52] Charles Thomas Davis, 'Fulfilment of Creation: A Study of Matthew's Genealogy', *Journal of the American Academy of Religion* 41 (1973), 520–35.

[53] Mary Coloe, 'The Structure of the Johannine Prologue and Genesis 1', *Australian Biblical Review* 45 (1997), 40–55.

[54] Gerard Siegwalt, 'Der Prolog des Johannesevangeliums als Einführung in eine christliche Theologie der Rekapitulation', *Neue Zeitschrift für systematische Theologie und Religionsphilosophie* 24 (1981), 150–71.

[55] See the study of Edward Adams, *Constructing the World: A Study in Paul's Cosmological Language*. Edinburgh: T&T Clark, 2000.

redemption. Christ is thus to be seen as the ground and guarantor of continuity of salvation history within the Pauline corpus. As Nils Dahl points out:[56]

> The Christian correlation of salvation and creation is not merely derived from the eschatological idea that the end should be like the beginning; it has also antecedents in the applications of the creation-pattern to historic and actual experiences of God's dealing with men.

The Pauline motif of Christ as the Second Adam (e.g. Romans 5:14; 1 Corinthians 15:45–49) is of especial importance in both developing the connection between creation and redemption, and also consolidating the Christological substructure of both doctrines. Having affirmed that God 'calls into existence the things that do not exist' (Romans 4:17), Paul establishes a link between Christ and the entire span of the economy of salvation:[57]

> The Pauline parallel between Christ and Adam implies that God's design for Adam has been effectively realized in Christ. Adam was intended to be son of God; he was created in the image of God. Christ is God's son; he is the image of God; he is 'in the form of God'; he is truly Adam, which means that he is truly and completely human. The sonship to God which was fully realized in Christ belongs to the nature of all; it characterizes humanity as the Creator intends it to be.

Paul's statement (Philippians 2:6) that Christ was 'in the form of God (ἐν μορφῇ θεοῦ)' has attracted considerable attention from commentators, and is of no small importance to any discussion of the relation of Christology and the doctrine of creation. Might Paul be using the term μορφῇ in its technical Greek philosophical sense, meaning something like 'the essential nature and character of God'?[58]

The New Testament writings thus offer a critically important hermeneutical grid, which is to be laid over the Old Testament creation accounts. The New Testament – in a variety of manners – sets Christ in a place of ontological and epistemological priority in relation to the affirmation of the creation. Christ is declared to be both the agent

---

[56] Nils Dahl, 'Christ, Creation and the Church', in W. D. Davies and D. Daube (eds), *The Background of the New Testament and Its Eschatology.* Cambridge: Cambridge University Press, 1964, 422–43, 432.

[57] G. W. H. Lampe, *God as Spirit.* London, Oxford: Clarendon Press, 1977, 178.

[58] The suggestion of J. B. Lightfoot, *Saint Paul's Epistle to the Philippians.* London: Macmillan, 1881. For a full discussion of the possibilities, see Peter T. O'Brien, *Commentary on Philippians.* Grand Rapids, MI: Eerdmans, 1991, 205–16.

and final goal of the creation, and the ground and goal of the event and process of redemption. The New Testament does not present us with a worked-out theology of creation, but provides a series of statements concerning creation which require creation to be viewed in a Christologically focused and trinitarian manner.

The doctrine of creation also plays an important apologetic role within the New Testament, especially in the Areopagus address (Acts 17), to which we shall return in greater detail later (pp. 260–2).[59]

Our concern, however, is to note the way in which the New Testament develops the notion of creation through Christ, thus establishing a link between creation and Christology, which will be explored in greater detail presently. Our attention now focuses on the emergence of the doctrine of creation *ex nihilo*.

Creation *ex nihilo*: the development of a doctrine

Christianity expanded from its origins in Palestine to engage with the intellectual world of late classical antiquity. Within this world, a number of ideas had become firmly established as virtually self-evidently correct. Although a degree of diversity on the issue can be discerned, the Hellenistic world of the first few centuries of the Christian era was convinced that the universe was eternal. An especially important issue concerns the doctrine of the origin of the universe found in Plato's *Timaeus*, which was especially influential in shaping Christian thinking on the issue.[60] In this work, Plato is concerned to deal with a number of questions of perennial philosophical importance. What is the nature of the world? In what way did it come into being? And what may be known of its author or creator? Plato's answer is that the world which is perceptible to the senses is fundamentally an image (εἰκών) or likeness of an eternal pattern or model (παράδειγμα). Despite all the weaknesses of the human ability to perceive things, at least some knowledge of this eternal pattern is possible, on the basis of reasoned reflection on the visible order. For Plato, the world (κόσμος) has been fashioned from existing material by a Demiurge.[61] While the world was

[59] See Bertil Gartner, *The Areopagus Speech and Natural Revelation*. Uppsala: Gleerup, 1955.

[60] Michael Landmann, *Ursprüngsbild und Schöpfertat: zum platonisch-biblischen Gesprach*. Munich: Nymphenburger Verlagshandlung, 1966; Jaroslav Pelikan, *What has Athens to do with Jerusalem? Timaeus and Genesis in Counterpoint*. Ann Arbor, MI: University of Michigan Press, 1997.

[61] *Timaeus* 29d–30c.

created according to the requirements of reason and necessity, the Demiurge was nevertheless restricted by the material from which he was obliged to construct the world. Some interpreted this dialogue to teach that the world had been created – that is, brought into being – at a specific point in time; others that the ordered world might have a definite point of origin, but that the matter from which it was fashioned was eternal. By the second century, however, there was growing sympathy within Platonist circles for the doctrine of the eternity of the world.

The Christian doctrine of creation *ex nihilo* can be regarded as, in part, a reaction against the Greek teaching of the eternity of the world.[62] In part, the doctrine can also be seen as an attempt to retain a more biblical perspective on the issue of the origins of the world. However, there was still debate within early Christian circles over what that biblical teaching actually was. As we have seen, the general tenor of the Old Testament teaching is somewhat fluid on this issue. The texts do not strictly demand a doctrine of creation *ex nihilo*; Genesis 1:1–3, for example, does not speak of creation from nothing, in that the text speaks of 'the earth' being 'formless and empty', and that 'darkness was over the surface of the deep'. We can see here immediately some statements concerning entities – 'the earth', 'darkness' and 'the deep' – which appear to exist before the act of creation. The emphasis upon the earth being 'formless' strongly suggests that creation is to be understood primarily as 'ordering' in this context. Yet the text is perfectly capable of being interpreted in another sense – namely, that creation is to be understood as the calling into existence of the universe, and the imposition of order upon this new entity.

Some scholars have suggested that some such notion can be seen in Jewish theological texts dating from the Maccabean period, when Jewish thought was brought into contact with Hellenistic ideas. The critical text is 2 Maccabees 7:28, which the Vulgate renders into Latin as *ex nihilo fecit illa Deus*. However, the evidence for this suggestion is weak,[63] and Jewish thought of this period is still best thought of in terms of God working with existent matter. It is indeed debatable whether Judaism developed a doctrine of creation *ex nihilo* at this stage, or even later. Even in the Middle Ages, a number of Jewish doctrines of creation

[62] For the best study, see Gerhard May, *Creatio Ex Nihilo: The Doctrine of 'Creation out of Nothing' in Early Christian Thought*. Edinburgh: T&T Clark, 1995.

[63] Georg Shmuttermayr, '"Schöpfung aus dem Nichts" in 2. Makk. 7:28? Zum Verhältnis von Position und Bedeutung', *Biblische Zeitschrift* 17 (1973), 203–28.

can be discerned.[64] The final acceptance of the doctrine of creation as the distinctive Jewish position on this matter emerged only during the fifteenth century, when Isaac Abravanel declared it to be the only cardinal dogma of Judaism – exceeding in importance even belief in the existence of God.[65] It can be argued that the polyvalence of the Old Testament on this matter contributed in no small way to the Jewish exposition of it. It is also of interest to note that Jewish elements appear to have become incorporated into Gnostic texts,[66] with the result that the ensuing debate between Christian and Gnostic theologians over the doctrine of creation can be seen as a battle over the correct interpretation of the Old Testament and related sources.

The doctrine of creation was not an issue to which Christian theologians of the patristic era would have given much attention, had not controversy forced the issue upon them. In general terms, most early Christian writers – such as Theophilus of Antioch, Origen and Diodore of Tarsus – developed critiques of the classic Greek idea of the eternity of the world, without necessarily developing a focused alternative.[67] One of the chief functions of theological debate is to stimulate clarification of issues, and there is no doubt that the Gnostic controversy forced explication of the doctrine of creation in a more precise manner than some would have liked.

For Gnosticism, in most of its significant forms, a sharp distinction was to be drawn between the God who redeemed humanity from the world, and a somewhat inferior deity (often termed 'the demiurge') who created that world in the first place.[68] The existence of evil in the world was thus to be explained on the basis of the intractability of this pre-existent matter. God's options in creating the world were limited by the poor quality of the material available. The presence of evil or

---

[64] H. Simon, 'Weltschöpfung und Weltewigkeit in der jüdischen Tradition', *Kairos* 14 (1972), 22–35. On the general context, see Herbert Davidson, *Proofs for Eternity, Creation and the Existence of God in Medieval Islamic and Jewish Philosophy*. Oxford: Oxford University Press, 1987. The position of Maimonides is of especial interest: see Marvin Fox, *Interpreting Maimonides: Studies in Methodology, Metaphysics and Moral Philosophy*. Chicago: University of Chicago Press, 1990.

[65] See Menachem M. Kellner, *Dogma in Medieval Judaism from Maimonides to Abravanel*. Oxford: Oxford University Press for the Littmann Library of Jewish Civilization, 1986, 213–17.

[66] Francis T. Fallon, *The Enthronement of Sabaoth: Jewish Elements in Gnostic Creation Myths*. Leiden: E. J. Brill, 1978.

[67] Henry A. Wolfson, 'Patristic Arguments against the Eternity of the World', *Harvard Theological Review* 59 (1966), 351–67.

[68] Hans Jonas, *The Gnostic Religion: The Message of the Alien God and the Beginnings of Christianity*. London: Routledge, 1992.

defects within the world are thus not to be ascribed to God, but to deficiencies in the material from which the world was constructed. The Old Testament was regarded by the Gnostics as dealing with this lesser deity, whereas the New Testament was concerned with the redeemer God. As such, belief in God as creator and in the authority of the Old Testament came to be interlinked at an early stage.

Of the early writers to deal with this theme, Irenaeus of Lyons is of particular importance.[69] Where the Valentinians argued for the creation of the world through Sophia, Irenaeus affirmed the ability of God to create the universe from nothing. Whereas human beings were incapable of creating, save from matter which required to be shaped into an appropriate form, God was able to create the material which was ordered in the act of creation. For Irenaeus, the term 'creation' thus embraces both the notions of 'bringing into existence' and 'imposing order and structure'.[70]

Irenaeus argued for a direct connection between creation and redemption in the economy of salvation. Both creation and redemption were to be seen as the work of the one and the same God, within the same economy of salvation. The *imago Dei*, which was bestowed in creation and blemished through sin, is being restored through Christ. The theme of *recapitulatio* allows Irenaeus to plot the trajectory of the work of reconciliation, seeing in it a 'going over the main points' of salvation history, and remedying the deficiencies and errors which had once occurred through Adam.[71] In the incarnation, God entered into the created order in order to restore it to its intended pattern. God thus did not enter into, or act to redeem, an alien world – that is, a world created by someone else – but maintained continuity of divine action by redeeming what that selfsame God had earlier created. Irenaeus sees salvation as a cosmic affair, extending beyond the realm of the spiritual, or simply humanity, and embracing the created order as a whole.

The doctrine of creation *ex nihilo* may be regarded as gaining the ascendancy from the end of the second century onwards. From that point onwards, it became the received doctrine within the

[69] J. Fantino, *La théologie d'Irénée: lecture des écritures en response à l'exégèse gnostique.* Paris: Editions du Cerf, 1994; Richard A. Norris, *God and World in Early Christian Theology: A Study in Justin Martyr, Irenaeus, Tertullian and Origen.* London: A&C Black, 1966.

[70] Irenaeus, *Adversus Haereses* II.x.2–4. For Clement of Alexandria's critique of Valentinianism at this point, see Everett Procter, *Christian Controversy in Alexandria: Clement's Polemic Against the Basilideans and Valentinians.* New York: Peter Lang, 1995.

[71] See the classic study of Emmeran Scharl, *Recapitulatio Mundi: Der Rekapitulationsbegriff des heiligen Irenäus und seine Anwendung auf die Körperwelt.* Freiburg im Breisgau: Herder, 1941.

church.[72] The importance of the decisive rejection of Gnosticism by the early church for the development of the natural sciences has been explored by Thomas F. Torrance, who argues that the affirmation of the fundamental goodness of creation 'established the reality of the empirical, contingent world, and thus destroyed the age-old Hellenistic and Oriental assumption that the real is reached only by transcending the contingent'.[73] Against any idea that the natural order was chaotic, irrational or inherently evil (three concepts which were often regarded as interlocking), the early Christian tradition affirmed that the natural order possessed a goodness, rationality and orderedness which derived directly from its creation by God.

A radical dualism between God and creation was thus eliminated, in favour of the view that the truth, goodness and beauty of God (to use the Platonic triad which so influenced many writers of the period) could be discerned within the natural order, in consequence of that order having been established by God. For example, Origen argued that it was God's creation of the world which structured the natural order in such a manner that it could be comprehended by the human mind, by conferring upon that order an intrinsic rationality and order which derived from and reflected the divine nature itself.

Augustine's development of the doctrine of creation *ex nihilo* is of particular interest on account of the vividness of his language and imagery. His discussion of the doctrine in the *Confessions* brings out the implications and difficulties of the doctrine:[74]

> How did you make heaven and earth, and what machine did you use for such a mighty work? You were not like a human craftsman who makes one physical body out of another according to the choice in his mind, which has the ability to impose on it a form which by an inner eye it can see itself. It only possesses this capacity on account of having been created by you. He imposes form on what already exists and possesses being – such as earth, stone, wood, gold or some such material.

The doctrine is clearly an important aspect of Augustine's polemic against the Manichees,[75] especially in relation to the implied dualism within the created order – which the doctrine of creation *ex nihilo*

---

[72] Tarsicius van Bavel, 'The Creator and the Integrity of Creation in the Fathers of the Church', *Augustinian Studies* 21 (1990), 1–33.

[73] Thomas F. Torrance, *Reality and Scientific Theology: Theology and Science at the Frontiers of Knowledge.* Edinburgh: Scottish Academic Press, 1985, 6.

[74] Augustine, *Confessions*, XI.v.7.

[75] N. Joseph Torchia, *Creatio ex nihilo and the Theology of St Augustine: The Anti-Manichaean Polemic and Beyond.* New York: Peter Lang, 1999.

precludes. Yet it is important to appreciate that the doctrine possesses a constructive, as well as a critical role, within the context of Augustine's theology, not least in its role as a bridge between the temporal and the eternal.

The debate over the doctrine of creation became of increasing importance in western Europe during the twelfth and thirteenth centuries, especially as the intellectual heritage of the Islamic philosopher Avicenna (980–1037) was debated. For Avicenna, the concept of creation implies origination. To say that a thing is created means that 'it receives its existence from another'.[76] A distinction is drawn between essence and existence, allowing Avicenna to affirm the contingency of the created order, within a context largely shaped by the categories of Greek metaphysics. Avicenna can be held to have 'fused the Aristotelian metaphysics of self-sufficiency with the monotheistic metaphysics of contingency'.[77] Yet although this at first sight might seem similar to Christian ways of thinking about the matter, a closer examination reveals some fundamental points of distinction. In effect, Avicenna adopts an emanationist understanding of creation, in which 'creation' is understood as the establishment of an ontological relationship between entities, rather than having any necessary reference to temporality. The universe is to be understood as eternal; within that universe, certain relationships are established within the order of being.[78]

It was not merely Christian writers of the period who felt uneasy about this approach. Islamic writers – such as al-Ghazālī (1058–1111) – argued that it was inconsistent with the Qu'ran, and demanded that Avicenna be declared an infidel. Yet the concept of eternal creation continued to gain acceptance within philosophical circles. Averroes (c. 1126–98) argued that the term 'eternal' could be understood in two senses: as meaning 'not limited in temporal duration', or 'being for ever self-sufficient, lacking a first cause'. For Averroes, creation was to be thought of as God's action of converting potentialities into actualities – in other words, as a change within the eternal universe, rather than the calling into being of that universe in the first place.[79]

---

[76] Avicenna, *La métaphysique du Shifa*, trans. Georges Anawati. 2 vols. Paris: Vrin, 1978, vol. 2, 83–4.

[77] Lenn E. Goodman, *Avicenna*. London: Routledge, 1992, 63.

[78] Goodman, *Avicenna*, 74.

[79] For the issues, see Barry S. Kogan, *Averroes and the Metaphysics of Causation*. Binghamton, NY: State University of New York Press, 1985. More generally, see Davidson, *Proofs for Eternity, Creation and the Existence of God in Medieval Islamic and Jewish Philosophy*.

Why is this debate of such importance? Averroes believed that the all-important idea of natural causation within the universe was called into question by a doctrine of creation *ex nihilo*:[80]

> [The doctrine of creation *ex nihilo*, which teaches] that life can proceed from the lifeless, and knowledge from what does not possess knowledge, and that the dignity of the First consists only in its being the principle of the universe, is false. For if life could proceed from the lifeless, then the existent might proceed from the non-existent, and then anything whatever might proceed from anything whatever, and there would be no congruity between causes and effects, either in the genus predicated analogically or in the species.

Without genuine natural causation, the network of causal relationships within the world would be reduced to arbitrary happenings. There could be no natural science, in that there were no general principles to discern.

The doctrine of the eternity of the world – however this was conceived – proved unacceptable to the medieval church, for a variety of reasons. In response to a variety of such debates, the Fourth Lateran Council (1215) formally defined the doctrine of creation *ex nihilo*, as follows:[81]

> We firmly believe and simply confess that there is only one true God . . . one origin (*principium*) of all things; creator of everything visible and invisible, spiritual and physical; who by his own omnipotent power all at once made all things out of nothing (*ab initio temporis utramque de nihilo condidit creaturam*).

In 1277, Etienne Tempier, bishop of Paris, condemned a series of Aristotelian propositions, including the teaching that the world was eternal.[82] The result of these measures was to enforce adherence to the doctrine of *creatio ex nihilo* While there is some doubt as to the precise position adopted by Albert the Great (*c.* 1200–80),[83] both Bonaventure and Thomas Aquinas offered rigorous defences of the doctrine. From this point onwards, the doctrine may be regarded as definitive for Christian orthodoxy.

---

[80] Cited by Kogan, *Averroes and the Metaphysics of Causation*, 353.

[81] Cap. 1, 'De fide catholica', in H. Denzinger (ed.), *Enchiridion Symbolorum*. 24–5th edn. Barcelona: Herder, 1948, 199.

[82] For details, see Luca Bianchi, *Il vescovo e i filosofi: la condanna parigini del 1277 e l'evoluzione dell'Aristotelismo scolastico*. Bergamo: Pierluigi Lubrina, 1990.

[83] See Steven Snyder, 'Albert the Great: Creation and the Eternity of the World', in R. James Long (ed.), *Philosophy and the God of Abraham*. Toronto, ON: Pontifical Institute of Biblical Studies, 1991, 191–202.

The doctrine of creation *ex nihilo* makes a number of significant assertions, which we shall consider in more detail presently. Among them, we may notice the following:

1. The doctrine of creation *ex nihilo* is primarily concerned with ontological origin, rather than with temporal beginnings. The doctrine is not primarily concerned – if, indeed, it is concerned at all – with issues of chronology or dating; the specific issue concerns the ontological dependence of the cosmos upon its creator.

2. The doctrine affirms that God, in creating the universe, was not constrained by the limitations of the already existing stuff from which that universe was to be fashioned, but was free to bring into existence a universe in which the divine will was recognizably embodied and enacted.

We shall therefore move on to consider some presentations of the Christian doctrine of creation dating from after this decisive development, and explore their relevance to the theme of this project.

Christian formulations of the doctrine of creation

Within Christian dogmatics, the doctrine of creation has generally been given a high profile. Two contributing factors to this may be noted:

1. The doctrine of creation is the first major theological statement to be encountered by the reader of the Bible, as set out in its canonical form.

2. The two most influential communal statements of faith to be recognized by the church – the Nicene Creed, and the Apostles' Creed – both open with an affirmation of God as creator. In that many classic Christian discussions of systematic theology tend to follow the credal ordering of doctrinal affirmations, the doctrine of creation is thus frequently to the fore in theological analysis.

Within evangelicalism, the doctrine has been affirmed as a matter of fidelity to the biblical witness and credal orthodoxy; however, the emphasis within evangelical reflection and proclamation has tended to fall upon the redemption of the world in Christ, rather than the creation of that world through Christ. This, however, is not to be seen as in any way indicating a lack of interest in the doctrine of creation within the movement. Three points may be made.

1. The question is one of emphasis, not substance. Evangelicalism has always asserted that it is, at heart, fundamentally credal orthodoxy, with certain emphases – for example, upon the importance of conversion and evangelism – which mark it off from other forms of Christian orthodoxy.[84] There is no question of evangelicalism having no place for a doctrine of creation; the movement has simply chosen to place its emphasis elsewhere.

2. If a distinction is drawn between *kerygma* and *dogma*, it can easily be shown that evangelicalism's especial concern with the doctrine of salvation is linked with the evangelistic imperative – something which is directly linked with the question of the saving work of Christ, and the manner in which this is to be appropriated by individuals. Evangelistic preaching is unquestionably related to a solid theological foundation; the two, however, represent distinct genres, with differing emphases.

3. There is no difficulty in assembling a range of theologians, both from within the evangelical tradition and others whom evangelicals regard highly, with a strong interest in the doctrine of creation. Jonathan Edwards' emphasis upon the doctrine is a case in point.

In that this project is envisaged as an engagement between the classic themes of Christian orthodoxy and the natural sciences, it is important to establish from the outset the contours of the engagement by setting out the classic Christian position on the matter. In what follows, we shall therefore explore both classic and contemporary approaches to the doctrine of creation.

The Middle Ages: Thomas Aquinas

There is no doubt that the most widely studied classic formulation of the doctrine of creation is that set out by the great medieval theologian Thomas Aquinas (*c.* 1225–74).[85] Although unquestionably Catholic in his thought, Aquinas has been receiving renewed and increasingly sympathetic attention from Protestant writers since the Second World War, not least on account of the considerable stimulus he offers to philosophical reflections on the nature of Christian

---

[84] On which see Alister E. McGrath, *Evangelicalism and the Future of Christianity.* Downers Grove, IL: InterVarsity Press, 1995.

[85] See Jan Aertsen, *Nature and Creature: Thomas Aquinas' Way of Thought.* Leiden: E. J. Brill, 1988; Norman Kretzmann, *The Metaphysics of Creation: Aquinas's Natural Theology in Summa contra Gentiles II.* Oxford: Clarendon Press, 1999.

theological orthodoxy.[86] Aquinas offers magisterial discussions of the doctrine at four points in his writings:

1. *Super libros sententiarum* book 2, distinction 1, question 1 (1252–5);
2. *Summa contra Gentiles* book 2, chapters 6–38 (1259–64);
3. *Quaestiones disputatae de potentia Dei* question 3 (1265–6);
4. *Summa theologiae* prima pars, questions 44–46 (1266–8).

Each of these texts offers different perspectives on the issues, within a context of a more or less fixed approach to the central point. Thus the discussion found in the *Summa theologiae* includes a discussion of the creation accounts in Genesis, which is not found elsewhere in Aquinas' writings. Aquinas also abandoned in his later life some of the views which he developed at an earlier stage – for example the idea that God is able to use some creatures as intermediaries of instruments in the work of creation. Thus we find this view defended in early writings, and refuted from the *Summa contra Gentiles* onwards.

We shall focus on Aquinas' earlier writings on this theme, specifically the comments on the 'Four Books of the Sentences' of Peter Lombard, and the *Summa contra Gentiles*, which is widely thought to have been written to counter Islamic criticisms of Christian theology.

Aquinas argues that there is only one first principle of all things. This argument will be developed to become the 'Five Ways', each of which can be seen as an examination of the effects observed within the world, and the necessity of tracing these back to a common source in God.[87] Aquinas depicts the whole of reality as a hierarchy of being, and argues that the diversity within the created order must be explained in terms of a single creator, who is the ultimate source of their existence. God as creator is the one who 'gives being to all' (*hoc est quod dat esse omnibus*).

At this point, we must introduce Aquinas' fundamental distinction between 'essence' and 'existence'.[88] The essence of an entity can be thought of as what it is that makes – for example – a dog be a dog, and not a stone. Yet essence does not imply existence. I can quite easily

---

[86] See Arvin Vos, *Aquinas, Calvin, and Contemporary Protestant Thought: A Critique of Protestant Views on the Thought of Thomas Aquinas.* Grand Rapids, MI: Eerdmans, 1985.

[87] *In II Sent.* Dist. 1, q. 1, a. 1.

[88] For discussion, see Arda Denkel, *Object and Property.* New York: Cambridge University Press, 1996; John Goheen, *The Problem of Matter and Form in the De ente et essentia of Thomas Aquinas.* Cambridge, MA: Harvard University Press, 1940.

describe the essential features of a hypothetical dog; this does not, however, imply that this specific dog exists. I am merely describing what kind of thing a dog is; the question as to whether a specific instance of a dog exists is quite another matter. There are thus two aspects of actually existing entities which require to be explained: their specific characteristics, and the fact that they exist in the first place. For Thomas, the essence of a thing relates to *what* a thing is; the existence (*esse*) of a thing relates to that fact *that* it exists. Aquinas thus argues that *esse* must be prior to all other aspects of actuality for the simple reason that a thing cannot exist in any specific manner unless it exists in the first place.

The creator is thus to be distinguished from the multiplicity of beings within the created order on account of the coincidence of essence and existence.[89] God exists, and gives being to others. As none other than God is capable of bestowing existence upon others, Aquinas affirms the doctrine of creation *ex nihilo*.[90] Creation is defined in terms of the emanation of the totality of being from its one and only source – God:[91]

> It is appropriate to consider, not only the emanation of a particular being from a particular agent (*oportet considerare emanationem alicuius entis particularis ab aliquo particulari agente*), but also the emanation of the whole of being (*emanatio totius entis*) from the universal cause, which is God. And it is this emanation which we designate by the name 'creation' ... Thus if the emanation of the whole universality of being from its first principle is considered, it is impossible that any being should be presupposed for that emanation. But 'nothing' is the same as 'no being' ... Therefore creation, which is the emanation of the whole of being, is out of non being, that is, nothing (*est ex non ente quod est nihil*).

Yet Aquinas insists that the doctrine of *creatio ex nihilo* does not contradict the existence of causes within nature – causes which human beings may discover and investigate. Creation gives rise to an ordered structure, whose various aspects are linked together in a regulated manner, governed by causes and effects.[92] The existence of real causality in nature cannot be understood as amounting to a challenge to, still

---

[89] On which see the classic study of Joseph Owens, 'The Accidental and Essential Character of Being', *Medieval Studies* 20 (1958), 1–40. On the subtle yet important divergence from the Greek tradition at this point, see Charles H. Kahn, 'Why Existence does not Emerge as a Distinct Concept in Greek Philosophy', in Parviz Morewedge (ed.), *Philosophies of Existence: Ancient and Medieval.* Bronx, NY: Fordham University Press, 1982, 7–17.

[90] *In II Sent.* Dist. 1, q. 1, a. 2.

[91] *Summa theologiae* Ia q. 45 a. 1.

[92] *In II Sent.* Dist. 1, q. 1, a. 4.

less a denial of, either divine omnipotence or divine omniscience. The resulting autonomy of nature – a fundamental working assumption of the natural sciences – cannot be interpreted as an indication of a lack of power or will within God, but is to be understood specifically as a consequence of the divine decision that there should be such autonomy in the first place. 'Creation is not dispersed among the works of nature, but is presupposed for the working of nature' (*sed praesupponitur ad operationem naturae*).[93] To argue otherwise – for example, by denying causality within the natural order – would be to 'eliminate the order of the universe, which is interwoven through the order and relation of causes'.[94] There is a particularly important discussion of this in the *Summa theologiae*, which demands to be considered fully:[95]

> Some understand God to work in every agent in such a way that no created power has any effect in things, but that God alone is the ultimate cause of everything that takes place; for example, that it is not fire that gives heat, but God in the fire, and so forth. But this is impossible. First, because the order of cause and effect would be taken away from created things: and this would imply lack of power in the Creator: for it is due to the power of the cause, that it bestows active power on its effect.
>
> Secondly, because the active powers which are seen to exist in things, would be bestowed on things without any purpose, if these effected nothing through them. Indeed, all things created would seem, in a way, to be purposeless, if they lacked an operation proper to them; since the purpose of everything is its operation. For the less perfect is always for the sake of the more perfect: and consequently as the matter is for the sake of the form, so the form which is the first act, is for the sake of its operation, which is the second act; and thus operation is the end of the creature. We must therefore understand that God works in things in such a manner that things have their proper operation.
>
> God thus works in every agent in three manners. (1) First as an end. For since every operation is for the sake of some good, real or apparent; and nothing is good either really or apparently, except in as far as it participates in a likeness to the Supreme Good, which is God; it follows that God is the cause of every operation as its end. (2) Again it is to be observed that where there are several agents in order, the second always acts in virtue of the first; for the first agent moves the second to act. And thus all agents act in virtue of God: and therefore God is the cause of action in every agent. (3) Thirdly, we must observe that God not only moves things to operate, as it were applying their forms and powers to

---

[93] *Summa theologiae* Ia q. 45 a.8.
[94] *de veritate* q. 11 a. 1.
[95] *Summa theologiae* Ia q. 105 a.5.

operation, just as the workman applies the axe to cut, who nevertheless at times does not give the axe its form; but God also gives created agents their forms and preserves them in being. Therefore God is the cause of action not only by giving the form which is the principle of action, as the generator is said to be the cause of movement in things heavy and light; but also as preserving the forms and powers of things; just as the sun is said to be the cause of the manifestation of colours, inasmuch as it gives and preserves the light by which colours are made manifest. And since the form of a thing is within the thing, and all the more, as it approaches nearer to the First and Universal Cause; and because in all things God Himself is properly the cause of universal being which is innermost in all things; it follows that God works intimately in all things. For this reason in Holy Scripture the operations of nature are attributed to God as operating in nature (*operationes naturae Deo attribuuntur quasi operanti in natura*), according to Job 10:11: 'You have clothed me with skin and flesh: You have put me together with bones and sinews.'

This important passage has been cited in full precisely because it represents such as important affirmation of two critically significant principles:

1. God works within nature;

2. Nature is autonomous, working according to the laws of causality.

For some, these principles were inconsistent; for Aquinas, they hold together with ease, on the basis of a rightly construed doctrine of creation.

The relevance of this point to 'naturalist' approaches to the world will be clear. Some argue that the natural sciences, through dealing with the observable world as an autonomous entity, governed by a set of rules and principles which do not explicitly invoke special divine action, are atheistic. Aquinas argues otherwise. The explanatory autonomy of the created order is itself a consequence of its creation by God.

Aquinas also develops a highly important account of the relation between the character of God as creator and the derivative character of the natural order. For Aquinas, there exists a fundamental 'likeness (*similitudo*) to God' within the created order as a consequence of God being the cause, in some sense of the word, of all created things. In that no created thing can be said to come into existence spontaneously, the existence of all things can be considered to be a consequence of a relationship of causal dependence between the creation and its creator. Using what are essentially Aristotelian categories of causality, Aquinas sets out a position which we may summarize as follows:

1. Suppose that A causes B;

2. Suppose also that A possesses a quality Q;

3. Then B will also possess that quality Q as a result of its being caused by A.

The full argument set out by Aquinas is complex, and not without its difficulties; nevertheless, its conclusion is clear. There is a presence in the effect of characteristics that could serve to identify its cause. There are, so to speak, physical or metaphysical fingerprints within what is caused, which provide the basis for an inductive argument to the existence of that cause, and allow at least some aspects of its nature to be established. As Kretzmann puts it, there is a 'presence in the effect of characteristics that could serve to identify, or at least to type, the agent – physical or metaphysical fingerprints providing the basis for an inductive argument to the agent's existence and some aspects of its nature'.[96] This does not mean that there is a similarity between all causes and effects; Aquinas notes that what he terms 'accidental effects' may arise, in which no such similarity exists. It is clear, however, that Aquinas regards creation as perhaps the clearest example of a purposeful causation, in which qualities of the agent are to be found in the generated outcome.

If God made the world, God's 'signature' (so to speak) may be found within the created order. Aquinas puts this point as follows:[97]

> Meditation on [God's] works enables us, at least to some extent, to admire and reflect on God's wisdom . . . We are thus able to infer God's wisdom from reflection upon God's works . . . This consideration of God's works leads to an admiration of God's sublime power, and consequently inspires reverence for God in human hearts . . . This consideration also incites human souls to the love of God's goodness . . . If the goodness, beauty and wonder of creatures are so delightful to the human mind, the fountainhead of God's own goodness (compared with the trickles of goodness found in creatures) will draw excited human minds entirely to itself.

Something of God's beauty can thus be known from the beauty of the creation, a point to which we shall return in due course. It is also important to note that Aquinas' highly important discussion of the use

---

[96] Norman Kretzmann, *The Metaphysics of Theism: Aquinas's Natural Theology in Summa contra Gentiles I.* Oxford: Clarendon Press, 1997, 146.

[97] *Summa contra Gentiles* Book II q. 2 aa. 2–4.

of analogies in theology is grounded in his theology of justification – an issue we shall explore in somewhat greater detail in a later volume, when we turn to deal with the issue of representation in Christian theology and the natural sciences.

The Reformation: John Calvin

The sixteenth century witnessed a theological renaissance throughout western Europe, largely fuelled by polemical concerns relating to contested issues such as the doctrine of justification by faith,[98] and the locus of authority in theological formulations.[99] A cluster of doctrines were not the subject of dispute between mainstream evangelical writers and their Catholic opponents: Christology, the doctrine of the Trinity and the doctrine of creation received relatively little theological attention precisely because there was a considerable degree of consensus on the issues within western Christendom.[100]

In what follows, we shall consider the theology of creation set out in the writings of John Calvin (1509–64), generally regarded as one of the most theologically organized and systematic thinkers of the Reformation period. Although unquestionably evangelical in his theological outlook, Calvin has receiving increasingly sympathetic treatment from Catholic commentators in recent decades, indicating a willingness to enter into dialogue with his theological heritage and achievement.[101] Calvin devotes considerable attention to the doctrine of creation, and its implications for a number of areas of human intellectual activity, making him a highly important resource for our reflections on this theme.[102]

One of the most important aspects of Calvin's doctrine of creation is his reaffirmation of the causal autonomy of the created order. Nevertheless, Calvin was aware that such an affirmation could be

[98] Alister E. McGrath, *Iustitia Dei: A History of the Christian Doctrine of Justification*. 2nd edn. Cambridge: Cambridge University Press, 1998.

[99] Gillian R. Evans, *Problems of Authority in the Reformation Debates*. Cambridge: Cambridge University Press, 1992; Alister E. McGrath, *The Intellectual Origins of the European Reformation*. Oxford: Blackwell, 1987, 122–90.

[100] It may be noted, however, that the Radical Reformation would offer critiques of many of these, particularly the doctrine of the Trinity, in the light of the movement's specific understanding of what it meant to be 'biblical': see George Hunston Williams, *The Radical Reformation*. 3rd edn. Kirksville, MO: Sixteenth Century Journal Publishers, 1992.

[101] See, for example, Alexandre Ganoczy, *Calvin, théologien de l'église et du ministère*. Paris: Editions du Cerf, 1964.

[102] Richard Stauffer, *Dieu, la création et la Providence dans la prédication de Calvin*. Berne: Peter Lang, 1978; Peter Wyatt, *Jesus Christ and Creation in the Theology of John Calvin*. Allison Park, PA: Pickwick Publications, 1996.

misinterpreted as tantamount to atheism, at least at the functional level – that is to say, that the universe could be understood to function without reference to God. Calvin's strong emphasis upon divine providence made him regard such a possibility with intense distaste, and it should therefore come as no surprise to find many statements throughout Calvin's writings reaffirming God's special providence *within* the operation of the created order. Thus the regularities within nature are not to be thought of as being intrinsic to it, but reflect the ordering imposed upon it by God in creation. Thus Calvin stresses that the rain does not fall, nor the sun rise, by some 'blind instinct of nature'; rather, such regularities reflect the ordering of the world in creation, and subsequent general influence of God through providence. *Non id fieri caeco naturae instinctu, sed quia Deus ita decrevit.*[103]

At this point, we need to introduce the theme of the fall, which plays a particularly important role in Calvin's reflections on the creation. Nature, as we see it, is not nature as God intended it to be. The *ordo* established within creation as a result of God's ordering activity was disrupted through the fall. Calvin uses a series of images to illustrate the violation of divine order which he associates with the fall. In his commentaries on the opening chapters of Genesis, Calvin speaks of the serpent 'overstepping its limits' in language which parallels the Old Testament imagery of God setting bounds to the forces of nature; Adam's sin is described in terms of a subversion of 'well-constituted order'. Creation is now characterized more by disorder than order, even though vestiges of that primal ordering may still be discerned. It is for this reason that the doctrine of providence plays such an important role in Calvin's account of creation. The autonomy of creation is compromised through the fall, in that the creation is now dependent upon its creator for the maintenance of its increasingly precarious ordering.

Calvin's emphasis upon the intrusion of disorder within the created order as a consequence of the fall is to be seen as one of his most important contributions to a scientific theology. His theological analysis offers us a double perspective on the natural order, in that nature is to be seen as God's *fallen* creation. One of the less satisfactory aspects of Aquinas' exposition of creation is that perhaps it offers something falling short of a full account of the impact of sin upon the ontology of nature. Aquinas tends to regard sin as a falling short of perfection, and thus to locate any absence of perfection within the created order as a direct

---

[103] Commentary on Psalm 135:7; CO 32.360; *Institutes* I.xvi.2–4.

result of its creatureliness. Calvin, however, locates sin as a significant presence at two levels within creation:

1. *Ontologically*, in terms of the structuring of the world itself. Disorder is not merely something that the human mind perceives within creation; it is something that exists prior to the human recognition of it.

2. *Noetically*, in terms of the capacities of the human mind in reflecting upon the ordering of the world.[104]

If a fallen human mind reflects upon the structures and patterns of a fallen world, is it surprising that misjudgements abound?

This emphasis on the present disorder of the creation naturally leads Calvin to stress the importance of the hope of redemption in Christ. In his important exegesis of Romans 8:20, which speaks of the universe being subjected to corruption and standing in need of renewal on account of the pervasive influence of sin, Calvin stresses the need for reordering of the world, and a restoration of the world to its primal ordering.[105] This theme in Calvin's thought has been picked up by a number of interpreters within the Reformed tradition, including Thomas F. Torrance.

Torrance argues that the significance of the doctrine of the atonement can be seen in relation to the 'reordering of creation'. At first sight, this might seem to be little more than a restatement of the cosmic notions of redemption which are particularly associated with the Greek patristic tradition.[106] On closer inspection, a more nuanced approach emerges, based on an analysis of the notion of the ordering discerned within the world by scientific investigation. Torrance notes how the universe requires 'redemption from disorder':[107]

> In Christian theology that redemption of the universe is precisely the bearing of the cross upon the way things actually are in our universe of space and time. It represents the refusal of God to remain aloof from the distintegration of order in what he has made, or merely to act upon it 'at a distance'. It is his decisive personal intervention in the world through the incarnation of his Word and love in Jesus Christ. In his life and passion he who is the ultimate source and power of all order has

[104] Stauffer, *Dieu, la création et la Providence*, 118–19.
[105] Susan Elizabeth Schreiner, *The Theater of His Glory: Nature and the Natural Order in the Thought of John Calvin*. Durham, NC: Labyrinth Press, 1991, 97–111.
[106] See H. E. W. Turner, *The Patristic Doctrine of Redemption*. London: Mowbray, 1952.
[107] Thomas F. Torrance, *The Christian Frame of Mind: Reason, Order, and Openness in Theology and Natural Science*. Colorado Springs: Helmers & Howard, 1989, 103.

penetrated into the untouchable core of our contingent existence in such a way as to deal with the twisted force of evil entrenched in it, and thereby to bring about an atoning reordering of creation.

This 'atoning reordering of creation' is to be understood as an engagement with the 'source of disorder'. The resurrection of Christ is understood as the means by which God 'triumphs over all the forces of disintegration and disorder in the cosmos'.[108] Redemption can thus be understood as reordering – that is, restoring the God-given order in which the cosmos came into being. Torrance notes that the disorder which has crept into the universe affects human nature in particular; nevertheless, redemption must be understood to embrace the whole created order, which has now fallen into disorder, and not simply humanity.

A contemporary statement: Karl Barth

Karl Barth is widely regarded as one of the most influential and important theologians of the twentieth century. Yet the decision to include a discussion of Barth's theology of creation at this point may initially seem misguided. After all, Barth himself appears to have little genuine knowledge of or interest in the natural sciences, apparently regarding them as having little relevance for theology.[109] For example, Barth's discussion of Darwinianism within the context of his doctrine of creation is brief and rather unsatisfactory; it might, of course, be argued that the point which Barth wishes to make in relation to Darwin's theory of evolution does not require a detailed engagement with Darwin's ideas.[110] Similarly, Barth shows no inclination to engage with Einstein's theory of relativity in particular, or the intellectual achievement of Einstein in general, at any point in the *Church Dogmatics*. In effect, Barth treats Christian theology and the natural

---

[108] Thomas F. Torrance, *Divine and Contingent Order*. Oxford: Oxford University Press, 1981, 138.

[109] For a detailed analysis, see Harold P. Nebelsick, 'Karl Barth's Understanding of Science', in John Thompson (ed.), *Theology beyond Christendom: Essays on the Centenary of the Birth of Karl Barth*. Allison Park, PA: Pickwick Publications, 1986, 165–214. The contrast at this point with Barth's colleague Emil Brunner is of interest. In a 1929 essay, Brunner argued that Christian theology possessed an apologetic and correlational role, which both enabled and encouraged dialogue with other intellectual disciplines: Emil Brunner, 'Die andere Aufgabe der Theologie', in *Ein offenes Wort: Vorträge und Aufsätze 1917–1962*. 2 vols. Zurich: Theologischer Verlag, 1981, vol. 1, 171–93. Close observers of the Barth–Brunner relationship will, of course, be aware that it was the publication of this article which led to the personal coolness and theological hostility between the two thinkers, which eventually manifested itself publicly in the 1934 debate over natural theology.

[110] *Church Dogmatics* III/2, 88.

sciences as non-interactive disciplines, each with their respective magisterial fields of competence.

While fully conceding the merit of such considerations, two points may be made in response. First, Barth's doctrine of creation is not merely one of the most thorough and comprehensive such theologies of the twentieth century; it is of especial interest to a scientific theology on account of the emphasis placed upon the notion of God's covenant, and the priority which Barth assigns to this concept in the theological explication of creation. As the importance of Barth's approach to the doctrine of creation for the natural sciences has not been explored in anything like the detail which it merits, the analysis provided here is more extensive than might at first appear to be warranted. Second, the substantial theological project of Thomas F. Torrance has demonstrated that the Barthian programme is capable of being modified and developed to be of considerable potential importance in relation to the natural sciences.[111] This suggests that, providing Barth's concerns about the dilution or distortion of theology from competing ideologies can be met,[112] the Barthian heritage has considerable potential as a dialogue partner between Christian theology and the natural sciences.

Barth's initial position may be regarded as a polemic against any possibility of discovering, discerning or encountering God through any natural resource, whether this is to be understood in terms of the categories of creation, nature or culture.[113] One of the central themes of Barth's theological enterprise is the elimination of any dependence of theology upon any form of natural mediation – such as human culture, or natural theology. Similar themes can be discerned within the later writings of Barth's Marburg teacher Wilhelm Herrmann, who regularly stressed the importance of liberating theology from any science (*Wissenschaft*) which is grounded in nature.[114] There is a chasm between

---

[111] Alister E. McGrath, *Thomas F. Torrance: An Intellectual Biography.* Edinburgh: T&T Clark, 1999, 195–235.

[112] On which see the useful study of Arie L. Molendijk, 'Ein heidnische Wissenschaftsbegriff. Der Streit zwischen Heinrich Scholtz und Karl Barth um die Wissenschaftlichkeit der Theologie', *Evangelische Theologie* 52 (1992), 527–45.

[113] Ray S. Anderson, 'Barth and a New Direction for Natural Theology', in John Thompson (ed.), *Theology beyond Christendom: Essays on the Centenary of the Birth of Karl Barth.* Allison Park, PA: Pickwick Publications, 1986, 241–66; Andrew Louth, 'Barth and the Problem of Natural Theology', *Downside Review* 87 (1969), 268–77; Eugene Rogers, *Thomas Aquinas and Karl Barth: Sacred Doctrine and the Natural Knowledge of God.* Notre Dame, IN: University of Notre Dame Press, 1995; Thomas F. Torrance, 'The Problem of Natural Theology in the Thought of Karl Barth', *Religious Studies* 6 (1970), 121–35.

[114] Bruce L. McCormack, *Karl Barth's Critically Realistic Dialectical Theology: Its Genesis and Development 1909–1936.* Oxford: Clarendon Press, 1995, 54–8.

the creator and the creation, which prevents human beings from making any valid epistemological judgements concerning the former from the latter. This point is stressed in the second edition of the *Romans* commentary (1922), which vigorously affirms the Kierkegaardian 'infinite qualitative distinction (*unendliche qualitative Unterschied*)' between God and human beings. God 'stands over and against humanity and everything human in an infinite qualitative distinction, and is never, ever (*nie und nimmer*) identical with anything which we name, experience, conceive or worship as God'. God cannot and must not be constructed or conceived in human or natural terms. God is *totaliter aliter*, wholly and absolutely different from us. Any form of natural theology – understood as the autonomous human attempt to know God on the basis of reflection on any aspect of the created order – is to be rejected. How, then, may mediation between God and humanity take place? Barth's answer, stated in the preface to the second edition of the *Romans* commentary, is highly significant for our purposes:[115]

> If I have any system, it is restricted to bearing in mind, as much as possible, what Kierkegaard called the 'infinite qualitative distinction' between time and eternity, in its negative and positive aspects. 'God is in heaven, and you are on earth.' For me, the relation of this God and this person, the relation of this person and this God, is, in a nutshell, the theme of the Bible and the totality of philosophy. The philosophers term this crisis of human knowledge the prime cause; the Bible sees Jesus Christ at this cross-roads.

Barth stresses that there is nothing intrinsic to nature which endows it with revelatory potential. It is this theme which can be discerned as lying behind his doctrine of creation.

Barth's magisterial discussion of the doctrine of creation is set out in the third volume of the *Church Dogmatics*. Creation is here affirmed to be a free act of the divine will:[116]

> The proposition that God created heaven and earth and humanity asserts that this whole reality is distinct from God. It thus affirms negatively that God does not exist alone, that the being of God is not the only being, to the exclusion of all others; and positively, it affirms that another exists before, near and with God, having its own being distinct from the being of God.

---

[115] Karl Barth, *Römerbrief*. 2nd edn. Munich: Kaiser Verlag, 1922, xiii.
[116] Karl Barth, *Church Dogmatics* III/1, 5. I have altered the English translation to bring out the sense of the original German more clearly.

Barth immediately sets this doctrine on a Christological foundation, picking up the themes developed earlier in his *Romans* commentary. God created all things in Christ (John 1:3). It is thus 'in Jesus Christ that we finally find all the individual elements in the biblical witness which go to make up the creation dogma'.[117] Barth distinguishes a number of aspects to this important statement. In the first place, there is a noetic dimension: the reality of creation only can be known with clarity and certainty in the person of Jesus Christ. Yet in addition to this noetic aspect of the matter, there is an ontological issue:[118]

> Jesus Christ is the Word by which the knowledge of creation is mediated to us because he is the Word by which God has fulfilled creation and continually maintains and rules it.

Having established the Christological dimension of creation, Barth turns to a discussion of the relation between creation and covenant – perhaps the most original and interesting aspect of his theology at this point.

'The purpose and therefore the meaning of creation is to make possible the history of God's covenant with humanity.'[119] With these words, Barth makes it clear that God's creation of the world must be set in the context of the purposes of God. Reconciliation – or 'atonement', which remains a perfectly acceptable translation of the German term *Versöhnung* – and redemption are presupposed in creation. While creation is the first of God's works, it is to be seen as the direct consequence of God's decision and plan. God willed from all eternity to become incarnate in Christ, and thus to achieve reconciliation with humanity. Yet this act of redemption required a place within which this act could take place. Creation therefore sets the stage for the execution of God's covenantal history.

Barth stresses that both the event and the form of creation are the result of a free act and decision of God, in which nothing save the divine will was involved. 'Creation as such is the immediate correlate and realization of the divine purpose to begin with the revelation of his glory.' That purpose is expressed particularly in the divine covenant with humanity:[120]

> As God's first work, again according to the witness of Scripture and the confession, creation stands in a series, in an indissolubly real connexion, with God's further works. And these works . . . have in view the

---

[117] *Church Dogmatics* III/1, 27.
[118] *Church Dogmatics* III/1, 28.
[119] *Church Dogmatics* III/1, 42.
[120] *Church Dogmatics* III/1, 43.

institution, preservation and execution of the covenant of grace, for partnership in which he has predestined and called humanity . . . Creation sets the stage for the story of the covenant of grace.

For Barth, creation is the external basis of the covenant, just as the covenant is the internal basis of creation. It is the divine decision to enter into this covenantal relationship that underlies the creation of the world in general, and humanity in particular.[121]

> The creature is not self-existent. It has not assumed its nature and existence of itself or given to itself. It did not come into being by itself. It does not consist by itself. It cannot sustain itself. It has to thank its creation and therefore its creator for the fact that it came into being and is and will be. Nor does the creature exist for itself. It is not the creature itself but its creator who exists and thinks and speaks and cares for the creature. The creature is no more its own goal and purpose than it is its own ground and beginning. There is no inherent reason for the creature's existence and nature, no independent teleology of the creature introduced with its creation and made its own. Its destiny lies entirely in the purpose of its creator as the one who speaks and cares for it. The creature's right and meaning and goal and purpose and dignity lie – only – in the fact that God the creator has turned towards it with purpose. Any other attitude than that of God's free acceptance of this turning towards it and therefore of this advocacy and care; any claim to a right inherent in its being and nature, to a meaning which has not first been received, to a goal which it has fixed for itself, to a purpose which it has in and for itself, to a dignity independent of the free will of the creator – all this is just as meaningless as the illusion that it came into existence of itself, that it consists in itself and that it can sustain itself. By its very creation, and therefore its being as a creature, all such views are shown, like this illusion, to be basically impossible, and thus disclosed as falsehoods.

This passage has been cited at length because it conveys some of Barth's most important insights concerning the nature and status of the creation, including its capacity to disclose God. In what follows, we shall pick up and explore some of these issues.

1. The doctrine of creation *ex nihilo* is seen as undergirding the fact that the entire created order owes its existence and purpose to God. There is nothing intrinsic to creation which demanded or permitted it to come into existence. Creation is a direct consequence of the divine decision to create, the divine *fiat* which is grounded in the freedom and sovereignty of God.

[121] *Church Dogmatics* III/1, 94–5.

2. Barth rejects any notion of the autonomy of the creation over and against the creator. Any purpose or meaning within creation is the consequence of the divine will, not something possessed by right or by nature. Meaning is given by God and received by the creation; it is not something which exists prior to or independent of the divine will that such a meaning shall exist. For Barth, the divine freedom is such that God is free to impose such meaning as God determines upon the creation – and that meaning is to be articulated in terms of a covenant between God and humanity.

3. It therefore follows that the created order cannot be allowed to possess an ontological or revelatory autonomy – for example, by becoming the basis of an alleged 'revelation' of the nature and purposes of God.

The implications of Barth's theology of creation for his understanding of the propriety of natural theology, or the nature of any 'analogy' between God and the creation, will be clear.

It will also be clear that Barth's doctrine of creation offers a powerful corrective to the quasi-deistical tendencies of many liberal Protestant theologies of the nineteenth and early twentieth centuries. This raises an important issue, which is conveniently addressed at this point. Is a particular interest in the doctrine of creation tantamount to Deism?

An emphasis upon creation: a Deist strategy?

Our discussion thus far has focused on the Christian understanding of creation, and its implications both for the concept of nature in general, and the natural sciences in particular. It is at this point that some readers will wish to raise a point of concern with the approach being set out in this work. 'Is there not', it might reasonably be asked, 'a serious risk that the approach being commended leads to a position which is regarded as widely discredited within Christian orthodoxy – namely, Deism?' This is a matter of considerable importance, and demands full discussion.

The nature of Deism

The movement that is generally known as 'Deism' arose in England as a result of the triumph of the Newtonian mechanistic world-view.[122]

---

[122] Peter A. Byrne, *Natural Religion and the Religion of Nature*. London: Routledge, 1989; Peter Gay, *Deism*. Princeton, NJ: van Nostrand, 1968; J. O'Higgins, 'Hume and the Deists', *Journal of Theological Studies* 22 (1971), 479–501; R. E. Sullivan, *John Toland and the Deist Controversy*. Cambridge, MA: Harvard University Press, 1982.

There is a significant debate about the origins of the term 'Deist' and the identity of the early advocates of the movement. Lord Herbert of Cherbury (1582–1648) is generally referred to as the 'father of English deism', although a careful study of his writings suggests that such an attribution is not without its difficulties.[123] Although 'Deism' is perhaps less theologically coherent than has been assumed, it is known to have defended the idea that God created the world, and endowed it with the ability to develop and function without the need for his continuing presence or interference. This viewpoint, which became especially influential in the eighteenth century, regarded the world as a watch, and God as the watchmaker. God endowed the world with a certain self-sustaining design, such that it could subsequently function without the need for continual intervention. Thomas Hobbes, for example, takes the view that God is essentially a retired constitutional monarch, having a certain role as a cosmic figurehead but divorced from any involvement in the day-to-day affairs of the universe.

The emphasis placed upon the doctrine of creation in this project might therefore be held to align it with a discredited approach to Christianity, rendering it of little value to its intended audience. This is clearly not the case, and it is hoped that the following points will indicate why the approach adopted throughout this series of works is quite distinct from the Deist position.

1. The present series of works is grounded on the fundamental principles of Christian orthodoxy, as set out in the Nicene Creed. There is no question of denying any fundamental Christian belief; the issue is merely that of identifying which aspect or aspects of Christian theology have particular relevance for the relation of Christian theology and the natural sciences. This project aims to develop and explore a strategic emphasis, within the context of an overall commitment to credal orthodoxy. For other purposes, it is possible that a different emphasis might have been adopted and explored. Deism, however, is not about emphases; it is about significant denials of substantial sections of Christian belief. Such denials might include the possibility and necessity of divine revelation, the continuing involvement of God with the creation, the Trinity, and the divinity of Christ.

2. Deism places an emphasis upon the concept of creation in that this is the focus of a 'natural religion', which can be known through

[123] David Pailin, 'Should Herbert of Cherbury be regarded as a "Deist"?', *Journal of Theological Studies* 51 (2000), 113–49.

reason or solely through the reading of the 'book of nature'. The characteristic Deist rejection of the notion of divine revelation in favour of a conception of Christianity as a 'republication of the religion of nature' (Matthew Tindal) leads to an emphasis upon God as creator being the consequence of a prior stance on the issue of revelation. The present project is fully committed to the notion of divine revelation; the emphasis upon the doctrine of creation is a result of the decision to identify those aspects of the Christian revelation which are especially significant in relation to the trajectory of this project.

3. Within Christian orthodoxy, the doctrine of creation is not treated as an isolated tenet of belief, which may be maintained and discussed without reference to other beliefs. The 'coherence of Christian doctrine' (Charles Gore) is such that doctrines interact and interrelate, so that the doctrine of the person of Christ interlocks with that of the Trinity, and the doctrine of redemption in Christ with the Christian understanding of human nature. Whereas Deism tended to insulate the doctrine, making it the lynchpin of a 'reasonable Christianity', Christian orthodoxy insisted that it be located within a web of doctrines, including the following:

(a) the doctrine of the Trinity; creation is to be seen as an action of the triune God.

(b) the doctrine of redemption; both creation and redemption are set within the one economy of salvation of God, with the latter 'recapitulating' the former.

(c) The doctrine of divine providence; God does not cease to tend for the creation, but sustains and upholds it.

(d) The doctrine of the person of Christ; there is a strongly Christological dimension to creation. In particular, for many Christian theologians there is a close link between the doctrines of creation and incarnation.

Deist writers would disagree, though perhaps to varying extents, with each of these four points.

In view of the importance of this fourth point (d) to our project, we shall explore it in more detail in what follows. One of the more significant achievements of the final decades of the twentieth century has been the recovery of a distinctively Christian approach to theology. Instead of loose and general talk about God, often couched in language and conceptualities which recognizably derive from Deism or Hegelianism,[124] we encounter an increasingly focused discussion of a specifically Christian approach to the matter, generally formulated in terms of the doctrine of the Trinity,[125] and a new realization of the importance of Jesus Christ for Christianity in general, and its theological enterprise in particular.

This development is evident in relation to the doctrine of creation, where there has been increased interest in formulating a specifically Christian – as opposed to a generally theistic – approach to the doctrine. The trinitarian and Christological aspects of the doctrine have been the subject of close study in recent years, and it is important to ensure that these are properly reflected in our formulation of a scientific theology. In what follows, we shall therefore make it clear that an emphasis upon creation cannot be taken to imply any, save the most superficial, semblance of affinity with Deism.

Creation and providence

Deism proposes an understanding of God as an absentee landlord who has no day-to-day involvement with the affairs of the creation. Without in any way denying that the universe is the creation of God, Deist writers were of the view that, having accomplished the work of creation, God was able to function as a retired potentate from whom no further gubernatorial duties were required or expected. Yet the Christian understanding of creation does not refer to a single divine action, which is now totally accomplished. A specifically Christian understanding of creation enfolds the related idea that God continues to uphold and preserve the ensuing created order.[126] While the first Genesis creation account could indeed depict creation as being a completed process, this must be set against the biblical affirmations of the continuing work of God (John 5:17), and the future hope of a new heaven and earth (Isaiah 65:17–19). What God creates, God preserves.

In an important discussion of the concept of providence, Colin Gunton points out that one of the more interesting theological

---

[124] See, for example, Peter C. Hodgson, *Winds of the Spirit: A Constructive Christian Theology.* Louisville, KY: Westminster/John Knox Press, 1994.
[125] See, for example, Colin E. Gunton, *The Promise of Trinitarian Theology.* 2nd edn. Edinburgh: T&T Clark, 1996; John Thompson, *Modern Trinitarian Perspectives.* Oxford: Oxford University Press, 1994; Thomas F. Torrance, *The Trinitarian Faith: The Evangelical Theology of the Ancient Catholic Church.* Edinburgh: T&T Clark, 1988.
[126] Wolfhart Pannenberg, *Systematic Theology.* 3 vols. Grand Rapids, MI: Eerdmans. Edinburgh: T&T Clark, 1991, 1994, 1998, vol. 2, 35–59.

achievements is the re-establishment of a connection between creation and providence through a robust Christology.[127] Where Schleiermacher generally thought of the doctrine of creation primarily in terms of providence, Barth developed an account of the continuing relationship between the creator and the creation which rests upon a trinitarian conception of mediation, and is thus ultimately grounded in Christology. Barth's discussion of this point demonstrates how a proper integration of Christology and creation is both important and theologically fruitful. This can be seen in terms of the high role Barth allocates to Christ in his doctrine of creation – to which we shall turn presently. However, it is also reflected in the link between creation and redemption.

Creation and redemption

One of the most distinctive features of Deism is its disinclination to posit any connection between the notions of creation and redemption. Perhaps the most compelling reason for this lack of interest in redemption is the general Deist conviction that redemption is not an essential aspect of the Christian faith. While the theological diversity evident within the loosely-defined Deist movement makes generalizations concerning its stance on critical issues more than a little problematical at times, it is generally accepted that Deism regards redemption as a matter of relative unimportance. The general Deist critique of orthodox Christian belief in the seventeenth century includes explicit criticism of both the necessity of redemption of humanity in the first place, and also any potential involvement of Jesus Christ in the process of redemption.

This can be seen by considering the various theological works of the later Deist writer Thomas Chubb (1679–1747), in which a strongly exemplarist approach is taken to the work of Christ.[128] Humanity does not require redemption, but guidance. That moral guidance is provided through conscience and the moral law, which the Christian faith reflects. The idea that human redemption is necessary is rejected as contrary to right reason; humanity requires no more than guidance and appropriate opportunities to repent. The further idea that redemption is in some sense dependent upon Christ is treated as an irrational hangover from

---

[127] Colin E. Gunton, *The Triune Creator: A Historical and Systematic Study*. Edinburgh: Edinburgh University Press, 1998, 182–4.

[128] See especially Thomas Chubb, *An Enquiry concerning Redemption*. London: J. Cox, 1743.

an earlier, more superstitious era, for which the modern period has no time. Ideas[129]

> . . . such as that men are rendered acceptable to God, and that sinners are recommended to his mercy, either through the perfect obedience or the meritorious sufferings or the prevailing intercession of Christ . . . may fairly be presumed to be no parts of the Christian revelation.

Such ideas were taken up and developed by the Enlightenment, and came to represent the predominant sentiment of German intellectual life in the second half of the eighteenth century.

To place an emphasis upon the doctrine of creation is not, however, to endorse the Deist rejection of the necessity of redemption, nor the connection presupposed in orthodox Christian theology between Christology and soteriology.[130] The Christian theological tradition has always proposed a close mutual relationship between the doctrines of creation and redemption. This can be found at a number of important junctures within the New Testament, especially the Christological hymn of Philippians 2.[131] The theme is developed extensively within the patristic period, perhaps most notably through Irenaeus' formulation of the concept of the 'economy of salvation', in which creation, redemption and consummation are linked together as a single process, initiated and sustained by the one God. There is thus an important eschatological element to the doctrine of creation, just as the Christian doctrine of the last things cannot be properly formulated without reference to the doctrine of creation.[132]

The Christian correlation of creation and redemption is understood and framed primarily in Christological terms. For this reason, we shall move on to consider the link between Christology and creation in more detail.

Creation and Christology

Credo in unum Deum . . . factorem coeli et terrae, visibilium omnium et invisibilium. These familiar words of the Nicene Creed would be taken

---

[129] Thomas Chubb, *The Posthumous Works of Mr Thomas Chubb.* 2 vols. London: J. Cox, 1748, vol. 2, 112–13. For responses to Chubb's critique of original sin and redemption in Christ, see John Rede, *The Doctrine of Original Sin Stated and Defended.* London, 1727.

[130] On which see Friedrich Schleiermacher, *The Christian Faith.* Edinburgh: T&T Clark, 1928, 374–75; Charles Gore, 'Our Lord's Human Example', *Church Quarterly Review* 16 (1883), 282–313; Thomas F. Torrance, *The Trinitarian Faith.* Edinburgh: T&T Clark, 1988, 151–4.

[131] John G. Gibbs, 'The Relation between Creation and Redemption according to Phil. II.5–11', *Novum Testamentum* 12 (1970), 270–83.

[132] Gunton, *The Triune Creator,* 212–25.

by many as an adequate summary of the Christian doctrine of creation. It is especially attractive to those wishing to stress the similarities of Christianity, Judaism and Islam, in that some degree of consensus can be identified across these different religious traditions. Yet this credal statement cannot be taken as a complete summary of the Christian doctrine of creation. The same Nicene Creed continues its exposition of the doctrine of creation by affirming belief in *unum Dominum Jesum Christum . . . per quem omnia facta sunt.*

This has often been misinterpreted as a reference to God the Father as creator, on account of the structure of the preceding phrase, which affirms that Christ is 'consubstantial with the Father', *per quem omnia facta sunt.* Especially in English translation, this could be understood to mean that it is God the Father through whom all things were made. Yet the Nicene Creed as a whole does not admit this interpretation. The second article is Christological in its focus, and its terse set of statements relate to Christ. Those statements which include reference to God are an explication of the identity and significance of Christ, not a duplication of ideas already mentioned in the first article. Thus the Nicene Creed speaks of Christ as *Deus verus de Deo vero, genitus non factus.* This is clearly a statement that Jesus Christ is, in the first place, 'true God from true God', and in the second, 'begotten, not made'. Both statements are Christological in substance and focus. In no way is it being asserted that the 'true God' is 'begotten, not made'. The statement of faith: *et in unum Dominum Jesum Christum . . . consubstantialem Patri, per quem omnia facta sunt* is an unconditional and unambiguous statement that Christ is, in the first place, 'consubstantial with the Father' – an extremely significant anti-Arian affirmation – and in the second place, that it is 'through him [that is, Christ] that all things were made'. The Christian doctrine of creation thus possesses an important Christological orientation which distinguishes it from those of other monotheistic religions.

It is for this reason that Karl Barth affirms that 'it is specifically in Christ, as the Father of our Lord Jesus Christ, that God is called our Creator'.[133] The implications of this linkage between Christology and creation is important, not least on account of its role in ensuring that the doctrines of creation and redemption are not treated as watertight and unrelated areas of Christian theology. In the New Testament, for example, it is clear that there is an implicit continuity between creation

[133] *Church Dogmatics* I/1, 398.

and redemption, focused on the person and work of Christ.[134] In recent theological discussion, there has been a welcome and somewhat overdue realization of the need to return to a trinitarian understanding of creation, which recognizes the Christological dimensions of that doctrine and explores their implications.[135] One such implication, which will be justified and unfolded in this present study, is that the divine rationality – whether we choose to refer to this as *logos* or *ratio* – must be thought of as being *embedded in creation and embodied in Christ.*

Thomas Aquinas developed this point by making a distinction between the efficient and exemplary cause of creation. In his discussion of the doctrine of creation, Aquinas considers the following objections to a Christological reading of the doctrine of creation:[136]

> It seems wrong to explain 'in the beginning (*in principio*) God created the heavens and the earth' as 'in the Son'. The Father is the beginning of the entire divinity, as Augustine says. By 'beginning', therefore, it is appropriate to understand 'the Father'.

Part of the difficulty here is that the Latin term *principium* can bear a number of meanings, including 'principle', 'cause' and 'beginning'. Aquinas' consideration of this point is an excellent example of the medieval concern to clarify the meaning of words before drawing extravagant theological conclusions. His response to these objections is immensely important:

> To the first objection, it should be said that the designation of being the efficient cause is to be appropriated to the Father, whereas that of being the exemplar cause for a work of art is appropriated to the Son, who is the wisdom and art of the Father.

Why is this point so important to this study? Because it affirms that the same divine rationality or wisdom which the natural sciences discern within the created order is to be identified within the *logos* incarnate, Jesus Christ. If indeed Christian theology is concerned, in part, with the unfolding of the significance of Jesus Christ – as traditional Christian orthodoxy has suggested that it is – there is a direct continuity between

---

[134] Peter Stuhlmacher, 'Erwägungen zum ontologischen Charakter der *kaine ktisis* bei Paulus', *Evangelische Theologie* 27 (1967), 1–35.

[135] Colin E. Gunton, *The Triune Creator: A Historical and Systematic Study.* Edinburgh: Edinburgh University Press, 1998, 99–102; 146–74. See also the important account of the Christological aspect of creation set out in Colin E. Gunton, *Christ and Creation.* Grand Rapids, MI: Eerdmans, 1992.

[136] *In II Sent.* Dist. 1 q. 1 a.6.

the study of the creator and of the redeemer. The *duplex cognitio Domini* – which Calvin found so useful a theological device[137] – can be put to fresh use. The study of the creation and of Jesus Christ are contiguous, not unrelated activities. Both creation and Christ bear witness to the one God, and the one divine rationality.

As will become clear during this study, this kind of consideration leads to the possibility of seeing theology as a science in its own right, yet related to other sciences, each of which has its own distinctive subject-matters and means of investigation appropriate to that subject. Such a unitary conception of the human intellectual enterprise is not without its attractions and importance, just as it is not without accompanying difficulties. The exploration of this matter is therefore of considerable interest for the long-standing discussion of the theme of 'theology as a science', which we shall consider in the second volume in this series.

The role of the homoousion *in the scientific theology of T. F. Torrance*

One of the most important contributions to the formulation of a scientific theology in the twentieth century owes its origins to Thomas Forsyth Torrance.[138] One of the most distinctive features of Torrance's exploration of the relation between Christian theology and the natural sciences is the emphasis which he places, not simply on Christology, but upon the *homoousion*, in his approach.[139] This has puzzled some of his more sympathetic readers, not least on account of his extensive engagement with the theological heritage of the eastern Christian church in developing this theme. In what follows, we shall give a critical account of this approach, with a view to identifying its usefulness for the development of a scientific theology.

In keeping with his high view of divine revelation as the foundation and criterion of all authentically Christian theology, Torrance argues that the 'word of God' plays a decisive role in a theological science. Yet he refuses to limit the category of 'the Word' to Scripture; it must also and primarily be understood as referring to Christ:[140]

---

[137] Edward A. Dowey, *The Knowledge of God in Calvin's Theology*. New York: Columbia University Press, 1952; T. H. L. Parker, *Calvin's Doctrine of the Knowledge of God*. Edinburgh: Oliver & Boyd, 1969.

[138] For an introduction, see Alister E. McGrath, *Thomas F. Torrance: An Intellectual Biography*. Edinburgh: T&T Clark, 1999. Torrance prefers to speak of 'theological science', where I have chosen to speak of 'scientific theology'.

[139] See Kang Phee Seng, 'The Epistemological Significance of *Homoousion* in the Theology of Thomas F. Torrance', *Scottish Journal of Theology* 45 (1992), 341–66.

[140] Thomas F. Torrance, *Theology in Reconstruction*. London: SCM Press, 1965, 88.

[This is] the epistemological import of the *homoousion* – the Word is eternal reality and resides as Word in the eternal Being of God himself, and proceeds from him without being less than God. The Word is in fact God himself speaking to us personally, for he personally resides in his Word even when he communicates it to us.

Knowledge of God is thus dependent upon God's decision that such knowledge shall be possible, and that this knowledge will be embodied in Christ as *Deus loquentis persona*. 'Everything hinges upon the reality of God's *self*-communication to us in Jesus Christ . . . so that for us to know God in Jesus Christ is really to know him as he is in himself.'[141] Torrance thus insists that the distinctive nature of theology is determined by its object, which is defined as God revealed in Jesus Christ. Torrance invokes the theological principle of the *homoousion* in making the point that this epistemological insight is ontologically determined. God already is what God's historical self-revelation in Christ discloses God to be. Epistemology is thus directly correlated with ontology.

Torrance had stressed this point as early as 1938, in a series of un-published lectures delivered at Auburn Theological Seminary, New York. The *ordo cognoscendi* is only possible on account of the *ordo essendi* – and the *ordo essendi* is disclosed in the incarnate God, Jesus Christ. Torrance's affirmation of the ontological and epistemological centrality of the incarnation is quite remarkable, and has highly important implications for his understanding of theological science. Any form of scientific knowledge – including Christian theology – must be reached 'strictly in accordance with the nature (κατὰ φύσιν) of the reality being investigated, what is, knowledge of it reached under the constraint of what it actually and essentially is in itself, and not according to arbitrary convention (κατὰ θέσιν).'[142] And how is the nature of that reality to be established in the case of theological science? For Torrance, the answer is as simple as it is profound: in Christ, as God incarnate.

The connection between the doctrines of incarnation and creation should be noted before proceeding further. Torrance argues that the Christian doctrine of creation lays the foundation for a 'created intelligibility' which can be discerned by the human mind.[143] Yet the

---

[141] Thomas F. Torrance, *Reality and Evangelical Theology*. Philadelphia: Westminster Press, 1982, 23.

[142] Torrance, *The Trinitarian Faith*, 51.

[143] Thomas F. Torrance, *The Ground and Grammar of Theology*. Belfast: Christian Journals Ltd, 1980, 99.

Christian doctrine of creation cannot be separated from the Christian doctrine of God – and, in that this specific doctrine is Christologically determined, it cannot be separated from Christ. There is a seamless connection between creation, creator and Christ. 'The very centre of a saving faith is the belief, not merely in God, but in God as Father, and not merely in Christ, but in Christ as the Son of God, in him, not as a creature, but as God the Creator, born of God.'[144] God is known through Christ – and through Christ, we have access to the same divine rationality which is embedded within the created order.[145]

> The full concept of contingency of the creation carries with it the idea that God is related to the universe, neither arbitrarily or necessarily, but through the freedom of his grace and will, when out of sheer love he created the universe and grounded it in his own transcendent Logos or Rationality.

Torrance here stresses that the ordering we discern within nature is not the consequence of any intrinsic property of matter which God was somehow obligated to respect in the act of creation. For Torrance, the doctrine of creation *ex nihilo* means that the ordering of the universe reflects only the divine rationality, in that no external considerations or pressures had to be taken into account in the act of creation. Creation represents the imposition of an ordering upon things which is contingent in the sense that God was not coerced by any external factors in ordering things in this specific manner.

From what has been said in this section, it should be clear that the scientific theology set out in these volumes has nothing of any great importance in common with Deism. The Christological and trinitarian aspects of an authentically *Christian* approach to creation immediately establish links with a network of interlocking doctrines, which must be regarded as present (and presupposed) even when the emphasis falls upon the doctrine of creation, rather than another locus.

This therefore brings us to the important question: what are the implications for a Christian doctrine of creation, both for a scientific theology and for a right understanding of the relation between a positive and constructive Christian theology and the natural sciences? We shall begin to explore this in the following chapter (Ch. 5).

---

[144] Torrance, *The Trinitarian Faith*, 53, citing Hilary of Poitiers.
[145] Torrance, *The Trinitarian Faith*, 105.

Chapter 5

Implications of a
Christian Doctrine of Creation

arlier (Ch. 4), we explored the contours of a Christian understanding of creation, setting out some of its leading features,
and making some preliminary comments concerning the impact
of this framework for a scientific theology. It is now appropriate to
explore the consequences of a Christian understanding of creation in
rather more detail.

The rendering of God in creation

The Christian understanding of creation leads directly to the conclusion
that there is a correspondence – the degree of which requires clarification
– between the works of God and the being of God. Creation and
redemption are not merely interconnected within the economy of
salvation; they can each be argued to embody the character of God. For
the Christian, the creation is not divine, but bears the hallmarks of
divine crafting. The fundamental assumption of a responsible natural
theology, to which we shall return later in this project, is that we are
authorized by Scripture to seek a partial disclosure of the glory of God
through the works of God in creation. God is rendered in and through
the creation.[1]

This insight is characteristic of Christian theology, and is not to
be identified with any specific period or school of thought. It was, as

---

[1] I borrow this way of speaking from the important study of Dale Patrick, *The Rendering
of God in the Old Testament*. Philadelphia: Fortress Press, 1981. While this work focuses on
the use of narratives, its general method is easily applied to the specific narrative of creation.

M. D. Chenu has argued, developed with particular sensitivity during the Middle Ages. At this time, 'nature' was seen and read as 'creation' – a physical entity which was encrusted with divine 'signatures', pointing to its origins in God and its capacity to offer an indirect knowledge of the divine will and character.[2]

> All natural or historical reality possessed a *signification* which transcended its crude reality and which a certain symbolic dimension of that reality would reveal to man's mind . . . Giving an account of things involved more than explaining them by reference to their internal causes; it involved discovering the dimension of a mystery.

As Chenu points out, the Christian doctrine of creation affirms that it is not the individual believer who gives signs their meaning. Rather, the meaning is intrinsic to the sign, in that it is those objective elements themselves which, 'before anything else and by their very nature, were so many representations, so many analogies'.[3] This kind of approach runs counter to the general direction of the postmodern deconstruction of any such claims to representation. Writers such as Barthes and Derrida would argue that this understanding of the symbolic potential of creation represents the improper and inept attribution of human-generated meanings to an external source. Yet it is an essential element of the Christian understanding of both the nature of the created order, and the nature of human observers and interpreters of that order, as those who have been created in the image of God.

It is also important to note the implications of the Christian notion of creation *ex nihilo*. In an important study of the creation motif, Charles Long argues that a doctrine of creation *ex nihilo* possesses four distinctive characteristics:[4]

1. The god who creates is affirmed to be all-powerful. Neither this power nor the work of creation is assigned to an inferior being.

2. God exists prior to the creation itself. There is no other being, power or created entity which exists before God.

3. The mode of creation is such that this act is to be considered as conscious, ordered and deliberate. Creation is a purposeful and directed action, revealing a 'plan of action'.

---

[2] M. D. Chenu, *Nature, Man and Society in the Twelfth Century*. Chicago: University of Chicago Press, 1968, 102.

[3] Chenu, *Nature, Man and Society in the Twelfth Century*, 126.

[4] Charles Long, *Alpha: The Myths of Creation*. New York: George Braziller, 1963, 149.

4. The creator is to be regarded as free of limitations imposed by the 'inertia of a prior reality'.

To understand the importance of these points (especially the fourth), we must consider the implications of a cosmogony which declines to regard God as creator, and entrusts this task to a lower being within a celestial hierarchy. There can be little doubt that the doctrine of creation set forth by the second-century Gnostic theologian Valentinus was seen as posing a particular threat to the teaching of the early church. There are certain difficulties in identifying this teaching with precision, partly due to the fact that we know Valentinus' ideas largely through citations in writings of his opponents, including Clement of Alexandria.[5] The Valentinian school is better known and understood, partly through extensive citations in the writings of Irenaeus of Lyons, and partly through a number of additional sources, including the *Excerpta ex Theodoto*. This important source – which is summarized in Irenaeus' *adversus haereses* – gives a full account of the creation of the Demiurge, and its subsequent activity.[6] In the course of an exposition of Genesis 1:1–4 – the only commentary on this text, incidentally, to have survived from a Gnostic source – we learn that the Demiurge is created by Sophia, who then uses the Demiurge as the agent through which she creates the world from pre-existing 'psychic' and 'hylic' substances.[7] There are strong affinities here with Middle Platonist concepts, particularly in relation to the idea that the original substances of the cosmos were initially in a state of chaos, and required to be separated out and ordered by the Demiurge.[8] The *Excerpta ex Theodoto* interprets the separation of light and darkness (Genesis 1:4) in terms of the Demiurge's separation of psychic and hylic matter within the primeval chaotic mixture, prior to ordering them.

Our concern is not, however, to offer a detailed account of the Valentinian cosmogonic myth, but to explore its implications for how the nature of God is rendered in the work of creation. There would appear to be two highly significant consequences of this.

---

[5] The best study is Jens Holzhausen, *Der 'Mythos vom Menschen' im hellenistischen Ägypten: eine Studie zum 'Poimandres' (=CH I), zu Valentin und dem gnostischen Mythos*. Bodenheim: Athenaum Hain Hanstein, 1994. See also Everett Procter, *Christian Controversy in Alexandria: Clement's Polemic Against the Basilideans and Valentinians*. New York: Peter Lang, 1995.

[6] *Excerpta ex Theodoto* 47.2 – 48.1; summarized in Irenaeus, *adversus haereses* I.v.2.

[7] On the Sophia myth, see G. C. Stead, 'The Valentinian Myth of Sophia', *Journal of Theological Studies* 20 (1969), 75–104.

[8] Walter Spoerri, *Späthellenistische Berichte über Welt, Kultur und Götter*. Basel: Reinhardt, 1959, 69–113.

1. The character of the creation is determined in part by the primeval matter from which the cosmos is fashioned. Limitations are thus placed upon the work of creation by lack of malleability of the original material. The ideas of the creator are thus imperfectly enacted in the resulting creation, and cannot be taken to represent a direct and complete expression of the mind of God. The Valentinian cosmogonical myth allows a ready explanation of the origins of evil; this is held to result from the intractability of the pre-existing material.

2. The Valentinian myth places ontological distance between God and the creation, through the role of intermediaries in the work of separation and ordering. We are not talking about 'God' as creator, but a subsidiary agent of questionable status. For Plato, and forms of Gnosticism influenced by the creation myth of the *Timaeus*, creation is the work of the Demiurge. The cosmos originated through the fall of an aeon, and neither the fact nor the specific form of its existence corresponds to the mind of God. The work of creation is to be ascribed to the lower ranks of the hierarchy of entities proposed within the Valentinian cosmology.[9]

Created rationality and the possibility of theological reflection

Our concern in this chapter is not to establish a detailed account of the nature of humanity, viewed from a theological perspective, but to begin the exploration of the manner in which human beings are able to grasp something of the rationality of the created order, and give an ordered account of what they discern. John Polkinghorne identifies the point we wish to consider as follows:[10]

> We are so familiar with the fact that we can understand the world that most of the time we take it for granted. It is what makes science possible. Yet it could have been otherwise. The universe might have been a disorderly chaos rather than an orderly cosmos. Or it might have had a rationality which was inaccessible to us . . . There is a congruence between our minds and the universe, between the rationality experienced within

---

[9] There is a useful account in the older study of Werner Foerster, *Von Valentin zu Herakleon: Untersuchungen über die Quellen und Entwicklung der valentinianischen Gnosis.* Giessen: Topelmann, 1928.

[10] John Polkinghorne, *Science and Creation: The Search for Understanding.* London: SPCK, 1988, 20–1. The allusion to the theories of Michael Polanyi will be obvious: see Michael Polanyi, *Personal Knowledge.* New York: Harper & Row, 1964.

and the rationality observed without. This extends not only to the mathematical articulation of fundamental theory but also to all those tacit acts of judgement, exercised with intuitive skill, which are equally indispensable to the scientific endeavour.

That human beings have been remarkably successful in investigating and grasping something of the structure and workings of the world is beyond dispute. Precisely why the rationality of the world should be so accessible to human beings remains rather more puzzling. Polkinghorne is quite clear as to how a Christian might offer an explanation of this observation:[11]

> If the deep-seated congruence of the rationality present in our minds with the rationality present in the world is to find a true explanation, it must surely lie in some more profound reason which is the ground of both. Such a reason would be provided by the Rationality of the Creator.

Human rationality and the imago Dei

One of the fundamental themes of the Christian understanding of human nature is that humanity has been created in the *imago Dei* (Genesis 1:28). The right understanding of this issue has been debated down the centuries within the Christian theological tradition.[12] The Old Testament description of humanity as created 'in the image and likeness of God' is agreed to be foundational to an authentically Christian conception of humanity.[13] The language of this statement immediately implies relationship within a framework of divergence: human beings may in some sense be 'like' God, or bear the divine image – but humanity is *not* divine. Humanity is part of the created order, and distinguished from the remainder of that order by its unique role as the divine image-bearer. It can be said to 'stand out' (*existere*) for that reason. Humanity thus finds itself in an ambivalent position within creation, being at one and the same time part of that creation yet also bearing a particular and significant relationship with the creator which has not been granted to the remainder of the created order.[14]

---

[11] Polkinghorne, *Science and Creation*, 22.

[12] For its interpretation in recent Old Testament scholarship, see A. Jónsson Gunnlaugur and S. Cheney Michael, *The Image of God: Genesis 1:26–28 in a Century of Old Testament Research*. Stockholm: Almqvist & Wiksell International, 1988.

[13] Tryggve N. D. Mettinger, 'Abbild oder Urbild? "Imago Dei" in traditionsgeschichtlicher Sicht', *Zeitschrift für Alttestamentlicher Wissenschaft* 86 (1974), 403–24.

[14] See further James Barr, 'The Image of God in the Book of Genesis: A Study of Terminology', *Bulletin of the John Rylands Library* 51 (1968), 11–26.

It must be stressed that the Christian interpretation of the *imago Dei* is Christological. I make this point partly in response to the theological exaggerations and posturings which have, sadly, emerged from an overzealous and perhaps rather uncritical reading of the notion of the *imago Dei*, which links it with the doctrine of the Trinity to yield a syllogism along the following lines:

> God, as Trinity, is X.
> Humanity is created in the image of God.
> Therefore humanity is also X.

The doctrine of the Trinity would seem to be singularly ill-suited to functioning as a criterion or point of access to other theological insights in this manner. From an evangelical perspective, this tendency is especially disturbing, in that it marks a serious erosion of any willingness to be closely attentive to the biblical text, heading off into what Luther and Calvin would regard as the less impressive type of scholastic speculation. The new vocabulary which has emerged from this style of theological speculation – 'perichoretic dancing' being a particularly luminous example – may be regarded as illustrating precisely the kind of unanchored speculation which a scientific theology aims to discourage.

Now perichoretic dancing might be fun, and might even have a significant impact on popular culture if it was to be done well. But it cannot be taken seriously as responsible theology. In response to those who rather like perichoretic dancing, three things may be pointed out. First, the question of the extent to which the *imago Dei* in humanity has been corrupted or distorted remains a point of serious theological debate, so that the simplistic assumption that some direct transposition may be made between God and humanity in this manner is potentially unrealistic. Second, such puzzling (and to those *extra muros ecclesiae*, absurd) theological ramblings are the inevitable outcome of a failure to be attentive and responsive to the biblical texts. Third, Scripture affirms that the image of God, in which we are created, is rendered (or, better, is made incarnate) in Christ – that is, in a specific historical figure, rather than a conceptual abstraction.[15] The God whose image is rendered

---

[15] This is an especially important theme of the writings of two leading British theologians of the twentieth century, Hugh Ross Mackintosh and Thomas Forsyth Torrance. See Robert R. Redman, *Reformulating Reformed Theology: Jesus Christ in the Theology of Hugh Ross Mackintosh*. Lanham, MD: University Press of America, 1997; Kang Phee Seng, 'The Epistemological Significance of *Homoousion* in the Theology of Thomas F. Torrance', *Scottish Journal of Theology* 45 (1992), 341–66.

in humanity is the 'God and Father of our Lord Jesus Christ' (1 Peter 1:3). The Christian tradition has always insisted that Christ is the true image of God (Colossians 1:15), and that humanity has been created according to this image. To use the language and conceptualities of the Alexandrian theology of the fourth century, the divine *logos* is the prototype which God used in the creation of humanity; Christ is thus the archetype of what it is and means to be human.[16]

Related ideas can be found in the writings of Marius Victorinus, particularly in his two treatises against Arius (359). Victorinus here argues that a clear distinction must be drawn between the *logos*, who is the true *imago Dei*, and human rationality, which is created *ad imaginem* – that is, after the pattern of the *logos*.[17] Augustine rejected this idea, and insisted that human rationality was not simply created *ad imaginem*, but was such that it was in itself a true *imago Dei*.[18]

The interpretation of the *imago Dei* motif within the Christian theological tradition has resulted in some immensely rich insights. Origen pointed out that the theme did more than reflect distinctive aspects of human nature; it allowed the unique goal of humanity to be identified:[19]

'And God said, "Let us make man in our image and likeness"' (Genesis 1:26). He then adds: 'In the image of God he made him' (Genesis 1:27), and is silent about the likeness. This indicates that in his first creation man received the dignity of the image of God, but the fulfilment of the likeness is reserved for the final consummation; that is, that he himself should obtain it by his own effort, through the imitation of God. The possibility of perfection given to him at the beginning by the dignity of the image, and then in the end, through the fulfilment of his works, should bring to perfect consummation the likeness of God.

Other theologians reflected on the impact of sin upon this image; what sin distorted or disfigured would be restored at the final perfection of all things.[20]

---

[16] Walter J. Burghardt, *The Image of God in Man according to Cyril of Alexandria*. Woodstock, MA: Woodstock Press, 1957.

[17] Marius Victorinus, *contra Arium* IA.20. See further Pierre Hadot, 'L'image de la trinité dans l'âme chez Victorinus et chez Saint Augustin', *Studia Patristica* 6 (1962), 409–42.

[18] Augustine, *de Trinitate*, VIII.vi.12.

[19] Origen, *de principiis*, III.iv.1. See further Henri Crouzel, *Théologie de l'image de Dieu chez Origène*. Paris: Aubier, 1956.

[20] For an account, see Peter Schwanz, *Imago Dei als christologisch-anthropologisches Problem in der Geschichte der Alten Kiche von Paulus bis Clemens von Alexandrien*. Halle: Niemeyer, 1970.

Perhaps the most important and influential discussion of the issue can be found in the tradition which identifies the *imago Dei* with human reason – a resource which is meant to be used to seek and apprehend God. The idea can be found in Augustine, especially in *de Trinitate*.[21] According to Augustine:[22]

> The image of the creator is to be found in the rational or intellectual soul of humanity . . . Although reason and intellect may at times be dormant, or may appear to be weak at some times, and strong at others, the human soul cannot be anything other than rational and intellectual. It has been created according to the image of God in order that it may use reason and intellect in order to apprehend and behold God.

Human rationality thus corresponds to – but is not identical with – divine rationality.

This idea finds further development in the writings of Thomas Aquinas.[23] Aquinas' discussion of the relationship of human rationality to its origins in the mind of God has achieved classic status within the Christian theological tradition, and merits close analysis on account of its sustained engagement of what it means for humanity to be created in the *imago Dei*. Aquinas argues that the divine image is specifically to be identified with rationality, so that only intellectual beings – by which he means angels and humans – can be regarded as true image-bearers.[24] Three general levels of this *imago* can be discerned:

1. At the most basic level, all human beings may be said to possess this image, in that they possess a natural aptitude or capacity for understanding at least something of God, and responding to God in love.

2. At a more developed level, this capacity becomes an actuality, when people 'actually or habitually know and love God, even though imperfectly'.

[21] John Sullivan, *The Image of God: The Doctrine of St Augustine and its Influence*. Dubuque, IA: Priory Press, 1963.

[22] Augustine, *de Trinitate* XVI.iv.6.

[23] For rich documentary illustration of the background to Aquinas' ideas here, see the rather jumbled collection of material presented in Robert Javelet, *Image et ressemblance au douzième siècle*. Paris: Letouzey et Ané, 1967. A more analytical and critical account may be found in Stephan Otto, *Die Funktion des Bildbegriffes in der Theologie des 12. Jahrhunderts*. Münster: Aschendorff, 1963.

[24] E.g., see Aquinas, *Summa theologiae* Ia q. 93, aa. 2, 6.

3. At the most advanced level, the image is perfected when God is seen face to face, in the beatific vision.[25]

Our concern in the present chapter is to consider Aquinas' understanding of the 'lowest' actualization of the *imago Dei*. According to Aquinas, in the fall, humanity lost any supernatural gifts of grace, yet retained the natural powers of the soul, including its ability to think and reason.

Aquinas is clear that God, as an intellective being, must create a world in which there are other intellectual beings, precisely because of the ontologically grounded correspondence between the creator and the creation.[26]

All that moves God to the production of created beings is God's own goodness, which God willed to share with other entities by way of assimilation . . . But a likeness of one thing can be found in another in two different manners. First, in respect of the being of nature, as when the likeness of the heat of a fire can be said to be in a thing which has been heated by that fire. Second, in respect of cognition, as when the likeness of a fire can be said to be found in a sense of sight or touch. Therefore, in order that a likeness of God might be in things as perfectly as possible, the divine goodness had to be shared with things though a likeness that is shared both in being and in cognition. Yet it is the intellect alone which can have cognition of the divine goodness. Therefore it was necessary for there to be intellectual creatures.

Aquinas thus argues that the divine intellect, which patterned the creation, can also be discerned within the operation of the human intellect. This leads to a clear link emerging in Aquinas' thought between the rationality of God and that of the created order on the one hand, and that of the human soul on the other. Perhaps the most obvious implication of this concerns the question of natural law, which we shall consider presently. As one commentator points out:[27]

For Aquinas, reason and the principles of rational organization are central to understanding the universe. God too follows some version of rationality. Aquinas suggests that since God created human beings in a certain way – i.e. through the divine archetypes in the eternal law, after which human nature is patterned – then it follows, so Aquinas argues, that the

---

[25] William J. Hoye, *Actualitas omnium actuum: Man's Beatific Vision of God as apprehended by Thomas Aquinas.* Meisenheim: Hain, 1975; Anton C. Pegis, *At the Origins of the Thomistic Notion of Man.* New York: Macmillan, 1963.

[26] Aquinas, *Summa contra Gentiles*, II.46.6.

[27] Anthony J. Lisska, *Aquinas' Theory of Natural Law: An Analytic Reconstruction.* Oxford: Clarendon Press, 1996, 113–14.

moral principles commanded must be in accord with the moral principles derived from the dispositional analysis of human nature. It would be inconsistent, therefore, for God to have commanded moral prescriptions which would go against the natural law. To do this would entail that God acted inconsistently, going against the content of a human essence as defined foundationally in the divine archetype.

For Aquinas, there is a congruence of rationality between the creator and the creation. This general approach has found wide acceptance within the Christian tradition, although some modifications have been advocated. We note two in what follows.

In an important discussion of the theme of the *imago Dei*, John Calvin argues that Adam was created with 'right understanding'.[28]

> The integrity with which Adam was endowed is expressed by this word [*imago*]. He had full possession of a right understanding, with his affections kept within the limits of reason and his senses were tempered in right order . . . Though the primary seat of the divine image was in the mind and the heart, or in the soul and its powers, there was nevertheless no part of humanity in which some sparks did not glow . . . From this we may conclude that, when this image was placed within humanity, a distinction is introduced which raises humanity above all other creatures.

A significant point of divergence from Aquinas becomes clear when Calvin turns to consider the effect of sin upon human rationality. Calvin regards the fall of humanity to have a significant and detrimental effect on the *imago Dei*. This image is not destroyed by sin; on the basis of Calvin's analysis, this would result in humanity being reduced to the level of other creatures. Nevertheless, both the human intellect and will are corrupted. The human mind is now unable completely to recognize and respond to 'right reason'; the human will becomes enslaved to desires and passions focusing on the creation, rather than the creator.[29]

> Now since reason, by which humanity distinguishes good and evil, understands and judges, is a natural gift, it could not be completely eliminated [through the fall], but was partly weakened and partly corrupted . . . [Humanity remains] a rational being, different from the animals because it has been endowed with understanding . . . Likewise the will, because it cannot be separated from human nature, has not perished, but is so enslaved to wicked desires that it cannot pursue the right.

[28] Calvin, *Institutes* I.xv.3.
[29] Calvin, *Institutes* II.ii.12.

One of Calvin's more significant theological conclusions to depend upon this analysis is that the natural human tendency is towards idolatry – that is, a worship of the creature in place of the creator. This has important consequences for Calvin's views on natural theology, which he regards to have a genuine yet limited role in positive theological reflection. It also compromises the relational capacity of the *imago Dei*, in that what was intended to lead humanity towards God now has the potential to deflect it from precisely that relationship.

This point is developed further by the Swiss theologian Emil Brunner, who distinguishes two aspects of the *imago Dei*. Brunner argues that what he terms the 'formal' aspect of the divine image has to do with human identity. In this sense, the *imago Dei* serves to distinguish humanity from other aspects of God's creation; this status is not compromised by sin.[30]

> In the Old Testament, the Bible describes this formal aspect of human nature by the concept of 'being made in the image of God'. In the thought of the Old Testament the fact that humanity has been 'made in the Image of God' means something which humanity can never lose; even when they sin, they cannot lose it. This conception is therefore unaffected by the contrast between sin and grace, or sin and obedience, precisely because it describes the 'formal' or 'structural', and not the 'material' aspect of human nature . . . Thus the formal aspect of human nature, as beings 'made in the image of God', denotes being as Subject, or freedom; it is this which differentiates humanity from the lower creation; this constitutes its specifically *human* quality; it is this which is given to humanity – and to humanity alone – and under all circumstances by Divine appointment.

Alongside this, Brunner postulates a second aspect of the *imago Dei* – the 'material' aspect of the matter. Where the formal dimension of the image of God has to do with the structure of humanity, the material aspect is concerned with human relationality towards God, which Brunner finds developed especially in the New Testament:[31]

> The New Testament simply presupposes this fact that humanity – in its very nature – has been 'made in the image of God'; it does not develop this any further. To the Apostles what matters most is the 'material' realization of this God-given quality; that is, that humanity should really give *the* answer which the Creator intends, the response in which God is honoured, and in which He fully imparts Himself, the response of

---

[30] Emil Brunner, *The Christian Doctrine of Creation and Redemption*. London: Lutterworth Press, 1952, 57.

[31] Brunner, *Creation and Redemption*, 58.

reverent, grateful love, given not only in words, but in its whole life. The New Testament, in its doctrine of the *Imago Dei*, tells us that this right answer has not been given; that a quite different one has been given instead, in which the glory is not given to God, but to human beings and to creatures, in which humanity does not live in the love of God, but seeks itself. Secondly, the New Testament is the proclamation of what God has done in order that he may turn this false answer into the true one. Here, therefore, the fact that humanity has been 'made in the image of God' is spoken of as having been lost, and indeed as wholly, and not partially lost. Humanity no longer possesses this *Imago Dei;* but it is restored through Him, through whom God glorifies and gives Himself: through Jesus Christ. The restoration of the *Imago Dei,* the new creation of the original image of God in humanity, is identical with the gift of God in Jesus Christ received by faith.

In this way, Brunner brings together a cluster of important concepts, including rationality and relationality. Created human nature is such that it is able to discern the divine ordering of the universe, and enter into a relationship with the creator God – not by right, but by grace.[32]

It would be possible to extend this discussion at length, exploring in some detail the various ways in which Christian theologians have understood human nature and its capacity to discern the rationality within creation.[33] Our concern, however, is to explore the importance of the fundamental congruence – but not identity – of the divine rationality on the one hand, and that found within the creation, including humanity itself, for a scientific theology. In what follows, we shall explore the importance of a Christian doctrine of creation for reflection upon the spiritual, intellectual and moral aspects of the created order.

In turning to do so, it is important to recall a point which was stressed throughout the previous analysis (Ch. 4) – that an authentically Christian doctrine of creation interconnects with a network of other Christian doctrines, including the person of Christ, the Trinity, and redemption.

Spiritual rationality: responding to Feuerbach

We begin by considering the criticism of religion made by Ludwig Feuerbach (1818–83), which is generally taken to assert that the

---

[32] For the differences between Barth and Brunner at this point, see Joan O'Donovan, 'Man in the Image of God: The Disagreement between Barth and Brunner Reconsidered', *Scottish Journal of Theology* 39 (1986), 433–59.

[33] A good starting point here is David Cairns, *The Image of God in Man.* London: Collins, 1973.

conception of God is essentially a projection of human emotions on to an imaginary transcendent screen.[34] The idea of God is nothing more than the objectification of human attributes. Feuerbach's critique was developed by both Karl Marx (religion as the product of socio-economic alienation) and Sigmund Freud (religion as wish-fulfilment), and has been of major importance in underpinning the plausibility of atheism in western culture.[35] The general thrust of Feuerbach's argument, as it has been received and developed within western culture, can be summarized thus: human beings long for the existence of a God, and therefore invent such a God. It is therefore important to explore how the doctrine of creation relates to the charge that God is the construct of the human imagination.

The background to Feuerbach's work must be taken into account at this point. During the period of the Enlightenment, the German universities came to be seen as centres of social protest against the con-servativism of the *ancien régime*. They fostered the progressive and modernist ideology of the Enlightenment, in conscious opposition to that of the past. A critical attitude to the religious past was seen as an integral element of this programme of social protest: the emphasis on present religious experience and rational reflection was partly due to a determination that the authority of the past should not be allowed to intrude on the present. The churches were widely regarded as embodying conservative political and social attitudes, and thus became a target – both as institutions, and in terms of their underlying theologies – for radical criticism.

There was a widespread reaction against institutional Christianity on the part of a 'Young Germany' which had expected the French Revolution to usher in a new and progressive period in German history. Nothing of the sort happened, and many young people were con-sequently disillusioned and alienated from the establishment, whether church or state. And if direct attacks upon the church were unrealistic, given the political situation of the time, then that church could nevertheless be attacked indirectly, by way of its foundational doctrines.

---

[34] The language of 'projection' is due to George Eliot's influential English translation of Feuerbach's *Das Wesen des Christentums* ('The Essence of Christianity', 1841), which used this word to render the German term *Vergegenständlichung*, which is better translated as 'objectification'.

[35] See Heinz Fastenrath, *Ein Abriss atheistischer Grundpositionen: Feuerbach, Marx, Nietzsche, Sartre*. Stuttgart: Klett, 1993; Werner Schuffenhauer, *Feuerbach und der junge Marx: Zur Entstehungsgeschichte der marxistischen Weltanschauung*. Berlin: Deutscher Verlag der Wissenschaften, 1972.

If the existence of the church depended upon its central legitimating doctrines, then a critique of the plausibility of such doctrines would serve to undermine the social credibility and status of the churches. The sensation accompanying the publication of D. F. Strauss' *Life of Jesus* (1835) was partly due to its appeal to socially and religiously alienated progressive elements, who recognized it as a useful propaganda weapon in their concerted attack on each and every aspect of the German establishment.[36]

Feuerbach's *Essence of Christianity* reflects this mood of rebellion against the past, and a longing for political and religious liberation. In the foreword to the first edition of his work, Feuerbach states that the purpose of the work is 'to show that the supernatural mysteries of religion are based upon quite simple natural truths'. The leading idea of the work is deceptively simple: human beings have created the gods, who embody their own idealized conception of their aspirations, needs and fears. Nevertheless, to suggest that Feuerbach merely reduces the divine to the natural is to inhibit appreciation of his full significance. The permanent significance of the work lies not in its repetition of the reductionist theology of Xenophanes or Lucretius, which affirmed that human beings constructed gods in the likeness of themselves. Rather, it lies in its detailed analysis of the means by which religious concepts arise within the human consciousness.

Feuerbach argues that human consciousness of feelings, such as fear or love, leads to their objectification and externalization:[37]

> Consciousness of God is human self-consciousness; knowledge of God is human self-knowledge. By the God you know the human, and conversely, by the human, you know the God. The two are one. What God is to a person that too is the spirit, the soul; and what the spirit, the soul, are to a person, that is the God. God is the revealed and explicit inner self of a human being . . . The historical progress of religion consists therefore in this: that what an earlier religion took to be objective, is later recognized to be subjective; what formerly was taken to be God, and worshipped as such, is not recognized to be something human. What was earlier religion is later taken to be idolatry: humans are seen to have adored their own nature. Humans objectified themselves but failed to recognize themselves as this object. The later religion takes this step; every advance in religion is therefore a deepening in self-knowledge.

---

[36] M. C. Massey, 'The Literature of Young Germany and D. F. Strauss' *Life of Jesus*', *Journal of Religion* 59 (1979), 298–323.

[37] Ludwig Feuerbach, *Das Wesen des Christentums*. 2 vols. Berlin: Akademie Verlag, 1956, vol. 1, 51–2. For a detailed account of Feuerbach at this point, see Wartofsky, *Feuerbach*, 220–6.

For Feuerbach, religious experience is nothing more than an expression or an embodiment of the feeling that human beings have of their own sensible nature. As such, they are liable mistakenly to objectify such feelings in terms of an imaginary God: 'If feeling is the essential instrumentality or organ of religion, then God's nature is nothing other than an expression of the nature of feeling . . . The divine essence, which is comprehended by feeling, is actually nothing other than the essence of feeling, enraptured and delighted with itself – nothing but self-intoxicated, self-contented feeling.'

Thus for Feuerbach, the doctrine of the incarnation enshrines the insight that God is human, and enables human beings to value their own humanity as they would otherwise value deity. 'Religion is the reflection, the mirroring of human nature in itself.' 'God-consciousness' is merely human self-awareness, not a distinct category of human experience. Even if Feuerbach did not totally reduce theology to anthropology, he at least succeeded in creating formidable difficulties for any theology which began with human feelings and inferred the existence of external or objective realities from them.

The criticism of religion which has developed from Feuerbach – whether it is expressed in its Marxian or Freudian variants – argues that because humans long for a divine being, such a being is to be dismissed as an illusion or construct of the human imagination. It is a demonstrable fact that humans long for such a divine being; therefore the alleged existence of such a being is nothing more than the result of the unrequited pinings of the human imagination and emotions. 'What human beings want to exist, they make their god.' As Hans Küng summarizes the matter:[38] 'The notion of God is seen as a psychological product of man.'

Feuerbach's criticism of Christianity may, however, itself be critiqued on the basis of a Christian doctrine of creation. The fundamental point which needs to be made here is that that Christian doctrine of creation can be argued to posit such a longing for God, as an aspect of the situation of fallen humanity. What Feuerbach proposes as an extrasystemic critique of Christian theology can be reformulated as its intrasystemic confirmation. To illustrate this, we shall consider Augustine of Hippo's reflections on the doctrine of creation, especially as set out in his *Confessions.*

From its outset, the *Confessions* develop the view that human beings have been created to worship God. Humanity has been created in order

[38] Hans Küng, *Does God Exist? An Answer for Today.* London: Collins, 1980, 208.

to relate to God, and until that relationship is established, human nature will be empty and dissatisfied.[39]

> To praise you is the desire of humanity, a small piece of your creation. You stir humanity to take pleasure in praising you, because you have made us for yourself and our heart is restless until it rests in you.

A human longing for God is thus built into the fabric of creation, precisely because creation is a purposeful and directed process.[40] Humanity has been created for a reason, and endowed with the resources to discern, apprehend and behold God – as we have seen, through the created faculties of the human soul. Augustine thus depicts fallen humanity as questing for God, experiencing emptiness and dissatisfaction, and finally achieving rest only when relationality with God has been achieved.

The idea was developed further in commentaries on Augustine, especially within the medieval spiritual tradition, for which the question of human longing for God was of particular importance. In his prayers, Anselm of Canterbury develops Augustine's reflections on God's creation of humanity.[41] The following extract from the 'Prayer to Christ' develops Augustine's idea that the human longing for God is implanted within humanity by God, in order to draw humanity back to fellowship with their creator and redeemer:[42]

> Lord, if what you inspire is good,
> or rather because it is good, that I should want to love you,
> give me what you have made me want:
> grant that I may attain to love you as much as you command.
> I praise and thank you for the desire that you have inspired;
> and I offer you praise and thanks
> lest your gift to me be unfruitful,
> which you have given me of your own accord.
> Perfect what you have begun,
> and grant me what you have made me long for,

---

[39] Augustine, *Confessions* I.i.1.

[40] There are some especially important reflections in Book XI of the *Confessions*: see E. P. Meijering, *Augustin über Schöpfung, Ewigkeit und Zeit: das elfte Buch der Bekenntnisse.* Leiden: E. J. Brill, 1979.

[41] Some useful related material is to be found in Katherin A. Rogers, *The Anselmian Approach to God and Creation.* Lewiston, NY: Edwin Mellen Press, 1997.

[42] *The Prayers and Meditations of St Anselm*, translated by Benedicta Ward. Harmondsworth: Penguin, 1973, 94–5.

not according to my deserts but out of your kindness
that came first to me.

The point being made by Anselm is that the human longing for God is
itself the work of God, and is to be seen as an aspect of the economy
of salvation. God, having created humanity in order to enter into a
living and loving relationship with their creator, graciously provides
resources and assistance to bring this process of return and renewal
possible. The human sense of longing is therefore not to be interpreted
– as in Feuerbach – as a misdirection of purely natural human feelings,
hopes or fears, which leads to the illegitimate construction of the notion
of God when there is, in fact, no such God. Rather, it is to be seen as
an integral aspect of a coherent Christian doctrine of creation, set within
the economy of salvation. The rationality of faith thus offers a very
different interpretation of the same phenomenon, observed yet interpreted in a very different manner by Feuerbach.

Nothing can be proved from this discussion. Feuerbach proposes –
but cannot verify, still less falsify – his theory that God is essentially a
human construction. Within a culture which is predisposed to regard
belief in God as odd, perhaps even insane, Feuerbach offers a reassuring
theory which purports to explain why anyone might develop such an
idea. Yet its plausibility is primarily cultural, rather than intellectual, in
its derivation. The Christian doctrine of creation offers a quite different
account of the matter, equally unverifiable and unfalsifiable. Yet it
possesses a certain coherence, offering an explanation of an important
phenomenon within a Christian theological context. Some such argument underlies Paul's address at the Areopagus in Acts 17,[43] and has
been used subsequently in both Christian apologetics and spirituality.[44]
The Christian doctrine of creation possesses more explanatory potential
than is often appreciated. With this point in mind, we turn to consider
another aspect of that explanatory role.

Intellectual rationality: the unreasonable effectiveness of mathematics

One of the most fundamental innovations to result from the Scientific
Revolution of the sixteenth century and beyond was the quantification
of the created order. In his influential studies of Galileo, Alexandre

[43] Hans Conzelmann, 'The Address of Paul on the Areopagus', in L. E. Keck and J. L.
Martyn (eds), *Studies in Luke-Acts: Essays in Honor of Paul Schubert*. Nashville, TN: Abingdon
Press, 1966, 217–30.

[44] I venture to mention my own small contribution to the field: Alister E. McGrath, *The
Unknown God: Searching for Spiritual Fulfilment*. Oxford: Lion, 1999.

Koyré used the phrase 'the geometrization of space' to describe the new appreciation of the power of mathematics, and especially Euclidean geometry, to describe what experimental observation was disclosing concerning the motion of celestial bodies.[45] This new emphasis upon the importance of mathematics to be able to account for observations concerning nature was initially focused on astronomy. In his work *de harmonice mundi*, Johann Kepler argued that, since geometry had its origins in the mind of God, it was only to be expected that the created order would conform to its patterns:[46]

> In that geometry is part of the divine mind from the origins of time, even from before the origins of time (for what is there in God that is not also from God?) has provided God with the patterns for the creation of the world, and has been transferred to humanity with the image of God.

We see here a classic statement of the Augustinian interpretation of the doctrine of the creation of humanity in the *imago Dei* – and that this image conveys the likeness of divine rationality, which embraces mathematics. Kepler's idea is also developed in the writings of Galileo:[47]

> Philosophy is written in this grand book, the universe, which stands continually open to our gaze. But the book cannot be understood unless one first learns to comprehend the language and read the letters in which it is composed. It is written in the language of mathematics, and its characters are triangles, circles, and other geometric figures without which it is humanly impossible to understand a single word of it.

A common theme to emerge from this formative period of the scientific universe is that mathematics is able to represent experimental observation, and that the universe cannot be comprehended quantitatively without recourse to mathematical formulae.[48]

The belief that mathematical description was the foundation of theoretical explanation gained increasing acceptance with advances in

[45] Alexandre Koyré, *Etudes galiléennes*. Paris: Hermann, 1939, *passim*. See also the earlier study of Edwin. A. Burtt, *The Metaphysical Foundations of Modern Physical Science: A Historical and Critical Essay*. London: Routledge & Kegan Paul, 1932.

[46] Johann Kepler, *Gesammelte Werke*, ed. Max Caspar. Munich: C. H. Beck, 1937–83, vol. 6, 233.

[47] *The Assayer: Discoveries and Opinions of Galileo*, trans. and ed. Stilman Drake. Garden City, New York: Doubleday, 1957, 237–8. For a more detailed assessment, see Julius Pomerans Arnold and Maurice Clavelin, *The Natural Philosophy of Galileo: Essay on the Origins and Formation of Classical Mechanics*. Cambridge, MA: MIT Press, 1974.

[48] See, for example, Joella G. Yoder, *Unrolling Time: Christiaan Huygens and the Mathematization of Nature*. Cambridge: Cambridge University Press, 1988.

physics in the eighteenth and nineteenth centuries.[49] This can be illustrated from a fascinating episode during the 1880s. The remarkable advances made in spectroscopy during the nineteenth century allowed the spectrum of the sun to be examined for the first time, with results which proved to be of foundational importance. During 1859–60, a number of spectral lines were identified by the Swedish physicist A. Ångström, and their wavelengths measured with what, for those days, was an astonishing accuracy – roughly one part in ten thousand.[50] The precision of these measurements of the visible line spectrum of atomic hydrogen led to the development of a new science: 'spectral numerology'.[51] This was an attempt to account for the relationship of the wavelengths of the observed spectral lines with some fundamental mathematical equation. It was widely believed, on the basis of the belief that mathematics was the chosen language of nature, that there simply had to be some mathematical formula which could account for these very precise and fixed wavelengths, and that any such formula would offer insights into some aspects of the workings of the universe which were not yet understood.

The breakthrough, when it came, was simple and elegant. Working only on the basis of the wavelengths reported by Ångström, J. J. Balmer found that he could reproduce the wavelengths (λ) of the four lines in the solar spectrum *exactly* – not approximately – by means of the following formula:

$$\frac{1}{\lambda} = R\left(\frac{1}{b^2} - \frac{1}{a^2}\right)$$

where R is a constant now known as the 'Rydberg constant', b = 2, and a = 3, 4, 5 and 6 respectively. Balmer (who was then a teacher in a Basle high school) mentioned his observations to the professor of physics at the University of Basle. By this time (1885), 12 more frequencies had been established, although this fact was unknown to Balmer. On learning of them from his colleague, Balmer found that they could all

---

[49] Christa Jungnickel and Russell McCormmach, *Intellectual Mastery of Nature: Theoretical Physics from Ohm to Einstein*. Chicago: University of Chicago Press, 1986; Rochelle Newman and Martha Boles, *Universal Patterns*. Bradford, MA: Pythagorean Press, 1992; Joe Rosen, *Symmetry Discovered: Concepts and Applications in Nature and Science*. Cambridge: Cambridge University Press, 1975.
[50] A. Ångström, *Recherches sur le spectre solaire*. Uppsala: Uppsala University Press, 1868.
[51] Abraham Pais, *Niels Bohr's Times in Physics, Philosophy and Polity*. Oxford: Clarendon Press, 1991, 142.

be fitted into his equation – again, *exactly* – without any difficulty, by setting a = 2 and b = 5, 6, . . . 15, and 16. In fact, Balmer's formula allows an entire series of spectral lines to be predicted (one of which is now known by his name), as follows:

b = 1, a = 2, 3 . . .	Lyman series (ultraviolet)
b = 2, a = 3, 4 . . .	Balmer series (visible)
b = 3, a = 4, 5 . . .	Paschen series (infrared)
b = 4, a = 5, 6 . . .	Brackett series (far infrared)
b = 5, a = 6, 7 . . .	Pfund series (far infrared)
b = 6, a = 7, 8 . . .	Humphreys series (far infrared)

The sheer beauty of the equation – matched, it has to be said, by experimental evidence, both retrodictive and predictive – will be clear. An elegant formula proved capable of representing something fundamental, which subsequently proved to be of major importance in uncovering the principles of atomic structure, and contributed significantly to the development of quantum theory.[52]

Yet this mathematical representation would prove to be more than a mere intellectual curiosity; it became the basis of theoretical development and explanation. Such was the interest in Balmer's analysis that his results were published in the 1912 edition of the *Encyclopaedia Britannica*. It was clear that the elegance of the mathematical formula was such that it was saying something very important about something very fundamental. But what? By 6 March 1913, the Danish physicist Niels Bohr realized the significance of what Balmer had uncovered.[53] On the basis of a quantum mechanical interpretation of the hydrogen atom, Bohr was able to derive Balmer's formula in two manners. For the first time, it became clear that Balmer's formula corresponded to aspects of the fundamental structure of the hydrogen atom.

It has often been argued – and on occasion rather tendentiously – that there is a correlation between mathematics, beauty and nature.[54] While this is open to some dispute, at least in regard to its

[52] Peter W. Atkins and R. S. Friedman, *Molecular Quantum Mechanics*. 3rd edn. Oxford: Oxford University Press, 1997, 202–39; R. D. Cowan, *The Theory of Atomic Structure and Spectra*. Berkeley, CA: University of California Press, 1981; E. U. Condon and G. Shortley, *The Theory of Atomic Spectra*. Cambridge: Cambridge University Press, 1964.

[53] Pais, *Niels Bohr's Times*, 143–55.

[54] Vagn L. Hansen, *Geometry in Nature*. Wellesley, MA: A. K. Peters, 1993; Rochelle Newman and Martha Boles, *Universal Patterns*. Bradford, MA: Pythagorean Press, 1992.

interpretation, there is widespread agreement of the ability of mathematics to describe the patterns and symmetries found at every level of the created order.[55] There have been important changes; for example, the 'geometry of space' is no longer understood to be Euclidean – but the principle of the geometrization of space continues to be maintained.

Interest in this mathematical depiction of nature has arisen in recent years both from fractals and string theory.[56] Both these areas of mathematics must be regarded as free creations of the human mind; yet both appear to have an inbuilt propensity to describe the natural order. In an account of a mathematician's view of modern physics, Roger Penrose stresses how such theories – including Newtonian dynamics, Maxwellian electrodynamics, special and general relativity, thermodynamics and quantum electrodynamics – have a 'superb' ability to mirror nature.[57] Mathematics offers a puzzling degree of correlation with the natural world – puzzling, that is, unless one operates with a Platonic notion of 'recollection' or a Christian doctrine of creation, which postulates a direct collection of the mind of God with the rationalities of the created order and the human mind, as created in the image of God.

Three main streams of the philosophy of mathematics may be discerned today: formalism, intuitionism and Platonism. Roger Penrose is among those mathematicians to defend this third position, which he defines as:[58]

> . . . the view that mathematical truth is absolute, external, and eternal, and not based on man-made criteria; and that mathematical objects have a timeless existence of their own, not dependent on human society nor on particular physical objects.

[55] Ian Stewart, *Life's Other Secret: The New Mathematics of the Living World*. London: Allen Lane, 1998; Ian Stewart, *Nature's Numbers: Discovering Order and Pattern in the Universe*. London: Weidenfeld & Nicolson, 1995; Anthony J. Tromba and Stefan Hildebrandt, *The Parsimonious Universe: Shape and Form in the Natural World*. New York: Copernicus, 1996.
[56] John Briggs, *Fractals: The Patterns of Chaos. Discovering a New Aesthetic of Art, Science, and Nature*. London: Thames & Hudson, 1992; Benoit B. Mandelbrot, *The Fractal Geometry of Nature*. New York: W. H. Freeman, 1982; Joe Rosen, *Symmetry Discovered: Concepts and Applications in Nature and Science*. Cambridge: Cambridge University Press, 1975.
[57] Roger Penrose, 'The Modern Physicist's View of Nature', in John Torrance (ed.), *The Concept of Nature*. Oxford: Oxford University Press, 1992, 117–66. For reflections on Penrose's personal agenda, see S. A. Huggett et al., *The Geometric Universe: Science, Geometry and the Work of Roger Penrose*. Oxford: Oxford University Press, 1998.
[58] Roger Penrose, *The Emperor's New Mind*. London: Vintage, 1990, 151.

A similar approach is found in the writings of Paul Davies, who offers a vigorous defence of Galileo's declaration that the language in which the book of the universe is written is that of mathematics:[59]

> To the outsider, mathematics is a strange, abstract world of horrendous technicality, full of weird symbols and complicated procedures. To the scientist, mathematics is the guarantor of precision and objectivity. It is also, astonishingly, the language of nature itself. No one who is closed off from mathematics can ever grasp the full significance of the natural order that is woven so deeply into the fabric of physical reality.

Davies stresses that the fact that mathematics works 'stunningly well' in this respect – a fact which Eugene Wigner described as the 'unreasonable effectiveness of mathematics' – points strongly to there being some deep similarities between the abstract world of mathematical concepts and the underlying order and structure of physical reality. Penrose thus asserts that there must be 'some deep underlying reason for the accord between mathematics and physics, i.e. between Plato's world and the physical world'.[60]

The use of the term 'Platonism' to refer to such an understanding of mathematics is understandable, in that it was a topic which concerned Plato in several of his dialogues.[61] Yet it must be stressed that such an understanding arises directly from any responsible Christian understanding of human nature as reflecting the *imago Dei*. Kepler's belief that there existed a fundamental congruence between the mind of God, human rationality and the fabric of the universe rests upon a classic insight of Christian theology, rigorously grounded in a Christian doctrine of creation. A scientific theology will wish to reclaim this neglected theme, and reaffirm its importance, not merely for a right understanding of the relation between Christian theology and the experimental sciences, but for a proper grasp of the nature and scope of theology itself.

Moral rationality: responding to the Euthyphro dilemma

The 'Euthyphro dilemma' is set up through a question posed by Socrates in one of Plato's early dialogues, as follows:[62]

[59] Paul Davies, *The Mind of God: Science and the Search for Ultimate Meaning*. Harmondsworth: Penguin, 1992, 93.

[60] Penrose, *The Emperor's New Mind*, 556–7.

[61] See D. H. Fowler, *The Mathematics of Plato's Academy: A New Reconstruction*. New York: Oxford University Press, 1999; Anders Wedberg, *Plato's Philosophy of Mathematics*. Westport, CT: Greenwood Press, 1977. More generally, see W. W. Tait, 'Truth and Proof: The Platonism of Mathematics', *Synthese* 69 (1986), 341–70.

[62] Plato, *Euthyphro* 10a.

Consider this question: Is that which is holy loved by the gods because it is holy, or is it holy because it is loved by the gods?

The two options in question are whether the gods endorse a previously existing standard of morality, or the same gods independently create the standards of morality. The two options appear to be mutually exclusive.

It is important to set this discussion against the background of Greek thought at the time, rather than treating it as if it were some timeless discussion, devoid of a context which gave it particular significance. Homer's divine heroes behaved in a manner which often raised the question of whether there was any correlation between human and divine notions of morality and justice. The 'will of Zeus' was understood to be an occasionally morally indeterminate force exercising 'a vague general control over events', knowledge of which was not without advantage to those plotting future events.[63] The general Greek belief in the pre-Socratic era was that no historical event was without some form of divine causality – whether the event was wise or foolish, eminently rational or apparently mad, or even apparently malicious and spiteful.[64] Even the irrational madness which led humans to make bizarre judgements and otherwise unaccountable errors was to be ascribed to divine action – in this case, through the work of the goddess Ate, whom Homer identified as a daughter of Zeus.[65] One could therefore say – perhaps playing on a related theme in Barth? – that the Homeric tradition envisages all events as taking place twice – once on Olympus, and then on earth, with the latter being the recapitulation in history of what has already happened in the timeless world of the gods.[66]

It is the apparent immorality of the prior divine events which gives Socrates' question its potency. All too often, events in the world seemed to rest on the outcome of power politics on Mount Olympus,[67] without

---

[63] Hugh Lloyd-Jones, *The Justice of Zeus*. 2nd edn. Berkeley, CA: University of California Press, 1983, 4–5.

[64] E. R. Dodds, *The Greeks and the Irrational*. Berkeley, CA: University of California Press, 1966, 6–8. For a series of examples drawn from Homer, see Walter F. Otto, *The Homeric Gods: The Spiritual Significance of Greek Religion*. New York: Pantheon, 1954, 169–228.

[65] William Chase Greene, *Moira: Fate, Good and Evil in Greek Thought*. New York: Harper & Row, 1963, 13–15, 20–1.

[66] Cedric H. Whitman, *Homer and the Heroic Tradition*. Cambridge, MA: Harvard University Press, 1958, 248.

[67] See the careful study of Jenny Strauss Clay, *The Politics of Olympus: Form and Meaning in the Major Homeric Hymns*. Princeton, NJ: Princeton University Press, 1989.

any perceptible 'moral' foundation. Can justice or holiness *really* be defined in terms of the occasionally highly dubious actitivities and judgements from Olympus? Or is there not some law or moral principle to which even the gods of Olympus are subject and by which their actions and decisions may be judged?

Euthyphro is an early dialogue, in which engagement with the Homeric tradition is of particular importance. The specific Socratic question noted above cannot be divorced either from its context within the dialogue, or from its specific location within the tradition of the critical evaluation of the Homeric tradition. Even the popular restatement of the Euthyphro dilemma in terms of 'God' rather than 'the gods' reveals a serious lack of awareness of the cultural context which gives the dilemma its particular force.

Yet the Socratic question raises an issue of considerable relevance to our discussion, which goes beyond the ongoing critique of the Homeric tradition in fifth-century Athenian society. The issue at stake can be summarized along the following lines. If the gods determine what is right and wrong, they are liberated from any accountability, and free to act as they please. If, on the other hand, the gods are under obligation to respect a prior or higher notion of justice, then there is no need to invoke the behaviour of the gods in any account of human morality – providing, of course, that this standard of justice can be known by humans. Socrates' line of questioning suggests that he endorses the view that the favour of the gods is not an adequate ground for making a course of action or decision holy or righteous. This is widely held to endorse the view that 'humanity is the measure of all things',[68] a view which is developed in the writings of David Hume, especially his *Natural History of Religion* (1757) and *Dialogues Concerning Natural Religion* (1779).

The Euthyphro dilemma gains its force precisely because we are asked to consider the relationship between two allegedly independent entities: what *human beings* recognize as good, and what *God* recognizes as good. The dilemma forces us, through the terms in which it is posited, to choose between human and divine conceptions of goodness or justice. But if these can be shown to be related to each other in any way, the force of the dilemma is lost. The choice we are forced to make is then seen as false.

As we have seen in our exploration of the Christian reflection on the implications of creation in relation to the *imago Dei*, there is a

---

[68] A view noted in Plato, *Theaetetus*, 160d.

congruence between divine notions of truth, beauty and goodness and proper human notions of the same through the creaturely status of humanity. The fourth of Thomas Aquinas' 'Five Ways' works on the assumption that human notions of goodness are derived from God as their ultimate cause and foundation.[69]

> The fourth way is from the gradation that occurs in things, which are found to be more good, true, noble and so on, just as others are found to be less so. Things are said to be more and less because they approximate in different degrees to that which is greatest. A thing gets hotter and hotter as it approaches the thing which is the hottest. There is therefore something which is the truest, the best, and the noblest, and which is consequently the greatest in being, since that which has the greatest truth is also greatest in being . . . Now that which most thoroughly possesses the nature of any genus is the cause of all that the genus contains. Thus fire, which is most perfectly hot, is the cause of all hot things . . . There is therefore something which is the cause of the being of all things that are, as well as of their goodness and their every perfection. This we call 'God'.

A Christian doctrine of creation affirms a congruence between the moral ordering of creation – including humanity as the height of that creation – and the mind of God. One of the most interesting expositions of this point in the last few decades has been Oliver O'Donovan's *Resurrection and Moral Order* (1986), a seminal work which explores the way in which the moral ordering of creation is disclosed through the economy of salvation, supremely the resurrection.[70]

> The order of things that God has made is *there*. It is objective, and mankind has a place within it. Christian ethics, therefore, has an objective reference because it is concerned with man's life in accordance with this order. The summons to live in it is addressed to all mankind, because the good news that we *may* live in it is addressed to all mankind. Thus Christian moral judgements . . . are founded on reality as God has given it. In this assertion, we may find a point of agreement with the classical ethics of Plato, Aristotle and the Stoics which treated ethics as a close correlate of metaphysics. The way the universe *is* determines how man *ought* to behave himself in it.

O'Donovan thus sets out how creation and redemption have both epistemological and ontological relevance to both the nature of this order, and the manner of how it may be known.

[69] Thomas Aquinas, *Summa theologiae* Ia q. 2, a. 3.
[70] Oliver O'Donovan, *Resurrection and Moral Order*. Grand Rapids, MI: Eerdmans, 1986, 17.

This emphasis upon the importance of created order from an ethical perspective naturally leads us to consider this matter in considerably more detail.

The ordering of creation

One of the most significant parallels between the natural sciences and Christian theology is a fundamental conviction that the world is characterized by regularity and intelligibility. As one modern cosmologist has suggested, without any trace of irony, 'the God of the physicists is cosmic order'.[71] So important is this notion that it could be argued that the natural sciences are founded on the perception of explicable regularity to the world, which is capable of being represented mathematically. In other words, there is something about the world – and the nature of the human mind – which allows patterns within nature to be discerned and represented.

This perception of ordering and intelligibility is of immense significance, at both the scientific and religious levels. As Paul Davies points out, 'in Renaissance Europe, the justification for what we today call the scientific approach to inquiry was the belief in a rational God whose created order could be discerned from a careful study of nature'.[72] This insight is, as we have seen (Ch. 4), a direct consequence of the Christian doctrine of creation. In view of the deeply religious nature of the world-view of the medieval and Renaissance periods, even the most 'secular' of activities – whether economic, political or scientific – were saturated with the themes of Christian theology.

This foundational assumption of the natural sciences – that God has created an ordered world, whose ordering could be discerned by humanity, which had in turn been created 'in the image and likeness of God' – permeates the writings of the period, whether it is implicitly assumed or explicitly stated. The natural order had been created as both *analogue* and *anagogue* – that is, with a capacity to represent the Godhead, and lead the human mind upwards through the dynamic symbols of the natural world to their *fons et origo* in God.[73] Whereas medieval writers were content to treat the natural order as pointing to the mystery of God, later Renaissance writers – such as Leonardo da Vinci, Galileo Galilei and Johann Kepler – were not satisfied with the 'imagistic and sensible force' of the signs in which we read the spiritual

---

[71] Heinz R. Pagels, *The Cosmic Code: Quantum Physics and the Language of Nature*. Harmondsworth: Penguin, 1984, 83.
[72] Davies, *The Mind of God*, 77.
[73] Chenu, *Nature, Man and Society in the Twelfth Century*, 123–4.

structure of the universe. Instead, they demanded that these signs should 'form a system, a thoroughly ordered whole'.[74] The concept of order could thus be articulated either in terms of the perceived ordering of the natural world, or the ordering of the systems devised to account for or explain such perceptions. Yet in each case, the grounds of that ordering – whether primary or secondary – were understood to be grounded in the mind and will of God. The subsequent secularization of western thought has meant that the controlling influence of such leading ideas has been removed from the public realm, and effectively relegated to the world of the private views of individuals.[75]

Yet this does not mean that they have lost their credibility or relevance for Christian thinkers. The modern shift in the social function or corporate plausibility of foundational religious beliefs cannot be equated with a demonstration of their falsity or their marginalization within the reflection of individual natural scientists operating within a framework influenced by Christian theology. As will be clear from our previous discussion (Ch. 4), a Christian doctrine of creation is an intellectual consideration and influence which is by no means restricted to past epochs in cultural or intellectual history, such as the Renaissance. It remains an essential element in a scientific theology, both in terms of offering a specific approach to doing theology, and also in demonstrating the fundamental consilience of Christian theology and the natural sciences.

Some have argued that the Christian emphasis upon the created order within the world is of fundamental importance in establishing a positive causal connection between Christianity and the natural sciences;[76] while appreciating the merits of this point, it is not my intention to pursue this historical issue. The question we shall be addressing is this: what might the importance of a Christian doctrine of creation be for the natural sciences, and for the notion of a scientific theology in general?

The contingent ordering of creation

The noted philosopher of religion Richard Swinburne identifies the importance of observable ordering within the natural world as follows:[77]

[74] Ernst Cassirer, *The Individual and the Cosmos in Renaissance Philosophy*. Philadelphia: University of Pennsylvania Press, 1972, 54.

[75] On which see Owen Chadwick, *The Secularization of the European Mind in the Nineteenth Century*. Cambridge: Cambridge University Press, 1975.

[76] Such as R. Hooykaas, *Religion and the Rise of Modern Science*. Edinburgh: Scottish Academic Press, 1972.

[77] Richard Swinburne, *The Existence of God*. Oxford: Clarendon Press, 1979, 136.

Regularities of succession are all-pervasive. For simple laws govern almost all succession of events. In books of physics, chemistry and biology we can learn how almost everything in the world behaves. The laws of their behaviour can be set out by relatively simple formulae which men can understand and by means of which they can successfully predict the future. The orderliness of nature to which I drew attention here is its conformity to formula, to simple, formulable, scientific laws. The orderliness of the universe in this respect is a very striking fact about it. The universe might so naturally have been chaotic, but it is not – it is very orderly.

The specific nature of the created order is thus to be seen as of critical importance. The universe has been created in a particular manner, reflecting the mind of God. Its orderedness is contingent, in the sense that it could have been created in another manner altogether. One of the most important consequences of the Christian doctrine of creation *ex nihilo* is that God was not operating under any constraints in the work of creation – such as the nature of pre-existing matter, which might have obligated God to fashion the world in a manner not entirely of God's own choosing. God, according to the Christian tradition, created the world in an ordered manner, expressing the distinctive divine rationality.

This point has been explored and developed extensively in the writings of Thomas F. Torrance. For Torrance, the order which is evident within the natural world is to be understood as *contingent*. On the basis of the Christian understanding of the nature of God and the creation, there is no tension between the concepts of 'contingency' and 'orderliness'. There exists what Barth termed a 'created correspondence' between the world and God. Torrance sets this point out in some detail in his essay 'Divine and Contingent Order':[78]

> [The notion of contingent order] is the direct product of the Christian understanding of the constitutive relation between God and the universe, which he freely created out of nothing, yet not without reason, conferring upon what he has made and continues to sustain a created rationality of its own dependent on his uncreated transcendent reality . . . [This doctrine of creation] liberated nature conceived as the time-less embodiment of eternal forms from a necessary relation to God, which made it impossible to distinguish nature from God; and it

---

[78] Thomas F. Torrance, 'Divine and Contingent Order', in A. R. Peacocke (ed.), *The Sciences and Theology in the Twentieth Century*. Notre Dame, IN: University of Notre Dame Press, 1981, 81–97; quotation at 84–5.

destroyed the bifurcation of form and matter, affirming each as equally created out of nothing and equally real in their indissoluble unity with one another in the pervasive rational order of the contingent universe under God.

The order that is discerned within the world – and, indeed, upon which so much scientific reasoning is dependent – is thus to be understood as a consequence of the creative action of God. One of the fundamental dilemmas of natural science, Torrance notes, is that it cannot be proved that there is order in the world, in that such proof would imply the prior assumption of precisely such an order.[79]

Torrance regards this point as an important and significant indication of the fundamental convergence between Christian theology and the natural sciences, and a clear illustration of the advantages of undertaking scientific investigation from the perspective of a Christian world-view. The fact that such order exists, and that the human mind is such that it can discern and appreciate it, is closely linked with the doctrine of the incarnation:[80]

> As the doctrines of the Incarnation and Creation began to be thought out in their bearing upon one another, the Hebraic idea that God had freely brought the universe into being from nothing was both strengthened and radicalized, with emphasis upon the creation of all things . . . out of nothing. Thus all rational form immanent in nature, including the mind of man, was held to be created out of nothing . . . The whole universe of created being was thought of as given an authentic reality and integrity of its own, and as endowed by God with a creaturely rational order grounded beyond itself in his own transcendent reality. This was the conception of the contingent nature of the creation, and its inherent rational order.

Torrance went on to link the discernment of ordering within the world with the classic concept of 'wisdom'. In a lecture published in 1991, Torrance noted the significance of the distinction between *sapientia* and *scientia* in the thought of Augustine. The concept of 'wisdom', as developed by Augustine, is to be understood as referring to:[81]

---

[79] Thomas F. Torrance, *The Ground and Grammar of Theology*. Belfast: Christian Journals Ltd, 1980, 131–2.

[80] Thomas F. Torrance, *The Christian Frame of Mind: Reason, Order, and Openness in Theology and Natural Science*. Colorado Springs: Helmers & Howard, 1989, 39–40.

[81] Thomas F. Torrance, 'The Transcendental Role of Wisdom in Science', in Evandro Agazzi (ed.), *Science et sagesse: Entretiens de l'Académie Internationale de Philosophie des Sciences, 1990*. Fribourg: Éditions Universitaires Fribourg Suisse, 1991, 63–80; 67.

... the unique insight that arises when the eye of the human mind discerns an invisible transcendent realm of immutable eternal truth upon which all *scientia* of the truths of the visible corporeal realm, gained through the rational operations of the human reason, are ultimately contingent.

What the natural sciences are forced to assume – in that it cannot be formally demonstrated without falling into some form of circularity of argument or demonstration – the Christian understanding of 'wisdom' allows to be affirmed on the basis of divine revelation, and correlated with the existence of a transcendent creator God, responsible both for the ordering of the world and the human ability to grasp and discern it.

[The concept of order] arises compulsorily in our minds through direct intuitive contact with the intelligible nature of reality which we acknowledge to be the ultimate judge in all questions of truth and falsity, order and disorder. That is to say, our concept of order presupposes an ultimate ground of order transcending what we can comprehend but of which we are implicitly aware in the back of our mind, and under the constraint of which we generate order in all intellectual activity. Belief in order, the conviction that, whatever may appear to the contrary in so-called random events, reality is finally and intrinsically orderly, thus constitutes an ultimate regulating factor in all rational and scientific activity.

Similar ideas can be discerned in other writers to have addressed this theme. In his unjustly neglected 1956 Bampton Lectures at Oxford University, Eric L. Mascall considered the theme of 'cosmology and contingency' in some detail. Mascall devoted particular attention to the question of what kind of world the Christian God might be expected to have created, on the basis of what could be known of that God on the basis of the Christian revelation. For Mascall, the answer was clear:[82]

It will be both contingent and orderly, since it is the work of a God who is both free and rational. It will embody regularities and patterns, since its Creator is rational, but the particular regularities and patterns which it embodies cannot be predicted *a priori*, since he is free; they can only be discovered by examination. The world of Christian theism will thus be one whose investigation requires the empirical method, that is to say, the method of modern natural science, with its twin techniques of observation and experiment.

[82] Eric L. Mascall, *Christian Theology and Natural Science: Some Questions on their Relations*. London: Longmans, Green & Co., 1956, 94.

We may see here important affinities with Torrance's stress upon the *a posteriori* nature of both scientific and theological knowledge, and also anticipations of the manner in which Torrance would develop and exploit the concept of contingent order.[83]

It could, of course, be argued that this perception of 'orderliness' reflects a propensity to discern patterns and impose coherence within the human mind, rather than any intrinsic structuring of the natural world itself. Regularity is thus an imposition of the human observer, rather than a feature of the world which is being observed. For Immanuel Kant, 'ordering' was not to be seen as something which exists in the world independently of human minds. Rather, Kant argues that things in the world owe their fundamental structure or ordering to the noetic activity of the human mind. In other words, the existence and fundamental structure of natural entities are not intrinsic to them, but have been conferred upon them by the conceptual activity of human agents. According to this view, the phenomenal world receives its fundamental 'structure' from the constitutive activity of the human mind. Thus Kant regards the category of 'quantity' as a human category which is imposed upon the world.[84] In this, Kant clearly builds on foundations erected by David Hume.[85]

Kant's use of the 'imposition' model is complex, and occasionally difficult to interpret – in part, due to Kant's evolving views on the matter.[86] The fundamental distinction which Kant wishes to draw is between a 'thing in itself (*Ding an sich*)' and things 'as they appear'. For Kant, the appearance is what may be known (or, better, experienced) on account of the organizing, imprinting and shaping activity of the human mind. The mental interpretation of sense-data as representing something such as 'order' involves the imposition of something which is not itself given empirically in the sense-data.

It must, of course, be conceded that the human mind is perfectly capable of discerning order or imposing patterns which are entirely of its own making. The popular image of the 'man in the moon' rests on

[83] See the comments of Torrance in Thomas F. Torrance, *Theological Science*. Oxford: Oxford University Press, 1969, 61.

[84] Robert Paul Wolff, *Kant's Theory of Mental Activity*. Cambridge, MA: Harvard University Press, 1963; Jonathan Bennett, *Kant's Dialectic*. Cambridge: Cambridge University Press, 1974, 9–65.

[85] Peter Urbach, 'What is a Law of Nature? A Humean Answer', *British Journal of Philosophy of Science* 39 (1988), 193–210.

[86] H. J. de Vleeschauwer, 'Wie ich jetzt die Kritik der reinen Vernunft entwicklungsgeschichtlich lese', *Kant-Studien* 54 (1962), 351–68.

the perception that the features of the lunar surface, viewed around the time of a full moon, resemble a human face. Ancient astronomers saw patterns in the heavens, and created the constellations, which they believed to resemble the physical appearances of mythological heroes. It could therefore be argued that, since it belongs to human nature to impose patterns upon our experience, 'order' would be discerned even if the universe were disordered. The perception of order is therefore not to be explained in terms of the way the world is, but in terms of the way in which the human mind works.

While it must be conceded immediately that the human mind does indeed demonstrate a propensity to identify patterns and impose structure, this cannot be taken to mean that no such patterns or structures exist within nature. The explanatory and predictive successes of the natural sciences pose a serious difficulty to this position, in that they posit the existence of a publicly observable and replicable regularity to the world. This ordering would then be held to be true even if there were no human mind to discern it; on the basis of contemporary cosmological theories, it can reasonably be argued that the laws of physics operated long before human minds evolved in order to notice them.

As Heinz Pagels has pointed out, the hidden order of the world has only proved amenable to interpretation in the last three centuries; this cannot by any stretch of the imagination be taken to mean that they were not present before then:[87]

> Although the idea that the universe has an order that is governed by natural laws that are not immediately apparent to the senses is very ancient, it is only in the last three hundred years that we have discovered a method for uncovering the hidden order – the scientific-experimental method. So powerful is this method that virtually everything scientists know about the natural world comes from it. What they find is that the architecture of the universe is indeed built according to invisible universal rules, what I call the cosmic code.

Pagels' language of the 'architecture of the universe . . . built according to invisible universal rules' immediately established a connection between order and fabrication, and naturally leads us into a discussion of the vitally important theme of the laws of nature, and their relevance to our theme.

---

[87] Pagels, *The Cosmic Code*, 156.

The laws of nature

Earlier, we had cause to note the reflections of the English philosopher Michael Foster on the implications of a doctrine of creation for a right understanding of the concept of nature. Foster himself was clear that the natural order did not proceed from God by an act of necessary emanation, but by a free and sovereign act of will. In particular, Foster stressed that the idea of regularity within nature – as expressed in the notion of the 'laws of nature' – was the outcome of a reaction of Christian theologians against various forms of cosmic necessitarianism within Greek philosophy. Views of nature, he argued, were ultimately dependent upon a view of God:[88]

> The method of natural science depends upon the presuppositions which are held about nature, and the presuppositions about nature in turn upon the doctrine of God. Modern natural science could begin only when the modern presuppositions about nature displaced the Greek ... but this displacement itself was possible only when the Christian concept of God had displaced the pagan, as the object of systematic understanding. To achieve this displacement was the work of medieval theology, which thus laid the foundations both of much else in the modern world which is specifically modern, and of modern natural science.

If developed in a more theological direction (for example, through the use of the biblical concept of covenant to express the divine decision to act in certain reliable ways) Foster's arguments lead to the vision of an order – moral, natural, political, salvific and social – within nature which is not grounded in the very nature of things, but which is rather founded on God's will, promise and covenant. Such a view is, of course, reinforced by Barth's strongly covenantal approach to the concept of creation, which we considered earlier.

The phrase 'law of nature' appears to have begun to be used systematically during the late seventeenth century. It is generally agreed that the phrase reflects the widely held notion, prevalent within both orthodox Christianity and Deism, that the world was ordered by a divine law-giver, who laid down the manner in which the creation should behave. This idea plays a central role, for example, in Descartes' philosophy of nature.[89] While there remain important areas of scholarly

---

[88] Michael B. Foster, 'The Christian doctrine of Creation and the Rise of Modern Science', *Mind* 43 (1934), 446–68, 465.

[89] Margaret J. Osler, 'Eternal Truths and the Laws of Nature: The Theological Foundations of Descartes' Philosophy of Nature', *Journal of the History of Ideas* 46 (1985), 349–65.

debate on the issue, there are good reasons for suggesting that the concept of a 'law of nature' has its theological origins in the new emphasis upon divine voluntarism in the fourteenth century, and that its extensive use within the emerging natural sciences dates from the seventeenth.[90] In that God had imposed an order upon the creation which was grounded in the divine will, it was only to be expected that certain 'laws of nature' could be discerned. Robert Boyle spoke of God as the 'supreme and absolute Lord' of creation who 'established those rules of motion, and that order among things corporeal which we are wont to call the laws of nature'. For Newton, the sovereignty of God over the creation was to be expressed in terms of a divinely imposed ordering and regularity within nature, which human intelligence could discern. Such was Newton's impact on the perception and explanation of regularity within the created order that Alexander Pope was moved to refer to this in his epitaph for the founder of the new celestial mechanics:

> Nature and Nature's Law lay hid in Night
> God said, let Newton be, and all was Light.

A 'law of nature' was thus held to be rather more than a mere description or summary of observable features of the world; it reflected a divine decision that the world was intended to behave in this manner.[91] With the widespread secularization of western culture, this general belief has been eroded, both inside and outside the scientific community. The phrase 'laws of nature' remains in use today, although it has acquired something of the status of a dead metaphor. It is, however, a concept with profound theological implications, whose theological associations may continue to be used and developed by Christian theologians. The strong degree of convergence between Christian theology and the natural sciences on this point is of considerable importance and interest, and shows how a Christian doctrine of creation continues to play a highly constructive role in this ongoing discussion.

We may begin by attempting to clarify the concept of a 'law of nature'. The term is used widely, and consequently with a degree of imprecision, not least on account of the variety of nuanced meanings

    [90] See the classic study of Francis Oakley, 'Christian Theology and the Newtonian Science', in Daniel O'Connor and Francis Oakley (eds), *Creation: The Impact of an Idea*. New York: Charles Scribner's Sons, 1961, 54–83.
    [91] A. J. Ayer, 'What is a Law of Nature?', in A. J. Ayer (ed.), *The Concept of a Person*. London: Macmillan, 1956, 209–34; Bas C. van Fraassen, *Laws and Symmetry*. Oxford: Clarendon Press, 1989, 1–14.

associated with the word 'law'.[92] It can be used to refer to universally true statements of non-limited scope that embody only qualitative predicates.[93] Examples of this might include 'all metals conduct electricity' or 'at constant pressure any gas expands with increasing temperature'. This approach to a definition excludes what might be termed 'accidental laws', such as 'all the animals in my garden this afternoon are cats'; or 'vacuously true generalizations', such as 'all solid gold spheres are less than ten metres in diameter' or 'all unicorns weigh five kilograms'.[94]

A general consensus on the nature and scope of the 'laws of nature' within the scientific community has been set out by Paul Davies. In general terms, the 'laws of nature' can be considered to have the following features.[95]

1. They are *universal.* The laws of physics are assumed to be valid at every place and every time. They are held 'to apply unfailingly everywhere in the universe and at all epochs of cosmic history'. There is an interesting parallel here with the criterion introduced in the fifth century by Vincent of Lérins for Christian doctrines, which were required to be things which were believed 'everywhere, always and by all (*quod ubique, quod semper, quod ab omnibus creditum est*)'.

2. They are *absolute* – that is to say, that they do not depend on the nature of the observer (for example, his or her social status, gender or sexual orientation). The state of a system may change over time, and be related to a series of contingent and circumstantial considerations; the laws, which provide correlation between those states at various moments, do not change with time. This aspect of the laws of nature causes serious difficulties for a postmodern world-view, which we shall examine in a later chapter of this work.

3. They are *eternal,* in that they are held to be grounded in the mathematical structures which are used to represent the physical world. The remarkable correlation between what we shall loosely term 'mathematical reality' and the observed physical world is of

[92] Peter Achinstein *Law and Explanation.* Oxford: Clarendon Press, 1971, 2.

[93] C. G. Hempel and P. Oppenheim, 'Studies in the Logic of Explanation', in B. A. Brody (ed.), *Readings in the Philosophy of Science.* Englewood Cliffs, NJ: Prentice-Hall, 1970, 8–27.

[94] John Carroll, 'The Humean Tradition', *Philosophical Review* 99 (1990), 185–219, especially 191–2.

[95] Davies, *The Mind of God,* 72–92.

considerable significance, and we shall return to this matter later. It is of considerable importance in this context to note that all known fundamental laws are mathematical in form.

4. They are *omnipotent*, in that nothing can be held to be outside their scope.

It will not have escaped the reader's notice that these attributes which are, by common agreement and convention, applied to the 'laws of nature', show remarkable affinities with those which are traditionally applied to God in theistic religious systems, such as Christianity. Davies' analysis thus raises the question of the relation between God and the 'laws of nature', to which we now turn.

A particularly important discussion of the theological foundations of the 'laws of nature' can be found in the writings of Emil Brunner. For Brunner, the act of creation involves the expression of divine ordering within the creation, in the form of the 'orders of creation'.[96]

> God has given to that which has been created – to *all* that has been created – a certain definite order which, because it has been created by Him, is the expression of His will. The way in which a creature has been made is an expression of the divine will . . . What we call the 'laws of nature' are God's orders of creation. This, and only this, is the way in which God has ordered the world. God is a God of order, not of disorder; He works according to law, and not in an arbitrary manner.

But according to *which* law does God work? Does not the very idea of such a law pose a fatal challenge to the notion of divine sovereignty within creation? This point has been noted by many writers, including Paul Davies, who argues that God therefore cannot be 'omnipotent, for he could not act outside the laws of nature'.[97]

So what response might be offered to such a comment? How can God be said to act reliably, in a manner which conforms to such laws, without making the concomitant statement that God is subject to such laws – and hence acts under an external constraint? This is not a new debate; the same question was debated with some heat at the University of Paris during the thirteenth century, in response to the forms of determinism developed by Averroes. For Averroes, the reliability of God ultimately rested upon God's obligation to respond in certain fixed

---

[96] For what follows, see Emil Brunner, *The Christian Doctrine of Creation and Redemption*. London: Lutterworth Press, 1952, 24–6.
[97] Paul Davies, *God and the New Physics*. New York: Penguin, 1984, 209.

ways to external pressures. In that God was coerced to act in certain ways, God may be said to act reliably, precisely because God's actions were dictated and constrained by outside agencies. If this were not so, then God would act in a whimsical or arbitrary manner. The only means of ensuring regularity and continuity of divine action within the creation was to hold that God was obligated to act within fixed limits, according to predetermined laws.

This position was regarded with distaste by writers such as Duns Scotus and William of Ockham, who argued that God's reliability could be affirmed by grounding it in the constant will of God, rather than a constant external set of laws. God did not act according to established laws; God established laws by his actions. The fundamental principle here is that the reliability of God is ultimately grounded in the divine nature itself. God does not act reliably because someone or something makes God act in this way, but because of a deliberate and free divine decision to act like this. This decision was not a result of coercion or external constraint, but a free decision reflecting the nature of God himself.

The theological framework which was developed to undergird this affirmation is often known as the 'two powers of God'.[98] In view of its importance, we shall discuss William of Ockham's exposition of this theme, and its relevance to the concept of a 'law of nature'. In his discussion of the opening line of the Apostles' Creed – 'I believe in God the Father almighty' – Ockham asks precisely what is meant by the word 'almighty (*omnipotens*)'. It cannot, he argues, mean that God is presently able to do anything and everything; rather, it means that God was once free to act in this way. God has now established an order of things which reflects a loving and righteous divine will – and that order, once established, will remain until the end of time. Ockham uses two terms to refer to these different options. The 'absolute power of God (*potentia Dei absoluta*)' refers to the theoretical possibilities prior to commitment to any course of action or world ordering. The 'ordained power of God (*potentia Dei ordinata*)' refers to the way things now are, which reflects the order established by God their creator. These do not represent two different sets of options now open to God. They represent two different moments in the history of salvation. The

[98] See Gijsbert van den Brink, *Almighty God: A Study of the Doctrine of Divine Omnipotence.* Kampen: Kok Pharos, 1993; Lawrence Moonan, *Divine Power: The Medieval Power Distinction up to Its Adoption by Albert, Bonaventure and Aquinas.* Oxford: Clarendon Press, 1994.

ordained power of God – the way in which God orders the creation at present – underlies the concept of a 'law of nature'.

Ockham thus invites us to consider two very different situations in which we might speak of the 'omnipotence of God'. The first is this: God is confronted with a whole array of possibilities – such as creating the world, or not creating the world. God can choose to actualize any of these possibilities. This is the absolute power of God, which refers to a situation in which God has not yet acted.[99]

We now move away from this scenario, in which we were invited to consider a range of possibilities which God had the potential to enact. We now consider the scenario which results from God's act – for example, by ordering the universe. God has chosen some options, and brought them into being, with the result that certain potentialities are now actualities. We are now in the realm of the ordained power of God – a realm in which God's power is restricted, by virtue of God's own decision. Ockham's point is that by choosing to actualize some potentialities, God has implicitly chosen not to actualize others. Choosing to do something means choosing not to do something else. Once God has chosen to create the world, the option of not creating the world is set to one side. This means that there are certain things which God could do once which can no longer be done. Although God could have decided not to create the world, God has now deliberately rejected that possibility. And that rejection means that this possibility is no longer open.

This leads to what seems, at first sight, to be a paradoxical situation. On account of the divine omnipotence, God is not now able to do everything. By exercising the divine power, God has limited options. For Ockham, God cannot now do everything. God has deliberately limited the possibilities. God chose to limit the options which are now open. Is that a contradiction? No. If God is really capable of doing anything, then God must be able to become committed to a course of action – and stay committed to it. God can thus be said to act according to established laws – but these are not laws which somehow have their origination outside God, or which can be thought of as contrary to the nature of God. They themselves are the creation of God, and reflect God's nature and character. In acting according to established laws,

---

[99] It should be noted that, for the sake of clarity of explanation of this specific issue, we have disregarded the question of whether God can be said to 'create time' or 'create *within* time'. This is an immensely important debate, which cannot be considered fully at this point.

God is remaining faithful to an expression of his now nature, brought about by his own free decision. Ockham expresses this as follows:[100]

> God is able to do some things by an ordained power (*de potentia ordinata*) and others by an absolute power (*de potentia absoluta*). This distinction should not be understood to mean that there are actually two powers within God, one of which is 'ordained' and the other of which is 'absolute', because there is only one power of God directed towards the external world, the exercise of which lies in all respects with God. Nor should this be understood to mean that God can do some things by an ordained power, and others by an absolute, not ordained, power, in that God does nothing without having first ordained it. But it should be understood in this way: God can do something in a manner which is established by laws which were ordained and established by God. In this respect, God acts according to an ordained power.

The relevance of this analysis to Davies' statement will be clear. Within a theistic perspective, such as that offered by Christianity, it is quite misleading to posit a tension between God and the laws of nature, as if the latter were somehow independent of the former, or in some way contradicted each other. We could thus say (very loosely and incautiously) that the absolute power of God refers to $t = 0$, whereas the ordained power of God refers to $t > 0$. As we have stressed, the Christian holds that God's nature is somehow *expressed and embodied in the ordering of the world*, which underlies the laws of nature. That God 'obeys' such laws cannot conceivably be taken to mean that God is subservient to another power or being, or is obligated or otherwise constrained to work within an alien framework which is not of God's own making. There is a fundamental line of continuity between the creator, the regularity of the creation, and the human perception and expression of this regularity in the form of 'laws of nature'.

At this point, we may try to bring together the various threads which have been explored in this chapter. The perceived ordering of the world is unquestionably one of the most important themes demanding to be investigated and explained by the natural sciences. In investigating such regularities, however, the natural sciences find themselves obliged to presuppose what they investigate – namely, that such ordering is a universal, rather than spatially or chronologically local, phenomenon. Three explanations of such perceptions of ordering may be noted, the third of which is adopted in the present study:

---

[100] William of Ockham, *Opera Philosophica et Theologica*. New York: St Bonaventure Publications, 1966, vol. 9, 585–6.

1. Such ordering is the result of the human mind, with its innate love of patterning, which leads it to impose pattern upon an essentially disordered world.

2. Such ordering is the result of innate properties of the matter from which the universe is composed.

3. Such ordering results from the character of God in the act of creation.

The beauty of creation

The human quest for beauty has graced the pages of many a treatise on the history of music, Renaissance architecture, and the artistic style of the Pre-Raphaelite painters. Plato placed beauty in his triad of enduring human values – along with truth and goodness – and can be seen as a stimulus to the well-known lines from John Keats' 'Ode on a Grecian Urn' (1820):

> 'Beauty is truth, truth beauty' – that is all
> Ye know on earth, and all ye need to know.

One of the most intriguing aspects of both the scientific reflection on nature, and the mathematical structure of scientific theories relating to nature, is the extent to which aesthetic considerations become involved at an early stage. The theoretical chemist Charles A. Coulson, bringing together his scientific and theological concerns, once commented that observations of the world 'set us going on a strange voyage where imagination, beauty and pattern are our signposts'.[101] There is no doubt that the elusive quality of 'beauty' has played a considerable role in the theoretical reflections of physicists.

What is increasingly being recognized as a classic discussion of this matter can be found in a 1979 lecture, delivered at the Fermi National Accelerator Laboratory by S. Chandrasekhar, who received the Nobel Prize for physics, entitled 'Beauty and the Quest for Beauty in Science'.[102] Chandrasekhar opens the lecture by reflecting on some comments of Henri Poincaré, who spoke of 'the intimate beauty' to be discerned within nature 'which comes from the harmonious order of its parts, and which a pure intelligence can grasp'. Chandrasekhar provides an extensive range of examples, drawn largely from physicists

---

[101] Charles A. Coulson, 'Fact and Fiction in Physics', *Bucknell Review* 9 (1960), 1–14; 11.

[102] S. Chandrasekhar, 'Beauty and the Quest for Beauty in Science', in *Truth and Beauty: Aesthetics and Motivations in Science.* Chicago: University of Chicago Press, 1990, 59–73.

and mathematicians of the twentieth century, to illustrate how beauty and truth appear to converge in scientific theorizing.

The very idea of 'beauty' is remarkably complex.[103] Indeed, for some writers, the concept has become so difficult to define that it has ceased to be meaningful. Especially in the twentieth century, recognition of the importance of such issues as cultural conditioning and growing suspicion of the power of those cultural élites who determine taste have combined to bring about something of 'a crisis not merely in the theory of beauty but in the very concept itself'.[104] The Humean critique of the objectivity of beauty has continued to have a significant influence on contemporary reflection. For Hume, 'beauty is no quality in things themselves; it exists merely in the mind which contemplates them'.[105] Just as Hume argued that the perception of 'order' within nature was the imposition of the human mind, so 'beauty' was to be seen as a concept imposed upon, rather than discerned within, the natural world.

It might therefore seem a little unwise to invest any effort in exploring such a controverted and nuanced concept. However, despite the difficulties attending the notion, it seemed essential to include reflection on its relevance to our theme. There has been a growing interest within the learned literature in the linkage between theology and aesthetics – for example, in the way in which Victorian aesthetics were shaped by religious beliefs.[106] The Humean critique of beauty as an intrinsic property of things has itself been subjected to criticism – from within both a Thomist and the Anglo-American analytical tradition – and the idea of beauty as an intrinsic property of things vigorously defended.[107] More importantly for our purposes, the notion of beauty has come to play a significant role within the philosophy of science itself, especially in relation to the evaluation of theories.[108] In what follows, we shall

[103] Patrick Sherry, *Spirit and Beauty: An Introduction to Theological Aesthetics.* Oxford: Clarendon Press, 1992; Jerome Stolnitz, '"Beauty": Some Stages in the History of an Idea', *Journal of the History of Ideas* 22 (1961), 183–204; Richard Viladesau, *Theological Aesthetics: God in Imagination, Beauty and Art.* New York: Oxford University Press, 1999.

[104] Wladislaw Tatarkiewicz, 'The Great Theory of Beauty and Its Decline', *Journal of Aesthetics and Art Criticism* 31 (1972), 165–80, 169.

[105] Fergus Kerr, 'Aesthetic Theory', in A. E. McGrath (ed.), *The Blackwell Encyclopaedia of Modern Christian Thought.* Oxford: Blackwell, 1993, 1–2.

[106] Hilary Fraser, *Beauty and Belief: Aesthetics and Religion in Victorian Literature.* Cambridge: Cambridge University Press, 1986.

[107] See Mary Mothersill, *Beauty Restored.* Oxford: Clarendon Press, 1984; Armand A. Maurer, *About Beauty: A Thomistic Interpretation.* Houston, TX: Center for Thomistic Studies, 1983; Guy Sircello, *A New Theory of Beauty.* Princeton, NJ: Princeton University Press, 1975.

[108] J. W. McAllister, 'Truth and Beauty in Scientific Reason', *Synthese* 78 (1989), 25–35; A. Zee, *Fearful Symmetry: The Search for Beauty in Modern Physics.* New York: Macmillan, 1986.

explore this fascinating aspect of the relationship between religion and the sciences. We may therefore begin by considering the religious aspects of the matter.

The theological aspects of beauty

The theme of 'the beauty of God' has figured prominently in Christian thinking. The Old Testament frequently dwells upon the 'beauty of the Lord', particularly in the Psalter.[109] In his dialogue *Phaedrus*, Plato had argued that the concept of beauty had already been laid down in the human soul, so that the perception of beauty was essentially a resonance between what was perceived and the pattern which had already been laid down for it. A similar view is found in classical Christian theology, but given additional intellectual rigour through the doctrine of creation in the image of God. This can be seen throughout the Christian theological tradition, whether the writers in question have drawn on Platonic (Augustine) or Aristotelian (Aquinas) resources in the exposition of their theologies.

Augustine of Hippo argued that there was a natural progression from an admiration of the beautiful things of the world to the worship of the one who had created these things, and whose beauty was reflected in them.[110] Beauty, for Augustine, was grounded ontologically in the being of God, evoking a response from humanity on account of the congruity between God and the height of the creation. The most celebrated statement of this point is found in his *Confessions*:[111]

> Late have I loved you, beauty so old and so new, late have I loved you. And see, you were within me, and I was in the world outside and sought you there. I threw myself in my unlovely state into those lovely things that you had created. You were with me, but I was not with you. Those lovely things kept me away from you, things which would not even exist if it were not for you. You called and cried out, and shattered my deafness. You were radiant and gleaming, and put my blindness to flight. You blew fragrant breath towards me, and I drew in my breath and now long for you. I tasted you, and I hunger and thirst for you. You touched me, and I was inflamed with a longing for your peace.

Beauty, for Augustine, possessed the ability to draw humanity to God, through an ascent of the mind through external beauty to the

---

[109] Gerhard von Rad, *Old Testament Theology*. 2 vols. London: SCM Press, 1975, vol. 1, 364–8; Chaim Reines, 'Beauty in the Bible and the Talmud', *Judaism* 24 (1975), 100–7.

[110] Hans Urs von Balthasar, *The Glory of the Lord: A Theological Aesthetics*. 7 vols. Edinburgh: T&T Clark, 1982–91, vol. 2, 123–9.

[111] Augustine, *Confessions*, X.xxvii.38.

final source of that beauty, which is God. To fail to discern God in the created order is to attach affection to the created order, rather than to its creator:[112]

> I loved beautiful things of a lower order, and I was sinking down to the depths. I used to say to my friends: 'Do we love anything other than that which is beautiful? Then what is a beautiful object? And what is beauty? What is it that charms us and attracts us to the things that we love? It must be the grace and loveliness which is inherent in him; otherwise they would in no way draw us to them.'

A similar theme can be found in the writings of C. S. Lewis, perhaps one of Augustine's more eloquent interpreters in the twentieth century:[113]

> The books or the music in which we thought the beauty was located will betray us if we trust to them; it was not in them, it only came *through* them, and what came through them was longing. These things – the beauty, the memory of our own past – are good images of what we really desire; but if they are mistaken for the thing itself they turn into dumb idols, breaking the hearts of their worshippers. For they are not the thing itself; they are only the scent of a flower we have not found, the echo of a tune we have not heard, news from a country we have not visited.

Lewis here affirms the existence of beauty within the created order, while simultaneously stressing that such beauty is intended to lead the beholder to the origins and ground of that created beauty in the creator.

Thomas Aquinas set out 'Five Ways' of inferring from the orderliness of the world to the reality of God; the fourth of those ways is based upon the observation of the existence of perfection in the world. Although Aquinas does not specifically identify 'beauty' as one of these perfections at this point, it is clear that this identification can be made without difficulty, and is made elsewhere in Aquinas' works.[114] The idea is also developed in some detail in the writings of Bonaventure, especially in the highly significant work *Itinerarium mentis in Deum*.[115] Bonaventure develops the same general line of argument: the character

---

[112] Augustine, *Confessions*, IV.xiii.20.

[113] C. S. Lewis, 'The Weight of Glory', in *Screwtape Proposes a Toast*. London: Collins, 1965, 97–8.

[114] Umberto Eco, *The Aesthetics of Thomas Aquinas*. London: Radius, 1988.

[115] Emma Jane Spargo, *The Category of the Aesthetic in the Philosophy of Saint Bonaventure*. St Bonaventure, NY: Franciscan Institute, 1953; Karl Peter, *Die Lehre von der Schönheit nach Bonaventura*. Werl in Westfalie: Dietrich-Coelde-Verlag, 1964.

of God – including God's truth, beauty and goodness – is reflected in God's creation:[116]

> The creatures of the world lead the souls of the wise and contemplative to the eternal God, since they are the shadows, echoes and pictures; the vestiges, images and visible images of the most powerful, wise and best first principle of that eternal origin, light and fulness; of that productive, exemplary and order-inducing art. They are set before us in order that we might know God. We are given signs by God . . . every creature is by its very nature and kind of depiction and likeness of that eternal wisdom.

This general line of argument was developed in the early twentieth century by the noted philosophical theologian F. R. Tennant, who argued that part of the cumulative case for the existence of God was the observation of beauty within the world.[117]

Within the Reformed tradition, a recognition of the importance of 'beauty' as a theological theme can be discerned in the writings of Calvin.[118] However, its most powerful exposition within this tradition is generally agreed to be found in the writings of the leading eighteenth-century American theologian Jonathan Edwards. Edwards argues that the beauty of God is to be expected – and duly found – in the derived beauty of the created order:[119]

> It is very fit and becoming of God who is infinitely wise, so to order things that there should be a voice of His in His works, instructing those that behold him and painting forth and shewing divine mysteries and things more immediately appertaining to Himself and His spiritual kingdom. The works of God are but a kind of voice or language of God to instruct intelligent beings in things pertaining to Himself. And why should we not think that he would teach and instruct by His works in this way as well as in others, viz. by representing divine things by His works and so painting them forth, especially since we know that God hath so much delighted in this way of instruction . . . If we look on these shadows of divine things as the voice of God purposely by them teaching us these and those spiritual and divine things, to show of what excellent advantage it will be, how agreeably and clearly it will tend to convey

---

[116] Bonaventure, *Itinerarium Mentis in Deum*, 2.

[117] F. R. Tennant, *Philosophical Theology*. 2 vols. Cambridge: Cambridge University Press, 1930, vol. 2, 89–93.

[118] Léon Wencelius, *L'ésthétique de Calvin*. Geneva: Slatkine, 1979.

[119] Jonathan Edwards, *The Images of Divine Things*, ed. Perry Millar. New Haven, CT: Yale University Press, 1948, 61–9. See further Diana Butler, 'God's Visible Glory: The Beauty of Nature in the Thought of John Calvin and Jonathan Edwards', *Westminster Theological Journal* 52 (1990), 13–26; Roland Delattre, *Beauty and Sensibility in the Thought of Jonathan Edwards*. New Haven, CT: Yale University Press, 1968.

instruction to our minds, and to impress things on the mind and to affect the mind, by that we may, as it were, have God speaking to us. Wherever we are, and whatever we are about, we may see divine things excellently represented and held forth.

The most theologically sustained and sophisticated exploration of the significance of 'beauty' of the present century can be found in the writings of the Swiss Roman Catholic theologian Hans Urs von Balthasar (1905–88). The theme of 'beauty' dominates his *magnum opus*.[120] 'The fundamental principle of a theological aesthetics . . . is the fact that, just as this Christian revelation is absolute truth and goodness, so also it is absolute beauty.'[121] Von Balthasar thus describes his own work as 'an attempt to develop a Christian theology in the light of the third transcendental, that is to say: to complement the vision of the true and the good with that of the beautiful'.[122] There are obvious parallels here with the Platonic triad of truth, goodness and beauty, which has led some critics to suggest that von Balthasar has himself adopted a form of Platonism, similar to that which is so striking a feature of the writings of pseudo-Dionysius.

Beauty as a criterion of scientific theories

It will be clear from what has just been stated that the concept of beauty is of major importance to a religious understanding of the nature of the world. Its importance has long been appreciated in pure mathematics,[123] although the new interest in fractals has opened up the issue in a new and highly exciting manner.[124] In the present century, that interest in beauty has also become significant for the natural sciences. While 'beauty' can be understood to refer to the natural world itself, it is generally understood to refer to the manner in which that world is to be interpreted and represented, especially at the theoretical level.[125]

[120] See Noel O'Donoghue, 'A Theology of Beauty,' in John Riches (ed.), *The Analogy of Beauty: The Theology of Hans Urs von Balthasar.* Edinburgh: T&T Clark, 1986, 1–10; John O'Donnell, *Hans Urs von Balthasar.* London: Chapman, 1992.

[121] Von Balthasar, *The Glory of the Lord,* vol. 1, 607.

[122] Von Balthasar, *The Glory of the Lord,* vol. 1, 9.

[123] Roger Penrose, 'The Role of Aesthetics in Pure and Applied Mathematical Research', *Bulletin of the Institute of Mathematics and Its Applications* 10 (1974), 266–71.

[124] Francis C. Moon, *Chaotic and Fractal Dynamics.* New York: John Wiley & Sons, 1992; Heinz-Otto Peitgen, Hartmut Jürgens and Dietmar Saupe, *Chaos and Fractals: New Frontiers of Science.* New York, Berlin and London: Springer-Verlag, 1992; Roger Penrose, *The Emperor's New Mind.* London: Vintage, 1990, 98–128.

[125] McAllister, 'Truth and Beauty in Scientific Reason'; Zee, *Fearful Symmetry*; Peter Barrett, 'Beauty in Physics and Theology', *Journal of Theology for Southern Africa* 94 (1996), 65–78.

The beauty of theories is often associated with their symmetry, as we noted when dealing with the elegance of Maxwell's equations. Steven Weinberg, who received the 1979 Nobel Prize for physics, comments as follows on the beauty of scientific theories:[126]

> The kind of beauty that we find in physical theories is of a very limited sort. It is, as far as I have been able to capture it in words, the beauty of simplicity and inevitability – the beauty of perfect structure, the beauty of everything fitting together, of nothing being changeable, of logical rigidity. It is a beauty that is spare and classic, the sort we find in the Greek tragedies.

This is especially clear from the writings of Paul Dirac, who managed to establish a connection between quantum theory and general relativity at a time when everyone else had failed to do so. Dirac's approach appears to have been based on the concept of 'beauty', in that an explicitly aesthetic criterion is laid down as a (not the only) means of evaluating scientific theories:[127]

> It is more important to have beauty in one's equations than to have them fit experiment . . . It seems that if one is working from the point of view of getting beauty in one's equations, and if one has a really good insight, one is on a sure line of progress.

At first, this might seem an outrageous suggestion. Surely it is the degree of empirical fit which determines the adequacy of a theory, rather than its intrinsic beauty? However, the situation is not quite as simple, as a cursory survey of the history of science will make clear.

An excellent example of this point is provided by Einstein's theory of general relativity. This theory allowed three correlations with empirical data: a retrodiction (i.e. accounting for something which was already known) of the anomalous precession of the planet Mercury (which had been known, but not accounted for, since about 1865); the prediction of the deflection of a beam of light on account of the gravitational mass of the sun; and the prediction of a solar gravitational redshift of light. The theory also possessed considerable conceptual elegance and simplicity. The noted physicist H. A. Lorentz commented that it 'has the very highest degree of aesthetic merit: every lover of the beautiful must wish it to be true'.

[126] Steven Weinberg, *Dreams of a Final Theory: The Search for the Fundamental Laws of Nature*. London: Hutchinson Radius, 1993, 119.
[127] Paul Dirac, 'The Evolution of the Physicist's Picture of Nature', *Scientific American* 208.5 (1963), 45–53; 47.

The theory undoubtedly possessed a high degree of beauty; the experimental evidence, however, obstinately refused to support it fully. This seemed to be a classic instance of T. H. Huxley's famous aphorism concerning 'the great tragedy of science – the slaying of a beautiful hypothesis by an ugly fact'.[128] But this was not, in fact, the case. It is now known that the instrumental techniques available in the 1920s simply were not good enough to allow the predicted effects which would have confirmed the theory to be observed; it was not until the 1960s that final confirmation was forthcoming. The intrinsic beauty of the theory could at last be seen to be correlated with its truth.[129]

Earlier, we noted Niels Bohr's explanation of Johann Balmer's mathematical representation of the atomic spectrum of hydrogen. It is important to note how the concept of 'beauty' played an important part in the development of the quantum mechanical explanation of this spectrum. During the period 1925–6, Werner Heisenberg and Erwin Schrödinger were both working on ways of describing atomic events,[130] especially in the light of the work of Louis de Broglie. Their younger colleague Paul Dirac described their different approaches as follow:[131]

> Heisenberg worked keeping close to the experimental evidence about spectra . . . Schrödinger worked from a more mathematical point of view, trying to find a beautiful theory for describing atomic events . . . He was able to extend de Broglie's ideas and to get a very beautiful equation, known as Schrödinger's wave equation, for describing atomic processes. Schrödinger got this equation by pure thought, looking for some beautiful generalization of de Broglie's ideas, and not by keeping close to the experimental development of the subject in the way Heisenberg did.

The differences in approach are highly significant. Heisenberg worked outwards from the experimental evidence; Schrödinger sought an elegant theory which would then account for that evidence. The two, as it proved, converged. The quest for beauty and the quest for truth met at a common point. This point is clearly hinted at in Heisenberg's reflections on his work:[132]

---

[128] T. H. Huxley, 'Biogenesis and Albiogenesis', in T. H. Huxley (ed.), *Collected Essays*. London: Macmillan, 1894, vol. 8, 227–91; 244.

[129] See the influential 1986 lecture of S. Chandrasekhar, 'The Aesthetic Base of the General Theory of Relativity', in *Truth and Beauty*, 144–64.

[130] Pais, *Niels Bohr's Times*, 267–89.

[131] Dirac, 'The Evolution of the Physicist's Picture of Nature', 46–7.

[132] Werner Heisenberg, *Physics and Beyond: Encounters and Conversations*. New York: Harper & Row, 1971, 59, 68. For similar themes in the work of another leading physicist, see George Johnson, *Strange Beauty: Murray Gell-Mann and the Revolution in Twentieth-Century Physics*. London: Jonathan Cape, 2000.

> I had the feeling that, through the surface of atomic phenomena, I was looking at a strangely beautiful interior, and felt almost giddy at the thought that I now had to probe this wealth of mathematical structures nature had so generously spread out before me . . . If nature leads to mathematical forms of great simplicity and beauty – coherent systems of hypotheses, axioms, etc. – . . . we cannot help thinking that they are 'true', that they reveal genuine features of beauty.

The general drift of this analysis will be clear. A strong doctrine of creation (such as that associated with Christianity) leads to the expectation of a fundamental convergence of truth and beauty in the investigation and explanation of the world, precisely on account of the grounding of that world in the nature of God. The correlation in question is not arbitrary or accidental, but corresponds to the reflection of the nature of the creator in the ordering and regularity of creation. It is a simple, yet important, indication of an area in which there is clearly convergence between the sciences and a religious world-view.

In drawing out the consequences of the Christian doctrine of creation, it has been argued that there is a very satisfactory degree of resonance between the implications of this doctrine and the world of experience which it seeks to address and interpret. It must be stressed that this is in no way to be understood as an implicit *proof* of the doctrine. The point being made can be stated like this: Christians, who accept a doctrine of creation such as that set out in this work, will use it as a framework for the engagement with experience of the world, as a Kantian net thrown over experience. As this chapter will indicate, they will find a strong degree of resonance between this doctrine and this world of experience.

The situation can be compared to Thomas Aquinas' 'Five Ways', which some have been unwise enough to regard as proofs for the existence of God. In fact they are not; Aquinas regards them as operating within the context of faith, and demonstrating the high degree of internal consistency within Christian theology, as well as a high degree of correspondence with the external world. These *rationes* can thus be argued to function primarily at an intrasystemic level, while at the same time indicating potential extrasystemic correlation.

On the basis of what has been said, it will be clear that it is essential to move on to deal with a cluster of questions which have traditionally been discussed under the general category of 'natural theology' – to which we now turn.

Chapter 6

The Purpose and Place of Natural Theology

I t is impossible to offer any account of the interaction of Christian theology and the natural sciences without engaging with the question of the legitimate place and purpose of natural theology. Defining this notion is far from easy, not least because of the intrusion of polemical considerations into any discussion of the issue.[1] In his major study *Perceiving God* (1991), William P. Alston sets out what he regards as a responsible and realistic approach. Alston defines natural theology as 'the enterprise of providing support for religious beliefs by starting from premises that neither are nor presuppose any religious beliefs'.[2] While such a definition is vulnerable at points – for example, it avoids any specific reference to the category of the 'natural' – the general position which it reflects would appear to be an excellent starting point for our discussion.

The historical origins of modern natural theology

We must be clear from the outset that Christian theologians have always been interested in the natural world, and the exploration of the place of reason in Christian life and thought. It is thus perfectly proper to speak of the 'natural theology' of Aquinas, Augustine or

---

[1] This point is made by H. J. Birkner, 'Natürliche Theologie und Offenbarungstheologie: Ein theologiegeschichtlicher Überblick', *Neue Zeitschrift für systematische Theologie und Religionsphilosophie* 3 (1961), 279–95.

[2] William P. Alston, *Perceiving God: The Epistemology of Religious Experience.* Ithaca, NY: Cornell University Press, 1991, 289.

Calvin. Yet it is clear that natural theology – as this notion would now be understood – is a recent invention, and is to be seen as a response to upheavals in the intellectual world in England during the seventeenth and eighteenth centuries. Natural theology, as this term is now understood, arose within the English theological tradition, and reflects the social and ecclesiastical conditions of the seventeenth and early eighteenth centuries.

In the modern sense of the term, natural theology has its origins in the English context of the seventeenth century, through a number of developments which caused increasing attention to be paid to the natural world as a confirmation of the Christian revelation. The earlier dominance of German-language discussions of the development of the discipline has tended to obscure, rather than illuminate this historical issue, but it is well attested in the literature of the period. Works such as John Wilkins' *Discourse concerning the Beauty of Providence* (1649), Walter Charleton's *The Darkness of Atheism Dispelled by the Light of Nature* (1652) and John Ray's *Wisdom of God Manifested in the Works of the Creation* (1691) set out the principles of the science of what was then termed 'physico-theology',[3] but is now more generally referred to as 'natural theology'.[4] The Boyle Lectures – established at Cambridge in memory of the great natural philosopher Robert Boyle – rapidly became established as a vehicle for the propagation of this new discipline, often using Newtonian physics as a means of confirming the reliability of the Christian world-view.[5] The English-language tradition of reflecting upon natural theology has, of course, been given considerable impetus in more recent English-language discussions through the Gifford Lectures, delivered annually at Scottish universities.[6] Among important contributions to the series, the contribution by Charles Raven may be noted as being

---

[3] See Ray's 1692 work *Physico-Theological Discourses*, and especially the seminal work of William Derham, *Physico-Theology; or; A Demonstration of the Being and Attributes of God from his Works of Creation* (1713). For a discussion of the apologetic factors which nourished this enterprise, see Hans-Martin Barth, *Atheismus und Orthodoxie: Analysen und Modelle christlicher Apologetik im 17. Jahrhundert*. Göttingen: Vandenhoeck & Ruprecht, 1971, 251–4.

[4] See Charles E. Raven, *John Ray, Naturalist: His Life and Works*. Cambridge: Cambridge University Press, 1986; Barbara J. Shapiro, *John Wilkins, 1614–1672: An Intellectual Biography*. Berkeley, CA: University of California Press, 1969.

[5] John J. Dahm, 'Science and Apologetics in the Early Boyle Lectures', *Church History* 39 (1970), 172–86. Derham's *Physico-Theology* was the published version of the Boyle Lectures for the academic year 1711–12.

[6] Stanley L. Jaki, *Lord Gifford and his Lectures*. Edinburgh: Scottish Academic Press, 1986.

of especial interest,[7] although other outstanding volumes should also be noted.[8]

Our concern at this stage, however, is with the impact of English 'physico-theology' upon the theological debates of the time. It is clear that these ideas were taken up with enthusiasm throughout Europe as a new means of defending the intellectual coherence of the Christian faith at a time when many perceived it to be under attack. This was especially the case at Geneva, where Protestant theologians found themselves increasingly drawn to the writings of the English physico-theologians in their defence of Reformed Orthodoxy. The writings of John Calvin might have suited the needs of earlier generations at Geneva; the theology of Geneva during the eighteenth century would be better served by the writings of Wilkins, Ray or Derham. Thus in 1726, Jean-Alphonse Fatio defended the 'truth of the Christian religion against the difficulties of non-believers' with an appeal to Ray and Derham.[9] There was nothing unusual in this; the intellectual climate throughout Europe made such an appeal as attractive as it was perceived to be necessary.

What was distinctive about the English situation was the manner in which natural theology was seen as a stabilizing influence during a critically important period in English social history. The upheavals of the Puritan commonwealth and the reign of James II (1685–8) led to a pronounced dislike for any form of religious enthusiasm. A natural religion, which was grounded in the regularities of the natural world, was widely seen as offering a more restrained and stable basis for polite English society. Newtonianism came to be seen as offering a more persuasive theological basis for English religion than either Puritan or Roman Catholic theological systems, even if the criteria of judgement deployed in drawing this conclusion were more pragmatic and social than intellectual.[10]

[7] Charles E. Raven, *Natural Religion and Christian Theology*. 2 vols. Cambridge: Cambridge University Press, 1953. See further Frederick W. Dillistone, *Charles Raven: Naturalist, Historian, Theologian*. London: Hodder & Stoughton, 1975.

[8] Perhaps most notably, William James, *The Varieties of Religious Experience: A Study in Human Nature*. New York: Longmans Green, 1917; William Temple, *Nature, Man and God*. London: Macmillan, 1935; Jaroslav Pelikan, *Christianity and Classical Culture: The Metamorphosis of Natural Theology in the Christian Encounter with Hellenism*. New Haven, CT: Yale University Press, 1993.

[9] See Michael Heyd, 'Un rôle nouveau pour la science: Jean Alphonse Turrettini et les débuts de la théologie naturelle à Genève', *Revue de théologie et philosophie* 112 (1982), 25–42.

[10] See the important study of Margaret C. Jacob, *The Newtonians and the English Revolution 1689–1720*. Ithaca, NY: Cornell University Press, 1976.

Four interconnected developments took place during this period, which encouraged a new interest to develop in the revelatory capacities of the natural world.

1. The rise of biblical criticism, which called into question the reliability or intelligibility of Scripture, and hence generated interest in the identification and exploitation of more accessible knowledge of the divine.

2. A growing impatience with and dislike of ecclesiastical authority, which caused more libertarian individuals to seek for sources of knowledge which were seen to be independent of ecclesiastical control. The church might have control of the Bible; nobody could control the natural order.

3. A dislike of the pomposity of organized religion and the apparent complexity of Christian doctrines caused many to seek for a simpler form of religion, free of complications and distortions. A highly idealized quest for an original 'religion of nature' thus began to take place, in which nature was given priority as source of revelation and object of worship over the Christian equivalents.

4. The continuing successes of the mechanical world-view prompted many to wish to gain a deeper knowledge of God through the intricacies of creation. The invisible God could be studied through God's visible works.

These four factors led to a new interest in a specific form of natural theology which went far beyond anything known to the first sixteen centuries of Christian theological reflections. Each of these factors is the result, to varying degrees, of specific intellectual and social developments, which must cause us to conclude that, at least to some extent, both the importance attached to this form of natural theology, and the specific form which it took, are to be regarded as socially mediated and polemically construed.

Given the importance of this matter, we shall explore each of these four matters in a little more detail.

The rise of biblical criticism

One central aspect of the rational criticism of religion in England, which began in earnest with the restoration of Charles II as king of England in 1660 after the collapse of the Puritan commonwealth, was the criticism both of the religious ideas of the Bible, and of the manner in which these were developed and appropriated by the Christian churches.[11] The Bible was declared to be difficult to interpret, laden with ideas and values which reflected the archaic religious beliefs and practices of an obsolete Judaism, and to represent at best a poor embodiment of notions which could be developed and justified through the judicious exercise of unaided human reason.

At this juncture, the tradition of the 'two books' was developed in a significant direction. Within the Reformed tradition, a distinction had been drawn between the 'book of nature' and the 'book of Scripture'. Both were written by the same God, but using different idioms. With a perceptible faltering in confidence in the 'book of Scripture', a new emphasis came to be placed upon the 'book of nature'. This latter book was publicly accessible, and more amenable to rational interpretation than the complexities of Scripture.

The rejection of ecclesiastical authority

Deism can be seen as an important anticipation of the agenda of the Enlightenment, in terms of both its pursuit of personal autonomy and its demand for emancipation from the constraints of traditional modes of thought. The 'Age of Reason' demanded liberation, and saw reason as the liberator in waiting.[12] As Jeffrey Stout points out, 'modern thought was born in a crisis of authority, took shape in flight from authority, and aspired from the start to autonomy from all traditional influence whatsoever'.[13] This desire for intellectual and political emancipation was often linked with the mythical figure of Prometheus, who came to be seen as a symbol of liberation in European literature.[14] Prometheus was now unbound, and humanity poised to enter a new era of autonomy and progress.

The church was often seen as a bulwark of conservatism, linked with the social and political establishment, and responsible for the repression of free thinking. This perception was partly the result of the European context, in which a 'national church' came to be the religious

---

[11] For an excellent introduction to this immensely complicated matter, see Henning Graf Reventlow, *The Authority of the Bible and the Rise of the Modern World.* London: SCM Press, 1984, 289–384.

[12] Edward H. Davidson, William J. Scheick and Thomas Paine, *Scripture and Authority: The Age of Reason as Religious and Political Ideal.* Bethlehem, PA: Lehigh University Press, 1994.

[13] Jeffrey Stout, *The Flight from Authority: Religion, Morality and the Quest for Autonomy.* Notre Dame, IN: University of Notre Dame Press, 1981, 2–3.

[14] On the literary significance of Prometheus, see Raymond Trousson, *Le thème de Prométhée dans le littérature européene.* Geneva: Droz, 1976; Linda M. Lewis, *The Promethean Politics of Milton, Blake and Shelley.* London: University of Missouri Press, 1992.

institution of the state. The Church of England represents a particularly perspicuous example of this phenomenon. As a result, political and social protest often took the form of criticism of both the church and its foundational legitimating dogmas.

Natural theology was thus seized upon as a weapon by which the institution of the church might be undermined. Knowledge of God – to the extent that this was conceded to be a good thing – was not limited to the sources recognized by the church, but was open to all, through the contemplation of nature. The authority of the church could be completely bypassed through a direct appeal to nature. The knowledge of God which had hitherto been the jealous preserve of the ecclesiastical establishment could thus be stolen, and made accessible to a wider audience.

The rise of the mechanical world-view

The rise of the mechanical world-view of the late seventeenth and eighteenth centuries was of considerable importance to the development of a natural theology. The rise of this discipline as a significant branch of Christian theology is widely held to be a direct result of the Newtonian revolution.[15] It should be noted that both the defenders of orthodox Christianity and their Deist and rationalist critics initially regarded the Newtonian world-view as being something which they could exploit. An appeal to nature was an indirect appeal to a divine being.

The amalgam of Newtonian natural philosophy and certain forms of Anglican theology – such as that developed by the 'Great Tew Circle'[16] – proved popular and plausible in post-revolutionary England.[17] Nevertheless, it was an inherently unstable amalgam. As Odom has pointed out, it was not long before the 'estrangement of celestial mechanics and religion' began to set in.[18] Celestial mechanics seemed to many to suggest that the world was a self-sustaining mechanism which had no need for divine governance or sustenance for its day-to-day operation. This danger had been recognized at an early stage by one of Newton's interpreters, Samuel Clark. In his correspondence with

[15] See Gascoigne, 'From Bentley to the Victorians: The Rise and Fall of British Newtonian Natural Theology', *Science in Context* 2 (1988), 219–56.

[16] Hugh Trevor-Roper, 'The Great Tew Circle', in H. R. Trevor-Roper (ed.), *Catholics, Anglicans and Puritans: Seventeenth Century Essays.* Chicago: University of Chicago Press, 1988, 166–230.

[17] James R. Jacob and Margaret C. Jacob, 'The Anglican Origins of Modern Science: The Metaphysical Foundations of the Whig Constitution', *Isis* 71 (1980), 251–67.

[18] H. H. Odom, 'The Estrangement of Celestial Mechanics and Religion', *Journal of the History of Ideas* 27 (1966), 533–58.

Leibniz, Clark expressed concern over the potential implications of the growing emphasis on the regularity of nature:[19]

> The notion of the world's being a great machine, going on without the interposition of God, as a clock continues to go on without the assistance of a clockmaker; is the notion of materialism and fate, and tends (under the pretence of making God a supramundane intelligence) to exclude providence, and God's government in reality of the world.

The image of God as a 'clockmaker' (and the associated natural theology which appealed to the regularity of the world) was thus seen as potentially leading to a purely naturalist understanding of the universe, in which God had no continuing role to play.

Such a development might cause distress to some within the ecclesiastical establishment; it was welcomed by Deist agitators and their successors within the Enlightenment. An appeal to the Newtonian conception of the natural world increasingly came to be seen as an important strategy in undermining the intellectual credibility of Christianity, and accelerating its replacement with a rational 'religion of nature'. A natural theology was to be seen as a polemical device, with both critical and constructive aspects. Negatively, it undermined traditional Christian thinking concerning providence and God's action in the world (and the Church of England); positively, it encouraged the development of simpler, more reasonable forms of religion. We shall pursue this latter point further in what follows.

The quest for a religion of nature

As we have seen, both Deism and the later Enlightenment were critical of the ideas and institution of the Christian churches. With important exceptions, however, the Enlightenment was not especially anti-religious. Criticism was directed against Christianity in particular on account of its dominant role in the social order of the late seventeenth and eighteenth centuries. Rather than eliminate religion – an agenda which later came to be associated with the French Revolution – many Enlightenment thinkers preferred to develop their own, taking their cues from nature. Robert Boyle was one of several influential writers to adopt the important metaphor of 'nature as a temple', with the natural scientist serving as a priest to nature.[20]

---

[19] H. G. Alexander, *The Leibniz–Clark Correspondence*. Manchester: Manchester University Press, 1956, 14.

[20] Harold Fisch, 'The Scientist as Priest: A Note on Robert Boyle's Natural Theology', *Isis* 44 (1953), 252–65.

The quest for a primordial 'religion of nature' – which had later been hijacked and distorted by the ecclesiastical establishment – thus became an important element of Enlightenment religious thought. Christianity was, at best, simply a republication of an older religion of nature; at worst, it represented the corruption of this earlier vision.[21] It was widely argued that religions were the invention of priests or other cultic leaders, whose prime interest was the furthering of their own personal ends. The notion of a 'religion of nature' was thus seen as a potent weapon against both the clergy and the church, with natural theology as the source of the creeds of this polemically focused movement.

This brief analysis leads to the inevitable conclusion that the development of natural theology as an autonomous area of human intellectual activity was encouraged and shaped by the social agenda of the late seventeenth century. Yet Christian theologians – such as Thomas Aquinas and John Calvin – had developed what might legitimately be styled 'natural theologies' long before this polemical turn had led to this enterprise being seen in this new light. It is therefore imperative to be aware that the intellectual climate of the 'Age of Reason' has had a major, yet largely unacknowledged, impact on the manner in which modern theologians view premodern styles of natural theology – often inadvertently imposing a modern agenda upon ages which were innocent of the polemical considerations which are today taken for granted. This insight allows us to approach Barth's seminal critique of natural theology from a helpful perspective, to which we shall return in due course.

Our attention now turns to a more detailed examination of possible approaches to natural theology. The most appropriate place at which to begin a discussion of the legitimacy of natural theology is the question of the 'natural' realm upon which such a theology might be based. The first major consideration which must be addressed in this respect is the problematic status of the category of 'nature' itself, which has a significant impact upon how a natural theology might be construed and defended.

---

[21] See, for example, William Wollaston, *The Religion of Nature Delineated.* London: S. Palmer, 1725; Matthew Tindal, *Christianity as Old as the Creation: or, The gospel, a Republication of the Religion of Nature.* London: [s.n.], 1730; and the response by Thomas Broughton, *Christianity Distinct from the Religion of Nature.* London: W. Bickerton, 1732; Thomas Bott, *The Principal and Peculiar Notion Advanc'd in a Late Book, intitled: The Religion of Nature Delineated.* London: J. Noon, 1725. More generally, see Peter A. Byrne, *Natural Religion and the Religion of Nature.* London: Routledge, 1989.

'Nature' and natural theology

To speak of 'natural theology' is to make an implicit judgement concerning the 'nature' which constitutes the foundation for any such
theology. As we have stressed throughout this work, the notion of
'nature' is intensely problematic, in that it is heavily conditioned by a
series of prior assumptions, and mediated through a complex network
of social constructions. If nature is seen as creation, a theological
foundation of some importance can be developed for a responsible
natural theology, which takes into account the specifically Christian
understanding of creation as a trinitarian event, and the concept of the
creation of humanity in the *imago Dei*.[22]

Nevertheless, there are still some difficulties which demand attention.
The most serious of these relate to the extent to which the notion of
'nature' may be developed away from the natural world to embrace
human culture. To indicate the importance of this point, we shall
explore how such a development might take place, and what its
implications would be.

Nature as the observable world

The classic understanding of nature is the world of the star-studded
night skies, plants and animals, landscapes and sunsets, which have
inspired the vision of artists as much as the attention of theologians.
The importance of nature, in this sense, for natural theology will be
self-evident. Richard Bentley developed a sophisticated natural theology,
based on the Newtonian system, which argued that the regularities of
planetary motion, as explained by Newton, constituted a significant
reinforcement of the Christian world-view in general, and its doctrine
of creation in particular. Bentley delivered the first series of Boyle
Lectures on natural theology in 1692, published the following year as *A
Confutation of Atheism*. One of the central themes of these lectures is
that a cosmogony (such as that set out by Newton) implies a creator – a
theme which Newton himself strongly endorsed.[23]

The appeal to the botanical world as the basis of a natural theology
is an important theme in the writings of the eighteenth-century

---

[22] On which see Stanley Grenz, 'The *Imago Dei* and the Dissipation of the Self', *Dialog*
38 (1999), 182–98.
[23] Gascoigne, 'From Bentley to the Victorians'; A. Rupert Hall, *Isaac Newton: Adventurer
in Thought*. Cambridge: Cambridge University Press, 1996, 246–8.

Swedish naturalist Linnaeus (Carl von Linné, 1707–78).[24] It has been persuasively argued that the perception and explanation of order within nature is the single most important question to be addressed by Linnaeus. Linnaeus believed that the patterns of ordering which he discerned within the world of plants, and which he expressed in his classification of species, were an important instance of a natural theology. Such ordering, he argued, either rested upon or otherwise reflected the divine creation of the world.

Such biological themes were further developed in important works of English natural theology in the early nineteenth century, especially the apologetic writings of William Paley (1743–1805). _Natural Theology; or Evidences of the Existence and Attributes of the Deity, Collected from the Appearances of Nature_ (1802) had a profound influence on popular English religious thought in the first half of the nineteenth century, and is known to have been read by Charles Darwin. Paley was deeply impressed by Newton's discovery of the regularity of nature, especially in relation to the area usually known as 'celestial mechanics'. It was clear that the entire universe could be thought of as a complex mechanism, operating according to regular and understandable principles.

For Paley, the Newtonian image of the world as a mechanism immediately suggested the metaphor of a clock or watch, raising the question of who had constructed the intricate mechanism which was so elegantly displayed in the functioning and ordering of the world. One of Paley's most significant arguments is that mechanism implies 'contrivance' – a word reflecting the interest in mechanical technology of the period, and which stresses the importance of _design_ and _purpose_. Writing against the backdrop of the emerging Industrial Revolution, Paley sought to exploit the apologetic potential of the growing interest in machinery within England's literate classes.

The general lines of Paley's approach are well known. At the time, England was experiencing the Industrial Revolution, in which machinery was coming to play an increasingly important role in industry. Paley argues that it is ludicrous to believe that such complex mechanical technology came into being by chance. Mechanism presupposes both a

---

[24] Margaret J. Anderson, _Carl Linnaeus: Father of Classification._ Springfield, NJ: Enslow Publishers, 1997; Gunnar Broberg, _Homo Sapiens: L. Studier i Carl von Linnés naturuppfattning och människolära._ Uppsala: Almqvist & Wiksell, 1975; James L. Larson, _Interpreting Nature: The Science of Living from Linnaeus to Kant._ Baltimore: Johns Hopkins University Press, 1994; James L. Larson, 'The Species Concept of Linnaeus', _Isis_ 59 (1968), 291–9.

sense of purpose, and an ability to design and fabricate. Both the human body in particular, and the world in general, could be seen as mechanisms which had been designed and constructed in such a manner as to achieve harmony of both means and ends. It must be stressed that Paley is not suggesting that there exists an analogy between human mechanical devices and nature. The force of his argument rests on an identity: nature *is* a mechanism, and hence was intelligently designed.

The opening paragraphs of Paley's *Natural Theology* have become so widely known that it will be helpful to cite them, and offer some comments.[25]

> In crossing a heath, suppose I pitched my foot against a *stone*, and were asked how the stone came to be there. I might possibly answer, that for any thing I knew to the contrary it had lain there for ever; nor would it, perhaps, be very easy to show the absurdity of this answer. But suppose I had found a *watch* upon the ground, and it should be inquired how the watch happened to be in that place. I should hardly think of the answer which I had before given, that for any thing I knew the watch might have always been there. Yet why should this answer not serve for the watch as well as for the stone; why is it not admissible in the second case as in the first? For this reason, and for no other, namely, that when we come to inspect the watch, we perceive – what we could not discover in the stone – that its several parts are framed and put together for a purpose, e.g. that they are so formed and adjusted as to produce motion, and that motion so regulated as to point out the hour of the day; that if the different parts had been differently shaped from what they are, or placed after any other manner or in any other order than that in which they are placed, either no motion at all would have been carried on in the machine, or none which would have answered the use that is now served by it.

Paley then offers a detailed description of the watch, noting in particular its container, coiled cylindrical spring, many interlocking wheels and glass face. Having carried his readers along with this careful analysis, Paley turns to draw his critically important conclusion:

> This mechanism being observed – it requires indeed an examination of the instrument, and perhaps some previous knowledge of the subject, to perceive and understand it; but being once, as we have said, observed

[25] William Paley, 'Natural Theology', in *The Works of William Paley*. London: William Orr, 1844, 25–8. For comment, see Neal C. Gillespie, 'Divine Design and the Industrial Revolution: William Paley's Abortive Reform of Natural Theology', *Isis* 81 (1990), 214–29; D. L. LeMahieu, *The Mind of William Paley: A Philosopher and His Age*. Lincoln, NE: University of Nebraska Press, 1976.

and understood, the inference we think is inevitable, that the watch must
have had a maker – that there must have existed, at some time and at
some place or other, an artificer or artificers who formed it for the purpose
which we find it actually to answer, who comprehended its construction
and designed its use.

Paley's essential point is that nature bears witness to a series of
biological structures which are 'contrived' – that is, constructed with a
clear purpose in mind. 'Every indication of contrivance, every manifestation of design, which existed in the watch, exists in the works of
nature.' Indeed, Paley argues, the difference is that nature shows an
even greater degree of contrivance than the watch. Perhaps it is fair to
say that Paley is at his best when he deals with the description of
mechanical systems within nature, such as the immensely complex
structure of the human eye, or the heart. In this second instance, Paley
is able to treat the heart as a machine with valves, and draw the
conclusion that it has been designed with a purpose in mind.

The influence of Paley upon English attitudes to natural theology
was immense. The celebrated *Bridgewater Treatises* show his influence
at many points, even if they develop an independent approach at others.
The noted anti-theistic evolutionary biologist Richard Dawkins pays
him a somewhat backhanded compliment in the title of one of his best-
known anti-teleological works – *The Blind Watchmaker*. For Dawkins,
the 'watchmaker' whom Paley identified with God was none other than
the blind and purposeless process of natural selection. The growing
acceptance of a Darwinian account of natural selection later in the
nineteenth century called into question the plausibility of an appeal to
the living world as the basis of a natural theology, and led to a growing
tendency of Christian apologists to focus on the physical, rather than
biological worlds, in their quest for support for the plausibility of faith.[26]
Yet Paley's natural theology raised an important question. Paley
appealed explicitly to details of human anatomy in his arguments,
suggesting that the complexity of the human body was such that it
implied purposeful design. We see here an important development –
to regard the human body as an element of nature. Nature does not
merely include stars, trees and rivers; it embraces humanity. So is not
an appeal to nature also an appeal to *human* nature? Should not a
natural theology therefore extend to the human body, including its

[26] For some of the issues, see James R. Moore, *The Post-Darwinian Controversies: A Study
of the Protestant Struggle to come to terms with Darwin in Great Britain and America, 1870–
1900.* Cambridge: Cambridge University Press, 1979.

resources of reason and imagination? This leads us to an extension of our original conception of nature, which includes explicit acceptance of the human faculties as a resource for natural theology.

Nature as human rationality

The doctrine that humanity is created in the image of God is widely interpreted to mean that there exists some correspondence between humanity and its creator. While a variety of approaches to the interpretation of the phrase *imago Dei* may be noted,[27] the classic interpretation of this concept views human rationality as reflecting the mind of God. Athanasius develops this idea in his important treatise *de incarnatione Verbi*:[28]

> God knew the limitations of humanity; and though the grace of being made in the image of God was sufficient to give them knowledge of the Word, and through Him of the Father, as a safeguard against their neglect of this grace, God also provided the works of creation as a means by which the Maker might be known . . . Humanity could thus look up into the immensity of heaven, and by pondering the harmony of creation, come to know its Ruler, the Word of the Father, whose sovereign providence makes the Father known to all.

The divine *logos* is embedded within the structures of the created order – including human rationality – thus allowing humanity to gain at least some access to a knowledge of God through creation, as an anticipation and preparation for the recognition of the *logos* incarnate in Christ.

Perhaps the most celebrated analysis of human rationality is to be found in the writings of Augustine. Augustine of Hippo addresses this question at some length in his major work *de Trinitate*, written between 400 and 417. The general line of argument developed by Augustine in this important work can be summed up as follows. If God is indeed to be discerned within the creation, we ought to expect to find the self-expression of God at the height of that creation. Augustine argues that the culmination of God's creation is to be found in human nature. And, on the basis of the neo-Platonic presuppositions which he inherited from his cultural milieu, Augustine further argued that the apex of human nature is the human capacity to reason. Therefore, he concluded, one should expect to find traces of God (or, more accurately, 'vestiges

[27] See, for example, James Barr, *Biblical Faith and Natural Theology*. Oxford: Clarendon Press, 1993, 156–73.

[28] Athanasius, *de incarnatione Verbi*, 3.

of the Trinity') in human processes of reasoning – that is, in the human *intelligentia, ratio,* or *mens.* On the basis of this belief, Augustine develops what have come to be known as 'psychological analogies of the Trinity'.[29] The two most important triads which Augustine thus identifies are *mens – notitia sui – amor sui* and *memoria – intelligentia sui – voluntas sui.* It is not our intention to develop these further; our concern is simply to note the manner in which Augustine believes that the investigation of human rationality discloses traces of the trinitarian creator of humanity:[30]

> This trinity of the mind is thus not to be understood to be the image of God because the mind remembers itself, understands itself, and loves itself. Rather, it is because it is able to remember, understand and love the one by whom it was created in the first place.

This appeal to human rationality as the basis of a natural theology can easily be extended beyond the Augustinian notion of the *shape* of such a rationality to the more general notion of the outcome of its *application.* This progression from the structure of human rationality to its formalized outcomes would lead some to argue that the general philo-sophical discussion of the existence of God – such as the classical or more recent variants of the ontological argument[31] or Thomas Aquinas' 'Five Ways' – would properly belong to this aspect of natural theology.[32]

Our analysis of human rationality as a possible basis for a natural theology has thus far focused on the individual. Yet humanity, as Aristotle pointed out, is not solitary; humans are political – or perhaps even *urban* – animals.[33] Can one therefore appeal to humanity without considering human societies and cultures? Aristotle drew a distinction between art (τέχνη) and nature (φύσις); yet many would question whether this distinction can be maintained in practice. Some have

---

[29] See the important study of Lewon Zekiean, *L'interioriso agostiniano: la struttura onto-psicologica dell'interioriso agostiniano e la 'memoria sui'*, Genoa: Studio editoriale di cultura, 1981.

[30] Augustine, *de Trinitate* XIV.xii.15.

[31] Such as Graham Oppy, *Ontological Arguments and Belief in God.* Cambridge: Cambridge University Press, 1995; Alvin Plantinga, *The Ontological Argument from St Anselm to Contemporary Philosophers.* London: Macmillan, 1968; Josef Seifert, *Gott als Gottesbeweis: eine phänomenologische Neubegrundung des ontologischen Arguments.* Heidelberg: Universitätsverlag C. Winter, 1996.

[32] William Lane Craig, *The Cosmological Argument from Plato to Leibniz.* London: Macmillan, 1980; C. F. J. Martin, *Thomas Aquinas: God and Explanations.* Edinburgh: Edinburgh University Press, 1997; William L. Rowe, *The Cosmological Argument.* New York: Fordham University Press, 1998.

[33] Aristotle, *Politics* I, 1253a 2–3.

therefore argued that a natural theology cannot limit itself to an appeal to nature, nor even the human faculties; it must be extended to include human culture. In what follows, we shall consider this development.

Nature as human culture

The appeal to human culture as either a foundation or norm of Christian theology can be argued to lie in the patristic period – for example, in Eusebius of Caesarea's 'imperial theology', which treated the culture of the Roman empire as being in some manner reflective of the divine will or character. The systematic development of the potential of culture as a theological resource is, however, generally regarded as dating from the nineteenth century, particularly through the rise of 'Culture Protestantism' – as the critics of the movement dubbed it.[34] Writers such as A. B. Ritschl, perhaps unduly influenced by the rise of evolutionary theory, transposed ideas originally deriving from a biological context into a social framework which saw the moral and spiritual evolution of humanity as theologically luminous. By the end of the nineteenth century, liberal Protestant theologians had come to regard human culture as endowed with revelatory potential.

This was a development which was regarded with alarm by Karl Barth, who regarded this approach as fraught with danger for authentic Christian theology. Might not such an approach lead to someone such as Adolf Hitler becoming authoritative for Christian theology? The Barmen Declaration insisted that true Christianity could have no source of revelation or authority other than Jesus Christ:[35]

> Jesus Christ, as he is attested for us in Holy Scripture, is the one Word of God which we have to hear and which we have to trust and obey in life and in death. We reject the false teaching, that the church could and should acknowledge any other events and powers, figures and truths, as God's revelation, or as a source of its proclamation, apart from or in addition to this one Word of God.

For Barth, a church which failed to define itself in relation to Christ and to judge its cultural context would be judged by and defined with respect to the prevailing culture. Barth's concerns were further

---

[34] Gangolf Hübinger, *Kulturprotestantismus und Politik: zum Verhältnis von Liberalismus und Protestantismus im wilhelminischen Deutschland.* Tübingen: Mohr, 1994; George Rupp, *Culture-Protestantism: German Liberal Theology at the Turn of the Twentieth Century.* Missoula, MT: American Academy of Religion, 1977.

[35] 'The Theological Clarification of the Present State of the German Evangelical Churches' (1934), article 1; in *Bekenntnisschiften und Kirchenordnungen der nach Gottes Wort reformierten Kirche,* ed. W. Niesel. Zurich: Evangelischer Verlag, 1938, 335.

fuelled by the Ansbacher Consultation, issued by the 'German Christians' in June 1934 in response to the Barmen Declaration, which declared that theology and the church should be governed by German culture and the German state.[36] The church should adapt itself radically to conform to the new German situation, recognizing that God had given the German people 'a pious and faithful ruler' in the person of Adolf Hitler.

Yet such concerns, strictures and criticisms have not dissuaded others from appealing to culture as a theological norm for a new style of natural theology. An example of a writer who seeks to ground Christian theology in culture is Gordon Kaufman, who argues as follows:[37]

> The roots of theology are not restricted to the life of the church or to special dogmas or documents venerated in the church, nor are they to be found in something as inchoate as 'raw experience'. They are to be found, rather, in the ordinary language(s) of western culture at large.

Such a statement raises a number of fundamental difficulties. Why, for example, should theological priority be given to *western* culture in this matter? Kaufman seems to make the same error of judgement which underlies Lawrence Kohlberg's analysis of the development of moral stages from infancy to adulthood.[38] Kohlberg believed that he had uncovered a universal cultural pattern; his many critics made the point that his 'moral stages' related only to white males in western post-Enlightenment culture.[39] Allegedly 'universal' judgements or truths are thus adduced on the basis of highly ethnocentric and particular values and beliefs. The theological implications of such reflections for any kind of appeal to 'culture' as a foundational theological resource will be obvious. Culture, like nature, is a social construction. It can be interpreted theologically; it cannot, however, be allowed to become the foundation of a natural theology.

[36] For the text of this document, see Gerhard Niemöller, *Die erste Bekenntnissynode der Deutschen Evangelischen Kirche zu Barmen*. 2 vols. Göttingen: Vandenhoeck & Ruprecht, 1959, vol. 1, 142–6. See also the disquieting analysis of Robert P. Ericksen, *Theologians under Hitler: Gerhard Kittel, Paul Althaus, and Emanuel Hirsch*. New Haven, CT: Yale University Press, 1985.

[37] Gordon Kaufman, *Essay on Theological Method*. Missoula, MT: Scholars Press, 1975, 15. See also his appeal to a concept of God rooted in western culture in *Theology for a Nuclear Age*. Philadelphia: Westminster, 1985, 22–3.

[38] Lawrence Kohlberg, *The Philosophy of Moral Development*. New York: Harper & Row, 1981.

[39] See especially Carol Gilligan, *In a Different Voice: Psychological Theory and Women's Development*. Cambridge, MA: Harvard University Press, 1982; Albert Borgmann, *Crossing the Postmodern Divide*. Chicago: University of Chicago Press, 1992, 53–4.

The present chapter has considered some of the frustrations and difficulties facing those who hold that it is possible to develop a reliable and authoritative knowledge of God through an appeal to nature. While there is no doubt that the somewhat elastic notion of 'nature' complicates matters in this respect, the more fundamental difficulty is that the concept of 'nature' lacks the epistemic autonomy required to permit it to be, or become, a theological resource in its own right. As we have stressed throughout this work, 'nature' is itself a construct, rather than something which can act as the foundation for an ideational construction.

Our attention must now be directed to an exploration of the biblical witness to the legitimacy of a natural theology.

The biblical foundations of a natural theology

While an engagement with the biblical material is essential if an authentically Christian formulation of any theological statement is to be achieved, it has particular importance for the specific topic of natural theology. Part of the battery of arguments assembled by Karl Barth against natural theology having any legitimate place in Christian thought is a sustained insistence that such a move undermines the authority of the Bible.[40] Natural theology, Barth argued, is inconsistent with the Protestant emphasis on biblical authority – a principle which Barth believed that Brunner had betrayed.

It is therefore a matter of no small importance to establish what the general features of the biblical witness on this matter might be. If the Bible itself sanctions or makes use of a natural theology, Barth's position would be seriously undermined. We therefore turn to consider the biblical witness to whether anything of God can be known in nature. The Bible does not have an explicit category of 'nature', which makes discussion of a putative notion of 'natural theology' problematic. For this reason, we shall explore the question in terms of more biblical ways of speaking – namely, whether God may be known apart from direct divine revelation. We begin by considering the Old Testament witness on this point.

Old Testament

There is widespread consensus within the scholarly community that the Old Testament includes a significant number of appeals to both

---

[40] See Barth's comments in Karl Barth and Emil Brunner, *Natural Theology*. London: SCM Press, 1947, 82, 87, 107.

what we might call 'natural theology' and 'natural law'.[41] Such passages cause no small difficulty to those who wish to maintain that the Old Testament permits or acknowledges no true knowledge of the Lord God of Israel apart from specific divine revelation.[42] Nevertheless, it is critically important not to draw hasty conclusions from such passages, but to consider their function.

It is within the wisdom literature of the Old Testament that we might expect to find the greatest number of positive references to the possibility of God being known in and through the created order.[43] God created the world 'in wisdom' (Proverbs 3:19) – and traces of that wisdom may be discerned by the spiritually enlightened human mind. Wisdom is regularly depicted as being engaged in a search for order within the world, including the human and the natural realms. The fundamental assumption here is that certain patterns may be discerned by the 'wise' within their experience of the world. While this assumption can be shown to be dispersed widely in the literature of the ancient near east,[44] the Old Testament wisdom literature generally links the theme of a natural knowledge of God with the divine activity of creation and the preservation of Israel.

Psalm 19 opens with a declaration that the 'heavens declare the glory of the Lord' (Psalm 19:1).[45] The clear sense of the Psalm's argument is that the works of God declare the glory of God. Just as all on the face of the earth recognize and receive the light of the sun, so all can recognize the glory of God in the heavens. The Psalm falls into two parts, the first of which emphasizes that God is to be known through the created order, and the second through the specific revelation of the law. Unless we follow Hermann Gunkel (who argued that the Psalm should be seen as two separate poems), it is clear that the general thrust of the

---

[41] See the excellent analyses of Barr, *Biblical Faith and Natural Theology*; John Barton, 'Natural Law and Poetic Justice in the Old Testament', *Journal of Theological Studies* 30 (1979), 1–14.

[42] See the issues explored by Jean Daniélou, *The Holy Pagans of the Old Testament*. London: Darton, Longman & Todd, 1957.

[43] See here John Day, *Wisdom in Ancient Israel: Essays in Honour of J. A. Emerton*. Cambridge: Cambridge University Press, 1995; Gerhard von Rad, *Wisdom in Israel*. Nashville, TN: Abingdon Press, 1972; Franz-Josef Steiert, *Die Weisheit Israels – ein Fremdkörper im Alten Testament? Eine Untersuchung zum Buch der Sprüche auf dem Hintergrund der ägyptischen Weisheitslehren*. Freiburg im Breisgau: Herder, 1990.

[44] See H. Brunner, 'Die Weisheitsliteratur', in Bertold Spuler (ed.), *Handbuch der Orientalistik*. Leiden: E. J. Brill, 1952, 90–110, especially 93, which stresses that 'primal order' is of central important to the ancient wisdom.

[45] See the comment and literature citations in Barr, *Biblical Faith and Natural Theology*, 85–9.

Psalm is to celebrate and proclaim that God may be known both generally through the created order, and specifically through the revelation of the law.

The passage can be construed in a Barthian manner, but not without doing some violence to the text. It would be necessary to suggest that, while the heavens do indeed declare the glory of God, this 'declaration' is either inaccessible or unintelligible to fallen humanity. The Psalm does not make any such suggestion, which would require the imposition of a quite alien framework upon the text. The basic theme here, and in other passages, is that the glory of the Lord can be discerned in the works of the Lord, both in history and in the created order.

Yet while the Old Testament clearly endorses that something of God may be known through creation, it does not endorse any notion of nature as an autonomous source of knowledge of God. Psalm 19 is clearly intended to be used within the covenant community of Israel, who already knew that their Lord was creator, law-giver and redeemer. The Psalm affirms that Israel may see the glory of her God in every aspect of the created order; it does not imply that this God may be known independently of the divine revelation to Israel. Many other passages could be explored in making the same point. After a careful exploration of the Old Testament evidence, James Barr concludes that a 'biblical' natural theology is very limited in scope:[46]

> The elements which we have detected, which we may call a 'biblical' natural theology, seem very limited in character. They do not amount to the fuller natural theology with which we have been familiar. They do not offer philosophical proofs of the existence of God, they do not work by means of pure reason, they do not appear to amount to the total system of classical theism or anything like it.

These legitimate observations must serve to reinforce the point we made earlier: that we have come to understand 'natural theology' in a manner which has been heavily conditioned by the polemical concerns of earlier generations, especially in the eighteenth century. There is a serious risk of reading the Old Testament material in the light of a modern (as opposed to classical or postmodern) world-view, thus merely reinforcing the opinions of a past generation of interpreters which our own age finds no pressing reason to follow.

---

[46] Barr, *Biblical Faith and Natural Theology*, 138.

New Testament

One of the most important audiences envisaged by New Testament writers for the gospel proclamation were 'the Greeks'. In Paul's first letter to the Corinthians, 'Greeks' are set alongside 'Jews' as a defining group of considerable importance (1 Corinthians 1:22). It is quite clear that sections of the Acts of the Apostles show at least some degree of familiarity and affinity with Hellenistic rhetoric,[47] as well as the beliefs and practices of the classical period.

It is widely thought that one of the most important descriptions of the early confrontation between Christianity and these classic philosophical beliefs is found in Paul's Areopagus address at Athens, the site of the Platonic Academy. Although Athens had been a major political and cultural centre in the classical period under Pericles, it had entered into a period of decline. Greece had become little more than a provincial city within the Roman empire, having lost its former glory and importance. The city suffered a serious setback when it was unwise enough to back the losing side in the Roman civil war. Nevertheless, the city retained an iconic significance, even if the reality no longer quite matched up to the image which it sought to project.[48] The development of Christianity in the city would both presuppose and entail an engagement with the city's formidable philosophical heritage.

According to Luke, Paul opens his address to the Athenians with a gradual introduction of the theme of the living God, allowing the religious and philosophical curiosity of the Athenians to shape the contours of his theological exposition.[49] The 'sense of divinity' present in each individual is here used as an apologetic device, by which Paul is able to base himself upon acceptable Greek theistic assumptions, while at the same time demonstrating that the Christian gospel goes beyond them. Paul shows a clear appreciation of the apologetic potential of Stoic philosophy, portraying the gospel as resonating with central Stoic concerns, while extending the limits of what might be known. What the Greeks held to be unknown, possibly unknowable, Paul proclaims to have been made known through the resurrection of Christ. The entire episode illustrates the manner in which Paul is able to exploit

---

[47] See W. S. Kurz, 'Hellenistic Rhetoric in the Christological Proofs of Luke-Acts', *Catholic Biblical Quarterly* 42 (1980), 171–95.

[48] For discussions of Athens, see Leslie Shear, 'Athens: From City State to Provincial Town', *Hesperia* 50 (1981), 356–77.

[49] See the full study of Bertil Gärtner, *The Areopagus Speech and Natural Revelation.* Uppsala: Gleerup, 1955.

the situation of his audience, without compromising the integrity of faith.

At this point, we need to pause and consider the inscription on an altar to which Paul refers: 'to an unknown god' (Acts 17:23). There are certainly classical precedents for this, especially according to the writings of Diogenes Laertius. Numerous Christian writers of the early patristic period explained Paul's meaning at this point by appealing to the 'anonymous altars' which were scattered throughout the region at that time. Several (including Didymus of Alexandria) suggested that Paul may have altered the inscription from the plural ('to unknown gods') at this point. However, there is no reason to suppose that Paul made any such change.

The fundamental point being made is that a deity of whom the Greeks had some implicit or intuitive awareness through the natural order is being made known to them by name and in full. According to Paul, the God who is known indirectly through creation can be known fully in redemption. Paul explicitly appeals to the idea of creation as a basis for his apologetic approach, apparently using it as a *praeparatio evangelica*, a way of introducing the theme of redemption in Christ. While the precise apologetic strategy deployed by Paul at Athens is the subject of some dispute, it is clear that the address presupposes some form of natural theology. The notion of the created order corresponding to the mind of a God who may be known plays a critical role in Paul's preaching on this occasion. The passage indicates that an apologetic, based in part on a natural theology, was a recognized option within the early Christian church.[50]

It has been argued that there is a tension between Paul's views in this passage, and his ideas as they are set out in his letters.[51] There is doubtless truth in this observation; yet it fails to take account of the very different audiences envisaged by Paul. In the Acts of the Apostles, we find Paul addressing a number of audiences, and tempering his language and modes of argumentation to the audience in question. For example, the 'forensic speeches' of Acts 26 are clearly modelled on classic Roman forensic paradigms, making use of contemporary Roman conventions on evidence and argumentation.[52] More than 250 papyri of official court

[50] Heinz Kulling, *Geoffenbartes Geheimnis: Eine Auslegung von Apostelgeschichte 17, 16–34.* Zurich: Theologischer Verlag, 1993.

[51] E.g. John Ziesler, *Pauline Christianity.* Oxford: Oxford University Press, 1983.

[52] Bruce W. Winter, 'Official Proceedings and the Forensic Speeches in Acts 24–26', in B. W. Winter and A. D. Clarke (eds), *The Book of Acts: Ancient Literary Setting.* Grand Rapids, MI: Eerdmans, 1994, 305–36.

proceedings in the early Roman empire are extant, and offer important insights into the way in which forensic proceedings were conducted, and the manner in which they were recorded. In general terms, forensic speeches – whether offered by the prosecution or defence – tended to consist of four or five standard components. In the case of a speech for the defence, this would include a refutation of the specific charges brought against the accused. The importance of this point can be seen by examining Paul's speech at Acts 24:10–21, in which he responds to the charges brought against him by the professional orator Tertullus (Acts 24:1–8). It is important to note the way in which Paul follows – in the view of many scholars, with great skill – the 'rules of engagement' laid down by Roman legal custom as he subjects Tertullus' accusations to a point-by-point refutation. In particular, he stresses the continuity between his own beliefs and those of the Jews who had accused him, particularly in regard to the Scriptures and the resurrection. But most significant is his appeal to Roman rules of evidence; his accusers (some Asian Jews) were not present to witness against him.

Here, we find Paul represented as using rhetorical conventions which he does not use, for example, in his New Testament letters. Yet the envisaged audiences are rather different. What Paul needed to say before the Roman courts – and the manner in which he said it – were quite different from the substance and manner of what he wished to say to his Christian readership in the case of his letters. Similarly, Paul's discourse at Athens shows a clear and principled intention to communicate the Christian gospel in a manner fitting and appropriate to the audience.[53] The radical divergence between his pagan audience on the Areopagus and his Christian readership in the epistles cannot be ignored. Given the conventions of classical rhetoric,[54] it is hardly surprising that Paul should have accommodated both the substance and the mode of presentation of the Christian faith to the specific characteristics of the respective audiences.

In his letter to the Romans, we find Paul setting out a line of thought which is specifically directed to a Christian audience. If Paul's concern

[53] David L. Balch, 'The Areopagus Speech: An Appeal to the Stoic Historian Posidonius against Later Stoics and the Epicureans', in D. L. Balch, E. Ferguson and W. Meeks (eds), *Greeks, Romans and Christians: Essays in Honor of Abraham J. Malherbe*. Minneapolis, MN: Fortress Press, 1990, 52–79; Dean Zweck, 'The *Exordium* of the Areopagus Speech, Acts 17.22, 23', *New Testament Studies* 35 (1989), 94–103.

[54] See here Frederick W. Danker, 'Graeco-Roman Cultural Accommodation in the Christology of Luke-Acts', in K. H. Richards (ed.), *Society of Biblical Literature 1983 Seminar Papers*. Chico, CA: Scholars Press, 1983, 391–414.

in the Areopagus address was apologetic, that in Romans is more dogmatic – the explication of the universal divine condemnation of human sinfulness. Part of Paul's argument is that, since all humanity had the capacity to know God, their failure to do so is 'without excuse', as is their refusal to respond appropriately to what they knew of God. For Paul, God's anger is revealed against those who refuse to respond to 'what can be known of God (τὸ γνωστὸν τοῦ θεοῦ)' which is manifest (φανερόν) among them (or perhaps 'in them'), in that God has revealed (ἐφανέρωσέν) this to them (Romans 1:18). From the creation of the world onwards, Paul continues, the invisible things (τὰ ἀόρατα) of God have been plainly made known; the context makes it clear that Paul specifically has God's eternal power and divine nature in mind. The general line of argument is that sufficient of God's nature and requirements has been manifested within the created order to render humanity without excuse for any failure to respond to God, in particular recognizing their status as creatures.[55]

Our intention is not to offer a detailed development of a natural theology on the basis of the biblical material. To do so would go beyond the intended limits of the texts upon which any such theology would ultimately be based. The issue is whether the Bible can be seen as legitimating any knowledge of God outside what would generally be taken as the domain of divine revelation, and where the locus of such a natural knowledge of God might be. The traditional Christian response – within Anglican, Catholic, Lutheran, Orthodox and Reformed circles – has been that there is indeed proper biblical warrant for such a supposition.

In the twentieth century, however, this consensus has been challenged, perhaps more at the rhetorical than theological level, by the sustained polemic of Karl Barth, directed against any autonomous human inquiry into God, and the gaining of any knowledge of God on terms other than those authorized by God. While the force of Barth's challenge increasingly lies in the past, the issues raised must be dealt with. A question of particular importance concerns whether Barth can here be seen as an authentic representative of the Reformed tradition in general, or whether he is to be regarded as departing from a previously existing Reformed consensus on the matter. For this reason, we shall

---

[55] For the literature, see James D. G. Dunn, *Romans 1–8*. Dallas: Word Books, 1988; Robert Jewett, 'Major Impulses in the Theological Interpretation of Romans since Barth', *Interpretation* 36 (1980), 17–31; J. A. Ziesler, *Paul's Letter to the Romans*. London: SCM Press, 1989.

presently explore the views of Calvin and Theodore Beza, with a view to establishing whether Barth continues – or departs from – the Reformed tradition at this point, before offering a positive account of the place of a natural theology within a Christian view of the world. We begin our engagement with the contemporary debate over natural theology by considering recent philosophical engagement with the issues.

The philosophical debate over natural theology

In recent years, philosophers of religion working within a Reformed theological perspective – such as William P. Alston, Alvin Plantinga and Nicholas Wolterstorff – have made substantial contributions to a number of philosophical and theological debates, including the question of the place and purpose of a natural knowledge of God.[56] In view of the particularly luminous quality of Plantinga's thought and writings, we shall consider his evaluation of the propriety and viability of a natural theology. Plantinga understands 'natural theology' to be an attempt to prove or demonstrate the existence of God, and vigorously rejects it on the basis of his belief that it depends on a fallacious understanding of the nature of religious belief.[57] The roots of this objection are complex, and can be summarized in terms of two fundamental considerations:[58]

1. Natural theology supposes that belief in God must rest upon an evidential basis. Belief in God is thus not, strictly speaking, a basic belief – that is, something which is self-evident, incorrigible or evident to the senses. It is therefore a belief which requires to be itself grounded in some more basic belief. However, to ground a belief in God upon some other belief is, in effect, to depict that latter belief as endowed with a greater epistemic status than belief in God. For Plantinga, a properly Christian approach is to affirm that belief in God is itself basic, and does not require justification with reference to other beliefs.

---

[56] Dewey J. Hoitenga, *Faith and Reason from Plato to Plantinga: An Introduction to Reformed Epistemology.* Albany, NY: State University of New York Press, 1991

[57] Alvin Plantinga, 'Reason and Belief in God', in Alvin Plantinga and Nicholas Wolterstorff (eds), *Faith and Philosophy: Reason and Belief in God.* Notre Dame, IN: University of Notre Dame Press, 1983, 16–93.

[58] Evan Fales, 'Plantinga's Case against Naturalistic Epistemology', *Philosophy of Science* 63 (1996), 432–51; D. D. Todd, 'Plantinga and the Naturalized Epistemology of Thomas Reid', *Dialogue* 35 (1996), 93–107.

2. Natural theology is not justified with reference to the Reformed tradition, including Calvin and his later followers.

As will become clear from our analysis of the development of the Reformed tradition, the latter point is inaccurate historically. However, the first line of argument has met with growing interest and sympathy.

Plantinga regards Aquinas as the 'natural theologian *par excellence*', and directs considerable attention to his methods.[59] For Plantinga, Aquinas is a foundationalist in matters of theology and philosophy, in that '*scientia*, properly speaking, consists in a body of propositions deduced syllogistically from self-evident first principles'. The *Summa contra Gentiles* shows, according to Plantinga, that Aquinas proceeds from evidential foundations to argue for a belief in God, which clearly makes such belief dependent upon appropriate evidential foundations. This point was set out with some force in a major paper of 1980, significantly entitled 'The Reformed Objection to Natural Theology'.[60] Here, Plantinga argues that the fundamental error of any programme including a natural theology is that it entails a commitment to 'strong foundationalism' – that is, to a belief that a 'proposition is properly basic for a person only if it is self-evident to him . . . or "evident to the senses"'.[61] Plantinga has no particular difficulties with what he terms 'weak foundationalism', which includes the beliefs that:

1. every rational noetic structure has a foundation; and
2. in a rational noetic structure (or system of beliefs), the strength of a nonbasic belief is directly related to the support it receives from these foundations.

Plantinga's concern here is with the Cartesian notion that there exist certain presuppositionless or neutral standpoints, isolated from any historical or social context, which function as the foundation of other beliefs. Plantinga fully concedes the importance of offering critically examined warrants for judgements.

Plantinga interprets Aquinas to hold that, if belief in God is to be rational, it must be based on other propositions or evidence available

[59] See the careful study of Hunter Brown, 'Alvin Plantinga and Natural Theology', *International Journal for Philosophy of Religion* 30 (1991), 1–19.

[60] Alvin J. Plantinga, 'The Reformed Objection to Natural Theology', *Proceedings of the American Catholic Philosophical Association* 54 (1980), 49–62. See further the analysis in Laura L. Garcia, 'Natural Theology and the Reformed Objection', in C. Stephen Evans and Merold Westphal (eds), *Christian Perspectives on Religious Knowledge*. Grand Rapids, MI: Eerdmans, 1993, 112–33.

[61] Plantinga, 'Reformed Objection', 56.

to the senses. If this line of argument is pursued, he argues, belief in God ultimately becomes dependent upon a natural theology. Plantinga's critique of natural theology is partly grounded in his belief that, at least as the enterprise is construed in the writings of Aquinas, it is associated with an intention to prove the existence of God.

This point is open to challenge. Historically, it is clear that patristic writers did not see natural theology as offering proofs of God's existence. The existence of God was taken for granted. The purpose of natural theology was understood to relate to the question of the specific nature, not the existence, of God. Natural theology was seen as a significant element in the clarification of the divergences between the Christian and classical philosophical notions of God – for example, those set forth in the writings of Thales of Miletus and Anaximander.[62] Such was the diversity within Greek divinity that the term θεός did not necessarily convey much information concerning the being in question.[63]

This broad tradition of natural theology is continued in the writings of Aquinas, who does not appear to make faith in God dependent upon any philosophical argument or appeal to natural theology.[64] Aquinas does not regard natural theology as offering proofs for faith, but as offering support for faith from within the context of an existing faith.[65] Plantinga's argument has force when directed against certain forms of evidentialism; Aquinas, however, does not develop any such approach. Second, it is perfectly possible to frame a natural theology in such a manner that it does not involve such an intention to prove God's existence. It is not necessary that a natural theology should make any such assumption; indeed, there are excellent reasons for suggesting that, as a matter of historical fact, natural theology is better to be understood as a demonstration, from the standpoint of faith, of the

---

[62] Ulrich Hölscher, 'Anaximander und die Anfänge der Philosophie,' in Hans-Georg Gadamer (ed.), *Um die Begriffswelt der Vorsokratiker*. Darmstadt: Wissenschaftliche Buchgesellschaft, 1968, 95–176.

[63] See the useful material provided in Alan B. Lloyd (ed.), *What is a God? Studies in the Nature of Greek Divinity*. London: Duckworth, 1997.

[64] See the substantial analysis offered by Norman Kretzmann, *The Metaphysics of Theism: Aquinas's Natural Theology in Summa contra Gentiles I*. Oxford: Clarendon Press, 1997; and idem, *The Metaphysics of Creation: Aquinas's Natural Theology in Summa contra Gentiles II*. Oxford: Clarendon Press, 1999.

[65] Thus the arguments set out in *Summa contra Gentiles* I.13 clearly presuppose certain beliefs concerning the relation of God to the creation. Aquinas' arguments at this point are best understood as *a posteriori* demonstrations of the consistency of the world with a Christian view of God, or the plausibility of the postulation of the Christian God as an explanation of the world. See Kretzmann, *The Metaphysics of Theism: Aquinas's Natural Theology in Summa contra Gentiles I*, 54–60.

consonance between that faith and the structures of the world. In other words, natural theology is not intended to prove the existence of God, but presupposes that existence; it then asks 'what should we expect the natural world to be like if it has indeed been created by such a God?' The search for order in nature is therefore not intended to demonstrate that God exists, but to reinforce the plausibility of an already existing belief.

This kind of approach can be found in the writings of William P. Alston, who can be seen as sharing at least some of Plantinga's commitments to a Reformed epistemology, while tending to take a considerably more positive attitude to natural theology. Conceding that it is impossible to construct a demonstrative proof of the existence of God from extra-religious premises, Alston argues that this is not, in any case, a proper approach to natural theology. Properly speaking, natural theology begins from a starting point such as a sense of the presence of God or the ordering of the world, and shows that this starting point leads us to recognize the existence of a being which would be accepted as God.

There is thus, in Alston's view, a strong degree of convergence between natural theology and traditional arguments for the existence of God, particularly those deriving from Thomas Aquinas. Yet his conception of natural theology goes beyond such narrow proofs, and encourages the engagement with other areas of human life and concern, amongst which he explicitly includes science. Natural theology thus offers 'metaphysical reasons for the truth of theism as a general world-view', and allows us to build bridges to other disciplines.[66]

Such philosophical critiques of certain styles of natural theology are of importance, and must be given due weight in any assessment of its proper role in the theological enterprise. However, there is little doubt that the most significant critique of natural theology during the twentieth century is explicitly theological in tone. In what follows, we shall offer a presentation and critique of Karl Barth's attempt to programmatically eliminate natural theology from Christian dogmatics.

The Barthian objection to natural theology: an evaluation

In recent years, there has been growing criticism of Barth's approach to natural theology. This criticism has been formulated at three distinct levels.

---

[66] Alston, *Perceiving God,* 270.

1. It is seen to rest on inadequate biblical foundations. Barth's engagement with the biblical texts is increasingly seen in terms of the
   imposition of Barth's views upon those texts, rather than a faithful
   attempt to expound them. 'Barth's rejection of natural theology
   was never really based on biblical exegesis . . . Its real foundation
   lay in trends and developments in modern theology, philosophy
   and society.'[67]

2. Barth's views on natural theology represent a significant departure
   from the Reformed tradition which he clearly regards himself as
   representing.

3. Barth's negative attitude towards natural theology appears to be
   linked to an indifferent attitude towards the natural sciences,
   stifling what potentially could be a significant theological exploration and engagement.[68]

Barth's critique of natural theology

Barth's formal critique of natural theology dates from the 1930s, and is
not strictly speaking part of his explicit agenda in his *Romans*
commentary or earlier writings.[69] The polemic which would later
be directed against natural theology is initially directed against the
category of 'religion'. In the second edition of his *Romans* commentary, Barth critiques the idea of 'religion' as a human construction
erected in opposition to God; we later find such a criticism directed
against natural theology – but this is *not* identified as the target in
1922.[70] Again, in 1927 we find Barth identifying the target of his criticisms as 'Schleiermacher's conversion of theology into anthropology'.[71]
Yet natural theology is still not identified as the enemy of Barth's
theological programme. It may be true to suggest that 'Karl Barth's
battle against natural theology was in respect of content a conflict with
the theology of the nineteenth century';[72] yet this conflict was not
conceptualized in this specific manner until around 1929–30.

[67] Barr, *Biblical Faith and Natural Theology*, 103. See also the more detailed argument at
1–20.
[68] Ray S. Anderson, 'Barth and a New Direction for Natural Theology', in J. Thompson
(ed.), *Theology beyond Christendom: Essays on the Centenary of Karl Barth*. Allison Park, PA:
Pickwick Publications, 1986, 241–66.
[69] As pointed out by Attila Szekeres, 'Karl Barth und die natürliche Theologie',
Evangelische Theologie 24 (1964), 229–42.
[70] Karl Barth, *Der Römerbrief*. 2nd edn. Munich: Kaiser Verlag, 1922, 213–55.
[71] Karl Barth, *Die christliche Theologie im Entwurf*. Munich: Kaiser Verlag, 1927, 82–7.
[72] Hans-Joachim Kraus and H. Berkhof, *Karl Barths Lichterlehre*. Zurich: Theologischer
Verlag, 1978, 39.

While it is entirely proper to stress that the challenging of natural theology is at least implicit in the development of a dialectical theology,[73] it is not until *Church Dogmatics* II/1 §26 that Barth offers an extended and systematic critique of natural theology. A 'natural theology (*natürliche Theologie*)' is here defined as a theology 'which comes to humanity from nature (*von der Mensch von Natur herkommt*)', which expresses humanity's 'self-preservation and self-affirmation (*Selbstbewahrung und Selbstbehauptung*)' in the face of God. Natural theology now becomes the paradigmatic instantiation of the human longing for self-justification, with the appearance of a controlling dialectic between a true theology based upon revelation and human self-justification based upon anthropology.[74]

Barth's hostility towards natural theology thus rests on his fundamental belief that it undermines the necessity and uniqueness of God's self-revelation. If knowledge of God can be achieved independently of God's self-revelation in Christ, then it follows that humanity can dictate the place, time and means of its knowledge of God.[75] Natural theology, for Barth, represents an attempt on the part of humanity to understand itself apart from and in isolation from revelation, representing a deliberate refusal to accept the necessity and consequences of revelation. One of Barth's central concerns is to expose the myth of human autonomy, and identify its consequences for theology and ethics.[76] The human desire to assert itself and take control over things is seen by Barth as one of the most fundamental sources of error in theology, leading to the erection of theological towers of Babel – purely human constructions, erected in the face of God. The quest for autonomy lies at the heart of original sin:[77]

> It is quite clear throughout Barth's analysis of sin that the target he had in view was the 'modern' idealistic conception of consciousness as structured by the autonomous generation (and realization) of tasks.

---

[73] Christof Gestrich, *Neuzeitliches Denken und die Spaltung der dialektischen Theologie: Zur Frage der natürlichen Theologie.* Tübingen: Mohr, 1977.

[74] See Karl Barth, 'Schicksal und Idee in der Theologie', in *Theologische Fragen und Antworten.* Zollikon: Evangelischer Verlag, 1957, 54–92, especially 85–7.

[75] On this general point, see Regin Prenter, 'Das Problem der natürlichen Theologie bei Karl Barth', *Theologische Literaturzeitung* 77 (1952), 607–11.

[76] On the theme of autonomy in Barth's writings, see John Macken, *The Autonomy Theme in the Church Dogmatics: Karl Barth and His Critics.* Cambridge: Cambridge University Press, 1990; Thies Gundlach, *Selbstbegrenzung Gottes und die Autonomie des Menschen: Karl Barths Kirchliche Dogmatik als Modernisierungschrift evangelischer Theologie.* Frankfurt/Berne: Peter Lang, 1992.

[77] Bruce L. McCormack, *Karl Barth's Critically Realistic Dialectical Theology: Its Genesis and Development 1909–1936.* Oxford: Clarendon Press, 1995, 167.

Where for the theologians of the Ritschlian school (as well as for neo-Kantian philosophy) the development of the 'free' (which is to say, autonomous) personality is synonymous with the creation of an ethical agent, for Barth, the desire for autonomy is the original sin. The quest for autonomy is the source of individualism, disorganization, and chaos in society.

For Barth, there is a close link between natural theology and the theme of human autonomy. As Barth understands the concept, natural theology concerns the human desire to find God on humanity's own terms. Natural theology thus appears to posit a second source of revelation alongside Jesus Christ, as he is attested in Scripture. The affirmation of a natural theology appears to contradict the fundamental principle that God reveals himself in Christ, implying that God reveals himself in nature independent of his self-revelation in Christ. For Barth, revelation is only to be had through the revelation of God, as a consequence of God's gracious decision that he is to be known. There is no manner in which God can be known outside and apart from God's self-revelation.[78]

Barth's view here would appear to represent an intensification of the consensus of the Reformed tradition. Calvin, as we have noted, argues that human nature has the capacity to know something of God from nature. Nevertheless, Calvin points out that the natural innate tendency of human nature is to use this capacity in an improper or misguided manner, and thus to fall into idolatry, worshipping the creation rather than its creator. For Calvin, it is necessary for this natural knowledge of God to be seen and interpreted in the light of revelation. There is thus a subtle and nuanced correlation between natural and revealed theology.

Barth, however, saw any form of affirmation of natural theology as tantamount to an assertion of human autonomy in theology. Thus Barth expressed serious anxieties concerning the statements set out by both the Gallic and Belgic Confessions:[79]

Natural theology was able to attain new forms and find new points of entry which were soon revealed in the teaching of the 16th century enthusiasts both inside and outside the Church. It could again recommend itself to a martyr Church – this time the French – in such a way that, in contradiction to Calvin's proposal, the mischief could be done

---

[78] This point is stressed at point after point: see, for example, *Church Dogmatics* II/1, 3–4; 69; 206–7. The general point at issue can be studied in Ingrid Spieckermann, *Gotteserkenntnis: Ein Beitrag zur Grundfrage der neuen Theologie Karl Barths*. Munich: Kaiser Verlag, 1985; McCormack, *Barth's Critically Realistic Dialectical Theology*, 241–88.

[79] *Church Dogmatics* II/1, 127.

which may now be read in article 2 of the *Confessio Gallicana*, from which it quickly spread to the *Confessio Belgica* (art. 2–3). And once the Reformers were dead . . . it could impress itself on their disciples as the indispensable prolegomena of theology, a part of the same development by which the Evangelical Churches allowed themselves, almost without thinking, to be steered into a new position as State Churches.

As can be seen from this citation, Barth saw a fatal connection between natural theology and allegiance to the state. Barth detected in the writings of Emil Brunner a particularly insidious approach to natural theology, given the political situation of the 1930s, as Nazism became a significant political and ideological force in Germany. For Barth, Brunner's concept of a 'point of contact' (*Anknüpfungspunkt*) seemed tantamount to a reversion to the classic pagan notion that the human soul represents a 'spark of the divine'. In addition, Brunner's essay on natural theology appeared at a highly contentious time (1934); Brunner's approach seemed to Barth to play into the hands of the pro-Hitler 'German Christians'.[80] Yet the validity of such an insight has been challenged.[81]

It will therefore be clear that Barth's attitude to natural theology rests partly on his concern that the assertion of the human autonomy to find God in whom or where it pleases inevitably leads to the enslavement of theology to prevailing cultural and ideological currents. Only by firmly anchoring theology to 'Jesus Christ, as he is attested for us in Holy Scripture' can theology maintain its true character as a response to God's revelation.

Yet it is important to note that in later sections of the *Church Dogmatics*, Barth appears to take a stance to the issue of the relation of knowledge of God in creation and knowledge of God through revelation which seems much closer to that associated with Calvin. For example, consider the following statement:[82]

It is given quite irrespective of whether the man whom it addresses in its self-witness knows or does not know, confesses or denies, that it owes this speech no less than its persistence to the faithfulness of the Creator . . . However corrupt man may be, they illumine him, and even in the depths of his corruption he does not cease to see and understand them

---

[80] For the reasons, see Joan O'Donovan, 'Man in the Image of God: The Disagreement between Barth and Brunner Reconsidered', *Scottish Journal of Theology* 39 (1986), 433–59.

[81] For an excellent criticism of Barth, see Barr, *Biblical Faith and Natural Theology*, 111–17.

[82] *Church Dogmatics* IV/3, 139.

... they are not extinguished by this light, nor are their force and significance destroyed ... As the divine work of reconciliation does not negate the divine work of creation, nor deprive it of meaning, so it does not take from its lights and language, nor tear asunder the original connection between creaturely *esse* and creaturely *nosse*.

Similarly, in the lecture fragments of the *Church Dogmatics*, published posthumously, Barth sets out reasons for supposing that something of God can be known from creation, so that God 'is objectively a very well known and not an unknown God'. Nevertheless, he stresses that these impressions should not be 'systematized in the form of a natural theology'.[83] These later statements seem to differ in tone from those found earlier in the *Church Dogmatics*; it is, however, probably improper to suggest that this softening in the tone of Barth's expression should be seen as representing a theological shift on the issue.

It is clear that Barth regards the rise of the human demand for autonomy in the eighteenth century as being of considerable importance to his own theological enterprise, especially in relation to countering this trend by the development of appropriate theological strategies. To identify possible reconstructions of the Reformed tradition which meet Barth's concerns – to the extent that these may be deemed to be legitimate – it will be helpful to compare a single influential stream of Reformed theology in the sixteenth and eighteenth centuries, and note the attitudes adopted at these different epochs to the question of natural theology. Such a tradition lies to hand in the stream of theological reflection arising from the the writings of John Calvin (1509–64) and his successors within the Reformed theological community in the city of Geneva. Calvin's rich approach to theology was based on a rigorous engagement with Scripture, strengthened by a judicious interaction with the pre-Calvinian theological tradition, especially during the formative patristic period.[84]

In that Karl Barth stands in conscious continuity with this tradition, and that Barth's discussion of the role of natural theology is of such importance to contemporary debates on the matter, it is clearly a matter of some importance to establish how Barth relates to this tradition, and what its future potential might be for a responsible Christian theology, such as the scientific theology which the present project seeks to develop.

---

[83] Karl Barth, *The Christian Life*. Edinburgh: T&T Clark, 1981, 120–2.

[84] See Robert H. Ayers, 'Language, Logic and Reason in Calvin's *Institutes*', *Religious Studies* 16 (1980), 283–97; Michael L. Czapkay Sudduth, 'The Prospects for "Mediate" Natural Theology in John Calvin', *Religious Studies* 31 (1995), 53–68; Anthony N. S. Lane, *John Calvin: Student of the Church Fathers*. Edinburgh: T&T Clark, 1999.

The early Genevan school: John Calvin and Theodore Beza

The early Genevan school took a critical yet generally positive attitude towards the question of the natural knowledge of God. Although the group identified by George H. Williams as 'evangelical rationalists' must be noted as important exceptions,[85] the sixteenth century was generally quite innocent of any emphasis upon the autonomy of reason. Calvin and his immediate successors were able to explore the question of the extent to which the natural order could be the basis for theological reflection and construction without any need to engage in polemical minimalization of the possibilities in response to the exaggerations of others.

The first book of the 1559 edition of Calvin's *Institutes* opens with discussion of one of the fundamental problems of Christian theology: how do we know anything about God?[86] Even before turning to discuss this question, however, Calvin stresses that 'knowledge of God and of ourselves are connected' (I.i.1). Without a knowledge of God, we cannot truly know ourselves; without knowing ourselves, we cannot know God. The two forms of knowledge are 'joined together by many bonds'; although they are distinct, they cannot be separated. It is impossible to have either in isolation. This principle is of fundamental importance to an understanding of Calvin's strongly world-affirming theology: knowledge of God cannot be detached from, nor allowed to merge with, knowledge of human nature or of the world. A dialectic is constructed, resting upon a delicately balanced interplay between God and the world, the creator and his creation.

In dealing with our knowledge of God as the 'creator and sovereign ruler of the world', Calvin affirms that a general knowledge of God may be discerned throughout the creation – in humanity, in the natural order, and in the historical process itself. Two main grounds of such knowledge are identified, one subjective, the other objective. The first ground is a 'sense of divinity (*sensus divinitatis*)' or a 'seed of religion (*semen religionis*)' implanted within every human being by God (I.iii.1; I.v.1). God has endowed human beings with some inbuilt sense or presentiment of God's existence. It is as if something about God has been engraved in the hearts of every human being (I.x.3). Calvin identifies three consequences of this inbuilt awareness of divinity:

[85] George Hunston Williams, *The Radical Reformation*. 3rd edn. Kirksville, MO: Sixteenth Century Journal Publishers, 1992, 1213–40.

[86] For full discussions, see Edward A. Dowey, *The Knowledge of God in Calvin's Theology*. New York: Columbia University Press, 1952; T. H. L. Parker, *Calvin's Doctrine of the Knowledge of God*. Edinburgh: Oliver & Boyd, 1969.

1. the universality of religion (which, if uninformed by the Christian revelation, degenerates into idolatry: I.iii.1);

2. a troubled conscience (I.iii.2);

3. a servile fear of God (I.iv.4). All of these, Calvin suggests, may serve as points of contact for the Christian proclamation.

The second such ground lies in experience of and reflection upon the ordering of the world. The fact that God exists and is the creator of the world, together with an appreciation of at least something of the divine wisdom and justice, may be gained from an inspection of the created order, culminating in humanity itself (I.v.1–15). 'God has revealed himself in such a beautiful and elegant construction of heaven and earth, showing and presenting himself there every day, that human beings cannot open their eyes without having to notice him' (I.v.1).

It is important to stress that Calvin makes no suggestion whatsoever that this knowledge of God from the created order is peculiar to, or restricted to, Christian believers. Calvin is arguing that anyone, by intelligent and rational reflection upon the created order, should be able to arrive at the idea of God. Drawing on the rich imagery used to depict nature at this stage in intellectual history, Calvin declares that the created order is a 'theatre' (I.v.5) or a 'mirror' (I.v.11) for the displaying of the divine presence, nature and attributes.[87] Although God is invisible and incomprehensible, God is made known under and through the form of created and visible things.

Calvin thus commends the natural sciences (such as astronomy), on account of their ability to illustrate further the wonderful ordering of creation, and the divine wisdom which this indicates (I.v.2). Significantly, however, Calvin makes no appeal to specifically Christian sources of revelation. His argument is based upon empirical observation and ratiocination. If Calvin introduces scriptural quotations, it is to consolidate a general natural knowledge of God, rather than to establish that knowledge in the first place. There is, he stresses, a way of discerning God which is common to those inside and outside the Christian community (*exteris et domesticis communem*: I.v.6).

Having thus laid the foundations for a general knowledge of God, Calvin stresses its shortcomings; his dialogue partner here is Cicero, whose *de natura deorum* is perhaps one of the most influential classical

---

[87] Diana Butler, 'God's Visible Glory: The Beauty of Nature in the Thought of John Calvin and Jonathan Edwards', *Westminster Theological Journal* 52 (1990), 13–26; Susan Elizabeth Schreiner, *The Theater of His Glory: Nature and the Natural Order in the Thought of John Calvin*. Durham, NC: Labyrinth Press, 1991.

expositions of a natural knowledge of God.[88] Calvin argues that the epistemic distance between God and humanity, already of enormous magnitude by virtue of God's status as creator and humanity's as the creature, is increased still further on account of human sin. Our natural knowledge of God is imperfect and confused, even to the point of contradiction on occasion. A natural knowledge of God serves to deprive humanity of any excuse for ignoring him; nevertheless, it is inadequate as the basis of a fully-fledged portrayal of the nature, character and purposes of God.

Calvin thus introduces the notion of biblical revelation; Scripture reiterates what may be known of God through nature, while simultaneously clarifying this general revelation and enhancing it (I.x.1). 'The knowledge of God, which is clearly shown in the ordering of the world and in all creatures, is still more clearly and familiarly explained in the Word' (I.x.1). It is only through Scripture that the believer has access to knowledge of the redeeming actions of God in history, culminating in the life, death and resurrection of Jesus Christ (I.vi.1–4). For Calvin, revelation is focused upon the person of Jesus Christ; our knowledge of God is mediated through him (I.vi.1).

We see here the basic theme of the 'twofold knowledge of God (*duplex cognitio Dei*)', which plays such an important role in Calvin's thinking, and subsequently that of the Reformed tradition.[89] God may be known as creator, and as redeemer. The former is a general knowledge of God, available to all of humanity; the latter is a saving knowledge, only available through Scripture. Knowledge of God as creator may be had through reflection on the creation, whether such reflection is based upon the structure of the created order, or the religious consciousness or rationality of the individual person. This knowledge is confirmed through a reading of Scripture, which reiterates the fragmentary insights concerning God made known through nature, and consolidates them – before leading on to a further knowledge of God as redeemer, which leads to salvation.

Calvin does not regard natural theology as offering an autonomous route to a full and saving knowledge of God, and it is of particular importance to avoid reading his statements on 'knowledge of God the creator' as if they were framed with the eighteenth-century discussion of the matter in mind. Calvin's primary concern is to explicate Paul's

[88] Emil Grislis, 'Calvin's Use of Cicero in the *Institutes* I:1–5: A Case Study in Theological Method', *Archiv für Reformationsgeschichte* 62 (1971), 5–37.

[89] Richard A. Muller, 'Duplex cognitio Dei in the Theology of Early Reformed Orthodoxy', *Sixteenth Century Journal* 10 (1979), 51–61.

insistence (Romans 1:18–21) that all of humanity has an awareness of the existence of God, and is thus responsible for any failure to respond properly to the demands of the creator upon the creatures. If the definition offered for natural theology by Alvin Plantinga – 'the attempt to prove or demonstrate the existence of God' – is applied to Calvin, a serious misreading of both his intentions and theological achievements will inevitably result. This is also true of his most notable intellectual disciple, Theodore Beza, to whom we now turn.

Calvin's theology was placed on a more systematic foundation by his successor Theodore Beza (1519–1605). Beza was of considerable importance in the consolidation of the rational foundations of Reformed theology, not least through his important discussion of the relation of faith and reason within a Reformed context.[90] Like Calvin, Beza has no particular polemic agenda for affirming the existence of a natural knowledge of God the redeemer; his concern is to remain faithful to Paul's general sentiments in Romans 1, while at the same time exploring the epistemic foundations of theology. This can be seen in his comments on Romans 2:2:[91]

> With great prudence, Paul carefully refutes each and every human being who is not in Christ of impiety and unrighteousness – not from the written Word of God (which the profane gentiles do not accept), but from the 'knowledge of God' which he describes in 1.19–21. In other words, he refutes them using those common and natural notions that each and every human being may discern within themselves.

While Beza stresses the impact of sin upon the human cognitive faculties, especially in relation to any intuitive human ability to discern and know God from nature, he nevertheless maintains the idea that at least something of God may be known in this way.

Like Calvin, Beza argues that a natural knowledge of God may be had both from contemplation of the structure of creation, and from an intuitive human knowledge of divinity:[92]

> It is true that the human understanding includes a general notion that there is some deity, the knowledge of whom is confirmed and sustained by a consideration of God's creation above us, around us, and beneath

---

[90] See Walter Kickel, *Vernunft und Offenbarung bei Theodor Beza: Zum Problem der Verhältnisses von Theologie, Philosophie und Staat.* Neukirchen-Vluyn: Neukirchener Verlag, 1967.

[91] Theodore Beza, *Iesu Christi Domini Nostri Novum Testamentum.* Geneva, 1598, 120.

[92] Theodore Beza, *Sermons sur l'histoire de la passion et sepultre de nostre Seignure Jesus Christ.* Geneva, 1592, 46.

us. God has engraved, as if with gigantic letters, his eternity and existence as creator above the creation onto even the smallest things. God shows his omnipotence, without which the world could not be created or governed; his omniscience, which is manifest in the arrangement and direction of so many creatures; and his absolute goodness.

Such ideas became well established in the Reformed tradition subsequent to Beza. While John Platt has argued persuasively that it is improper to speak of the recognition of an 'innate' natural knowledge of God within the later Reformed tradition,[93] Beza's language points strongly towards a natural knowledge of God within human nature which is *innata, insculpta* or *insita*. Beza does not for one moment entertain the notion that a natural theology may be developed which can function as an independent route to a true knowledge of God. His concern is to explore the manner in which natural yet fallen resources, whose ultimate source is God as their creator, may serve in an ancillary capacity in relation to the apologetic and systematic enterprises of his day.

The contrast with the later Genevan school, to which we now turn, will be apparent, and allows us to appreciate at least something of the anxiety which Barth felt concerning the potential of a natural theology to assert its autonomy as a means of acquiring knowledge of God.

The later Genevan school: Jean-Alphonse Turrettini

In many ways, the intellectual currents prevalent at the Genevan Academy illuminate the development of Protestant theology as a whole, from the sixteenth to the end of the eighteenth century. Beza's growing interest in questions of method in the 1570s can be seen as anticipating the increasing awareness within Protestant Orthodoxy as a whole of this issue, particularly in relation to apologetic issues.[94] Beza's ideas were formalized in the teaching of François Turrettini (1623–87), and were dominant in the Academy until the final decades of the seventeenth century. However, the appointment of Robert Chouet as professor of philosophy at the Academy in 1669 resulted in the introduction of Cartesianism into Reformed theological reflections – a development which appears to have done little to increase the credibility of Reformed

---

[93]   John E. Platt, 'The Denial of the Innate Idea of God in Dutch Remonstrant Theology: From Episcopius to van Limborch', in C. R. Trueman and R. S. Clark (eds), *Protestant Scholasticism*. Carlisle: Paternoster Press, 1999, 213–26.

[94]   Alister E. McGrath, *The Intellectual Origins of the European Reformation*. Oxford: Blackwell, 1987, 191–6.

Orthodoxy in an increasingly sceptical age.[95] Awareness of this fact was of some importance in creating a new interest in the apologetic possibilities of English 'physico-theology' at Geneva in the early eighteenth century. Might not this new form of natural theology offer apologetic resources superior to those of Cartesianism? This was certainly the view of Jean-Alphonse Turrettini (1671–1737) – the son, incidentally, of François Turrettini – who was called to the chair of theology at the Academy in 1705.

Turrettini's development of natural theology represents a significant shift away from the older Genevan approach, evident in Calvin and Beza. Perhaps aware of the growing pressure to offer rational demon-strations of the truth of the Christian religion, Turrettini conceived natural theology as providing a powerful refutation of the forms of scepticism then being directed against all forms of Christian belief in western Europe on the one hand, and the theological criticisms directed against Reformed Orthodoxy by its Roman Catholic opponents.[96]

Turrettini's assessment of the importance of natural theology is set out in his *Theses de theologia naturali*. Many of the arguments which he develops in this writing are clearly present in the earlier Genevan tradition – for example, the argument that the wisdom of the creator is evident in the design of the world. When one considers the excellence and wisdom of the created order, it is impossible to conclude that it has been brought into existence *sine mente, sine consilio, sine arbitrio*.[97] While Turrettini does not go so far as to make such a natural theology the foundation of his theological method, it is noteworthy that he modifies Calvin's traditional formulation of the *duplex cognitio Domini* motif by allowing that it is possible to be saved on the basis of a natural knowledge of God. Turrettini thus introduced natural theology into the theological curriculum at Geneva.

According to Michael Heyd, this development must be regarded as marking the beginnings of an Enlightenment mentality at the Genevan Academy.[98] The Academy which had once taken its stand on Scripture

---

[95] For a full account, see Michael Heyd, *Between Orthodoxy and the Enlightenment: Jean-Robert Chouet and the Introduction of Cartesian Science at the Academy of Geneva*. The Hague: Martinus Nijhoff, 1982.

[96] For details, see Heyd, 'Un rôle nouveau pour la science'; Martin Klauber, 'Jean-Alphonse Turrettini (1671–1737) on Natural Theology: The Triumph of Reason over Revelation at the Academy of Geneva', *Scottish Journal of Theology* 47 (1994), 301–25.

[97] *Theses de theologia naturali* I.iv.15. See further Klauber, 'Jean-Alphonse Turrettini (1671–1737) on Natural Theology: The Triumph of Reason over Revelation at the Academy of Geneva'.

[98] See Heyd, *Between Orthodoxy and the Enlightenment*.

had now succumbed to the rationalist pressures of the age; the new emphasis on natural theology was to be seen as a symptom of a greater malaise – namely, the reliance upon autonomous human reason as a foundational theological resource.

So how does this excursion into the intellectual history of one of Protestantism's leading theological centres illuminate Barth's critique of natural theology? It must certainly raise serious questions concerning Barth's judgements concerning Calvin's views on natural theology.[99] The simple fact of the matter is that Calvin espoused a theologically inoffensive and apologetically fruitful approach to a natural theology, whether Barth cares to admit this or not. Richard Niebuhr once wrote of his concern that 'something approaching a Barthian captivity of the history of modern Christian thought reigns';[100] this is nowhere more evident than in the confusion of those who learn their historical theology from the small-print sections of the *Church Dogmatics*. Barth's greatest achievement may well turn out to be the shaping of perceptions of Christian history for those who are too lazy to study it for themselves. It does not seem to have occurred to some of these people that Barth has a theological agenda, and that this agenda shapes his presentation and interpretation of the past. Barth's reluctance to acknowledge that Calvin concedes a natural knowledge of God is not simply a case of a nodding Homer; it is a piece of purposeful theological polemic involving the reinterpretation of the formative phase of the Reformed tradition to suit Barth's agenda.

When we come to the Genevan school in the eighteenth century, however, Barth begins to make sense. While Barth shows no great concern for Turrettini *fils* – reserving his critical interest for Turrettini *père* – it can be seen that Barth's polemic against natural theology, both as an autonomous discipline and as an independent means of gaining access to knowledge of God, resonates with the trends at Geneva reflecting the growing impact of the Enlightenment on Reformed theology in general.

Thomas F. Torrance on natural theology

In recent years, considerable attention has been directed to the concept of natural theology developed by Thomas F. Torrance, the leading

---

[99] E.g. see Gestrich, *Neuzeitliches Denken und die Spaltung der dialektischen Theologie*, 184.

[100] Richard R. Niebuhr, *Schleiermacher on Christ and Religion*. New York: Charles Scribner's Sons, 1964, 11.

British theologian of the twentieth century.[101] This interest reflects a number of factors, including Torrance's pivotal role in English-language Barth-reception,[102] his clear commitment to and familiarity with the Christian theological tradition, and his substantial contribution to the fostering of a creative and responsible dialogue between Christian theology and the natural sciences. Torrance's approach to natural theology can be viewed, not simply as a development within a clearly 'Barthian' approach to theology, but also as a significant contribution in its own right to the dialogue between theology and the natural sciences and the formulation of a scientific theology. In that the present project adopts an approach which is clearly related to Torrance's, it is important to explore his views in a little detail.

Torrance's evaluation of Barth

Torrance's most sustained engagement with Barth's views on natural theology is to be found in the 1970 study 'The Problem of Natural Theology in the Thought of Karl Barth'.[103] Torrance here stresses that Barth does not reject natural theology on the grounds of rational scepticism or some form of *via negationis* which denies a positive knowledge of God. The issue concerns the human desire to conduct theology on anthropocentric foundations. Torrance affirms that one of Barth's most fundamental objections to natural theology concerns the innate human tendency to develop and assert its own autonomy.[104]

> The claim to a natural knowledge of God, as Barth understands it, cannot be separated out from a whole movement of man in which he seeks to justify himself over against the grace of God, and which can only develop into a natural theology that is antithetical to knowledge of God as he really is in his acts of revelation and grace. From this point of view, the danger of natural theology lies in the fact that once its ground has been conceded it becomes the ground on which everything else is absorbed and naturalized, so that even the knowledge of God mediated through his self-revelation in Christ is domesticated and adapted to it until it becomes a form of natural theology.

---

[101] See Wolfgang Achtner, *Physik, Mystik und Christentum: Eine Darstellung and Diskussion der natürlichen Theologie bei T. F. Torrance*. Frankfurt/Berne: Peter Lang, 1991, 158–87.

[102] Alister E. McGrath, *Thomas F. Torrance: An Intellectual Biography*. Edinburgh: T&T Clark, 1999, 113–45.

[103] 'The Problem of Natural Theology in the Thought of Karl Barth', *Religious Studies* 6 (1970), 121–35.

[104] Torrance, 'Problem of Natural Theology', 125.

Torrance argues that Barth came to this conclusion as a result of his study of the development of German Protestant theology since the Enlightenment, and notes the particular importance of the rise of Nazism as a catalyst for Barth's misgivings in this matter.

If all theology proceeds from God's self-revelation in Christ, then it would seem that there is no place for natural theology. Yet Torrance makes the point that, even at this point, Barth is not denying the possibility or even the actuality of natural theology. His point is that natural theology 'is undermined, relativized and set aside by the actual knowledge of God mediated through Christ'. Torrance thus asserts that Barth neither denies the existence of a natural knowledge of God, nor mounts a metaphysical critique of its foundations. Barth's critique is directed against the doctrine that a natural theology is a self-sufficient and autonomous discipline, which leads to a knowledge of God apart from and in opposition to revealed theology. For Torrance, 'what Barth objects to in natural theology is not its rational structure as such, but its *independent* character, i.e. the autonomous rational structure which it develops on the ground of "nature alone" in abstraction from the active self-disclosure of the living God'.[105] As such, natural theology has a proper and significant place *within the ambit of revealed theology*. On Torrance's reading of Barth, his objection to natural theology lies in the perception that such a natural theology will be seen as an independent and valid route to knowledge of God, which may be had under conditions of our choosing – not God's.

Yet Torrance believes, not only that this danger is averted if natural theology is itself seen as a subordinate aspect of revealed theology, legitimated by that revealed theology rather than by natural pre-suppositions or insights; he further believes that Barth himself appreciated this point. The legitimation of natural theology lies not in its own intrinsic structures, nor in an autonomous act of human self-justification, but *in divine revelation itself. Theologia revelata* both legitimates *theologia naturalis* and defines its scope.[106]

Barth can say that *theologia naturalis* is included and brought to light within *theologia revelata*, for in the reality of divine grace there is included the truth of the divine creation. In this sense Barth can interpret, and claim as true, the dictum of St Thomas that grace does not destroy nature but perfects and fulfils it, and can go on to argue that the meaning of God's revelation becomes manifest to us as it brings into full light the

[105] Torrance, 'Problem of Natural Theology', 128–9.
[106] Torrance, 'Problem of Natural Theology', 128–9.

buried and forgotten truth of the creation. In other words, while knowledge of God is grounded in his own intelligible revelation to us, it requires for its actualization an appropriate rational structure in our cognising of it, but that rational structure does not arise unless we allow our minds to fall under the compulsion of God's being who he really is in the act of his self-revelation and grace, and as such cannot be derived from an analysis of our autonomous subjectivity.

Torrance believes that the situation is illuminated by exploring the relation of geometry and physics, in the light of Einstein's theory of relativity.[107]

> Since the rise of four-dimensional geometries which have brought to light a profound correlation between abstract conceptual systems and physical processes, geometry can no longer be pursued simply as a detached independent science, antecedent to physics, but must be pursued in indissoluble unity with physics as the sub-science of its inner rational structure and as an essential part of empirical and theoretical interpretation of nature. As such, however, its character changes, for instead of being an axiomatic deductive science detached from actual knowledge of physical reality, it becomes, as Einstein said, a form of natural science.

The point Torrance is making is that geometry may be viewed in two quite different manners. It can be seen as an independent discipline, having no essential relation to physics; or, following Einstein's approach, it can be seen as properly belonging within the discipline of physics as a whole, in which it can be seen in its proper light, and allowed to achieve its full potential. The same point can then be made concerning natural theology in relation to revealed theology.[108]

> Natural theology can no longer be pursued in its old abstractive form, as a prior conceptual system on its own, but must be brought within the body of positive theology and be pursued in indissoluble unity with it. But then its whole character changes, for pursued within actual knowledge of the living God where we must think rigorously in accordance with the nature of the divine object, it will be made *natural* to the fundamental subject-matter of theology and will fall under the determination of its inherent intelligibility.

While Barth does not deploy this comparison at any point within his writings, Torrance indicates that he discussed this with Barth prior to

---

[107] Torrance, 'Problem of Natural Theology', 129.
[108] Torrance, 'Problem of Natural Theology', 129.

his death, and secured Barth's approval for the comparison as a means of setting out his views on the matter.[109] Torrance thus argues that Barth can be interpreted to have sanctioned natural theology, providing natural theology is not seen as an independent, autonomous or detached discipline in its own right, but is viewed as an integral aspect of the overall project of theology.

Torrance on natural theology

Torrance follows Barth in arguing that revelation must be understood to be self-revelation of God. Any 'natural theology' which is understood as being independent of God's self-revelation must therefore be regarded as a serious challenge to authentic and responsible Christian theology. Natural theology has its place under the aegis of revelation, not outside it. In its improper mode, a 'natural theology' is an approach to theology which leads to the introduction of 'natural' concepts into theology without first establishing the warrant for doing so on the basis of revelation. In this sense of the term, Torrance believes that Barth was entirely justified in critiquing natural theology, which could only lead to the 'assimilation of God to nature and of revelation to history, and thus the reduction of theology to anthropology'.[110]

Yet Torrance insists that there exists an approach to natural theology which is grounded in God's self-revelation, and views itself as located within and subordinate to that revelation. It is this view of natural theology which Torrance seeks to defend, both in terms of its theological legitimacy and its relevance for the dialogue between Christian theology and the natural sciences. The doctrine of creation plays an especially important role in Torrance's reflections on the place of a reconstructed natural theology. The doctrine of creation *ex nihilo* is, for Torrance, the foundation of the idea that the world is contingent, and dependent upon God for its being and order. This allows for the notional separation of natural science and theology, while at the same time insisting that, rightly understood and conceived, the two enterprises can be seen as thoroughly compatible.[111] Torrance insists that creation can only be held

---

[109] See Thomas F. Torrance, *Space, Time and Resurrection*. Edinburgh: Handsel Press, 1976, ix–xi. The conversation referred to dated from the late summer of 1968, a few weeks before Barth's death. The essay in which Einstein explored this point may be consulted: Albert Einstein, 'Geometry and Experience', in *Ideas and Opinions*. London: Souvenir Press, 1973, 232–46.

[110] Thomas F. Torrance, *Karl Barth: Biblical and Evangelical Theologian*. Edinburgh: T&T Clark, 1990, 136.

[111] Thomas F. Torrance, *God and Rationality*. London: Oxford University Press, 1971, 39.

to 'reveal' God from the standpoint of faith. Nevertheless, to one who has responded to revelation (and thus who recognizes nature as God's creation, rather than an autonomous and self-created entity), the creation now has potential to point to its creator. The theologian who is thus a natural scientist (or vice versa) is thus in a position to make some critically important correlations. While the neutral observer of the natural world cannot, according to Torrance, gain meaningful knowledge of God, another observer, aided by divine revelation, will come to very different conclusions.

Torrance's most important analysis of the positive role of natural theology is to be found in the discussion of 'The Transformation of Natural Theology', which formed part of the 1978 Richards Lectures, given at the University of Virginia at Charlottesville.[112] In this lecture, Torrance developed the Athanasian insight that knowledge of God and knowledge of the world share the same ultimate foundations in the rationality of God the creator.[113]

> If natural theology is to have a viable reconstruction, it can only be on the basis of a restored ontology in which our thought operates with a fundamental unity of concept and experience, or of form and being, within a contingent but inherently intelligible and open-structured universe.

For Torrance, one of the great strengths of both Athanasius and Barth was their sustained exposition and defence of non-dualist modes of thought. Barth's critique of natural theology thus simultaneously identifies its vulnerability and points the way towards its reconstruction.[114]

> If the God whom we have actually come to know through Jesus Christ really *is* Father, Son and Holy Spirit in his own eternal and undivided Being, then what are we to make of an independent natural theology that terminates, not upon the Being of the Triune God – i.e. upon God as he really is in himself – but upon some Being of God in general? Natural theology by its very operation abtracts the existence of God from his act, so that if it does not begin with deism, it imposes deism upon theology. If really to know God through his saving activity in our world is to know him as Triune, then the doctrine of the Trinity belongs to the very groundwork of knowledge of God from the very start, which calls

---

[112] Published as Thomas F. Torrance, *The Ground and Grammar of Theology*. Charlottesville, VA: University of Virginia Press, Charlottesville, 1980.
[113] Torrance, *Ground and Grammar of Theology*, 86–7.
[114] Torrance, *Ground and Grammar of Theology*, 89.

into question any doctrine of God as the One God gained apart from his trinitarian activity – but that is the kind of knowledge of God that is yielded in natural theology of the traditional kind.

It will be clear that Torrance rejects 'natural theology of the traditional kind', by which he understands that approach to natural theology which was critiqued by Barth, and which may be regarded as an assertion of human autonomy, resting upon dualist foundations.[115]

> Barth's opposition to the traditional type of natural theology, which is pursued as an independent system on its own, antecedent to positive or revealed theology, rests upon a radical rejection of its dualist basis and constitutes a return to the kind of unitary thinking we find in classical Christian theology as exemplified by Athanasius, in which theology is committed to one coherent framework of thought that arises within the unitary interaction of God with our world in creation and incarnation, and in which we are unable to make any separation between a natural and supernatural knowledge of God.

Torrance then outlines his alternative, which explicitly sets a proper natural theology within a trinitarian context, linked with both revelation and salvation through Christ.[116] Torrance argues that there is an urgent need for theology to set to one side the disruption of the unity of form and being which underlies dualistic modes of thought, and restore this unity along the lines mapped out by classical Christian theology. Torrance is adamant that this is not 'a call to theology to submit itself to some alien way of thinking'; rather, it is to be seen as an invitation to rediscover and return to its own proper epistemic basis, which has become corroded and distorted through the intrusion of cosmological and epistemological influences.[117] Theology and the natural sciences thus stand together in their mutual affirmation of the rationality and intelligibility of the world.

Earlier, we noted the epistemically problematic status of nature. Torrance argues that the restoration of a legitimate and viable natural theology must rest upon a recovery of an authentically Christian understanding of nature. It is only when the theologian has deconstructed nature – that is to say, identified the ideological constraints which have shaped the manner in which 'nature' is conceived – and recovered a

---

[115] Torrance, *Ground and Grammar of Theology*, 93.
[116] For further discussion of this point, see Thomas F. Torrance, *Transformation and Convergence in the Frame of Knowledge*. Grand Rapids, MI: Eerdmans, 1984, 293.
[117] Torrance, *Ground and Grammar of Theology*, 96.

Christian construal of the natural order that a proper 'natural theology' may be restored.[118]

> Barth's thought, it must be understood, moves within the orbit of the Reformation's restored emphasis on the creation of the world out of nothing and thus upon its utter contingence, in which the natural is once again allowed to be natural, for nature is set free from the hidden divinization imposed upon it when it was considered to be impregnated with final causes – the notion of *deus sive natura*. That is the way nature is treated if God is actually thought of as deistically detached from it, so that nature can in some measure substitute for God by providing out of itself a bridge to the divine.

The recovery of a trinitarian theology of nature thus holds the key to the possibility of a reconstructed natural theology, which takes account of the objections raised by Barth – to the extent that these are justified – while at the same time going beyond Barth to offer new possibilities for a scientific theology.[119]

> If Barth's position is to be accepted, as I believe it is, then I also believe that there must be a deeper connection between the basic concepts of theological science and natural science than he seemed to allow: or, otherwise expressed, there is a *mutual* connection between theological science and natural science. If that is the case, then a proper natural theology should be *natural* both to theological science and to natural science. A natural theology in this full sense will have its proper place in the dialogue between theological science and natural science, with their common sharing of the rational structures of space and time conferred on the universe by God in his creating of it, and within their common sharing in the basic conceptions of the unitary rationality of the universe.

This vision offers important theological potential, both as a positive proposal in its own right, and as a critique of Barth, both of which are of some importance to a scientific theology.

The implications of sin for a natural theology

Up to this point, we have focused on the foundational role played by the Christian doctrine of creation in relation to a responsible natural theology. It is now necessary to explore the extent of modulation which is introduced by taking account of the concept of sin. This concept has

---

[118] Torrance, *Ground and Grammar of Theology*, 88.
[119] Torrance, *Ground and Grammar of Theology*, 94.

been treated with a certain degree of disdain in academic theological circles since the Enlightenment, possibly reflecting the perception that the notion of sin was anthropologically demeaning.[120] However, there has recently been renewed interest in reclaiming the concept as a theologically legitimate notion, of no small important to the central questions of Christian theology. This can be seen in Christof Gestrich's *Return of Splendor*, which sets out a renewed vision of the critical role of sin in the Christian scheme of things.[121] Gestrich sets out to reclaim the notion of sin as fundamentally the human attempt at self-justification through an insistence upon human autonomy at both the revelational and soteriological levels, refusing to concede that human dignity and identity are to be defined and affirmed in and through God.[122] There is no doubt that Gestrich is responding, often highly sympathetically, to a series of Barthian concerns, especially in relation to the theme of human autonomy in the face of God.[123] Sin is not to be conceived primarily – still less *essentially* – as a moral concept. In essence, sin is a failure to accept the limitations and possibilities placed upon human existence as a consequence of its creaturely status. If humanity possesses any glory, it is not a glory which is achieved through human achievements, but a glory which is 'lent' to humanity by its creator and redeemer.[124]

A Christian understanding of sin – such as that set out by Gestrich – does not call into question that the creation, as we observe it, is the work of the creator God. Rather, it raises questions concerning both the ability of the human agent to discern the character of God from its rendering in creation, and the direct correspondence of nature, as an empirically observed entity, with what God created, or ultimately intends that creation to become.

---

[120] One of the most important nineteenth-century works to deal with this theme is Julius Müller, *The Christian Doctrine of Sin*. Edinburgh: T&T Clark, 1885. The important study of Frederick R. Tennant, *The Concept of Sin*. Cambridge: Cambridge University Press, 1912, should also be noted.

[121] Christof Gestrich, *The Return of Splendor in the World: The Christian Doctrine of Sin and Forgiveness*. Grand Rapids, MI: Eerdmans, 1997.

[122] Gestrich, *The Return of Splendor*, 14–21.

[123] See, for example, his discussion of the autonomy theme in his earlier work *Neuzeitliches Denken und die Spaltung der dialektischen Theologie: Zur Frage der natürlichen Theologie*. Tübingen: Mohr, 1977.

[124] Gestrich, *The Return of Splendor*, 15; 53–5. Note that Gestrich sets his presentation of sin primarily within the context of the doctrine of forgiveness in Christ. It is thus identified, not simply as a *theological* (as opposed to a metaphysical or moral) concept, but as a Christologically shaped notion.

The phrase 'empirically observed entity' was chosen with care, in that it highlights two significant areas in which sin might be of importance to a natural theology. In the first place, the process of observation involves a 'seeing as' – that is, a process of discernment or perception. What if the human discernment of the created order were to be skewed or clouded by sin? And second, it relates to the created order as that which is observed. What if that created order itself had been affected by sin, having in some sense been disordered? The place and scope of a responsible natural theology will rest, at least in part, on the manner in which these issues are understood. The prospects for natural theology are not especially promising if this is to be understood as an attempt on the part of a rebellious humanity, unwilling to accept its designated place within the natural order and its accompanying limitations, involving reflection upon a fallen creation by a fallen human mind. But is this the case?

In what follows, we shall explore two issues of importance to this matter.

The renewed disorder of creation?

We have made much of the notion of the ordering of creation, and stressed its importance for the development and successes of the natural sciences. Yet the interplay between 'order' and 'chaos' is more complex than might at first appear. It is very easy to regard ordering as a static concept; in fact, it is better regarded as a dynamic notion, grounded in the flux of chaotic forces. While the existence of disorder within the cosmos was initially addressed in terms of the classical thermodynamical notion of 'entropy', more recent discussion of the theme has centred around chaos theory. Ilya Prigogine has argued that the emergence of chaos theory is to be seen as marking an irreversible break with the 'closed universe' or deterministic modes of thought which have characterized the classical origins of modern science.[125] The origins of this development are often traced to 1963, when Edward Lorenz, then a meteorologist at the Massachusetts Institute of Technology, noted that the use of mathematical modelling and computer prediction in the specific field of weather forecasting was subject to severe

---

[125] See Ilya Prigogine, *The End of Certainty: Time, Chaos and the New Laws of Nature.* New York: Free Press, 1997. For further studies, see James Gleick, *Chaos: Making a New Science.* New York: Penguin Books, 1987; John Holte, *Chaos: The New Science.* Lanham, MD: University Press of America, 1993; Stephen H. Kellert, *In the Wake of Chaos: Unpredictable Order in Dynamical Systems.* Chicago: University of Chicago Press, 1993; Roger Lewin, *Complexity: Life at the Edge of Chaos.* New York: MacMillan, 1992.

limitations.[126] It was soon realized that this was not a matter which could be confined to meteorology. The same general principles could easily be applied to all systems governed by Newtonian dynamics, yielding the alarming result that they do not necessarily exhibit the 'predictability' which would once have been regarded as an integral aspect of their behaviour.

The theological aspects of chaos theory have only begun to be explored.[127] However, it will be clear that one area of especial significance to our discussion of natural theology is whether the disordering to be discerned within the natural world has significant implications for a natural theology, and whether this can be regarded as reflecting or resting upon a concept of sin. There is no doubt that the Greek patristic tradition, with its firm commitment to the notion of cosmic redemption, saw a correlation between the necessity of cosmic redemption and the actuality of cosmic sin.[128] Sin was naturally understood as the disordering of the cosmos, which required restoration to its original integrity through redemption. Such an approach has found much sympathy in the twentieth century, particularly from those theologians with a particular affinity with the Greek tradition.

The importance of the theme of emergent disorder within a primordially ordered cosmos is brought out in the later writings of T. F. Torrance. Torrance notes how the universe has fallen into disorder – which he connects, incidentally, with the thermodynamical notion of 'entropy' – and thus requires 'redemption from disorder':[129]

> In Christian theology that redemption of the universe is precisely the bearing of the cross upon the way things actually are in our universe of space and time. It represents the refusal of God to remain aloof from the distintegration of order in what he has made, or merely to act upon it 'at a distance'. It is his decisive personal intervention in the world through the incarnation of his Word and love in Jesus Christ. In his life and

[126] Edward N. Lorenz, 'Deterministic Nonperiodic Flow', *Journal of the Atmospheric Sciences* 20 (1963), 130–41.

[127] For example, see D. J. Bartholomew, *God of Chance*. London: SCM Press, 1984; Robert John Russell, Nancey Murphy and Arthur Peacocke, *Chaos and Complexity: Scientific Perspectives on Divine Action*. Vatican City State: Vatican Observatory and Berkeley: Center for Theology and Natural Sciences, 1995; Keith Ward, *Divine Action*. London: HarperCollins, 1990, 74–133.

[128] See the classic study of H. E. W. Turner, *The Patristic Doctrine of Redemption: A Study of the Development of Doctrine during the first Five Centuries*. London: Mowbray, 1952.

[129] Thomas F. Torrance, *The Christian Frame of Mind: Reason, Order, and Openness in Theology and Natural Science*. 2nd edn. Colorado Springs: Helmers & Howard, 1989, 103. On the link with entropy, see 99–101.

passion he who is the ultimate source and power of all order has
penetrated into the untouchable core of our contingent existence in such
a way as to deal with the twisted force of evil entrenched in it, and thereby
to bring about an atoning reordering of creation.

Torrance here argues that sin affects the very fabric of creation, including
human nature and reason, at its deepest level, rather than merely at a
superficial level. The extent of this disordering of creation is such
that divine transformation of the cosmos is required to realign it
with the divine intentions and goals – a transformation which is
brought about through the death and resurrection of Jesus Christ,
by which the 'reordering of creation' may be initiated.[130] The
created order, as it presently exists and as it is presently conceived,
incorporates within it a deep-rooted dimension of disorder, with the
potential to skew and confuse our interpretation of its identity and
signification.

The question which must therefore be raised at this point is this:
does the disordering of the universe – whether we choose to explore
this in terms of entropy, chaos, or sin – raise a fundamental difficulty
for natural theology? At first sight, a positive answer would seem to
be called for. Reflection on a disordered universe could easily lead to
a seriously defective concept of divinity. Yet such considerations
ultimately serve to chasten, rather than to invalidate, a natural theology.
This conclusion rests upon reflection on both the nature and the extent
of the disorder within the world.

At a mathematical level, the origins of 'chaos' may be argued to lie
primarily in the complexity of the solutions to non-linear equations
rather than 'disordering' within the world. Whereas linear equations
offer exact solutions, their non-linear counterparts often defy precise
solution. It must be stressed that the difficulty is intrinsic to the mathematics, and does not result from a lack of precision concerning the
parameters of the equations in question. The origin of the unpredict-
ability thus does not lie so much in the 'disorder' of the world, but in
the intrinsic difficulty of predicting behaviour in complex systems. An
inability to predict the behaviour of a system does not necessarily mean
that the system itself is chaotic or disordered, but that the mathematical
equations which require to be solved in order to predict that behaviour
prove resistant to the precise solution needed. Such a view is especially
associated with the Nobel Prize winning physicist Ilya Prigogine, noted

for his work on non-equilibrium thermodynamics. As Prigogine argues forcefully, non-equilibrium is 'the source of order'.[131]

Yet a specifically theological concern must be raised at this point. A failure to concede the presence of disorder within the creation can easily lead to the notion that the creation, as it is now observed, is *perfect* – like its creator. This naïve and unrealistic inference fails to take account of any notion of the corruption of nature through sin, whether this is conceived in the modest language of 'deflection from an intended trajectory' found in the tradition of theological reflection deriving ultimately from Irenaeus, or the more forceful discourse of 'fall' or 'depravation' found within the Augustinian tradition. Yet there is within the Cartesian tradition a disturbing tendency to focus on the perfection of God,[132] so that any perceived imperfections within the natural order come to assume the role of disconfirmations of the God-hypothesis.[133]

Descartes' highly contestable construal of the divine perfection leads to the existence of suffering within the world becoming a reason for challenging the existence of God. The importance of these issues extends beyond the ambit of natural theology *per se*. There exists an at best difficult and imprecise distinction between a natural theology and a theodicy, in that reflections upon the current status of the natural order tend to lead to reflection on the competency and intentions of its originator.

These issues are intrinsically important, and cannot be overlooked in any responsible attempt to construct a natural theology. However, it is arguable that perhaps the most fundamental issue to be raised in this regard by the doctrine of sin concerns the ability of sinful humanity to discern the presence of God within the natural order – an issue to which we may turn immediately.

The human misreading of creation?

The human ability to discern God within the natural order is arguably fragile at the best of times. What if the already frail capacity of the

---

[131] Ilya Prigogine and Isabelle Stengers, *Order out of Chaos: Man's New Dialogue with Nature.* New York: Bantam Books, 1984, 287.

[132] See especially Emmanuel Faye, *Philosophie et perfection de l'homme de la Renaissance à Descartes.* Paris: Librairie philosophique J. Vrin, 1998. More generally, see Iris Murdoch, *The Sovereignty of the Good.* London: Macmillan, 1970; Frederick Sontag, *Divine Perfection: Possible Ideas of God.* London: SCM Press, 1962.

[133] This point has been made forcefully by Michael Buckley, *At the Origins of Modern Atheism.* New Haven, CT: Yale University Press, 1987.

human mind to discern the creator in the creation were in some sense to be clouded by sin? Such an idea plays an important role in the theology of Augustine of Hippo,[134] and can be argued to represent a recognition of the potentially distorting impact of sin upon the reading of the divine signatures embodied within creation. The idea is, of course, by no means limited to Augustine. Calvin argued that both the human mind and will were skewed through sin:[135]

> Since reason – by which humanity discriminates between good and evil, gains understanding, and makes judgements – is a natural gift, it cannot be completely eradicated. Rather, it was partly weakened, and partly corrupted . . . Similarly, the will, in that it is inseparable from human nature, did not cease to exist, but was so enslaved to evil desires that it was incapable of seeking the right.

The basic point that Calvin makes is open to criticism, but has found much sympathy within the Christian theological tradition. Sin does not eradicate or eliminate the gifts bestowed by God upon humanity in creation, but erodes them, and weakens their capacity both to discern what is right, and to act upon such a discernment.[136] Although there is an important discussion to be had concerning precisely how Calvin articulates the noetic impact of sin,[137] there is no doubt that he regards it as having significant implications for human knowing and willing. For Calvin, there is a depressing inevitability to the move from an imperfect knowledge of God through human reason to the worship of that imperfection as God.[138]

The extent to which the human mind and will have been affected by sin is contested within the Christian tradition, and it is not my intention to become involved in this intricate discussion. The point made is simple enough to require no further elaboration – namely, that while there is debate concerning the extent to which the human ability to behold the divine within the complex network of signatures which constitutes the created order has been compromised by sin, there is widespread

[134] See the careful study of G. R. Evans, *Augustine on Evil.* Cambridge: Cambridge University Press, 1990.

[135] Calvin, *Institutes* II.ii.12. See further L. Anderson, 'The *Imago Dei* Theme in John Calvin and Bernard of Clairvaux', in W. H. Neuser (ed.), *Calvinus Sacrae Scripturae Professor.* Grand Rapids, MI: Eerdmans, 1994, 180–97.

[136] Gunter Gloede, *Theologia naturalis bei Calvin.* Stuttgart: Kohlhammer, 1935, 72–146.

[137] Paul Helm, 'John Calvin, the *Sensus Divinitatis* and the Noetic Effects of Sin', *International Journal of Philosophy of Religion* 43 (1998), 87–107.

[138] See the discussion of Cicero's *de natura deorum* in the opening chapters of the *Institutes*: Emil Grislis, 'Calvin's Use of Cicero in the *Institutes* I:1–5: A Case Study in Theological Method', *Archiv für Reformationsgeschichte* 62 (1971), 5–37.

agreement that the human situation is characterized by some such diminution in the human epistemic capacity to discern, and subsequently to respond appropriately to, God.[139]

Nevertheless, some points of caution need to be registered. One of the more interesting features of many more recent discussions of sin is that the locus of such discussion has shifted away from the metaphysical or cognitive roles of sin.[140] Sin tends to be interpreted primarily in relational categories – for example, a dysfunctional relationship with the creation, or with Christ. A number of recent writers – such as Wolfhart Pannenberg and Colin Gunton – have given particular attention to the issue of relationality as a theological issue,[141] noting its implications for the Christian understanding of human nature in general, and sin in particular.

Nevertheless, the debate between Barth and Brunner must serve to demonstrate that it would be utterly premature to suggest that sin has ceased to be an issue in matters of the theology of revelation in general, and natural theology in particular. There is no doubt that some theologians, wedded to a general process of accommodation of the Christian tradition to modern understandings of human nature, have misgivings concerning traditional formulations of sin, and prefer to state the concept in terms of, for example, depth psychology rather than the incapacitation of human rational faculties.[142] Yet the issues raised by the debate between Brunner and Barth concerning the quality of *Wortmächtigkeit* and the epistemological implications of being created in the *imago Dei* make it clear that this is far from a settled issue.[143]

---

[139] See Colin E. Gunton, *A Brief Theology of Revelation*. Edinburgh: T&T Clark, 1995, 40–1. Further debates centre on the manner in which sin can be considered to have entered the world, and influenced individuals: see especially N. P. Williams, *The Ideas of the Fall and of Original Sin: A Historical and Critical Study*. London: Longmans Green & Co., 1927.

[140] For a useful survey, see Walter E. Wyman, 'Rethinking the Christian Doctrine of Sin', *Zeitschrift für neuere Theologiegeschichte* 2 (1994), 226–50.

[141] See Wolfhart Pannenberg, *Anthropology in Theological Perspective*. Philadelphia: Westminster Press, 1985; F. Leron Shults, 'Constitutive Relationality in Anthropology and Trinity: Shaping and *Imago Dei* in Barth and Pannenberg', *Neue Zeitschrift für systematische Theologie und Religionsphilosophie* 39 (1997), 304–22; Colin Gunton, 'Trinity, Ontology and Anthropology: Towards a Renewal of the Doctrine of *Imago Dei*', in Christoph Schwöbel and Colin Gunton (eds), *Persons Divine and Human: King's College Essays in Theological Anthropology*. Edinburgh: T&T Clark, 1991, 47–64.

[142] Gestrich, *The Return of Splendor in the World*, 44–7.

[143] See Brunner's reflections on the nature of sin in Emil Brunner, *Der Mensch im Widerspruch: Die christliche Lehre vom Wahren und vom wirklichen Menschen*. Zurich: Theologischer Verlag, 1985.

It will therefore be clear that the debate over the viability of a natural theology is framed on the one hand by the doctrine of creation, and on the other by a theological anthropology which is shaped by a proper emphasis upon both the *imago Dei* and sin. Wolfhart Pannenberg sets this point out as follows:[144]

> The doctrines of the image of God and sin thematize the two basic aspects found in the most varied connections between anthropological phenomena and the reality of God. To speak of the image of God in humans is to speak of their closeness to the divine reality, a closeness that also determines their position in the world of nature. To speak of sin, on the other hand, is to speak of the factual separation of God from human beings whose destiny is nonetheless union with God; sin is therefore to be thematized as a contradiction of human beings with themselves, an interior conflict in the human person.

Considerations such as these raise questions concerning the place of natural theology within an overall vision of the theological enterprise. In what follows, we shall consider some of the issues which must be addressed.

The place of natural theology within a scientific theology

Two main approaches may be discerned within Christian theology to the contested question of a natural theology.

1. Nature provides a foundational resource for Christian theology. Nature is thus treated as an *explicans*, an agent of explication with potentially revelatory status.

2. Christian theology provides an interpretative framework by which nature may be interpreted. This approach takes nature to be an *explicandum*, something which requires or demands explication, but is not itself possessed of the intrinsic capacity or ability to offer such an explanation.

The present project affirms and defends the theological viability of the second of these two options, for reasons that will become clear as our analysis proceeds. A natural theology, which sees nature as creation, has an important role in a scientific theology.

In what follows, we shall explore some of the issues relating to, and functions of, a natural theology within the overall context of a scientific

---

[144] Pannenberg, *Anthropology in Theological Perspective*, 20.

theology. Some of the issues have already been addressed in our historical and theological analysis thus far; the present chapter aims to consolidate and expand these.

Resonance, not proof: natural theology and revealed theology

One of the objections to natural theology raised – although in different ways – by both Karl Barth and Alvin Plantinga relates to the issue of the proof of God's existence. Natural theology, they suggest, improperly seeks to prove the existence of God, or some other aspect of Christian faith. From our earlier discussion, it will be clear that this is an important critique, not of natural theology itself, but of one particular approach to natural theology. It is not the only such approach, and must not be represented as being so. There exists a perfectly legitimate role for natural theology within the scope of a revealed knowledge of God.

As we have stressed, it is problematic to speak of a 'theology of nature', in that this rests upon the false and misleading assumption that 'nature' is a self-authenticating category, devoid of presupposed concepts or values, and isolated from any historical or social context. 'Nature' is an interpreted concept, irrespective of the nature of the assumptions shaping that interpretation, whether secular or religious. A legitimate Christian natural theology interprets nature in a Christian manner – namely, as God's creation. This involves construing natural theology in line with the foundational insights of the Christian tradition.

For this reason, natural theology cannot be conceived as an autonomous theological discipline, precisely because its foundational and legitimating insight – namely, that nature is to be viewed and recognized as God's creation – is derived from divine revelation. 'Nature' is not a self-sufficient category, capable of bearing the epistemological weight which an autonomous natural theology demands. In its legitimate and defensible form, natural theology is to be viewed as a legitimate and proper theological exercise to be conducted *within* the scope of a revealed knowledge of God, rather than as an autonomous discipline outside its bounds.

The framework offered by Christian theology includes both an account of the natural order as God's creation, and of humanity as created in the *imago Dei*. As we have seen, this double-headed insight offers a perspective by which nature may be viewed as reflecting the rationality of God as its creator. There is thus a fundamental resonance – but nothing more – between nature and theology, with the latter offering a prism through which the former may be viewed and understood. Such an approach is already present within the Christian tradition, whether in Calvin's musing on the insights of astronomy, John Ray's reflections on the wisdom of God in the created order, or Joseph Addison's poetic rendering of Psalm 19, published in 1712 in *The Spectator*:

> The spacious firmament on high,
> With all the blue ethereal sky,
> And spangled heavens, a shining frame,
> Their great Original proclaim.
> Th'unwearied Sun from day to day
> Does his Creator's power display;
> And publishes to every land
> The work of an Almighty hand.

The recovery of a properly configured natural theology can serve as the basis for a critical theological engagement with both the world and the sciences which seek to give an account of it. Perhaps the time has come for theology to recover from its Barthian captivity in this matter – however understandable the reasons for such isolationism may have been – and engage with the secular world, on the basis of its theological convictions concerning the 'nature of nature' – to which we now turn.

On seeing nature as creation

We noted earlier William Alston's definition of natural theology as 'the enterprise of providing support for religious beliefs by starting from premises that neither are nor presuppose any religious beliefs'.[145] Yet this definition can now be seen to be problematic. To have any validity, there has to be some implicit connection between nature and God – and it is impossible to frame such a connection without postulating something akin to a doctrine of creation, which both is, and pre-supposes, religious beliefs. It is wrong to treat natural theology and revealed theology as being opposed to each other, *provided* that nature is construed in a trinitarian manner as the creation of the self-revealing God.

If nature is to reveal the Christian God, it must be regarded as creation – that is, as bearing some relation to God, in order that this God may somehow be disclosed through it. Natural theology cannot become a totally autonomous discipline, independent of revelation, in that it depends for its credibility upon the revealed insight that God is creator of the natural order. If the Christian God is to be known through

---

[145] Alston, *Perceiving God: The Epistemology of Religious Experience*, 289.

the natural world, that world must have some relation of likeness or affinity to this God; otherwise it is not this God which is disclosed, however imperfectly, through it.

How is this relation to be understood? The traditional view, with which I can find no convincing reason to disagree, is to affirm that there is an intrinsic capacity within the created order to disclose God. Here, nature-as-creation is understood to have an ontologically grounded capacity to reflect God as its maker and originator. Yet it is also perfectly acceptable to conceive this as a covenantal relationship, in which the ability of the creation to disclose God is not intrinsic, resting on an *analogia entis*, but is rather grounded in a decision that this shall be the case. Such a shift from ontological to covenantal understandings of causality is one of the most distinctive features of the theology of the late fourteenth and early fifteenth centuries, and can be discerned within the writings of Pierre d'Ailly, Robert Holcot and Gabriel Biel.[146] A similar idea is developed by Karl Barth, whose concept of *analogia fidei* was intended to counter the ontological presuppositions of Aquinas' *analogia entis* – which Barth held to confer revelatory autonomy upon the creation.

A similar idea is developed in the earlier works of Thomas F. Torrance, in which the covenantal foundation of the created order's ability to disclose God is affirmed:[147]

> The whole world of signs which God in his covenant mercy has appointed to correspond to him only has revealing significance, and therefore can be interpreted only, in relation to his covenant will for communion with man and in the actualization of that covenant in the course of his redemptive acts in history. Thus while the whole of creation is formed to serve as the sphere of divine self-revelation, it cannot be interpreted or understood out of itself, as if it had an inherent likeness or being to the Truth, but only in the light of the history of the covenant of grace and its appointed signs and orders and events in the life of the covenant people . . . In this way, Reformed theology certainly holds that God reveals himself in creation, but not by some so-called 'light of nature', and it certainly holds that God's revelation makes use of and is mediated through a creaturely objectivity, but it does not hold that an examination of this creaturely objectivity of itself can yield knowledge of God.

---

[146] E.g. see W. J. Courtenay, 'Covenant and Causality in Pierre d'Ailly', *Speculum* 46 (1971), 94–119. For its impact on the doctrine of justification, especially in relation to the causality of grace, see Alister E. McGrath, *Iustitia Dei: A History of the Christian Doctrine of Justification*. 2nd edn. Cambridge: Cambridge University Press, 1998, 145–54.

[147] Thomas F. Torrance, *The School of Faith*. London: James Clarke, 1959, liii.

In this analysis, Torrance explicitly critiques the idea that there exists some intrinsic likeness between creator and creation arising from the creative action of God. The fact that there exists some form of correspondence between the creator and creation is not due to an inherent relation of likeness, but to the free and gracious decision of God that some such correspondence shall exist. We are thus dealing with an *analogia gratiae* rather than an *analogia entis*. There is no intrinsic capacity on the part of nature to convey God, nor is the created element as such part of the content of revelation.

The point at issue is best understood by returning to consider the Valentinian variant of Gnosticism, which held that creation was the work of a lower entity within a divine hierarchy. Creation is the work of the Demiurge, which bears no significant relation to God. If the natural order bears witness to any creative being, it is this Demiurge. Yet even here, the degree of witness must be open to challenge, on account of the Valentinian insistence that creation involves the crafting of matter already in existence. The importance of the Christian doctrine of creation *ex nihilo* for natural theology has not been adequately dealt with in the literature concerning this matter; it is simply not adequate to state that a doctrine of creation in general undergirds such a theology. The question of the *identity* of the creator and the extent to which *the character of the creator can be rendered* in and through the creation demand careful attention.

It is impossible simply to read theological insights from an allegedly epistemologically neutral 'nature'. Nature has to be seen in a certain way before it has revelatory potential; the manner in which it is seen – to continue using the language of N. R. Hanson in this matter – depends upon the assumptions which the observer brings to the act of observation. To slip into the language of phenomenology – for example, as used by Husserl and developed by Gadamer – the act of interpretation is based upon a *Vorverständnis*, a 'pre-understanding' which is brought to this act by the observer on account of his or her standing within a tradition of discourse which, at least initially, causes him or her to 'pre-judge' matters. Those who believe that they are observing nature devoid of any presuppositions – an error which graces the pages of Kant's main *Critiques* – have yet to appreciate that they are social beings, whose horizons are shaped by unacknowledged traditions.

But what framework of interpretation is to be brought to this act? A Valentinian approach declares that the natural order is the fabrication of a being who is *not* the supreme god, and whose handiwork was significantly influenced by the quality of the material on which this Demiurge was obligated to work. It is therefore impossible to establish any significant connection between the world as we observe it and the nature of God. Such a connection can only be held to exist if three conditions are satisfied:

1. That the created order is held to be the work of the Christian God, not any other entity, whether divine or otherwise;

2. That the act of creation was not determined or significantly influenced by the quality of the material which was ordered through this act;

3. That the human mind possesses the capacity to recognize this work of creation as such, and to draw at least some reliable conclusions concerning the nature and character of God from the created order.

These three insights are secured through the Christian revelation, and may be specifically linked to the doctrine of creation *ex nihilo* and the doctrine of the *imago Dei*, along lines such as those sketched out elsewhere in this work.

The question of whether there can be a legitimate natural theology is of considerable *apologetic* importance, through the recognition that, if God has indeed created the world and allowed this world to bear witness to its creator, the Christian evangelist will have a number of 'points of contact' for the gospel within the created order. The use of the phrase 'points of contact' in this context is not without its polemical overtones. The term *Anknüpfungspunkt* was used by Emil Brunner in his controversy with Karl Barth over the purpose and scope of natural theology, to indicate Brunner's fundamental belief that the creation of the world entailed the incorporation of a number of *vestigia* which might serve as 'signals of transcendence' (Peter Berger) to humanity, and to which an apologist might appeal in affirming the plausibility of the Christian faith.

It will also be clear that a natural theology has important implications for Christian spirituality, and also for the growing interest in the spirituality of the natural sciences. If nature is seen as creation, some exciting possibilities await exploration. 'It is not too much to say that the Gospel itself can never be fully known till nature as well as man is fully known,' wrote the leading Anglican writer F. J. A. Hort in his 1871 Hulsean Lectures, 'and that the manifestation of nature as well as

man in Christ is part of his manifestation of God.'[148] Such insights have
been characteristic of many Christian writers, who have argued that
the truth, goodness and beauty of God are disclosed through the created
order. We shall consider the implications of a scientific theology for
spirituality and apologetics in the second volume in this series; we now
turn to consider some issues raised by the public character of discourse
concerning the natural order.

Natural theology as discourse in the public arena

One of the more important debates to develop during the final decades
of the twentieth century concerns whether Christian theology offers an
account of its own privileged insights, or whether it can be seen as
engaging with publicly accessible resources, the interpretation of which
is open to debate. To offer an interpretation of nature is to engage with
the sciences, and avoid the ghetto mentality which occasionally descends
upon the Christian theological community. There is a public debate
taking place over the status of nature, in which theological insights
demand a hearing – and will fail to be heard unless Christian theology
appreciates the importance of engaging in this discourse within the
public arena. This discourse is taking place in public, and concerns a
publicly accessible entity, whose standing and place are under
exploration – namely, the natural world.

An emphasis upon the public accessibility of the legitimating
resources of the Christian faith is characteristic of the writings of
Wolfhart Pannenberg, whose contributions demand attention at
this point. Initially, Pannenberg's interests lay in the area of the
importance of the philosophy of history.[149] These issues were explored
throughout the 1960s, when the predominance of Marxism in
German intellectual culture made an examination of the role of
history particularly significant. Marxism emphasized the importance
of the correct interpretation of history, and Pannenberg responded
by arguing for the grounding of theology in what he termed
'universal history'. His views on this issue were developed and
justified in the 1961 volume *Offenbarung als Geschichte*, edited by
Pannenberg, in which these ideas are explored at some length. This
volume established Pannenberg as a leading young theologian of the

---

[148] F. J. A. Hort, *The Way, The Truth, The Life: The Hulsean Lectures for 1871*. Cambridge:
Cambridge University Press, 1893, 83.
[149] Kurt Koch, *Der Gott der Geschichte: Theologie der Geschichte bei Wolfhart Pannenberg
als Paradigma einer philosophischen Theologie in ökumenischer Perspektive*. Mainz: Matthias
Grünewald Verlag, 1988.

period.[150] This reputation was further consolidated by his 1968 work on Christology, *Gundzüge der Christologie*, in which he set out an approach to the identity and significance of Jesus of Nazareth which made a particular appeal to the resurrection as a public historical event.

Pannenberg's early essay 'Redemptive Event and History' opens with a powerful appeal to universal history:[151]

> History is the most comprehensive horizon of Christian theology. All theological questions and answers have meaning only within the framework of the history which God has with humanity, and through humanity with the whole creation, directed towards a future which is hidden to the world, but which has already been revealed in Jesus Christ.

These crucially important opening sentences sum up the distinctive features of Pannenberg's theological programme at this stage in his career. Christian theology is based upon an analysis of universal and publicly accessible history. For Pannenberg, revelation is essentially a public and universal historical event which is recognized and interpreted as an 'act of God'.

Pannenberg's argument takes the following form. History, in all its totality, can only be understood when it is viewed from its endpoint. This point alone provides the perspective from which the historical process can be seen in its totality, and thus be properly understood. However, where Marx argued that the social sciences, by predicting the goal of history to be the hegemony of socialism, provided the key to the interpretation of history, Pannenberg declared that this was provided only in Jesus Christ. The end of history is disclosed in advance proleptically in the history of Jesus Christ. In other words, the end of history, which has yet to take place, has been disclosed in advance of the event in the person and work of Christ.

Perhaps the most distinctive, and certainly the most discussed, aspect of this work is Pannenberg's insistence that the resurrection of Jesus is an objective historical event, witnessed by all who had access to the evidence. Whereas Rudolf Bultmann treated the resurrection as a private event within the experiential world of the disciples, Pannenberg declares that it belongs to the world of universal public history. Revelation is not something that takes place in secret. It is 'open to anyone who has

---

[150] See David P. Polk, *On the Way to God: An Exploration into the Theology of Wolfhart Pannenberg*. Lanham, MD: University Press of America, 1989, 1; Pierre Warin, *Le chemin de la théologie chez Wolfhart Pannenberg*. Rome: Universita Gregoriana Editrice, 1981.

[151] Wolfhart Pannenberg, 'Redemptive Event and History', in *Basic Questions in Theology* I. London: SCM Press, 1970, 15–80; 15.

eyes to see. It has a universal character.' Any concept of revelation which implies that revelation is either opposed to or distinct from natural knowledge is in danger of lapsing into a form of Gnosticism. The distinctively Christian understanding of revelation lies in the way in which publicly available events are interpreted. Thus the resurrection of Jesus, he argues, was a publicly accessible event. But what did it *mean*? Christian revelation concerns the distinctively Christian way of understanding that event, and its implications for our understanding of God. Such an emphasis upon the public accessibility of revelational resources has proved controversial,[152] in that it suggests that it is intelligent reflection on (at least in principle) publicly observable entities and events – rather than the guidance or inspiration of the Holy Spirit – which is of decisive importance.

During the 1970s, however, Pannenberg began to express an interest in the way in which theology relates to the natural sciences.[153] Just as he appealed to the publicly observable sphere of history in his theological analysis of the 1960s, so he appeals to another publicly observable sphere – the world of nature – from the 1970s onwards. Both history and the natural world are available to scrutiny by anyone; the critical question concerns how they are to be understood. In his essay 'Contingency and Natural Law', Pannenberg draws attention to the way in which these two spheres of history and nature interact, exploring in particular the idea of a 'history of nature'.[154]

Pannenberg is clear that the natural sciences and theology are distinct disciplines, with their own understandings of how information is gained and assessed. Nevertheless, both relate to the same publicly observable reality, and they therefore have potentially complementary insights

---

[152] For the hostile reaction to this notion of revelation, see Paul Althaus, 'Offenbarung als Geschichte und Glaube', *Theologische Literaturzeitung* 87 (1962), 321–30; Lothar Steiger, 'Offenbarungsgeschichte und theologische Vernunft', *Zeitschrift für Theologie und Kirche* 59 (1962), 88–113. For Pannenberg's response to Althaus at this point, see Wolfhart Pannenberg, 'Einsicht und Glaube: Antwort an Paul Althaus', *Theologische Literaturzeitung* 88 (1963), 81–92.

[153] For important studies, see Philip Hefner, 'The Role of Science in Pannenberg's Theological Thinking', *Zygon* 24 (1989), 135–51; Hans-Dieter Mutschler, 'Schöpfungstheologie und physikaler Feldbegriff bei Wolfhart Pannenberg', *Theologie und Philosophie* 70 (1995), 543–58; Mark William Worthing, *Foundations and Functions of Theology as Universal Science: Theological Method and Apologetic Praxis in Wolfhart Pannenberg and Karl Rahner*. Frankfurt am Main/Berlin: Peter Lang, 1996. There is a useful collection of material in Rausch Albright Carol and Joel Haugen, *Beginning with the End: God, Science, and Wolfhart Pannenberg*. Chicago, IL: Open Court, 1997.

[154] Wolfhart Pannenberg, 'Contingency and Natural Law', in *Toward a Theology of Nature: Essays on Science and Faith*. Louisville, KY: Westminster/John Knox Press, 1993, 72–122. For a critique, see Robert John Russell, 'Contingency in Physics and Cosmology: A Critique of the Theology of Wolfhart Pannenberg', *Zygon* 23 (1988), 23–43.

to bring. The area of the 'laws of nature' is a case in point, in that Pannenberg believes that the provisional explanations for such laws offered by natural scientists have a purely provisional status, until they are placed on a firmer theoretical foundation by theological analysis. There is thus a clear case to be made for a creative and productive dialogue between the natural sciences and religion; indeed, had this taken place in the past, much confusion and tension could have been avoided.[155]

> Much would have been gained with the insight that the themes of theology and the reality that natural sciences describe must not stand side by side without relationship. Rather, it must be possible and meaningful to think of reality as a whole with the inclusion of nature as a process of a history of God with his creatures . . . It is clear that faith in God has to be gained in other areas of life than that of scientific knowledge, but the significance of the idea of God for an interconnected understanding of nature is just as clear.

It has been stated before – and will be stated again in view of its critical importance to our theme – that there is no 'neutral' or 'presuppositionless' reading of nature. Pannenberg's approach thus has considerable importance to the theme of natural theology. Pannenberg argues for a creative exploration of the impact of a trinitarian doctrine of creation for a right understanding of 'nature', along with an incorporation of the insights of the *logos* doctrine of the ancient church.[156] Puzzlingly, Pannenberg seems unaware that such an enterprise underlies the theological programme of T. F. Torrance – whom Pannenberg does not mention at any point in the course of his 'Essays on Science and Faith'.

The proposal that we wish to advance in this chapter is that natural theology offers a comprehensive means by which theology may address the world, and engage in productive dialogue concerning the legitimation and consequences of belief systems. In a free market of ideas, in which competing conceptions of 'nature' clamour for attention, the question of how the natural order is to be interpreted is of critical importance. Presuppositionless exegesis of the book of nature being an impossibility – as is also the case with the book of Scripture – there is room for a proper and informed debate over how the natural order is to be construed.

---

[155] Pannenberg, 'Contingency and Natural Law', 112.
[156] Wolfhart Pannenberg, 'God and Nature', in *Toward a Theology of Nature: Essays on Science and Faith*, 50–71; 65–6.

This insight allows full engagement on the part of the theologian with the following:

1. the world of nature;
2. the interpretations of nature offered by the natural sciences;
3. the working assumptions of those sciences upon which such interpretations are based;
4. the interpretations of nature offered by the social sciences.

It will therefore be clear that such an approach to natural theology opens the way to liberating theology from any self-imposed imprisonment within an intellectual ghetto – 'self-imprisonment' precisely because of a failure on the part of theology to engage with the natural order and its interpreters.

A scientific theology is thus a public theology. Although grounded in the Christian tradition, it possesses a capacity to address issues beyond the community of faith. Yet it must be appreciated that any public engagement with nature rests upon a pre-understanding of what 'nature' denotes. The variety of answers offered within western culture serves to remind us that while the natural world is publicly accessible, its interpretation remains disputed.[157] There is no one public 'theory of nature', in that such a grand universal theory would demand agreement on the manner in which nature is to be conceived – an agreement which is conspicuously absent from the western intellectual community at present. That which is to be explained is publicly observable; the manner of its observation presupposes an informing theory. The Christian doctrine of creation is one such theory; others, however, compete for plausibility within the public arena. The Enlightenment belief that there was only one account of nature which could be taken seriously has not withstood critical scrutiny, leading to the post-Enlightenment notion of a range of equally plausible approaches to nature.

The now defunct Enlightenment project, which demanded a universally valid rationality for the investigation of the world, protested against what it unwisely termed 'the scandal of particularity' of Christian truth-claims. The collapse of this project – partly on account of the recogition

---

[157] Compare the very different understandings of nature found in sociobiology, traditional Christian theology, and the 'Gaia' movement – all of which are significant elements in North American intellectual culture at present: Edward O. Wilson, *Sociobiology: The New Synthesis.* Cambridge, MA: Harvard University Press, 1975; Paul Devereux, John Steele and David Kubrin, *Earthmind: Communicating with the Living World of Gaia.* Rochester, VT: Destiny Books, 1989; Rosemary Ruether, *Gaia and God.* San Francisco: HarperSanFrancisco, 1989.

that its own allegedly 'universal' rationality was actually strongly ethnocentric, and hence an instance of the same 'scandal of particularity' which it so deplored – has led to growing sympathy for the idea of a tradition-based rationality which, though particular in respects to its tradition, claims to have validity in a wider context. We shall be exploring the issue of tradition-mediated rationality later in this project; at this point, it is enough to note that the Enlightenment dream of a 'universal rationality', devoid of the specificities of time and culture, has been shown to be somewhat utopian.

It is for this reason that many have turned to explore the ideas of writers such as Alasdair MacIntyre, which we shall consider critically in the following volume,[158] as we turn to deal with the question of the reality of the external world, and the manner in which this is to be represented and explained. We shall return to exploring this matter in the third volume of this work.

---

[158] For my earlier reflections on this topic, see my 1990 Bampton Lectures at Oxford University, published as Alister E. McGrath, *The Genesis of Doctrine: A Study in the Foundations of Doctrinal Criticism.* Oxford: Blackwell, 1990, 172–98.

Moving On: Anticipating an Engagement with Reality

The present volume has offered a sustained engagement with the concept of nature, assessing its place within a scientific theology. It will be clear that this exploration has raised a host of questions and issues which demand fuller discussion. Is there an external world, and how may it be accessed and represented? Can transcendent ideas be developed by an appeal to the natural order – or is the naturalist position correct? How does a scientific theology offer an account of reality? And how does such a rendering relate to rival accounts, such as those of the natural sciences? Or the cultural and intellectual enterprises loosely gathered together as 'postmodernity'?

It is therefore necessary to move on to the agenda of the second volume in this series, entitled – doubtless provocatively to some – 'reality', which sets out a sustained presentation and defence of a realist approach to theology.

Bibliography

ADAMS, EDWARD, *Constructing the World: A Study in Paul's Cosmological Language*. Edinburgh: T&T Clark, 2000.

AERTSEN, JAN, *Nature and Creature: Thomas Aquinas' Way of Thought*. Leiden: E. J. Brill, 1988.

ALBERTZ, RAINER, *Weltschöpfung und Menschenschöpfung untersucht bei Deuterojesaja, Hiob und in den Psalmen*. Stuttgart: Calwer, 1974.

ANDERSON, BERNHARD W., 'A Stylistic Study of the Priestly Creation Story', in George W. Coats and Burke O. Long (eds), *Canon and Authority: Essays in Old Testament Religion and Theology*. Philadelphia: Fortress Press, 1977, 148–62.

ANDERSON, RAY S., 'Barth and a New Direction for Natural Theology', in John Thompson (ed.), *Theology beyond Christendom: Essays on the Centenary of the Birth of Karl Barth*. Allison Park, PA: Pickwick Publications, 1986, 241–66.

ANGERSTORFER, ANDREAS, *Der Schöpfergott des Alten Testaments: Herkunft und Bedeutungsentwicklung des hebräischen Terminus bara, 'schaffen'*. Frankfurt am Main: Peter Lang, 1979.

AYER, A. J., 'What is a Law of Nature?', in A. J. Ayer (ed.), *The Concept of a Person*. London: Macmillan, 1956, 209–34.

BARR, JAMES, 'The Image of God in the Book of Genesis: A Study of Terminology', *Bulletin of the John Rylands Library* 51 (1968), 11–26.

——, *Biblical Faith and Natural Theology*. Oxford: Clarendon Press, 1993.

BARRETT, PETER, 'Beauty in Physics and Theology', *Journal of Theology for Southern Africa* 94 (1996), 65–78.

BARTH, KARL, *Church Dogmatics*. 14 vols. Edinburgh: T&T Clark, 1957–75.

——, and EMIL BRUNNER, *Natural Theology*. London: SCM Press, 1947.

BIRKNER, H. J., 'Natürliche Theologie und Offenbarungstheologie: Ein theologiegeschichtlicher Überblick', *Neue Zeitschrift für systematische Theologie und Religionsphilosophie* 3 (1961), 279–95.

BROWN, HUNTER, 'Alvin Plantinga and Natural Theology', *International Journal for Philosophy of Religion* 30 (1991), 1–19.

BURGHARDT, WALTER J., *The Image of God in Man according to Cyril of Alexandria*. Woodstock, MA: Woodstock Press, 1957.

BURRELL, DAVID B., *Analogy and Philosophical Language*. New Haven, CT: Yale University Press, 1973.

——, *Knowing the Unknowable: Ibn Sina, Maimonides, Aquinas*. Notre Dame, IN: University of Notre Dame Press, 1986.

——, *Freedom and Creation in Three Traditions*. Notre Dame, IN: University of Notre Dame Press, 1993.

BYRNE, PETER A., *Natural Religion and the Religion of Nature*. London: Routledge, 1989.

CAIRNS, DAVID, *The Image of God in Man*. London: Collins, 1973.

CARROLL, JOHN, 'The Humean Tradition', *Philosophical Review* 99 (1990), 185–219.

CHADWICK, OWEN, *The Secularization of the European Mind in the Nineteenth Century*. Cambridge: Cambridge University Press, 1975.

CHANDRASEKHAR, S., *Truth and Beauty: Aesthetics and Motivations in Science*. Chicago: University of Chicago Press, 1990.

CLIFFORD, R. J., 'The Hebrew Scriptures and the Theology of Creation', *Theological Studies* 46 (1985), 507–23.

CROUZEL, HENRI, *Théologie de l'image de Dieu chez Origène*. Paris: Aubier, 1956.

CUNEO, TERENCE D., 'Combating the Noetic Effects of Sin: Pascal's Strategy for Natural Theology', *Faith and Philosophy* 11 (1994), 645–62.

CZAPKAY SUDDUTH, MICHAEL L., 'The Prospects for "Mediate" Natural Theology in John Calvin', *Religious Studies* 31 (1995), 53–68.

DAHM, JOHN J., 'Science and Apologetics in the Early Boyle Lectures', *Church History* 39 (1970), 172–86.

DAVIES, PAUL, *The Mind of God: Science and the Search for Ultimate Meaning.* Harmondsworth: Penguin, 1992.

DAY, JOHN, *God's Conflict with the Dragon: Echoes of a Canaanite Myth in the Old Testament.* Cambridge: Cambridge University Press, 1985.

DEROCHE, MICHAEL, 'Isaiah 45:7 and the Creation of Chaos', *Vetus Testamentum* 42 (1992), 11–21.

DREES, WILLEM B., *Religion, Science and Naturalism.* Cambridge: Cambridge University Press, 1995.

EICHRODT, WALTHER, 'In the Beginning: A Contribution to the Interpretation of the First Word of the Bible', in Bernhard W. Anderson and Walter Harrelson (eds), *Israel's Prophetic Heritage.* London: SCM Press, 1962, 1–10.

FALES, EVAN, 'Plantinga's Case against Naturalistic Epistemology', *Philosophy of Science* 63 (1996), 432–51.

FALLON, FRANCIS T., *The Enthronement of Sabaoth: Jewish elements in Gnostic Creation Myths.* Leiden: E. J. Brill, 1978.

FIELD MICHAEL, J., and MARTIN GOLUBITSKY, *Symmetry in Chaos: A Search for Pattern in Mathematics, Art and Nature.* Oxford: Oxford University Press, 1995.

FISCH, HAROLD, 'The Scientist as Priest: A Note on Robert Boyle's Natural Theology', *Isis* 44 (1953), 252–65.

FISCHER, HERMANN, 'Natürliche Theologie im Wandel', *Zeitschrift für Theologie und Kirche* 80 (1983), 85–102.

FISCHER, JOHANNES, 'Kann die Theologie der naturwissenschaftlichen Vernunft die Welt als Schöpfung verständlich machen?', *Freiburger Zeitschrift für Philosophie und Theologie* 41 (1994), 491–514.

FOSTER, MICHAEL B., 'The Christian Doctrine of Creation and the Rise of Modern Science', *Mind* 43 (1934), 446–68.

——, 'Christian Theology and Modern Science of Nature (I)', *Mind* 44 (1935), 439–66.

——, 'Christian Theology and Modern Science of Nature (II)', *Mind* 45 (1936), 1–27.

——, 'Man's Idea of Nature', *The Christian Scholar* 41 (1958), 361–6.

FOSTER, MICHAEL B., 'Greek and Christian Ideas of Nature', *The Free University Quarterly* 6 (1959), 122–7.

FOWLER, D. H., *The Mathematics of Plato's Academy: A New Reconstruction.* New York: Oxford University Press, 1999.

FRAASSEN, BAS C. VAN, *Laws and Symmetry.* Oxford: Clarendon Press, 1989.

GESTRICH, CHRISTOF, 'Die unbewältige natürliche Theologie', *Zeitschrift für Theologie und Kirche* 68 (1971), 82–120.

——, *Neuzeitliches Denken und die Spaltung der dialektischen Theologie: Zur Frage der natürlichen Theologie.* Tübingen: Mohr, 1977.

——, *The Return of Splendor in the World: The Christian Doctrine of Sin and Forgiveness.* Grand Rapids, MI: Eerdmans, 1997.

GIBBS, JOHN G., 'The Relation between Creation and Redemption according to Phil. II.5–11', *Novum Testamentum* 12 (1970), 270–83.

GRIFFIN, DAVID R., 'A Richer or Poorer Naturalism? A Critique of Willem Drees's *Religion, Science and Naturalism*', *Zygon* 32 (1997), 595–616.

——, *Religion and Scientific Naturalism: Overcoming the Conflicts.* Albany, NY: State University of New York Press, 2000.

GUNNLAUGUR, A. JÓNSSON, and S. CHENEY MICHAEL, *The Image of God: Genesis 1:26–28 in a Century of Old Testament Research.* Stockholm: Almqvist & Wiksell International, 1988.

GUNTON, COLIN E., *The Promise of Trinitarian Theology.* Edinburgh: T&T Clark, 1991.

——, *Christ and Creation.* Grand Rapids, MI: Eerdmans, 1992.

——, *The Triune Creator: A Historical and Systematic Study.* Edinburgh: Edinburgh University Press, 1998.

HABEL, NORMAN C., '"Yahweh, Maker of Heaven and Earth": A Study in Tradition Criticism', *Journal of Biblical Literature* 91 (1972), 321–37.

HADOT, PIERRE, 'L'image de la trinité dans l'âme chez Victorinus et chez Saint Augustin', *Studia Patristica* 6 (1962), 409–42.

HANSON, N. R., *Patterns of Discovery: An Inquiry into the Conceptual Foundations of Science.* Cambridge: Cambridge University Press, 1961.

HARNER, P. B., 'Creation Faith in Deutero-Isaiah', *Vetus Testamentum* 17 (1967), 298–306.

HARRIS, SCOTT L., 'Wisdom or Creation? A New Interpretation of Job 38:27', *Vetus Testamentum* 33 (1983), 419–27.

HEFNER, PHILIP, 'The Role of Science in Pannenberg's Theological Thinking', *Zygon* 24 (1989), 135–51.

HENDRY, GEORGE, *The Theology of Nature*. Philadelphia: Westminster Press, 1980.

HENRIKSEN, JAN-OLAV, 'How is Theology about Nature "Natural"?', *Studia Theologica* 43 (1989), 179–209.

HOITENGA, DEWEY J., *Faith and Reason from Plato to Plantinga: An Introduction to Reformed Epistemology*. Albany, NY: State University of New York Press, 1991.

HUGGETT, S. A., et al., *The Geometric Universe: Science, Geometry and the Work of Roger Penrose*. Oxford: Oxford University Press, 1998.

JACOB, JAMES R., and MARGARET C. JACOB, 'The Anglican Origins of Modern Science: The Metaphysical Foundations of the Whig Constitution', *Isis* 71 (1980), 251–67.

JACOB, MARGARET C., *The Newtonians and the English Revolution 1689–1720*. Ithaca, NY: Cornell University Press, 1976.

JAVELET, ROBERT, *Image et ressemblance au douzième siècle*. Paris: Letouzey et Ané, 1967.

JEREMIAS, JORG, *Das Königtum Gottes in den Psalmen: Israels Begegnung mit dem kanaanäischen Mythos in den Jahwe-König-Psalmen*. Göttingen: Vandenhoeck & Ruprecht, 1987.

JOHNSON, GEORGE, *Strange Beauty: Murray Gell-Mann and the Revolution in Twentieth-Century Physics*. London: Jonathan Cape, 2000.

JONES, WILLIAM FRANK, *Nature and Natural Science: The Philosophy of Frederick J. E. Woodbridge*. Buffalo, NY: Prometheus Books, 1983.

JUNGNICKEL, CHRISTA, and RUSSELL MCCORMMACH, *Intellectual Mastery of Nature: Theoretical Physics from Ohm to Einstein*. 2 vols. Chicago: University of Chicago Press, 1986.

KNIGHT, D. A., 'Cosmogony and Order in the Hebrew Tradition', in R. W. Lovin and F. E. Reynolds (eds), *Cosmology and Ethical Order: New Studies in Comparative Ethics*. Chicago: University of Chicago Press, 1985, 133–57.

KRETZMANN, NORMAN, *The Metaphysics of Theism: Aquinas's Natural Theology in Summa contra Gentiles I.* Oxford: Clarendon Press, 1997.

——, *The Metaphysics of Creation: Aquinas's Natural Theology in Summa contra Gentiles II.* Oxford: Clarendon Press, 1999.

KURTZ, PAUL, *Philosophical Essays in Pragmatic Naturalism.* Buffalo, NY: Prometheus Books, 1990.

LARSON, JAMES L., *Interpreting Nature: The Science of Living from Linnaeus to Kant.* Baltimore: Johns Hopkins University Press, 1994.

LEASE, GARY, 'Nature under Fire', in Michael E. Soulé and Gary Lease (eds), *Reinventing Nature: Responses to Postmodern Deconstruction.* Washington, DC: Island Press, 1995, 3–16.

LEE, T. D., 'Symmetry Principles in Physics', in A. Zichichi (ed.), *Elementary Processes at High Energies.* New York: Academic Press, 1971, 306–19.

LeMAHIEU, D. L., *The Mind of William Paley: A Philosopher and His Age.* Lincoln, NE: University of Nebraska Press, 1976.

LEVENSON, JON D., *Creation and the Persistence of Evil: The Jewish Drama of Divine Omnipotence.* Princeton, NJ: Princeton University Press, 1994.

LINK, CHRISTIAN, *Die Welt als Gleichnis: Studien zum Problem der natürlichen Theologie.* Munich: Christian Kaiser, 1976.

LLOYD-JONES, HUGH, *The Justice of Zeus.* 2nd edn. Berkeley, CA: University of California Press, 1983.

LOHFINK, NORBERT, 'God the Creator and the Stability of Heaven and Earth: The Old Testament on the Connection between Creation and Salvation', in Norbert Lohfink (ed.), *Theology of the Pentateuch.* Edinburgh: T&T Clark, 1994, 116–35.

LOUTH, ANDREW, 'Barth and the Problem of Natural Theology', *Downside Review* 87 (1969), 268–77.

LUDWIG, T. M., 'The Traditions of Establishing of the Earth in Deutero-Isaiah', *Journal of Biblical Literature* 92 (1973), 345–57.

MASCALL, ERIC L., *Christian Theology and Natural Science: Some Questions on their Relations.* London: Longmans, Green & Co., 1956.

MAY, GERHARD, *Creatio Ex Nihilo: the Doctrine of 'Creation out of Nothing' in Early Christian Thought.* Edinburgh: T&T Clark, 1995.

McCormack, Bruce L., *Karl Barth's Critically Realistic Dialectical Theology: Its Genesis and Development 1909–1936.* Oxford: Clarendon Press, 1995.

McGrath, Alister E., *The Foundations of Dialogue in Science and Religion.* Oxford: Blackwell, 1999.

——, *T. F. Torrance: An Intellectual Biography.* Edinburgh: T&T Clark, 1999.

McGuire, J. E., 'Boyle's Conception of Nature', *Journal of the History of Ideas* 33 (1972), 523–42.

Meijering, E. P., *Augustin über Schöpfung, Ewigkeit und Zeit: das elfte Buch der Bekenntnisse.* Leiden: E. J. Brill, 1979.

Mettinger, Tryggve N. D., 'Abbild oder Urbild? "Imago Dei" in traditionsgeschichtlicher Sicht', *Zeitschrift für Alttestamentlicher Wissenschaft* 86 (1974), 403–24.

Millar, P. D., 'Cosmology and World Order in the Old Testament: The Divine Council as Cosmic-Political Symbol', *Horizons in Biblical Theology* 9 (1987), 53–78.

Modiano, Raimonda, *Coleridge and the Concept of Nature.* Tallahassee, FL: Florida State University Press, 1985.

Moonan, Lawrence, *Divine Power: The Medieval Power Distinction up to Its Adoption by Albert, Bonaventure and Aquinas.* Oxford: Clarendon Press, 1994.

Nebelsick, Harold P., 'Karl Barth's Understanding of Science', in John Thompson (ed.), *Theology beyond Christendom: Essays on the Centenary of the Birth of Karl Barth.* Allison Park, PA: Pickwick Publications, 1986, 165–214.

Niditch, Susan, *Chaos to Cosmos: Studies in Biblical Patterns of Creation.* Chico, CA: Scholars Press, 1985.

Novak, David, *Natural Law in Judaism.* Cambridge: Cambridge University Press, 1998.

Oakley, Francis, 'Christian Theology and the Newtonian Science', in Daniel O'Connor and Francis Oakley (eds), *Creation: The Impact of an Idea.* New York: Charles Scribner's Sons, 1961, 54–83.

Odom, H. H., 'The Estrangement of Celestial Mechanics and Religion', *Journal of the History of Ideas* 27 (1966), 533–58.

O'DONOVAN, JOAN, 'Man in the Image of God: The Disagreement between Barth and Brunner Reconsidered', *Scottish Journal of Theology* 39 (1986), 433–59.

O'DONOVAN, OLIVER, *Resurrection and Moral Order*. Grand Rapids, MI: Eerdmans, 1986.

O'HIGGINS, J., 'Hume and the Deists', *Journal of Theological Studies* 22 (1971), 479–501.

OSLER, MARGARET J., 'Eternal Truths and the Laws of Nature: The Theological Foundations of Descartes' Philosophy of Nature', *Journal of the History of Ideas* 46 (1985), 349–65.

OTTO, STEPHAN, *Die Funktion des Bildbegriffes in der Theologie des 12. Jahrhunderts*. Munster: Aschendorff, 1963.

PAGELS, HEINZ R., *The Cosmic Code: Quantum Physics and the Language of Nature*. Harmondsworth: Penguin, 1984.

PAILIN, DAVID, 'Should Herbert of Cherbury be regarded as a "Deist"?', *Journal of Theological Studies* 51 (2000), 113–49.

PANNENBERG, WOLFHART, *Systematic Theology*. 3 vols. Grand Rapids, MI: Eerdmans; Edinburgh: T&T Clark, 1991, 1994, 1998.

———, *Toward a Theology of Nature: Essays on Science and Faith*. Philadelphia: Westminster/John Knox Press, 1993.

PELIKAN, JAROSLAV, *Christianity and Classical Culture: The Metamorphosis of Natural Theology in the Christian Encounter with Hellenism*. New Haven, CT: Yale University Press, 1993.

———, *What has Athens to do with Jerusalem? Timaeus and Genesis in Counterpoint*. Ann Arbor, MI: University of Michigan Press, 1997.

PENROSE, ROGER, 'The Role of Aesthetics in Pure and Applied Mathematical Research', *Bulletin of the Institute of Mathematics and Its Applications* 10 (1974), 266–71.

———, *The Emperor's New Mind*. London: Vintage, 1990.

PFEIFFER, GERHARD, 'Jahwe als Schöpfer der Welt und Herr ihrer Mächte in der Verkündigung des Propheten Amos', *Vetus Testamentum* 41 (1991), 475–81.

PLANTINGA, ALVIN J., 'The Reformed Objection to Natural Theology', *Proceedings of the American Catholic Philosophical Association* 54 (1980), 49–62.

PLATT, JOHN, *Reformed Thought and Scholasticism: The Arguments for the Existence of God in Dutch Theology*. Leiden: E. J. Brill, 1982.

PLATT, JOHN, 'The Denial of the Innate Idea of God in Dutch Remonstrant Theology: From Episcopius to van Limborch', in C. R. Trueman and R. S. Clark (eds), *Protestant Scholasticism*. Carlisle: Paternoster Press, 1999, 213–26.

POLKINGHORNE, JOHN, *Science and Creation: The Search for Understanding*. London: SPCK, 1988.

——, *Belief in God in an Age of Science*. New Haven, CT: Yale University Press, 1998.

POMERANS ARNOLD, JULIUS, and MAURICE CLAVELIN, *The Natural Philosophy of Galileo: Essay on the Origins and Formation of Classical Mechanics*. Cambridge, MA: MIT Press, 1974.

PRENTER, REGIN, 'Das Problem der natürlichen Theologie bei Karl Barth', *Theologische Literaturzeitung* 77 (1952), 607–11.

RANDALL, JOHN H., 'The Nature of Naturalism', in Yervant H. Krikorian (ed.), *Naturalism and the Human Spirit*. New York: Columbia University Press, 1945, 354–82.

REDHEAD, M. L. G., 'Symmetry in Intertheory Relations', *Synthese* 32 (1975), 77–112.

REID, MICHAEL, 'The Call of Nature', *Radical Philosophy* 64 (1993), 13–18.

RENDTORFF, ROLF, 'Die theologische Stellung des Schöpfungsglaubens bei Deuterjesaja', *Zeitschrift für Theologie und Kirche* 51 (1954), 2–13.

——, '"Where Were You when I laid the Foundations of the Earth?" Creation and Salvation History', in Rolf Rendtorff (ed.), *Canon and Theology: Overtures to an Old Testament Theology*. Minneapolis, MN: Fortress, 1993, 92–113.

ROBINSON, N. H. G., 'The Problem of Natural Theology', *Religious Studies* 8 (1972), 319–33.

ROGERS, EUGENE, *Thomas Aquinas and Karl Barth: Sacred Doctrine and the Natural Knowledge of God*. Notre Dame, IN: University of Notre Dame Press, 1995.

ROSEN, JOE, *Symmetry Discovered: Concepts and Applications in Nature and Science*. Cambridge: Cambridge University Press, 1975.

SCHILBRACK, KEVIN, 'Problems for a Complete Naturalism', *American Journal of Theology and Philosophy* 15 (1994), 269–91.

SCHMID, HANS H., *Gerechtigkeit als Weltordnung: Hintergrund und Geschichte des alttestamentlichen Gerechtigkeitsbegriffs.* Tübingen: Mohr, 1968.

——,'Jahweglaube und altorientalisches Weltordnungsgedanken', in H. H. Schmid, *Altorientalische Welt in der alttestamentlichen Theologie.* Zurich: Theologischer Verlag, 1974, 31–63.

SCHWANZ, PETER, *Imago Dei als christologisch-anthropologisches Problem in der Geschichte der Alten Kiche von Paulus bis Clemens von Alexandrien.* Halle: Niemeyer, 1970.

SENG, KANG PHEE, 'The Epistemological Significance of *Homoousion* in the Theology of Thomas F. Torrance', *Scottish Journal of Theology* 45 (1992), 341–66.

SHAPERE, DUDLEY, 'The Concept of Observation in Science and Philosophy', *Philosophy of Science* 49 (1982), 485–525.

SHEA, WILLIAM M., *The Naturalists and the Supernatural: Studies in Horizon and an American Philosophy of Religion.* Macon, GA: Mercer University Press, 1984.

SHELDON, W. H., 'A Critique of Naturalism', *Journal of Philosophy* 42 (1945), 254–69.

SHERRY, PATRICK, *Spirit and Beauty: An Introduction to Theological Aesthetics.* Oxford: Clarendon Press, 1992.

SHMUTTERMAYR, GEORG, '"Schöpfung aus dem Nichts" in 2. Makk. 7:28? Zum Verhältnis von Position und Bedeutung', *Biblische Zeitschrift* 17 (1973), 203–28.

SIEGWALT, GERARD, 'Der Prolog des Johannesevangeliums als Einführung in eine christliche Theologie der Rekapitulation', *Neue Zeitschrift für systematische Theologie und Religionsphilosophie* 24 (1981), 150–71.

SOULÉ, MICHAEL E., 'The Social Siege of Nature', in Michael E. Soulé and Gary Lease (eds), *Reinventing Nature: Responses to Postmodern Deconstruction.* Washington, DC: Island Press, 1995, 137–70.

STAUFFER, RICHARD, *Dieu, la création et la Providence dans la prédication de Calvin.* Berne: Peter Lang, 1978.

STEWART, IAN, *Does God Play Dice: The Mathematics of Chaos.* Oxford: Blackwell, 1989.

——, *Life's Other Secret: The New Mathematics of the Living World.* London: Allen Lane, 1998.

STOLZ, FRITZ, *Strukturen und Figuren im Kult von Jerusalem: Studien zur altorientalischen, vor- und frühisraelitischen Religion.* Berlin: de Gruyter, 1970.

STUHLMACHER, PETER, 'Erwägungen zum ontologischen Charakter der *kaine ktisis* bei Paulus', *Evangelische Theologie* 27 (1967), 1–35.

SULLIVAN, JOHN, *The Image of God: The Doctrine of St Augustine and its Influence.* Dubuque, IA: Priory Press, 1963.

SULLIVAN, R. E., *John Toland and the Deist Controversy.* Cambridge, MA: Harvard University Press, 1982.

SULLOWAY, FRANK J., 'Darwin and his Finches: The Evolution of a Legend', *Journal of the History of Biology* 15 (1982), 1–53.

TATARKIEWICZ, WLADISLAW, 'The Great Theory of Beauty and Its Decline', *Journal of Aesthetics and Art Criticism* 31 (1972), 165–80.

TODD, D. D., 'Plantinga and the Naturalized Epistemology of Thomas Reid', *Dialogue* 35 (1996), 93–107.

TORCHIA, N. JOSEPH, *Creatio ex nihilo and the Theology of St Augustine.* New York: Peter Lang, 1999.

TORRANCE, THOMAS F., *Theology in Reconstruction.* London: SCM Press, 1965.

——, 'The Problem of Natural Theology in the Thought of Karl Barth', *Religious Studies* 6 (1970), 121–35.

——, *The Trinitarian Faith: The Evangelical Theology of the Ancient Catholic Church.* Edinburgh: T&T Clark, 1988.

——, *The Christian Frame of Mind: Reason, Order, and Openness in Theology and Natural Science.* 2nd edn. Colorado Springs: Helmers & Howard, 1989.

——, 'The Transfinite Significance of Beauty in Science and Theology', in Luz García Alonso, Evanghelos Moutsopoulos and Gerhard Seel (eds), *L'art, la science et la métaphysique: Études offertes à André Mercier.* Berne: Peter Lang, 1993, 393–418.

TROMBA, ANTHONY J., and STEFAN HILDEBRANDT, *The Parsimonious Universe: Shape and Form in the Natural World.* New York: Copernicus, 1996.

TSUMURA, DAVID T., *The Earth and the Waters in Genesis 1 and 2: A Linguistic Investigation.* Sheffield: Sheffield Academic Press, 1989.

URBACH, PETER, 'What is a Law of Nature? A Humean Answer', *British Journal of Philosophy of Science* 39 (1988), 193–210.

VAN DEN BRINK, GIJSBERT, *Almighty God: A Study of the Doctrine of Divine Omnipotence*. Kampen: Kok Pharos, 1993.

VILADESAU, RICHARD, *Theological Aesthetics: God in Imagination, Beauty and Art*. New York: Oxford University Press, 1999.

VON RAD, GERHARD, 'Das theologische Problem des alttestamentlichen Schöpfungsglaubens', in *Gesammelte Studien zum Alten Testament*, vol. 1. Munich: Kaiser Verlag, 1965, 136–47.

WAGNER, STEVEN J., 'Why Realism Can't Be Naturalized', in Steven J. Wagner and Richard Warner (eds), *Naturalism: A Critical Appraisal*. Notre Dame, IN: University of Notre Dame Press, 1993, 211–53.

WEINBERG, STEVEN, *Dreams of a Final Theory: The Search for the Fundamental Laws of Nature*. London: Hutchinson Radius, 1993.

WOODBRIDGE, FREDERICK J. E., *An Essay on Nature*. New York: Columbia University Press, 1940.

YODER, JOELLA G., *Unrolling Time: Christiaan Huygens and the Mathematization of Nature*. Cambridge: Cambridge University Press, 1988.

YOUNG, FRANCES, '"Creatio ex Nihilo": A Context for the Emergence of the Christian Doctrine of Creation', *Scottish Journal of Theology* 44 (1991), 139–51.

ZEE, A., *Fearful Symmetry: The Search for Beauty in Modern Physics*. New York: Macmillan, 1986.

Index